CHALLENGE AND CHANGE

UNIVERSITY PRESS OF FLORIDA

Florida A&M University, Tallahassee
Florida Atlantic University, Boca Raton
Florida Gulf Coast University, Ft. Myers
Florida International University, Miami
Florida State University, Tallahassee
New College of Florida, Sarasota
University of Central Florida, Orlando
University of Florida, Gainesville
University of North Florida, Jacksonville
University of South Florida, Tampa
University of West Florida, Pensacola

To the Florida Book Awards

CHALLENGE AND CHANGE

Right-Wing Women, Grassroots Activism,
and the Baby Boom Generation

JUNE MELBY BENOWITZ

June Melby Benowitz

University Press of Florida
Gainesville · Tallahassee · Tampa · Boca Raton
Pensacola · Orlando · Miami · Jacksonville · Ft. Myers · Sarasota

This book may be available in an electronic edition.

20 19 18 17 16 15   6 5 4 3 2 1

Library of Congress Cataloging-in-Publication Data
Benowitz, June Melby, author.
Challenge and change : right-wing women, grassroots activism, and the baby boom
generation / June Melby Benowitz.
pages cm
Includes bibliographical references and index.
ISBN 978-0-8130-6122-1
1. Women—Political activity—United States—History—20th century.
2. Conservatism—United States—History—20th century. 3. Women's rights—
United States—History—20th century. 4. Baby boom generation—United States.
5. Women political activists—Training of—United States. 6. Right and left (Political
science) I. Title.
HQ1236.5.U6B47 2015
320.0820973'0904—dc23
2015014588

The University Press of Florida is the scholarly publishing agency for the State
University System of Florida, comprising Florida A&M University, Florida Atlantic
University, Florida Gulf Coast University, Florida International University, Florida
State University, New College of Florida, University of Central Florida, University of
Florida, University of North Florida, University of South Florida, and University of
West Florida.

University Press of Florida
15 Northwest 15th Street
Gainesville, FL 32611-2079
http://www.upf.com

For Elliot

CONTENTS

FIGURES

ACKNOWLEDGMENTS

Beginning with Martin Johnson who, following the publication of my study of rightist women of the 1930s and 1940s, suggested that I continue investigating the story of right-wing women into the post–World War II era, I am indebted to numerous people for their help on this project. With their invitation to join them on a panel at the 2006 American Historical Association's annual conference, Michelle Nickerson and Jennifer Burns offered me further encouragement to continue researching the topic. Thanks also go to the History of Education Society, Blackwell Publishing, and the editors at the *History of Education Quarterly* who worked with me as I revised and expanded the paper for publication as an article in their journal. Peter French, who during the early stages of my project was associate vice president and dean for academic affairs at the University of South Florida Sarasota-Manatee, helped fund my early research expeditions. Archivists and librarians at the Lyndon Baines Johnson Presidential Library, New York Public Library Manuscripts Division, Stanford University Libraries Department of Special Collections, National Archives II at College Park, Maryland, and the other repositories listed in the bibliography provided me with scholarly assistance and gracious hospitality while I conducted my research. I particularly wish to thank Bruce Tabb and others on the staff in Special Collections at the University of Oregon Libraries, where I spent many weeks. Brian Johnson of City of Portland Archives introduced me to some very useful photographs. I had research help from several of my students, including Carlton Stout, Luis Oliva, Evelyn Peters, Hope Black, Kim Godbee, and Andrea Burgess. Thanks also go to Barbara

Dubreuil, the interlibrary loan coordinator at the Jane Bancroft Cook Library, who gracefully and efficiently acquired scores of books, dissertations, and articles that I needed for my work. My college dean, Jane Rose, and Bonnie Jones, as regional vice chancellor for academic affairs, granted me extra research time for my project.

Justus Doenecke generously took the time to read several chapters of my work. He not only made careful and detailed suggestions in regard to the chapters but also made himself available to discuss my project whenever I had questions. I also received support and assistance from Christa Fowler and Jonathan Scott Perry who read and critiqued individual chapters. Mary Brennan, who reviewed the manuscript in its entirety, offered invaluable suggestions, as did other, unnamed, readers. Assistant Editor-in-Chief Sian Hunter and others on the staff of the University Press of Florida expertly and patiently guided me through the editorial process. Thanks also go to the baby boomers and mothers of baby boomers who took the time to speak with me, reminisce, and analyze past experiences. Throughout the process, colleagues and friends have been invaluable. I especially want to thank Jane Roberts, Silvia Blanco, Florence Hesler, Fawn Ngo, Thomas Jackson, and Marcelle Forbes.

Most of all, I wish to express my appreciation to my husband, Elliot Benowitz, whose blindness prevented him from being able to closely read my manuscript. Thus, he has patiently listened to me read the manuscript and revisions numerous times, has offered valuable critiques, and has encouraged me throughout the ups and downs of the research, writing, and publishing process. This book is dedicated to him.

INTRODUCTION

The year was 1970, the place New York City. People throughout the metropolis, and throughout America, were destitute and struggling to survive. Thousands each month were dying by their own hands to escape a life too horrible to bear. Citizens were prisoners of an all-powerful government, "The Democracy," "slaves of a monster they had fabricated in their demented dreams." Men and women aged fifty and older had betrayed the nation. Beginning in 1933, they had blindly followed as the new regime led the country deep into an abyss of tyranny. In just twenty years the government, with its imposition of increasingly severe regulations, had not only become intrusive but also, during World War II, had formed an alliance with Communist Russia. Matters worsened during the 1950s and 1960s as government leaders destroyed the Constitution and confiscated churches. "Had they not known that power delegated to government becomes the club of tyrants?"[1]

Popular writer Taylor Caldwell asks this question in *The Devil's Advocate* (1952). Her novel portrays a bleak prediction of what the United States might look like two decades later if the nation should continue on the political track established under the administrations of Franklin D. Roosevelt and Harry S. Truman. While placing the blame for this dire situation on the older generation, she predicts that it will be Americans born after the 1930s who will suffer most. "You never knew what freedom was and can be," a leading character tells two young men. "You were born when America had already lost a great part of her freedom. You were born into the age of tyrants and what you know of liberty and justice and all the old American virtues is only hearsay."[2] Despite this handicap, Taylor's hero, a young man, born in the 1940s, joins forces with others to topple The Democracy and restore America to its pre-1933 ideal.

Caldwell's novel expressed the fears of many on the political right during the postwar years. They claimed that, thanks to New Deal depression and wartime policies, disastrous political and social consequences awaited the next generation. Following the war, the Truman administration's continuation of many of Roosevelt's social and economic policies, along with new entanglements in international affairs, led many on the right to question the nation's direction. Adding to the right's anxiety, as well as that of many other Americans, was the advent of the Cold War and the threat of the spread of communism. They saw communism as evil and something that had to be defeated, not merely contained. The sudden appearance of the atomic bomb, with the accompanying revelation that nuclear fission was a new factor in the struggle for world power, brought an overwhelming sense of urgency to all, including those on the right. As with Caldwell, some rightists, including large numbers of women, believed it was up to them to take action. They would do whatever was necessary to see that the next generation, those born 1946–1964 and known as "the baby boomers," lived in a restored America that was safe from communism and statism.

In the years following the ravages of the Great Depression and World War II, Americans were putting their lives back together, making plans for the future, finding peacetime jobs, establishing homes, and beginning families. People wanted to see themselves as individuals, working for themselves and building stable and happy lives for their families. They wanted to help create and to enjoy an environment of peace and prosperity. As years passed and families grew, parents focused attention on their children, hoping that their lives would be free of turmoil such as that the older generation had so recently experienced. Mothers, in particular, sought advice for raising their children, often in such publications as Dr. Benjamin Spock's *Baby and Child Care* (1946). Parents joined the Parent Teachers Association and similar organizations and led youth groups such as Boy Scouts and Campfire Girls. Most were anxious to instill their values in their children as they prepared them for the future.

While many parents believed that planning for the future meant building upon institutions that were established during the presidency of Franklin Roosevelt, there were others, particularly those on the right who, like Taylor Caldwell, maintained that the country's best years were in the past, prior to FDR. The world that emerged following World War II was alien to their way of thinking. Political and economic philosophies had changed since the 1920s and, in their eyes, not for the better. Some on the right were uneasy as they perceived a shift of power from the established political and social order to the common masses, and they raised the issue that the United States was founded as a republic, not a democracy. Others, who identified themselves as grassroots Americans of a conservative social bent, pushed for more democracy in the sense of greater roles for individuals, families, and local and regional interests in political and cultural decision making. They differed from liberals and radicals in that they considered the government's adoption of ever larger roles, in matters of institutional and social reforms, as constricting the rights of individuals. Thus, social and political conservatives were finding that the world they envisioned for their children would take extra efforts to achieve.

Rightists believed that Communists were at the center of the problems that they perceived, but they saw the threats as wider. Particularly troubling for the right was what they saw as moral decay, the growing secularism in America, continued rapid growth in the power of government, and the ascendancy of political, scientific, and educational elites. No longer were the traditional elites—local clergy and other community patriarchs—in control. All of these changes contributed to what rightists saw as a marked decline in American values. They feared that if such deterioration continued, the United States would come to resemble the Soviet Union. In their search for simple explanations for the many, mostly undesirable changes, they attached themselves to the idea of "conspiracy." They believed that not only Communists but also the government, scientific elites, progressive educators, African American leaders, Jews, and other groups were part of a broad conspiracy to undermine American politics, economics, society, and culture.

To counter the attack, rightists joined in a struggle to educate the upcoming generation in a manner reminiscent of the way they remembered their own upbringing. As the world around them changed during the decades following World War II, they increasingly stressed the need for a solid grounding in Christianity, as they understood it, and placed a great emphasis on what they considered the strong traditions that had held American society together and made it great. Rightists focused considerable attention on using public schools to teach the younger generation the "American Way." The future of the nation would lie in the hands of the youth, and the right wing, especially its women, sought to ensure that the baby boom generation would later lead the country in the proper direction.

From the 1950s through the mid-1970s, the years during which the baby boom generation was growing up, the right encountered a variety of social and political issues that stirred them to action. Some were carryovers from the Roosevelt era, but others were quite new. While Cold War anxieties concerning the spread of communism were present from the beginning of this period, such issues as civil rights for blacks and equal rights for women climaxed during the 1960s and 1970s. As had been the case with women of the 1930s and 1940s,[3] most women of the postwar era, including the mothers of the baby boomers, chose their causes based not only upon where they stood socially and politically but also frequently took action depending upon how emerging issues might affect their personal lives and the lives of their families. How they defined what was best sometimes led women to take rightist points of view on some issues and more liberal positions on others. There was a growing conjunction between the personal and the political. Each of these spheres gained in potency from its link to the other. This was particularly true for groups outside the power elite, including women, minorities, and the upcoming baby boom generation, the latter group being much more mobile, much better educated, and much more numerous than earlier generations.

In telling its story of how right-wing women sought to shape the world in which the baby boom generation grew up, this book draws from a wide variety of manuscript collections, more than two dozen personal interviews, a broad range of printed sources from the period, and a large array of studies by other historians. It centers on the approximate time period of 1950 through the mid-1970s, and explores the development of the right-wing women's movement in terms of main issues that faced the country during those decades. The book includes historical background for the movement and for the issues and provides a loosely chronological, issue-oriented framework into which more localized studies can be placed. By exploring archival and other sources to bring out what was going on in the grassroots, this book sheds new light upon ways that issues and players in the history of the right have changed over time. This look at changes of focus on the right should help create a better understanding of how and why the New Right drew such massive support in the late 1970s and early 1980s. It also reveals a growing influence of rightist women over the decades under study, helping to explain how dozens of right-wing women emerged as leaders in the Tea Party movement of the twenty-first century.

In 1950, the earliest of the more than 77 million boomers, the largest such cohort in American history[4] were about to enter school; by the middle of the 1970s they were young adults. The mid-1970s also marks the emergence of the New Right and the waning of the older right, though the transition is not abrupt since some of the same leaders were active with both the old and the new. Also, many of the earlier issues still remained. Phyllis Schlafly, who began political activity during the 1950s and who has continued to speak for the right in the twenty-first century, is a prime example of the older right carrying on to the new. Right-wing women's efforts frequently met with resistance from moderates, the left, and, as they matured, from many of the youth themselves; thus, at times reactions from "the other side" are explored as well. Some areas existed in which left, middle, and right concurred. For example, many conservatives and liberals raised similar questions about the safety of fluoridation and government attempts to establish and enforce it.

This brings up the question of how one defines the "right wing." Certainly, it is difficult to pin labels because most people are complex; such naming often results in oversimplification. Too, the concept of what is "right" changes over time and from region to region, making it impossible to attempt an immutable definition. As historian Kim Nielsen points out, establishing a definition of what constitutes "right wing" is both "slippery and difficult."[5] Nevertheless, there are some commonly accepted identifiers of the "right" that were in use throughout the Cold War era. "Right" in any specific context denotes a conservative stance, championing older, established beliefs and forms of social and political organization. In contrast, "left" denotes supporting social and/or political changes from the established norms. But what the established norms consist of, and what the moral and behavioral bases for these norms are, is itself at times a matter of contention between various interest groups. In modern American political life there is a "right" and a "left" within both major political parties. However, in America, where social and political stratification has been less rigid than in Europe, the terms "right" and "left" usually appear in times of special crisis. Most of the time, the terms "conservative" and "liberal" have seemed to suffice. The terms "right" and "left" seem to appear when, due to specific crises, consensus diminishes and more and more sharply defined interest groups come to the fore.

A further complexity arises because the groups and individuals whom others might define as "right" or "left" often do not accept these descriptions as who they are, but see themselves as representing the center of what are defined as American social and political values. Recognizing all of this, for working purposes in this book, the term "right wing" refers to Americans who actively campaigned to halt changes in the nation's culture, society, and politics. These are changes that the right usually dated from the early twentieth-century Progressive Era, and changes they believed were reinforced under the Roosevelt administration.

In addition to the right's anger over the rapid growth of government during the New Deal and beyond and the growing secularization of American society, patriotism was an issue. While Americans who consider themselves "patriotic" are found across the political spectrum, many of those on the right, and especially on the far right, believed themselves to be the only true patriots. They considered "Un-American" anyone who did not see eye-to-eye with them. In its more extreme manifestation, the right is associated with hatred for "outsiders" including blacks, Jews, immigrants, and homosexuals. At the same time, the right is usually opposed to internationalism and egalitarianism, ideologies that are often defined as "liberal." While not all right-wing women equated liberalism with collectivism, most considered liberals to be "soft on communism," or at least naïve about the dangers of "red" infiltration into American institutions. As with the right-wing women active during the 1930s and World War II, the farther to the right the women were on the political spectrum, the more they tended to have a Manichaean outlook on issues and ideologies, viewing them in black and white, allowing for no middle ground.[6] Many right-wing women had an "us against them" attitude whether it was on issues of fluoridation, school integration, the Equal Rights Amendment, or in regard to the many other issues that sparked campaigns among women on the right.

In recent decades, scholars researching the right have found that there are several strands of rightist ideology in America. Sociologist Jerome L. Himmelstein, for example, describes three elements that are prevalent in rightist ideology—what he calls "economic libertarianism," which stresses the idea of less government intervention in the marketplace; "social traditionalism," which focuses upon traditional attitudes about family, gender roles, religion, and morality; and "militant anticommunism," which centers on national security and America's fight against communism wherever that nation's interests are threatened.[7] Friedrich Hayek, author of *The Road to Serfdom* (1944), was a proponent of economic liberty, as was libertarian Ayn Rand. While economic libertarianism plays a role in this book, the latter two elements are the primary focus, for it was usually their virulent anticommunism or their desire to maintain or to reignite traditional values that drove rightist women to join political campaigns.

Many rightist women's beliefs were aligned with those of rightist intellectuals Russell Kirk or Richard Weaver. Kirk, a leading exponent of traditional conservatism, believed that a divine intent ruled both society and conscience, and that, at their base, political problems were religious and moral problems. Weaver viewed the culture and values of the postwar world as being in a rapid decline and believed that Americans should look back to their ancient and medieval heritage for direction.[8] Similarly, many rightist women held the view that God had a plan that came to America via the nation's founders, an educated and propertied elite, who established the country's social and political foundations. By the mid-twentieth century, these women saw secular and other forces threatening those foundations. Many of them were concerned that too much power was now in the hands of an uninformed majority. They believed communists to be taking advantage of all weaknesses in American society, conspiring and manipulating to attain power for themselves.[9] While anticommunism was a widely held sentiment in America during that period, generally the farther right one was found on the political spectrum, the greater was their fear of a Communist takeover. Rather than being influenced by the deeper and more complex layer of conservative intellectual ideology, women whose greatest anxieties came from worries about Communist conspiracies found they held points of view that aligned with the more extreme right. These included such men as Wisconsin senator Joseph McCarthy and, later, Robert Welch, founder of the John Birch Society.

The socially traditional and intensely anticommunist elements of rightist ideology were prevalent, but libertarian elements were also present in the sentiments of many of the women studied here. Historian Donald T. Critchlow points out that the two strains, "libertarianism" and "religious traditionalism," could become intertwined.[10] Such was the situation in regard to many of the rightist women studied here. Although the traditionalist and anticommunist elements usually dominated the women's campaigns, many of the women exhibited a libertarian strand of rightist thought. Often their diagnoses of what was wrong in America included concerns that government was becoming involved in too many aspects of citizens' lives, impinging on both individual and states' rights. Such rightist leaders as Arizona senator Barry Goldwater, who advocated more individual freedom and less government, were frequently able to capture support from these women.

On education, those defined as "right wing" are women who objected to curricula that praised government reforms and expansion associated with the New Deal. Many of these women shared Taylor Caldwell's fear of "The Democracy," that if patriotic Americans were not alert to the danger and did not take action, they might soon be crushed in a nation overridden with tyranny. Right-wing women feared communist influences on such issues as education, health, morality, the civil rights movement, student rebellion, and equal rights for women. The farther to the right they were, the more rigid they tended to be; the more vehement they were in their campaigns, the more likely they were to see government programs and social change as threats to their lives. Indeed, there was a decided difference between middle-of-the-road conservatives and those on the far right. Both were anticommunist, but the far rightists saw conspiracy. They feared Soviet military power and ideology, but especially its technique of subversion. One example is the far right's assertion that government-sponsored fluoridation was a Communist plot to affect people's health and thereby weaken the United States. From coast to coast, most leaders on the far right found Communist-backed conspiracies in almost all of the new ideas and programs they were fighting against.

Useful for defining the far right, and placing it in the context of the time, is a list that a committee of concerned citizens of Sarasota, Florida, compiled in the mid-1960s while investigating "extremism" in the county's public schools. The committee included such defining criteria as: racial hatred, religious bigotry, and distrust of local, state, or federal policing agencies and organizations. Extremists used such tactics as censorship, "incitement to violence and hysteria," and "slanderous accusations such as treason, etc.," against the nation's leaders. They denied the "right to free interchange of ideas" and "the right of individuals to be heard." The committee also considered extreme those who ignored "educational advances" and urged withdrawal of the United States from "world affairs and alignments" and "abandonment of allies and [the] free world."[11] Such characteristics were common among the far right studied here.

Although mainstream Americans might at times promote some of the above ideas and methods of action, such as distrust of government policing agencies, overall the Sarasota committee provided a functional definition of extremism. The group decided that while their ultimate goals differed sharply, extremists on both the left and the right often held the same absolutist kinds of attitudes. Compiled in 1966, the list provides insight into many of the practices of radical dissenters during the 1950s through 1970s.

While most historians of the right wing in twentieth-century America focused on specific regions, organizations, issues, or leaders, this book casts a wider net, exploring a number of factors that drew women from various regions of the country into right-wing campaigns. The right has become a rather popular topic in recent years, with an increasing number of historians researching various manifestations. Their studies point out that the right has undergone transformations. The Old Right of the 1930s–1940s has evolved into a New Right that emerged in the 1970s when a new generation of conservative leaders sought to unite rightists backing specific causes into a larger political coalition. Among the changes was the discarding of the explicit racism of the Old Right, replacing it with more subtle discrimination. Also, the New Right updated its opposition to the New Deal, more recently denouncing social welfare programs as products of "tax-and-spend" liberal reforms. At the same time, the intense anticommunism that was so important to the Old Right was dropped and greater emphasis placed on the theme of building a strong military defense against possible new challenges.[12]

One theme that became stronger with the emergence of the New Right was that of "family values," though that issue had long been high on the agendas of women of the Old Right. The late 1970s saw the growth of the Christian Right, too, with an agenda that often reinforced the right's emphasis on "family values."[13] Mainstream perceptions of the right have undergone change as well, for right-wing columnists, radio and television commentators, activists, and politicians acquired audiences among politically and socially moderate Americans. Patrick Buchanan, Rush Limbaugh, Laura Ingraham, Ann Coulter, and Laura Schlesinger are some examples. The Tea Party movement, which emerged in 2009 to become so strong that it continues to have effects on local, state, and national elections, is another indicator of the growing strength of the right. Historians, political scientists, and sociologists are now unraveling processes by which the right went from being a small movement, often associated with extremism, to a powerful force in American politics and society.[14] This book will add to that conversation. It will provide further insight as to how many of the issues and ideas associated with the right of today have roots in the past.

Since this book examines the actions and opinions of both the baby boom generation and their elders, it is important to take a moment to look at the meaning of the term "generation." The term refers to the creation, over a delimited period of time, of new human beings, who begin without social experience, and who continue to develop after birth, both physically and mentally. These youngsters are imprinted to a major, but not absolute, degree with the language, values, and behavioral patterns of their elders. The elders themselves underwent similar patterns of growth in their development. So, on through the generations, a specific culture forms, carried on through time as generation succeeds generation. But, over time, individuals and cultures are modified, sometimes to a small and sometimes to a greater extent, including contact with other cultures. The modifications might come peacefully or perhaps through such events as wars, plagues, or forced religious conversions. Often the culture changes because of internal developments, as when the invention of the cotton gin or the railroad created both opportunities for some groups and severe stresses for others.

The characterization of the baby boomers as a generation is basically biological. The tremendous increase in the birth rate beginning in 1946, peaking in the late 1950s, and in a downward trend by the mid-1960s, had a fundamental impact on American society. Americans strove to address the needs of this vast and quickly growing population of young people by building homes, new schools, expanding medical facilities, and so forth. But within this generation there were also changes, as those born in its later years were born into a world already impacted by what the older part of this generation had experienced and, in their own turn, had effected.

Also, baby boomers differed to various extents according to the section of the United States they lived in, their sex, family circumstances, and individual differences, and through the influence of their peers. The rapid development of new mass media played a large role in shaping the generation. Such media as television and new forms of music brought the young generation together, giving them a chance to express their experiences and hopes for themselves and their country. Another unifying factor was the greatly increased availability of higher education, of which they made great use. As a result, they developed a strong sense of themselves as a cultural and political force. Some of what they absorbed put many, but not all, boomers on a collision course with their elders.

The concept of the "baby boom generation" is used in this book in several ways. Not only does it help define the study by addressing the years during which that generation grew from childhood to adulthood but also it reveals how concerns about their children prompted women, right-wing women in particular, to become activists during the 1950s and 1960s. It also shows right-wing women's reaction to liberal and radical student activists and reveals that by the 1970s, thousands of young baby boomer women (although a minority among their generation) were attaching themselves to emerging right-wing causes.

Each chapter of the book contains examples of letters and other documents that women wrote in response to various matters of concern, and the later chapters include baby boomers' thoughts as well. The documents quoted here do not give just one individual's opinion, but are representative of numerous others within the manuscript collections listed in this book's bibliography. Tens of thousands of women from the grassroots of America were speaking out, writing books and articles, and corresponding with representatives in government. Many of the issues that these women raised were in the minds of many other Americans and were issues that had great implications for the future of American society. Much depended upon how they were resolved. The selected examples of their statements on issues that rightist women, their opponents, and baby boomers deemed important, give voice to their values and concerns.

This book is divided into two sections. The first, "Our Schools, Our Children," examines right-wing women's efforts to direct the manner by which public schools and government-run institutions address matters relating to the education and physical and mental health of youth. The chronological focus of this section is on the years when most baby boomers were in elementary school or in their early years of high school. The second, "Protesting the Protests," addresses rightist women's reactions to the changes they perceived in the attitudes and behaviors of these youth in regard to moral, political, and social values during their teenage and young adult years. It marks a time when these women found they needed to go beyond efforts to build rightward-leaning foundations in society and culture and confront the youth themselves. By the mid-1960s, women on the right were dismayed by what they saw as a decline in American values overall, and they were determined to combat those changes.

One of the most important issues for right-wing women in the postwar era was education. This monograph, in the first chapter, begins with an exploration of right-wing women's attempts to shape curricula through textbook censorship and the elimination of those teachers and programs the right deemed leftist. Rightist women, many of them mothers of baby boomers, sought to control the very subjects being taught. Given the crucial role of education in forming America's entire society, the education theme will surface repeatedly as the story of the efforts of right-wing women and their campaigns unfolds.

The second chapter examines three health issues that affected baby boomers in particular, but other Americans as well. Frequently, it was mothers' fears of harmful effects on their children's health that led them to join campaigns on those issues. Fluoridation of public water systems became a prominent issue in the 1950s and 1960s, with activism on this matter frequently having a lasting impact upon American communities. Two other public health issues causing concern for the right during those years were mental health and polio vaccination programs. Rightists' suspicions of government intent in matters of community mental health, and their questions regarding the necessity for and safety of polio vaccines being administered to American children, led to their protesting government intervention in such matters. The third chapter focuses on right-wing women's opposition to the civil rights movement, particularly as it pertained to school desegregation. Thousands of right-wing women in both the South and the North were wholehearted participants in crusades against school desegregation, sometimes being in the forefront of anti-integration and antibusing campaigns.

The fourth chapter, and the first of the book's second section, examines the supposed decline in moral values among American youth. This includes such matters as school prayer, sex education, and patriotism. It explores rightist women's efforts to shape baby boomers' moral values, to restore religious teachings in public schools, to keep sex education out of schools, and to instill patriotism in young people. The war in Vietnam created a dilemma for right-wing women, which is a subject of the fifth chapter. Often these women struggled with the choice between supporting the war as a fight against communism and opposing the drafting of their sons to face an unknown fate. Chapter 5 also looks at the problem of student unrest during the Vietnam War era. For rightist women in particular, it seemed as if the struggle overseas was now being fought at home. The sixth and final chapter examines right-wing women's response to the "women's liberation" movement and the Equal Rights Amendment, in the process describing the expectations they had for young women in society and politics.

By the mid-1960s the older baby boomers were approaching adulthood and were realizing how many of these issues might directly affect their lives. While their elders, including rightist women, continued their attempts to shape their ideologies, youth were forming their own opinions on social and political matters. Some became activists themselves, for the right or for the left. Therefore, in addition to examining the older generation of rightist women, the latter chapters address baby boomers' reactions to the civil rights movement, changes in moral values, the Vietnam War, women's rights, and other issues, and draw conclusions as to the right's influence on America's youth.

As historians of the right have shown, rightist activism among both men and women existed throughout the entire twentieth century.[15] Nativism prevailed in the early decades, a time when immigration rates were soaring and World War I passions inspired hatred for German-Americans. The right was active, too, in promoting eugenics and disputing Darwinism. Post–World War I America experienced a Red Scare and the resurgence of the Ku Klux Klan, an order that focused on such "un-American" groups as Jews, Roman Catholics, and African Americans. In the early decades of the century, the growing emphasis on the sciences, as well as on changing moral values, drew reaction from traditionalist Americans. Hatred for the New Deal, campaigns to keep out of World War II, anti-Semitism, and anticommunism were major foci of right-wing activity during the years of Roosevelt's presidency, 1933–1945.

New issues arose during the postwar era, including special concern for the rapidly swelling baby boom generation, social, moral, and family issues, and the worldwide expansion of communism. While some right-wing women continued with their anti-Semitic diatribes, the revelation of the full extent of the Holocaust led to a quieting of blatant anti-Semitism. The decline of the numbers of foreign immigrants since the mid-1920s had lessened concerns about aliens destroying American values. Most moderates moved on, but some people continued to seek out elements in society that they deemed "un-American." As late as the mid-1960s, aging far right agitator Elizabeth Dilling continued in her newsletters to lash out at Jews as sexually depraved Christ-killers, out to destroy Christianity. Dilling, who was best known for authoring *The Red Network* (1934), an encyclopedia of alleged communists that included the names of many prominent Americans, was a leading anti–New Deal activist and a promoter of conspiracy theories during World War II. After the war, however, she lost much of her readership. Dilling revealed just how out of step she was with others on the right when she spoke out against the campaign of conservative candidate Barry Goldwater during the 1964 presidential campaign because the candidate's grandfather was Jewish.[16] There were others too, such as Marilyn Allen, who produced and distributed anti-Semitic materials in addition to her other far rightist propaganda throughout the 1950s.[17] Yet most right-wing women focused far more attention upon communists than upon Jews. This is not to say that anti-Semitism had disappeared. It had not, but it was usually more subtle. Indeed, a rigid and intolerant version of Christianity remained a powerful theme for many of these women. While such groups as the Minute Women of the U.S.A. claimed to welcome women of all creeds, the mastheads of their newsletters frequently included a prayer or a verse from the Bible's New Testament.[18]

While usually working within structured organizations, right-wing women also crusaded individually, often as authors, lecturers, or political lobbyists. Although much of their activity took place during a time when caring for home and family took priority, many of these women sought involvement in the political world, especially in local campaigns.[19] They stressed the protection of children, particularly if those children were

Christian, white, and middle class. Motherhood certainly played a role in inspiring some women to become active in rightist causes. They looked at how political, social, and cultural issues would affect their families and joined campaigns that addressed those issues. Others saw beyond their immediate families and strove to influence the development of the community as a whole.

Rightist women often collaborated with men and joined male-led organizations. But whether or not they also belonged to such organizations, the majority of the women studied here were members of gender-specific groups. As women, they saw themselves as possessing unique concerns, particularly regarding children. They also believed that, as women, they had special talents—including a heightened awareness of moral issues— that would enable them to be more effective than men. At times, the focus of their agendas differed for women. For example, while homosexuality was an important topic for right-wing men during the McCarthy era of the 1950s, right-wing women paid little attention to the issue before the women's equal rights movement of the late 1960s and 1970s. At the same time, long-standing ideas about "women's place" in society led many to feel more comfortable working in such organizations as the Minute Women of the U.S.A. that were limited to women only.

Yet some believed that they should involve themselves in both women's and predominantly male organizations. Such women usually seemed to disappear within men's organizations, for male leaders received most of the publicity. However, some studies, including this one, indicate that women often wielded significant influence within groups that outwardly appeared to be male-dominated.[20] Sociologist Kathleen McCourt, who investigated white working-class women's activism on Chicago's southwest side in the late 1960s and early 1970s, found that women were active in the local block clubs that organized when blacks moved into all-white neighborhoods, but that the presidents of these groups were almost always men.[21] The situation in left-of-center organizations was similar. Studies show that women in such leftist organizations as Students for a Democratic Society (SDS) were more likely to do office work and participate in (but not lead) demonstrations.[22] While receiving little publicity within such organizations, women nevertheless often supplied the backbone of local political groups. At the same time, they were effective organizers and campaigners within their own organizations, which at times received more publicity than men's groups. It was within these organizations that they were able to unite on issues most pertinent to women. Whether or not their children adopted the attitudes of their parents, most mothers had at least some influence on the social and political outlooks of their children.

Most of the women in this book considered themselves to be representative of traditional American womanhood, or the grassroots of the nation's women. They took pride in being ordinary Americans, with traditional values, rather than being associated with the intellectual or scientific elites whom they believed possessed low moral values and were sympathetic to communism. These women, however, did not see themselves as part of an all-encompassing sisterhood with other American women. Instead, they criticized women who did not share their points of view. Some rightist women openly criticized mainstream women's organizations, including some traditionally viewed as socially or politically conservative.

Rightist leader Lucille Cardin Crain, who was particularly active from the 1940s through the 1960s, led the way with the booklet *Packaged Thinking for Women* (1948), which she co-authored with Anne Burrows Hamilton. *Packaged Thinking* warned of subversive activity within mainstream women's groups and quickly became popular among right-wing women's organizations that were on the lookout for left-wing conspirators.[23] In addition to criticizing the more liberal League of Women Voters (LWV), the self-proclaimed "patriotic" organization the Minute Women of the U.S.A., Inc., and the Pasadena Anti-Communist League criticized the General Federation of Women's Clubs (GFWC), an association that is generally considered to be moderate to conservative on social and political issues. In 1956, the Pasadena group circulated a list of thirty-eight women's organizations it considered of questionable integrity, which included the LWV and GFWC, as well as such mainstream organizations as the Girl Scouts of the U.S.A., the National Federation of Business and Professional Women's Clubs, the National Association of Colored Women, and other lesser-known women's organizations.[24]

At the same time, there were some among the right, including rightist journalist Elizabeth Churchill Brown, who believed that members of "patriotic groups" should be active in their local church groups, parents-teachers associations, the League of Women Voters, and other mainstream organizations. Brown advised them to not "join these groups in order to raise a rumpus, but for the purpose of winning friends and influencing people."[25] If they wanted their patriotic organizations to grow, and their political ideas to spread, rightist women needed to work on a local and small-scale basis to create opportunities to convert other people to their point of view.

During the 1950s to 1970s, there were hundreds of right-wing women's groups, small and large, scattered around the United States.[26] This book focuses on the largest of these organizations as well as some smaller, but still influential, groups. A few, including Pro America, the Daughters of the American Revolution (DAR), and the Minute Women of the U.S.A., were national organizations with branches throughout the country. Founded in 1932, as an anti–New Deal organization, Pro America's campaigns during the era examined here focused on such issues as patriotism, school prayer, integration, and the Equal Rights Amendment. The DAR adopted those issues as well as those pertaining to fluoridation, sex education, and the Vietnam War. Minute Women were drawn to the same issues, but also were actively involved in protesting community mental health programs and the polio vaccine. These leading rightist women's organizations of the 1950s and 1960s claimed tens of thousands of members. For example, in 1958, the DAR claimed 180,000 members and chapters in every state of the Union.[27] In 1952 the Minute Women claimed 50,000 members, and an outside investigator found that there were branches of that organization in at least twenty-seven states.[28] In comparison, the more liberal League of Women Voters claimed 157,000 members at its high point in 1969.[29] As with most women in this book, whose race and social and marital statuses could be determined, the typical Minute Woman of the 1950s and 1960s was white and middle- or upper-class, and married.[30] The same was true for members of Phyllis Schlafly's Eagle Forum, founded in 1975. This organization, the leading right-wing force of women in the fight against the Equal Rights Amendment, reported having 60,000 members by the end of that campaign.[31]

Most right-wing women's groups were considerably smaller than the DAR, Minute Women, and Eagle Forum. The smaller organizations were usually regional, such as Texas Women for Constitutional Government, New Mexico Women Speak!, and the Southern California-based Network of Patriotic Letter Writers. Often a specific issue, such as water fluoridation, was the inspiration behind a group's forming, but many participated in a variety of crusades.

There was a core group of right-wing women who spoke out and led campaigns on a wide range of issues. These women, based in a variety of geographic regions of the United States, participated in right-wing causes spanning much of the era that this book encompasses. Some of these women gained prominence as individuals, many of them earning their recognition through their publications. Likely the best known was New Yorker Lucille Cardin Crain, editor of the *Educational Reviewer* and an activist for most of the right-wing causes discussed in this book. Another prominent rightist woman of the period was Ida Darden of Fort Worth, Texas, editor of the *Southern Conservative*. She was particularly interested in preventing integration, promoting patriotism, and battling community mental health programs. Focusing on education, Southern Californian Frances Bartlett, editor of *FACTS in Education*, sought to keep "subversives" out of education. Mental health testing and sex education were among the "subversive" ideas she wished to keep out of the schools. Phoebe Courtney, editor of the *Independent American* and *Tax Fax*, spoke out against integration, busing, fluoridation, the polio vaccine, sex education, and the Supreme Court decision to prohibit organized prayer in schools. During her career as an activist for the right, Courtney moved from Colorado to Louisiana. Although Phyllis Schlafly of Illinois was politically active throughout most of the period explored here, it was not until her campaign to stop the Equal Rights Amendment that she became particularly prominent among women's campaigns. During the 1970s, her Eagle Forum organization and her newsletter, the *Phyllis Schlafly Report*, attracted the attention of Americans nationwide. (See appendix for a listing of major organizations and individuals examined here, and the main issues with which they were associated.)

Right-wing women did not always get along with one another. In 1952, for example, Elizabeth Dilling denounced Suzanne Silvercruys Stevenson, founder of the Minute Women of the U.S.A. Dilling became upset when Stevenson rejected a movement for a new political party because the organizers appeared to be anti-Semitic.[32] Jealousy may have played a part in Dilling's pronouncement since Dilling's influence among rightist women was on the decline while the Minute Women were thriving. Stevenson's objection to being associated with an anti-Semitic political party was also a sign of the changes occurring among the right, its anti-Semitic emphasis gradually dissipating during the postwar years. Stevenson's sincerity is questionable, however, as anti-Semitic publications were on Minute Women's reading lists.[33]

There were also splits within organizations. The Charleston, West Virginia, chapter of the Minute Women withdrew from the national organization in 1966, and others threatened to do so as well, when they deemed the Minute Women's longtime national chairman, Dorothy Frankston, dictatorial. Nor was Pro America completely united. That organization had two branches in California because the Southern California members considered those in the North to be "far too liberal."[34] Such divisiveness usually resulted in loss of membership and a weakened organization.

There was fluidity within the right-wing women's movements studied here. While many of the leaders and organizations attached themselves to a variety of issues, others became activists when issues became personal. This was especially the case when they sensed a threat to their children. The health, education, morality, and security of their children and grandchildren were motivating forces for action for tens of thousands of women across America. For many of these women, participation in just one rightist organization was not enough. Lucille Cardin Crain was one of thousands who enlisted in several organizations with similar agendas, or who joined groups that adopted agendas that supplemented, but differed from those of the organization they had joined earlier. For instance, a woman might be in a group that focused on fighting leftist teachings in public schools and then join a group that campaigned against polio vaccinations. Both groups would have right-wing views, but were focusing on different causes.

Women in various groups corresponded with one another—within the membership and also from one organization to another. There were no formal national networks, but loose networks, many of which included Crain, who was based in New York City. Letter writing campaigns addressed to legislators and newspapers, rallies in women's hometowns and in Washington, D.C., were leading tactics in getting their points of view into the public sphere.

Rightist women had great successes in some of their campaigns, but were less fortunate in others. In some instances, including on the issues of education and fluoridation, they won victories in some parts of the country, but not in others. Just as the right's influence waxed and waned depending upon a specific issue, geographic region, or moment in time, the older women could not rely upon the younger generation's acceptance of their guidance. Indeed, there were times when vast numbers of youth rebelled against many of these women's basic principles. Civil rights, women's rights, and the Vietnam War were issues over which rightist women experienced the most profound generation clashes, but the generations clashed on other matters as well.

Even while issues came and went, most rightist women remained true to their convictions that the America they loved was under attack and that it was their duty to save it. They sought to establish a sound foundation, replete with "traditional" American values, upon which the baby boom generation would be nurtured. While many other Americans shared some of the ideas that right-wing women expressed on various issues, most rightist women pulled all the issues together and took it upon themselves to save the nation. They saw the shaping of the next generation as a means to uphold the values they held dear.

OUR SCHOOLS,
OUR CHILDREN

☼ 1

SHAPING AMERICAN EDUCATION

Rooting out radical influences in American education is women's job.
Lucille Cardin Crain, 1951

During the early 1950s, headlines in popular women's magazines and in educational journals asked, "Who's Trying to Ruin Our Schools?" and declared "Danger's Ahead in the Public Schools." They were referring to recent right-wing efforts to influence school curricula and to discredit teaching methods that diverged from the traditional methods of the past. "A bewildering disease that threatens to reach epidemic proportions has infected the public schools of America," warned author John Bainbridge in September and October 1952 in a two-part series for *McCall's*. "The disease does not attack the body but, rather, the mind and the spirit. It produces unreasoning fear and hysteria."[1] Bainbridge described efforts to censor textbooks; standardize the curriculum; eliminate teaching about communism, the United Nations, and the workings of foreign governments; and discredit teaching methods. Activists sought to ban from speaking before students and educational conferences anyone who did not subscribe to the political right's way of thinking. As a consequence, some American communities were wracked with disagreement over what the country's youth were being taught and who was doing the teaching.

Leading the campaign for censorship and standardization were several right-wing organizations. A few of their leaders were known extremists, such as Allen A. Zoll of the National Council for American Education, who had a reputation dating back to the late 1930s as an anti-Semite and a fascist.[2] Others were individual "ultraconservative" Americans who preached that American history, economics, and other courses must stay within the boundaries of their rigid thinking. Among these rightists were women who believed that, as women, they had a special role to play in the "cleaning up" of the schools.

Censorship in America was not new. In Boston during the 1920s, men, with some assistance from women, fought to ban books that "extolled" obscenity and political "radicalism." Textbooks too faced censorship. In 1923, the state of Wisconsin passed a law that banned schools from adopting history books that gave less than favorable information about the Revolutionary War and the nation's founders, or contained what lawmakers determined was "propaganda favorable to any foreign government."[3] While men stood out as the driving forces behind most of the earlier censorship campaigns, those of the 1950s found thousands of women involved, many of whom became leaders.

The late 1940s and early 1950s found Americans, including the right wing, in the process of adjusting to political and social changes that had emerged in postwar America. Franklin Roosevelt was dead, but many New Deal ideas and policies, foreign and domestic, continued under his successors. The country's involvement in World War II, and in the creation of the United Nations, indicated a far greater international consciousness on the part of its political leaders. If the right was to help determine the nation's future, it needed to advance its ideas without alienating the general public. As historian Eric F. Goldman pointed out, even during years when America was at peace, people found it difficult to discuss domestic issues without also bringing up foreign affairs.[4] Communism lay in the forefront of post–World War II political thinking, and many on the right pushed that theme to the extreme.

One place that the right's anticommunism crusade played itself out was in America's schools. In an era in which women's role was centered upon the home and family, campaigns to shape American education gave white, middle-class, right-wing women opportunities to exert considerable influence in the public sphere. Their campaigns were particularly influential during the early to mid-1950s. Fears of domestic communism were at a height at this time due to the highly public actions of Republican senator Joseph McCarthy to seek out communists in the public sector. Rightist women networked, joined like-minded women in organizations, wrote letters to newspapers and to government officials, published articles, newsletters, and books, and gave lectures designed to push their agendas. Such activism helped to keep the right wing alive in the 1950s and into the 1960s and to carry on some rightist agendas that were rooted in the era of Franklin Roosevelt's presidency. Concurrently, they were able to move the right in a new direction by attaching themselves to an issue—that is, the spread of communism—that caused anxiety for a broad segment of American society, while deemphasizing the anti-Semitism that was often associated with the right of the Roosevelt era.[5]

Following World War II, Americans no longer saw the Soviet Union as a wartime ally, but rather as threatening to dominate the world. At the same time, many Americans who had formerly balked at the idea of the United States becoming involved in international affairs were now suspicious of the new United Nations, fearing that Communist nations had too much power in the organization. The United Nations Educational, Scientific and Cultural Organization (UNESCO), created in November 1945, added fuel to these worries. UNESCO's programs promoting the sharing of cultures and educational methods throughout the world led to concerns that "un-American" philosophies would permeate this country's schools. As historian Stuart J. Foster points out in his study of the Red Scare in America's public schools, Americans feared that external forces "beyond their control" were challenging the American way of life.[6] News of Communist teachers and professors teaching in American schools and colleges permeated the press, although a government report estimated that at its peak in 1948, Communist Party membership among American teachers numbered only about 1,500.[7]

Despite the lack of numbers, such fears could not be set aside in an era in which communism had both overtaken Eastern Europe and was a driving force in Asia. As in the Roosevelt era, the right remained obsessed with fears of communist conspiracies and of other "un-American" ideas.[8] News that there were indeed communists in the New Deal, as revealed in the Alger Hiss case in the late 1940s and in the convictions of Ethel and Julius Rosenberg on espionage charges in 1951, was further evidence for those arguing that the New Deal was teeming with communists. Journalist John T. Flynn's The Roosevelt Myth (1948) raised questions regarding the president's associations with communists and cast doubt on his truthfulness with the American people. To many right-wing women, New Deal liberalism was as dangerous to the country as communism. They were distraught to realize that Roosevelt's welfare policies were not to be dismantled under Truman and Eisenhower. Proper education for the upcoming generation, however, might redeem the nation. But, as these women saw it, modern education was sending the country in the wrong direction.[9]

Lucille Cardin Crain, editor of the right-wing quarterly the *Educational Reviewer* (1949–1954), became a leading figure in the campaign to rid schools of "leftist influences." She often spoke on the importance of women's involvement in this issue. In an address before a group of Rotary Club women in 1951, Crain said, "In a very real sense, rooting out radical influences in American education is women's job. In every book of old sayings it is written that women by nature are conservative, and certainly they are in a pivotal position in helping to foster and preserve through their children the ideals of this great country of ours."[10] Two years later, in an address before the Michigan Women's National Security Council in Detroit, Crain expounded further on this theme asserting, "[T]he educational controversy is in a very real sense women's business. . . . We women have a reputation for getting things done once we set our hands to them."[11] Judging from letters to Crain and to others involved in the crusade, thousands of women answered the call for action and rose to protest "progressive education."[12] Confident in their capabilities, these women welcomed the opportunity to lead the country in what they believed was the appropriate direction.

The progressive education movement was by this time decades old, having emerged amidst the progressive movement—a broad program of social and political reform—of the early twentieth century. At the forefront of progressive education was philosopher and educational reformer John Dewey, who believed that the emphasis in education should be on the needs and interests of the child. He held that children should participate in planning their courses of study and also advocated group and experiential learning. Dewey believed that as active, organic beings, growing and changing, children should engage in courses of study that reflected their particular stages of development. At the same time, he considered schools to be a place where new ideas could be tested, challenged, and restructured, with the goal of improving the social order. Dewey and other progressives such as philosopher and educator Boyd H. Bode saw schools as the means to prepare children for life in a democratic society. They

Figure 1. Lucille Cardin Crain, ca. 1950. From front of published essay, Lucille Cardin Crain papers, Coll. 95, box 84. Courtesy of Special Collections and University Archives, University of Oregon Libraries, Eugene, Oregon.

eliminated such teaching methods as rote memorization and drill.[13] For a brief time, during the 1920s and early 1930s, some progressive educators flirted with Marxism but, by the late 1930s, most of the movement's leaders had repudiated that and other radical ideas, including "collectivism." Throughout the 1920s and 1930s schools implemented the ideas and tenets of progressive education. Although the extent of progressive practices varied from district to district, by the 1940s progressive education dominated the American pedagogy.[14] Many Americans, particularly those on the right, were suspicious of modern education, and right-wing attacks grew after World War II.

As several historians of the 1940s–1960s have shown, the grassroots played an important role in postwar right-wing activism.[15] The education fight was one that American women considered of utmost importance for their gender to adopt. Some women responding to the right-wing cause joined national organizations whose branches became involved in identifying "subversive" educators and textbooks. Chapters of such rightward-leaning groups as the Daughters of the American Revolution, the National Association of Pro-America, and the Minute Women of the U.S.A. actively campaigned on the issue. Outside of these groups, other women, particularly those on the right, joined local organizations to protest liberal teachings in their local schools. Crain believed the "communist assault" on American schools was not a new phenomenon, but a practice of long standing. In a speech before a group of Republican women in 1953, she explained, "The plans of the Communist conspirators for American education were not evolved only in recent years. These conspirators were not stupid men, and it was Lenin . . . who said 'Give us a child for eight years and it will be a Bolshevik forever.'"[16]

Critics of the public schools often blamed progressive education, with its experimentation, ideas of "learning by doing," and de-emphasis on grades and "The Three R's," for the problems they saw with the schools. They claimed the schools were neglecting American history, were involving children in too many extracurricular activities, and were failing to teach traditional moral values.[17] Educators frequently found that men and women of the far right were spearheading many of these complaints. These rightists first offered broad criticism, then focused on how these failings would bring about "Collectivist," "Socialist," or "Communist" indoctrination.[18] One attack centered on the Social Studies movement because it included the study of global, cultural, political, and economic issues, rather than concentrating on straight American history. Critics feared that students would come under the influence of un-American ideas if they studied other cultures. By concentrating on such matters, right-wing groups had some notable successes in ousting administrators and removing textbooks from school curricula. For example, in November 1950, in conservative Pasadena, California, rightists ousted Willard E. Goslin, a nationally respected educator, from his post as superintendent of schools. Similarly, many school districts removed a textbook, Frank Magruder's *American Government*, long considered a classic.[19] Such erstwhile vigilantes frequently consulted Lucille Cardin Crain's *Educational Reviewer*, citing its textbook reviews.

The Educational Reviewer

The founding of the *Educational Reviewer* quarterly resulted from efforts of Crain and oil magnate William F. Buckley Sr., under the auspices of the Conference of American Small Business Organizations (CASBO). They hoped to purge from schools' books any statements that appeared to support recent New Deal or Fair Deal policies or that appeared "communistic."

Crain and Buckley began plans for the creation of an organization that would carry the same name as their publication. They began outlining their ideas in December 1947, but the publication was not launched until July 1949. Their grand plan, however, went beyond the quarterly *Reviewer*. They hoped to organize groups by states or among college alumni who could distribute propaganda that the Educational Reviewer organization would supply. The plan was for Crain and her office staff to prepare a list of publications that espoused their political and economic points of view. These books included an edition of philosopher and sociologist Herbert Spencer's *The Man Versus the State* that contained an introduction by libertarian writer Albert Jay Nock, and CASBO member George S. Montgomery's *The Return of Adam Smith*. Crain and Buckley wanted similarly concerned alumni to purchase sets of these books and place them at strategic points in various colleges. They also sought like-minded correspondents in each college, asking them to prepare lists of "radical" professors, along with their backgrounds and connections. Crain proposed they organize a "cell" of students who shared their points of view "to report on matters of interest." In fact, Buckley considered it advantageous to issue what he described as "a 'Who's Who' of radicals among teachers in our schools." Crain sought to convince university presses to "print proper textbooks." Commencement speakers, too, should be monitored. If necessary, the Educational Reviewer organization would lodge protests against those they considered "inappropriate." Further, she suggested that alumni withhold contributions to educational institutions "until undesirable situations are corrected."[20]

Crain and Buckley first met when a member of CASBO suggested that they unite in ridding the schools of radical teachings. Buckley became the financial backer for the project, agreeing to pay Crain an annual salary of $5,000 for three years. He also paid travel, office, and other expenses incurred during the first three years of the Educational Reviewer's operation. Crain requested funds for "indispensable" publications, telling Buckley she would "feel quite lost" without the *Wall Street Journal* and the conservative weekly *Human Events*. Desiring to gain a sense of what liberal groups were promoting, Crain also requested memberships in Columbia University's Academy of Political Science and the Academy of Social Sciences at Philadelphia. Their start-up date was September 1, 1948, and the founders hoped that within three years their organization would be self-supporting, with funds coming in from subscriptions to the *Educational Reviewer* and from wealthy contributors.[21]

Crain and Buckley discovered that they had more than their political outlooks in common. Soon Crain and her husband, Kenneth, a businessman and magazine editor, began socializing with William F. Buckley Sr., and his wife, Aloise, and Lucille was corresponding with William ("Billie") F. Buckley Jr., and his sister Patricia. Shortly after the Educational Reviewer's founding, Patricia (Buckley) Bozell worked for Crain for at least several months. By 1950, the elder Buckley was calling upon Crain, "with [her] wealth of knowledge and experience," to give Billie "a few pointers" on what to include in his political writings and speeches. She occasionally sent the younger Buckley suggestions, contributing some materials for the younger Buckley's book *God and Man at Yale* (1951). Once published, the book was advertised as showing "how 'academic freedom' is being used to undermine traditional American values," a point of view completely in line with Crain's thinking.[22] Both Crain and the senior Buckley were Roman Catholics. Crain, who was of French Canadian descent, received her education in Catholic schools. While she occasionally referred to her religious faith, expressing pride that her teachers were nuns, there is no evidence that Buckley and Crain ever discussed theology or religious education.

Crain had been active on the political scene since the early 1940s, when, in November 1941, she founded a consumer advocacy group, We, the People, Inc. An economic conservative, she believed that national, state, and local governments were all wasting taxpayers' money. Her group floundered in 1943, but she remained active within the right-wing movement. As the war years passed, Crain's political outlook evolved from moderate right wing, with a libertarian strain of the old Jeffersonian bias against big government, to a position well outside of the mainstream. By the war's end, she was a passionate anti–New Dealer and anticommunist, and a believer in the theory that Winston Churchill and Franklin Roosevelt had conspired to involve the United States in World War II.[23] After the war, she remained politically active within right-wing circles. In 1948, with Anne Burrows Hamilton, she wrote *Packaged Thinking for Women*, in which she accused mainstream women's organizations of becoming increasingly left-wing and corrupted by "the beatitudes of internationalism." The authors were especially critical of the General Federation of

Women's Clubs for promoting the teaching of "world citizenship" in the public schools.[24] The booklet brought positive responses from the right, giving Crain recognition as a spokesperson in the fight against collectivism and internationalism.[25]

The *Educational Reviewer* periodical survived until February 1954. Crain believed that at least part of the reason for the publication's demise was that she and the *Reviewer* were "smeared" in the September 1951 issue of *McCall's*, her name being linked with Allen Zoll's in the article "Who's Trying to Ruin Our Schools?" She filed a lawsuit, charging *McCall's* with libel.[26] Crain also sued the ousted Pasadena schools superintendent, Willard E. Goslin, after he denounced, in a radio broadcast, those persons named in the *McCall's* article. His broadcast, she claimed, caused her to suffer "great anxiety of mind."[27] The lawsuit proved costly for the Educational Reviewer organization. The suit dragged on from 1951 to 1954, when Crain finally lost the case.[28] Subscriptions to the *Reviewer* never exceeded the low thousands, and at the end of the contracted three years, William Buckley Sr., withdrew his financial support. Donations and payments for individual reviews of texts were not sufficient to keep the publication afloat. A few wealthy men and large organizations contributed, including Lammot DuPont, who was a long-time opponent of the New Deal and a founding member of the American Liberty League.[29] Nevertheless, the Reviewer organization never drew enough financial support to remain on sound footing. A female acquaintance suggested that Crain take advantage of her gender and ask some vulnerable wealthy women to support the *Reviewer*: "You and I know of women who fall easy prey to propagandists, so why should you not have some of that kind of money?"[30] But it was too late to revive the publication.

The Educational Reviewer organization, however, which held tax-exempt status, was not dissolved. In 1955, Crain, as its president, offered to turn the corporation over to William F. Buckley Jr., when his conservative journal, *National Review*, began to run into financial trouble. The final transfer was not completed until 1960. Crain later said that following a desperate plea from Buckley Jr., she "made the transfer as an acknowledgement of his father's important contribution to the *Reviewer*." The transfer allowed the *National Review* to receive tax-exempt status.[31]

While the *Educational Reviewer* survived fewer than five years, the publication brought Crain considerable recognition as a leader in the right's attacks on modern education. Shortly after the launching of the *Reviewer*, the conservative *Chicago Tribune* endorsed "this modest little paper." Now school boards would have less excuse for allowing a textbook that "promotes socialism, ridicules the American system of government and presents a distorted account of this nation's history."[32] On January 29, 1950, a *Tribune* editorial suggested that all school trustees and administrators subscribe to the *Educational Reviewer* because the quarterly's reviewers were "liberals in the old and respectable sense of the word. They believe that the principles of the Declaration of Independence are good and that the principles of the Constitution . . . are valid." Acknowledging that few textbooks in the country openly advocated socialism or communism, the editorial noted that the *Reviewer* grasped subtle, but glowing accounts of "the gradual governmentalization of the American people."[33]

Crain's postsecondary education included only two or three summers of normal school, and her teaching experience lasted only three years,[34] yet during the early 1950s, many on the right considered her an authority on education. She was a popular speaker, especially before such right-wing women's groups as Pro America and the Minute Women.[35] She occasionally served as a guest speaker on conservative radio programs and wrote many articles condemning what she saw as "collectivist," "pseudo-liberal," and "internationalist" notions. Not only women, but men too, respected Crain's accomplishments. On July 2, 1952, conservative congressman Paul W. Shafer of Michigan read one of her articles, "The UNESCO Threat to Our Schools," into the *Congressional Record*.[36] Right-wing commentator John T. Flynn admired Crain's efforts, applauding "*The Educational Reviewer* [as] a key instrument in the movement to clean up the schools." Flynn praised Crain and her work in several radio broadcasts and sought financial support and positive publicity for her venture.[37]

Also backing the *Reviewer* was Paul Palmer, senior editor of *Readers Digest*, who in 1949 indicated that he was recommending Crain's work to others. He was an early subscriber to the *Reviewer*, but by 1951 was criticizing the quarterly. He wrote Crain that he objected to "the long sections of your review *telling* the reader that the textbook is collectivist or subversive or whatnot, instead of [providing] examples *showing* him that it is."[38] The following year Crain canceled her long-time subscription to *Readers Digest* "because," she wrote, "it is no longer the staunch defender of the American tradition. . . . the *Digest* has given in to a leftist trick with which

I am familiar, that of the 'both sides' formula."[39] Despite a letter from Burt MacBride of *Readers Digest*, enclosing a list of about 100 anticommunism articles the magazine had published over the previous ten years, Crain did not relent.[40] Obviously, Crain was farther to the right than the conservative *Digest*.

The Educational Reviewer enterprise was not a large operation. In 1950 its two offices were housed in the front parlor of an old brownstone in New York City, the office staff consisting of Crain, one secretary, and one clerk. To provide an intellectual base to the quarterly, the organization employed a consulting staff that included three professors: William Starr Myers, professor emeritus of politics, Princeton; Lewis H. Haney, professor of economics, New York University; and O. Glenn Saxon, professor of business administration, Yale University.[41] Every quarter the *Reviewer* printed critiques of several textbooks used in public schools and colleges. Frequently writing the reviews were professors, lawyers, and teachers holding graduate degrees, all of whom shared the basics of Crain's social, political, and economic outlook.

Hundreds of people wrote Crain, asking for recommendations for textbooks, particularly in the social sciences. If books had been reviewed in the quarterly, she would send correspondents the information; if not, she charged the correspondent a $50 fee to have a specified book reviewed.[42] A letter from C. W. Behrhorst was typical of scores that Crain received from concerned citizens and educators. Behrhorst, a county school board president, wrote Crain that local schools planned to purchase new textbooks and, in a three-year period, "to completely revamp [their] entire library of books." He then asked if she would provide help in evaluating those texts as well as information on how to "go about checking all the texts which we have in our school system."[43] She received considerable mail concerning the Magruder *American Government* text, which was extensively criticized in the first issue of the *Reviewer*.[44] That text was eventually banned in a number of school districts across the nation, from Oregon to Florida and California to Connecticut.[45]

While the quarterly *Reviewer* was at the center of Crain's organization, she took other steps to fight radicalism in education. Crain and her associates conducted investigations of those professors they suspected of leaning to the left, keeping files on them to supply "proof" of their allegations. For example, when the second issue of the *Reviewer* criticized the history text *The Building of Our Nation* by Eugene Barker, Henry Steele Commager, and Walter Prescott Webb, the book's publishers, Row, Peterson and Company, objected to the reviewer's charge that the text had a leftist slant. Defending the review, and giving some evidence as to how she investigated "leftist" writings, Crain wrote William Buckley Sr., that her files on Columbia University professor Henry Steele Commager revealed some "very slanted writing" on his part, including his support for "the Roosevelt court packing plan." She pointed out that both Barker and Webb were historians in the University of Texas History Department, writing, "It occurred to me that you might want to ask some of your Texas friends for information about both of them. How did these two Texans tie up with a Columbia University Professor? And who did write the book—the two Texans or Commager? And can anyone find any writings by either Barker or Webb that would reveal their slant?"[46] While the book's publishers may have been upset over the review, it does not appear that the review greatly affected the text's circulation. Written by three highly respected historians, it went through several subsequent editions over the next ten years.

The Educational Reviewer also proceeded with earlier plans to send like-minded students into colleges and universities to expose professors who were Communists or sympathetic to communism. In September 1951, Crain wrote right-wing journalist and conspiracy theorist John T. Flynn of two students, one male and one female, whom she found to be willing to "monitor" courses they would be taking at Columbia University and its Teachers College. She asked Flynn if he might be willing to pay the young people "a nominal fee for this research assignment." Indicating that she and Flynn were already working together on the plan, Crain concluded, "Both students were enchanted to learn that you would value their collaboration in this project and they are looking forward with the keenest anticipation to meeting you."[47]

Its proximity to Educational Reviewer headquarters as well as its history of association with radicalism likely influenced Crain's focus on Teachers College. In 1934 progressive educator George S. Counts and several male colleagues launched a publication, the *Social Frontier*, promoting the belief that education should lead the way in reconstructing American society. For the next year or more, the magazine lobbied against individualism and capitalism, in favor of collectivism and socialism. However, it was not long before disillusionment with the far left led Counts to leave the editorship of the *Social Frontier*. He quit the magazine in 1937 and became the leader of the anticommunist group within the college teacher's union. Others of the magazine's founders had also become disenchanted with Marxism and communism, and by May 1939 *Social Frontier* was anticommunist. Despite their turn away from communism, it would be decades before most of these men, their magazine, and Teachers College, Columbia University, were able to lose their "Communist sympathizer" reputations.[48]

Crain was eager to involve young people in efforts to clean up public education, and she was successful in attracting some young men to the organization. They were, as Crain described them, "students who somehow have escaped the indoctrination of their schools and who recognize the importance of the Reviewer. I call them the Reviewer Junior Group."[49] The April 1950 edition of the *Educational Reviewer* featured an article by student Roger MacBride, who had attended three years of high school in upscale Westchester County, followed by attendance at "a famous New England preparatory school," and was at the time of his writing attending Princeton. He claimed that until he became an upperclassman at his college, in practically all of his courses "the predominant slant was away from the individual and toward the collective." MacBride concluded that "very few people finish school today without having a tinge of collectivism ingrained into them."[50] Not mentioned in the newsletter was the fact that MacBride, since his early teens, had been a protégé of libertarian author Rose Wilder Lane, and he was a leader of a student libertarian group at Princeton.[51]

If Crain's vision was to survive, she needed such young people as MacBride to carry on the movement. In the meanwhile, she had help from other quarters. Thousands of women throughout the United States, many of whom were familiar with Crain's work, were joining with others of their sex to promote rightist ideas on education.

Rightist Women and Their Organizations

The late 1940s and early 1950s saw a number of right-wing women and right-wing women's organizations playing a role in influencing parents, voters, and school boards regarding who should be leading the nation's schools and what types of information America's children should be taught. Although she had no children of her own, Frances Bartlett, a

Pasadena, California, physician's wife, helped form a group known as the School Development Council. This agency sought to rid Pasadena public schools of "subversive" influences. A retired teacher, Bartlett had great respect for the work Crain was doing and for the *Educational Reviewer*. Bartlett kept Crain updated regarding the council's efforts to oust Superintendent Willard E. Goslin and also sent her material on people suspected of being communists or liberals and those who sought to modernize or change school curricula.[52]

Women who led right-wing organizations, as well as those who like Crain published newsletters, realized that it was important to keep one another informed of happenings in their locales. They helped spread word about vital issues, enlisting at least moral support from women in other regions of the country. Within their own organizations, women connected via meetings, letters, newsletters, and the telephone. For example, during the organization's early years, the Minute Women communicated within a pyramid-style telephone chain system in which chapter chairs designated women to make calls to five members on a list, and those members would then make calls to another five, and so on down the list until all members received the intended message.[53]

In the mid-1950s Bartlett took over the editorship of *FACTS in Education*, a bimonthly newsletter designed to keep like-minded thinkers informed of current educational issues.[54] Almost five years after Goslin resigned as superintendent, *FACTS* sought to keep the controversy alive by implying that Goslin's appointment had been part of a plot to transform Pasadena "from a stable, conservative community into a hot bed of socialism." Bartlett, in 1955, wrote of a dire situation. "We are," she warned, "witnessing today the actual destruction of the Constitution of this Republic and its Bill of Rights." Evidencing the right's fears of the rise of an intellectual elite, she continued, "We are presently engaged in a revolution, not one by force and violence, but one of ideas. [It is] a revolution begun and fostered by the intellectuals." Bartlett blamed much of the problem on the National Education Association (NEA), believing that due to negligence, ignorance, or both, teachers and parents had paid little attention to the NEA's rise to power. As a result, the public school systems of the nation were "drifting steadily to the LEFT." The next step, Bartlett surmised, would be federal aid to education, an act of government intervention that she and most rightists adamantly opposed. Aid from the federal government, they feared, would increase government interference in public school procedures and would diminish local control.[55]

During the early 1950s in particular, the Minute Women were prominent among the groups on the lookout for "subversive" materials in school texts and "left-leaning" school administrators. The organization's founder, Belgian-born Suzanne Silvercruys Stevenson, the daughter of a Belgian baron, shared Crain's belief that conservative women could wield considerable influence if they united for a cause. Stevenson, who became an American citizen in 1922, was married to a colonel in the United States Army Reserve. She detested communism and anything that resembled it, and by the late 1940s was concerned that American institutions were moving toward socialism. Her worries regarding the direction the country was taking led to the founding of the Minute Women of the U.S.A., Inc., in 1949. Stevenson was confident that she could lead rightist women as a united force determined to preserve traditional moral, political, and economic values. She led the Minute Women until early 1952, after which the organization's headquarters moved from Connecticut to Wheeling, West Virginia.[56]

In contrast to the centrally located enterprises of Bartlett and Crain, the Minute Women had branches in more than two dozen states by the time of the relocation of the group's headquarters. The group campaigned on a variety of issues in addition to education, including socialized medicine and integration, both of which they opposed. Although the group was officially nonpartisan, the women generally supported the right wing of the Republican Party. Members occasionally discussed foreign policy, but campaigns usually focused upon domestic issues. As might be expected from a group with a name that harkened back to the Minute Men of the American Revolutionary era, on the Minute Women's list of "Principles" was "Patriotic teaching in our schools and colleges."[57] They saw themselves as patriotic, on the alert for subversive influences in America. Some of the greatest successes of this mostly white, Christian, middle-class organization of women centered on their attempts to influence educational systems. In their November 1952 national newsletter, the group's leaders—like Crain—denounced the *McCall's* "Save Our Schools" article.[58] In Houston, Texas, local Minute Women succeeded in having their supporters elected to the board of the city's Independent School District. Founded in the spring of 1951, the Houston chapter was one of the strongest in the nation, with membership numbers exceeding five hundred by November 1952. Because of their agitation, Houston experienced resignations and firings of teachers and school officials, including the deputy school superintendent.[59]

Among the leaders of the Houston Minute Women was Helen Darden Thomas, daughter of Ida Darden, publisher of the right-wing newspaper the *Southern Conservative*. Thomas, a 1928 graduate of the University of Texas, served as the "intellectual" of the Houston group, poring over right-wing publications, discredited files of the House Committee on Un-American Activities, the *Congressional Record*, and other materials, to create dossiers on Texans she alleged to be associated with subversives.[60] Although New Yorker and fellow Minute Woman Lucille Cardin Crain did not become directly involved in the uproar in Houston, she did correspond with Texas Minute Women and was sought after and spoke before various branches of the organization.

Also entering the battle over what should be taught in the nation's schools was the Daughters of the American Revolution (DAR). Almost since its founding in 1890, the DAR placed heavy emphasis upon the role of history in education, propagating its version of American history, which emphasized patriotism and an iconic notion of the founding fathers and American values. Nevertheless, the association endorsed the majority of the progressive legislation of the early twentieth century, as did other mainstream women's organizations.[61] However, as historian Kim E. Nielsen points out, the organization took a rightward turn and joined the fight against radicalism during the post–World War I Red Scare. One of the DAR's concerns at the time was the perceived influence of Bolshevism within women's colleges.[62] Evidence of the organization's rightist leanings was reinforced during the 1930s, when chapters invited far right activist Elizabeth Dilling to speak to them. The organization's racism drew the public's attention too, particularly during 1939 when the DAR refused to allow the famed black contralto Marian Anderson to sing in its Constitution Hall.[63] Also during 1939, signs of the group's anti-Semitism emerged when it joined with various other "patriotic" groups in opposition to the Child Refugee Bill that would have admitted refugee Jewish children to the United States.[64] During the early 1950s, with fears about the spread of communism once again abounding, the organization put considerable stress upon young people having the opportunity to study America's early history. In July 1953, member Osie Smith Coolbaugh, writing in the *Daughters of the American Revolution Magazine,* maintained that knowledge of the history of the United States was the most powerful weapon to combat communism. "No one who knows the story of America can ever become a communist," she wrote. "The only reason any American ever does is because he doesn't know his country." Coolbaugh contended that children should begin studying American history as soon as they learned to read.[65]

But some DAR members believed there was a need for more than the emphasis upon American history if the nation was to defeat communism. Parents needed to be vigilant as to the ideologies their children were being exposed to in the classroom. In 1953, Frances B. Lucas, executive secretary for the National Defense Committee of the DAR, found some disturbing similarities while comparing Russian and American education. American children, she feared, were being taught to favor collectivism over individual freedom and private ownership. She asked readers of her newsletter, "What are YOUR children being taught?"[66]

The DAR's efforts to inculcate knowledge of American history and tradition into the nation's children did not go unnoticed among other rightists. An editorial in the *American Mercury* in 1958 recognized the group as "one organization which never wavers in its fight for the preservation of American ideals." With chapters in every state of the Union, the DAR "has been in the forefront of every hard fight against Communist and un-American subversion since it was launched in 1890." The editorial noted further that while other women's organizations were "notoriously infiltrated with socialistic and international activists," such was not the case with the DAR.[67] The DAR's strict requirement that potential members prove they are lineal descendants of an ancestor who actively participated in America's War for Independence was no doubt instrumental in keeping "infiltrators" out.

DAR representatives from all regions of the United States, North, South, East, and West, corresponded with Lucille Cardin Crain. They frequently sent lists of texts, along with requests for their review. Mrs. E. L. (Eunice) Harwell, of Abilene, Texas, and state chairman of the DAR, sent a transcript of that organization's "Investigation of Subversive Textbooks in Texas Public Schools," a report presented at the organization's state conference in March 1952.[68] At that time, the national DAR was also voicing opposition to federal aid to education, charging that such assistance would lead to federal control, which in turn would lead to "socialization" as well as to racial desegregation.[69] Other patriotic groups took similar positions, including the Daughters of American Colonies, which opposed federal aid in education while supporting the "return of old-fashioned American history again in the schools."[70]

DAR members, as well as members of other older patriotic women's associations, were frequently found in the right-wing women's groups of the 1950s and 1960s. For example, in his study of the "Red Scare" in Houston, Texas, during the 1950s, historian Don E. Carleton found that many of the Minute Women involved in the public school dispute in that city also belonged to the DAR or to the Daughters of the Republic of Texas.[71] The conservative ideologies of the traditional and the modern right merged in regard to a number of issues, particularly when the issues pertained to education.

Pro America, which began as the Lake Washington Garden Club in the suburbs of Seattle, was composed of a group of middle-class women who decided that devotion to their homes, children, and the cultural and civic life of their community was not enough. During the closing days of the 1932 presidential election campaign, the women organized Pro America to combat the rise of Franklin Roosevelt's New Deal. They worried that the new administration would not lead the country in a manner that would uphold their traditional values in respect to patriotism, religion, and morality. They wanted to return to an idealized "traditional" America, a time when there was less government bureaucracy and more power was in the hands of families and the community. They feared that the country was straying from the representative form of government as set forth in the Constitution, and they hoped to reverse the trend. If they were to do so, they needed to do more than vote; they needed to get together and create a national organization "dedicated to the rebirth of idealism in our national life." Pro America began as a nonpartisan organization, but by the time of the 1936 presidential election, it was aligned with the Republican Party.[72] By the 1950s it was a national association of right-wing women and involved in the public school controversies.

Often, women might belong to Pro America while at the same time be involved in local rightist organizations. Louise Hawke Padelford, founder of the Pasadena chapter of Pro America, is one example. Like Frances

Bartlett, she was an outspoken member of the School Development Council (SDC), the organization that played an important role in the removal of Superintendent Goslin. Some of Padelford's sister members of Pro America also belonged to the SDC. In fact, David Hurlburd found in his study of the public school controversy in Pasadena, that there were times when it was difficult to accurately determine where the operations of the School Development Council left off and Pro America took over.[73] Offering further evidence of the influence of rightist women in the Pasadena schools controversy, the Defense Commission of the National Education Association also noted the close connection between Pro America and the SDC. It reported that "The first intimation of hostility" toward Goslin's appointment to the superintendency "came from the Pasadena chapter of Pro America." As Defense Commission investigators saw the situation, the SDC "served largely as the action organization for the . . . Pasadena Chapter of Pro America."[74]

As was the case with other rightist women's groups, members of Pro America frequently corresponded with Crain. Evidence points to Crain being an important link in a loose network of rightist women who realized that they could more readily further their cause if they cooperated with one another. As early as June 1949, when the *Educational Reviewer* was just getting under way, Crain spent time with Pro America's president, Dorothy Bonny of Ellensburg, Washington. Bonny was campaigning against federal aid to education and making contacts with conservative leaders in New York.[75] Although battling against federal aid to education was not at the top of rightist women's agendas, almost every one of their organizations voiced opposition to such government interference.

Most of these women were particularly fearful of ideas they considered "collectivist" that encouraged people to work together in common causes. Rightist women believed that such collaboration was an early step in the direction of communism. In school curricula, some new programs that encouraged students to work in groups to solve problems and to share ideas fit into these women's definitions of "collectivism." Apparently they did not recognize that their own organizing and networking could fall under their definition. Also, they criticized schools that introduced studies of various countries associated with the United Nations, an organization which many if not most of these women opposed as "un-American." They believed that such curricula, with their aims of giving balanced views of the cultures of individual nations, would result in promoting socialistic or communistic forms of government.

In July 1953, Kathryn G. Alexander, the mother of two children who were attending Los Angeles schools, wrote Crain to describe the activities of local women involved in campaigns against collectivist influences in public schools. She referred to those she worked with as "a small group of very active women," all of whom were "good *Christian ladies* [Alexander's emphasis]" who believed God was on their side. Alexander, who was a Minute Woman, added that one of her practices was to "blast away at the school board." However, the last time she did so, the board invoked the "gag rule," and her group was no longer allowed to speak unless it sent in a script ahead of time. She was particularly concerned about the teaching of world government in the schools, but by the time of the letter she was resigned to the fact that such "un-American fundamentals" had penetrated too deeply to eradicate easily. Alexander claimed that her group had scored some small victories against the influence of UNESCO in Los Angeles schools, but was upset about "the sex line of UNESCO" in the high schools where "nothing [was] left untaught. That is what started me to fight," she said.[76] The invocation of the "gag rule" shows the women's behavior was not such as one might envision being associated with the "good Christian ladies" whom Alexander describes. Indeed, at least one woman, Dorothy Frank of the Women for Legislative Action, found these women's actions to be quite intimidating.

The education of the nation's children was of concern to men and women of all political views. Dorothy Frank was one woman who held a much more liberal attitude than Alexander regarding what was being taught in Los Angeles schools. As chairwoman of the education committee of Women for Legislative Action, Frank spoke before the Los Angeles school board in favor of teaching about UNESCO. She believed it important that children learn about other cultures of the world so as to enable greater tolerance of other peoples. In an article for *Collier's* magazine, she recalled testifying that "Participation in the United Nations is a vital part of our nation's program. We can't allow Los Angeles to become the ostrich city of our country!" UNESCO, Frank soon learned, was only one of many subjects that the right-wing opposition was trying to abolish in the schools. Anthropology, intercultural relations, mental hygiene, and current events were others. Frank found herself embroiled in a huge fight over what was being taught. By the time she next appeared before the school board, Frank had become "notorious" as a supporter of UNESCO. She was quite shaken when she next appeared before the board to give a two-minute presentation amidst a cacophony of boos and jeers from the right. The atmosphere of hate caused her to fear for her physical safety.[77]

Both men and women were active in the anti-UNESCO forces in Los Angeles, but several women emerged as leaders, particularly Florence Fowler Lyons the supposed "spark" behind the campaign, and Ruth Cole, a newly elected school board member. It was a woman who sent Frank two venomous letters. The woman (whose name Frank did not disclose) wrote, "In my estimation you are not fit for American citizenship. . . . I have two grandchildren and you may rest assured that, if I live, they will be taught the 'nationalism' that you besmirch, *and* they will be taught to hate the United Nations just as I do, and to spit upon its flag at every opportunity." Frank recognized she could never have a reasonable discussion with such a woman, who was so insistent upon viewing issues and ideas in black and white.[78]

While local battles were under way in places like Pasadena, Los Angeles, and Houston, other women with rightist leanings were reaching national audiences via the media. Journalist and radio pioneer Irene Corbally Kuhn, who with her daughter Rene produced a radio show for WNBC called "The Kuhns," was among those joined in the education controversy. Irene, a widow since 1925, became a conservative activist during the 1940s. In 1940 and again in 1944, she was associate director of publicity for the Republican National Committee during the presidential campaigns.[79] In January 1951, *American Legion Magazine* published Irene's "Why You Buy Books that Sell Communism." Eighteen months later, the magazine published her article, "Your Child Is Their Target." In the latter article she charged that for nearly three decades "a small but well organized minority" of educators had been attempting to make radical changes to the character of American education. As Kuhn saw it, these educators intended to "capture the 'whole child,' usurp parental authority, and so nullify moral and spiritual influences." She found that "these authoritarians in education" were trying to subvert teachers. Overall, however, "the majority of teachers have kept their integrity and sense of high responsibility to their calling."[80]

Unlike Crain and others on the right, Kuhn did not single out liberals

and the Left as the enemy, but wrote that "Many of the professional educators and lobbyists involved in the agitation are actually rightists, even
extreme conservatives," who sought to retain their jobs and power. They
protected "the pinkoes, collectivists, Marxists and commies" because they
all belonged to the same gang, "and the gang must stick together." Kuhn
was another who defended Crain against her detractors, agreeing with the
Reviewer editor that the *McCall's* article did a "smear job" on such critics.[81]
Historian Jonathan Zimmerman found that there was considerable opposition to Kuhn's ideas from Legionnaires throughout the country after
Kuhn's article was published, revealing that at least some of her beliefs
were well outside of the mainstream.[82] However, the publication of Kuhn's
article in the magazine, combined with letters from Legion post leaders to
Crain requesting textbook reviews, reveal that at least some of the organization's leadership shared the right wing's anxieties. There were other
connections between the American Legion and right-wing women. For
example, Minute Women often assembled in local Legion or Veterans of
Foreign Wars meeting halls, and a number of rightist women had husbands who belonged to the American Legion.[83]

Articles such as Kuhn's helped to inspire women to form such committees as the Citizens' Book Committee in San Antonio, Texas. After reading
Kuhn's "Why You Buy Books That Sell Communism" and other rightist
literature, Texan Myrtle G. Hance and six other women reviewed card index files in San Antonio's public libraries. She emphasized that they were
women from the grassroots of America. "We are not learned people with
PhDs. We are housewives and mothers." Taking a more moderate stance
than such rightists as Crain and the Minute Women, they did not ask that
the books with Communist connections be destroyed or removed from
the shelves, but that they be identified with a large red stamp, showing
that the author had Communist Front affiliations. "The reader," Hance
wrote, "will then realize that in many instances he is reading Communist
propaganda." Americans, she believed, were unwittingly supporting Communists during the very time that the country's soldiers were fighting in
Korea to "contain" communism.[84] In the early to mid-1950s, Hance assisted state representative Marshall O. Bell of San Antonio in the drafting
of legislation that would require the labeling of books that had authors
who were Communists or Communist sympathizers. Largely through the
efforts of another San Antonio representative, liberal Democrat Maury

Maverick Jr., the measure was defeated. Refusing to give up, Hance took her campaign to the public via radio addresses and lectures before various clubs.[85]

Spreading her message in a somewhat different way was novelist Taylor Caldwell, a rightist with a vast audience of readers. Born in England in 1900, Taylor Caldwell (nee Janet Miriam Taylor) immigrated to the United States in 1907. Her first encounter with what she described as "Communist jargon" came in 1928, when she met a young man who attempted to convert her to communism. She was an employee of the U.S. Immigration Service at that time, and found Communist doctrine distasteful. Nevertheless, it was not until after she became a prominent author that she became active in her opposition to communism.[86] In a letter to John T. Flynn in 1953, she declared that she had been fighting communism "by book and by lecture since 1944, a time when it was dangerous to breathe a word against Roosevelt's war or Stalin;" but now the Communist threat had become worse. Caldwell informed Flynn that her "depressed conviction that Communism has become so strong in America since 1933 that it can never be eradicated has now returned, with deeper conviction."[87]

Much of this pessimistic outlook resulted from her "prolonged investigation" into the "matter of Communistic Socialism in our public schools." Caldwell determined that youth attending secular colleges in the United States had become "thoroughly indoctrinated. And why not?" she asked. "They've never heard anything but radicalism in all their lives, from kindergarten on." Caldwell wrote that she knew a teacher who "had to leave the public school system . . . because she could not bear to teach the enforced Socialism to children." Caldwell's investigation into the schools led her to inquire, "So what are we going to do with these millions of children and youths and girls who have been poisoned all through the years? Their diseased minds are closed to the truth. The Constitution means nothing to them. Liberty is 'reaction.'"[88]

Caldwell addressed the issue of communism and socialism in the modern public school system in her novel *The Devil's Advocate*. Set in the future—1970—the book, she told Flynn, was "about the final results of Communism in America," and was written in hopes of influencing the 1952 presidential election. She believed that a vote for Democrat Adlai Stevenson was a vote for communism. The novel, a best-seller, presented a bleak picture of an America that entered into a social, economic, and political downward spiral when the Roosevelt administration came to power in 1933 and had not recovered. Citizens who foolishly voted for the Democrats in the 1930s and 1940s now found themselves in a country where the Common Man was reduced to the lowest common denominator. No one could trust one's neighbors, and even those who toed the party line could never feel secure in their more comfortable positions. Since Caldwell was a Minute Woman, it was apparently no coincidence that the hero of Caldwell's novel was a Minute Man. Caldwell's Minute Men were fighting to overthrow the new Communist-inspired government and return the country to conditions similar to those that the older people remembered—a happy, free, and prosperous America—that existed prior to 1933.[89]

In *The Devil's Advocate* Caldwell placed a large proportion of the blame for the nation's demise on teachers. One of the major characters of the novel, Arthur Carlson, leader of the Minute Men, spoke about education: "The teachers of America, as a class, are very docile, and always eager to serve the most powerful master. You know how their so-called 'liberalism' helped to enslave the people several decades ago. When America became completely regimented, the teachers followed every instruction." But, he believed, many of the teachers had come to realize the error of their ways and were angry with the government. "So," he announced to the Minute Men, "we have, now, many teachers and professors subtly and artfully teaching our children and our youth of the lost brave past."[90] Yet most of the schools of the time were maintaining curricula in line with the tyrannical government's requirements. The protagonist of the novel, Andrew Durant, at one point sadly "thought of the state schools, where history was perverted and where new slaves were trained to docility, obedience, and devotion to their masters."[91] Students were no longer taught about the American Revolution because that would induce them to study the Declaration of Independence. Students in this new United States were required to learn social studies instead of history.[92] As she told Flynn, Caldwell's novel was addressing the current issues in education. Many teachers who had been sympathetic toward communism during the 1930s and early 1940s had by 1952 been renouncing that philosophy. But, for Caldwell, the turnabout was too little and occurring too slowly to restore the country to the America of the past.

Educator and lawyer Bella Dodd might have been one of those teachers of whom Caldwell was writing. Dodd joined the Communist Party in 1936, and in 1944, she was officially installed as a party leader. However, by early 1946, she had become disillusioned and was expelled later that year. During the early 1950s her politics took an almost 180 degree turn, and she became a spokesperson for the right. As a former leader among American Communists as well as having been a leader of the New York Teachers' Union during the first half of the 1940s, she became a star witness for those charging that Communists were conspiring to hijack American education. In an appearance before the Senate Internal Security Subcommittee in 1952, she estimated that of the nation's approximately one million teachers, about 1,500 were card-carrying Communists, with about two-thirds of them in the New York area.[93] Dodd blamed herself for helping the Communist Party gain power in the area of American education, believing that her position within the Teachers Union allowed her to influence the union's leftward leanings.[94] When Crain found herself overburdened with legal costs associated with the Educational Reviewer's suit against McCall's, Bella Dodd helped her by providing legal services at a reduced cost.[95] Perhaps it was her feeling of guilt over her Communist associations that prompted her to offer that aid.

Dodd got into the education fray even more deeply when she published School of Darkness (1954), an autobiography focusing on her years as a teacher, professor, union leader, and Communist Party member. Her name appeared frequently in newsletters of right-wing organizations, as Dodd was considered one who had seen both sides of the issue of communist infiltration of schools and hence could confirm that the right was indeed fighting off a conspiracy to indoctrinate America's youth into communism. After hearing Dodd speak, a Texas woman gave her approval: "Put Dr. Dodd in office and she'll show you where the communists are and how to recognize them."[96]

In 1951, Dodd, a lapsed Roman Catholic, returned to the faith of her youth. In contrast to Crain, Caldwell, and others among the right who feared a loss of morality and spirituality in public education, Dodd was somewhat optimistic in this regard. In her 1954 autobiography, she observed that schools were leaning more toward teaching spirituality, not materialism, writing, "Students are beginning to realize that the training of the mind is of little value to man himself or to society unless it is placed in the framework of eternal truth."[97]

Other right-wing women reaching audiences with their opinions on public education included Mary Louise Allen of Pasadena and Rosalie Gordon, John T. Flynn's longtime secretary. Both women feared that government interference was destroying the nation's public schools by indoctrinating students with socialistic thought. In defense of the School Development Council's actions and those of other rightist citizens of Pasadena, Allen wrote *Education or Indoctrination* (1955). Allen, the mother of three children, considered such proposals as school-sponsored summer camps and group decision-making as radical ideas, and methods by which school administrators were pushing students to adopt leftist practices and ideas.[98] Gordon's *What's Happened to Our Schools?* (1956) revealed a point of view similar to that of Taylor Caldwell, warning that educators were using "progressive education" to create a new social order. Within the public school system, Gordon wrote, there was a conspiracy to under-educate children in order "to make them into an unquestioning mass who would follow meekly those who wish to turn the American Republic into a socialist society." Gordon urged parents to keep themselves informed of what was going on in their children's schools and to fight attempts to "get the hand of the federal government—directly or indirectly—on your schools."[99]

Not all criticism of modern education was coming from the far right. From the mainstream, prominent journalist Dorothy Thompson, a frequent contributor to *Ladies Home Journal,* addressed some of the questions being raised regarding public schools in the magazine's February 1953 issue. While Thompson had once observed that the most likely new recruit to the American Communist Party would be a young person between the ages eighteen to twenty-three,[100] she remained aloof from the fray over whether public schools were attempting to indoctrinate children toward specific religious (or antireligious), economic, or political concepts. Thompson denied that public schools were "riddled with subversives, red or otherwise. There are communist teachers and communist sympathizers in some schools," but she noted that such people could be found in a variety of occupations. At the same time, "There are also teachers who are violently racist, anti-Negro, anti-Semitic, anti-alien, anti-Catholic, or who see 'red' in anything or everything done by the state. But both types are a small minority."[101]

"The public schools," she wrote, "too quickly reflect the transient political and social changes of viewpoint, and imprint them on the minds of children and youth too young and inexperienced to digest them except in the form of slogans." She found too much attention given to current affairs, leading youth "who have no valid judgment" to merely echo the opinions of their teachers. Thompson fondly recalled the older form of education, the type that her former husband, author Sinclair Lewis, had received more than half a century earlier. For her a traditional education—with emphasis upon spelling, penmanship, knowledge of the history and topography of America, meticulous training in math and grammar, and considerable reading of the English classics—formed a truly solid groundwork.[102] Thompson was not worried about radical or subversive teachers, but she did maintain a conservative point of view regarding the state of American education.

Throughout the 1950s Thompson held to her opinion that American education was heading in the wrong direction, asking in 1958, "Do American Educators Know What They Are Up To?" She blamed American educators for allowing the Soviet Union to leap ahead in technology. As evidence, Thompson pointed to the Soviets' recent achievements in outer space. In particular, she criticized modern educators' practice of teaching to a "group" rather than attempting to bring out the best in an "individual." Displaying agreement with the rightist criticism of group or "collectivist" methods of teaching, she complained that educators were producing groups of conformists. However, Thompson differed from those farther to the right in that she sought to create critical individualists, while most of the right-wing women discussed here wanted to form a child's belief system. Thompson's concern was that group teaching was not conducive to creating "character" and would not encourage students to reach their highest potential.[103]

Anxiety over what was being taught to American children had indeed spread into the mainstream. In response to citizens' concerns about what was being taught to students in their local schools, school boards frequently formed committees to review textbooks and school curricula. At times, state departments of education went further, some forming committees to investigate the possibility of "subversive" teaching and many required that teachers take loyalty oaths, swearing that they did not in any way support communism. For example, in November 1951, the New York State Federation of Women's Clubs, which usually consisted of women and their organizations with a wide range of social and political views, adopted a controversial resolution. By a vote of 117 to 44, the Federation called upon the State Department of Education "to investigate teaching and textbooks in public schools 'as to the extent, if any, of subversive indoctrination found therein.'"[104] Among the opposition to the resolution were some politically moderate women from Scarsdale, New York, whose affluent community was in an uproar over an attack on its public schools by a right-wing extremist group, the Scarsdale Citizens Committee, or Committee of Ten.

The Federation's resolution passed, but the Scarsdale women successfully opposed the Federation's plan to have Rabbi Benjamin Schultz, director of the American Jewish League Against Communism, as the sole speaker at its state convention. Schultz had a reputation as a "professional Communist baiter." At the last minute, the board of the New York Federation of Women's Clubs agreed to have a second speaker who could provide an alternative viewpoint. In their protests, the Scarsdale Women's Club, along with women's groups from elsewhere in the state, noted that "patriotic American women concerned with the preservation of democracy have a right to hear all sides of a controversial question."[105] This attitude contrasts with that of Crain and others of the far right, who refused to acknowledge that other points of view might have merit. The controversy in Scarsdale lasted approximately five years. Finally, in April 1953 the Scarsdale Town Club submitted a report of its investigation into the charges of communist infiltration in the local schools. It was the finding of investigators that there was no organized infiltration of the schools. Instead, the group found that the controversy had caused unwarranted divisions within the community and had tended to arouse latent religious bigotry.[106]

The Late Fifties and Early Sixties

In his study of what he describes as "culture wars" in American schools, Jonathan Zimmerman determined that, after 1954, efforts to censor textbooks found little success outside of the South.[107] The televised Army-McCarthy hearings of April–June 1954, which discredited the veracity and tactics of the Wisconsin senator and led to his censure in the Senate in December, played a part in the quietening of the investigations into "subversive" textbooks. Gallup Polls revealed a decline among Americans who gave McCarthy a "favorable" rating, dropping from 50 percent in January 1954 to 34 percent by June.[108] By 1955, most mainstream Americans were deciding that the communist threat from within was not as great as they had been led to believe; thus, there was less need for investigations into educators and textbooks than previously thought.

Such was not the case for rightist women's groups. In 1958 the National Defense Committee of the DAR reported that their members' ongoing interest in school textbooks had not abated. The committee found so much interest that the group undertook a new study in 1958–1959 to determine if American youth were "emphatically taught love of God and Country or [were] being corrupted to accept socialism and materialism." They found that only 20 percent of the evaluated textbooks met "minimum DAR standards: that is, only one in five promotes pride, confidence and trust in our Country, its traditions and principles; refrains from partisan presentation of such political concepts as world government and the United Nations; takes care not to include in bibliographies the names of persons with documented records of Marxist or pro-Communist affiliation without informing to that effect." They objected to history and economics texts that contained "uncomplimentary pictures of slum areas or of long lines of the unemployed during 'The Great Depression,'" and to one book in particular that labeled "such a photograph as 'A Long Line of Unemployed Waiting for *Christmas Dinner.*'" The committee questioned "the inclusion of so much realistic literature" and "sordid and shocking" stories for which they supposed young readers were unprepared.[109]

In December 1960, Marian M. Strack of the DAR's National Defense Committee denounced the Department of Education and the State Department. According to Strack, the two departments were conspiring to "change the emphasis of our own textbooks so that the student would acquire a strong attachment for certain international concepts by developing less attachment to the United States." She contended that the use of language, such as "family of nations," and "our regional neighborhood" was designed to transfer some of a student's affection for his family, town, and nation to the international community. Strack worried that such rhetoric would lead students to identify with peoples of other nations.[110] Again, this DAR leader was giving indication that there was uneasiness among the organization's membership regarding the strength of American society and culture.

Anxiety over possible communist influences in American schools continued throughout the 1950s and into the 1960s, the years during which tens of millions of baby boomers were matriculating through elementary, junior high, and high school. While for most Americans, Joseph McCarthy and his crusade against communism had lost credibility by the late 1950s, neither the Minute Women nor the DAR lost their desire to be vigilant in assessing student curricula. "New math," for example, came under attack during the 1960s. Designed to teach students an understanding of the basic principles of mathematics, the "new math" replaced the "old math" that emphasized learning by rote. Teachers needed to be retrained, and parents found themselves unable to assist their children with their homework. For the right, the "new math" was yet another example of what appeared to be a conspiracy on the part of leftist educators to destroy all traditional methods of education and to experiment with and confuse young minds.[111]

During the 1960s, the Minute Women circulated a portion of a report of the Textbook Study Committee of the Alabama Society DAR, which included a report by Reverend Robert Ingram, a rector at an Episcopal Church and school in Houston, Texas. The report revealed that for some the "new math" went beyond being merely an assault on tradition in education; it was also an attempt to overthrow Christian morality. An excerpt from the report cites Ingram as calling "new math" an "attack on the competence of the general public's power to think straight." He maintained that a public that "has no God-given standards of how to think straight is helpless before the propaganda barrage of the steely-eyed atheist or the false religionist who has substituted the world for heaven." New math, he wrote, was part of a "Satanic movement" designed "to destroy the human soul."[112]

Throughout the 1960s, women continued to play important roles in the textbook fight. Such was the case in Los Angeles in January 1962, when women appeared before the Los Angeles Board of Education as individuals and with petitions opposing some of the state-recommended textbooks.

Their complaints that the texts were slanted toward "welfarism," socialism, and world government, and were "inadequate in presenting factual accounts of modern historical events," differed little from those of Crain and others who crusaded to keep communism and liberal ideas out of the textbooks of the early 1950s.[113]

In Florida, the state legislature took a different approach. Seeking to discourage youth from becoming attracted to communism, in 1961 the Florida Legislature passed a bill to require high schools to teach a course that would expose communism's evils. By 1962, five other states had passed similar legislation, and education departments in thirty-four others included instruction about communism in state curricula. However, that approach was not as readily accepted among Floridians as legislators might have anticipated. The Florida Federation of Women's Clubs denounced the bill as "dangerous," arguing that instructors might not teach the course properly. Rather than risking the possibility that students might somehow receive a message supportive of communism, the women advocated a substitute course that stressed "Americanism."[114] Similar to the New York Federation of Women's Clubs' position in the early 1950s, the majority of the members in Florida suspected that local school districts could not monitor themselves.

As teachings about communism were being debated, conservative and affluent Sarasota, Florida, was one of many communities to feel the impact of right-wing attacks on its public schools. Much of the disruption in Sarasota arrived with the growth of a local chapter of the John Birch Society (JBS). Founded in Indiana in 1958 by candymaker Robert Welch Jr., the right-wing organization spread the message that communist conspirators were in abundance in the United States, including in the administration of President Dwight D. Eisenhower. Despite Welch's rigidity in his claims of conspiracy, the JBS would claim 80,000 members nationally by the mid-1960s. It drew mostly conservative members of the Republican Party who, similar to those in right-wing women's organizations of the 1950s and 1960s, were disturbed over the direction American politics and society had been traveling since the New Deal era.[115]

Members of the Sarasota chapter, together with other rightists in the region, maintained that a communist conspiracy was at work within the local schools. They caused turmoil within that Florida Gulf Coast community that would last for more than five years, 1961 to 1966. Pressure from the far right led to the resignation, in 1962, of moderate Republican Philip Hiss from his position as chairman of the Sarasota County School Board. Rightists unjustly accused Hiss of being tied to the radical Left and being anti-Christian. (He was a cousin of Alger Hiss, who had been accused in the 1940s of being a Communist spy.)[116] After Hiss's resignation, the right attacked Superintendent Russell W. Wiley, who they saw as being responsible for the modernizing of the curriculum and the relaxing of some student behavior codes.[117] Wiley had complied with federal mandates to desegregate the school district, a highly controversial topic at the time. Faced with hostile voices and continued pressure coming from the community, Wiley resigned as superintendent in the summer of 1964.[118]

In a letter to the editor of the *Sarasota Herald-Tribune* in 1964, a Sarasota High School graduate (1958) and mother of two young children, revealed how confusing the controversy over school textbooks and curricula could become. Recounting her experiences as a high school student, she wrote, "I was told in a history class at SHS that the textbooks we were using were misleading. Pertinent facts concerning certain historical events had been omitted, purposefully, because they cast an unfavorable light on some of our politicians and policies. I was not, and our children are not, being taught important events in our history. Good or bad, they are still the history of our country, and we have a right to be informed." Although the above statements appear to indicate that she was open to modern, revisionist history, the kind of teaching that the right sought to eliminate, in the next paragraph her thinking appears closer to that of the right. It begins, "As a result of our up-bringing and our instruction, loyalty is a vague thing, patriotism is scoffed at." She goes on to describe the lack of school spirit at Sarasota High, writing that this apathy could be translated into a lack of loyalty toward one's country. She concludes, "These so-called 'far right' groups may be wrong in their opinions of the schools. I wish they were, but I fear that they are not."[119] This young woman's letter reveals how one's discontent with an institution can lead to their being influenced by extremists. She may not have understood the entire agenda of the right-wing activists in Sarasota, but the words "loyalty" and "patriotism" drew her attention to their cause.

Another local woman wrote the editor to express her amusement upon reading charges brought by former superintendent Wiley that right-wing extremists were infiltrating the local schools. "The infiltrating is being done . . . but not by parents trying to make themselves heard in behalf of their children. It is being done at the top level by those who would undermine our country, and is being condoned or ignored in key spots on down the line." "Who can deny," she asked, "that the Communists' first line of attack is our youth?" Although she denied being "a member of any of the so-called 'extremist' groups," she revealed a willingness to join, adding, "but surely if banding together openly and publicly is wrong, what recourse do we have?"[120] Her letter, written almost a decade after Mary Louise Allen's *Education or Indoctrination?* (1955), revealed similar anxieties over leftist school administrators and the lack of parental authority regarding their children's education.

In October 1964 another woman from Sarasota County inquired, "Can you tell me what is wrong with the John Birch Society? All I can find out is that they are trying to preserve the U.S.A. Is there anything wrong with that?"[121] Although it is impossible to determine just how many women were developing such sympathies, the uproar reveals that the JBS and other groups on the far right were having substantial success in gaining recruits to their point of view.

In 1966, still not satisfied that the school system in Sarasota had been cleaned up, the right began to attack the Sarasota County Council of the Parents Teachers Association. They mounted their campaign under the leadership of Sarasota physician William Campbell Douglass, who founded both a local chapter of the John Birch Society and a right-wing information network, "Let Freedom Ring." It was here that those on the far right met their match. Elizabeth McCall, president of the Sarasota District's PTA, at the suggestion of Jennelle Moorhead, national president of the PTA, established an ad hoc committee to investigate extremism in Sarasota.[122] Meanwhile, men and women from the right, mainstream, and left, sounded off in community forums and in local newspapers. The uproar eventually drew the attention of the national media, and NBC news taped the March 7, 1966, public presentation of the findings of the Extremism Committee. There, McCall and other committee members refuted, one by one, charges brought forth by the far right. As months passed, the controversy came to a gradual end. Moderation eventually triumphed, but the extremists had scored substantial victories, most notably the resignations of two of the school district's administrators.[123]

The situation in Sarasota was not unique. Forty miles to the north, the

PTA of Pinellas County, Florida, was fighting to keep far right-wing influences out of the local chapters. The *Evening Independent* of St. Petersburg reported that local PTA officials were receiving "ultra-conservative literature" in the mail, including from the *Spirit*,[124] a publication of the right-wing group Woman's Right to Know, Inc., based in Lakeland, Florida. In their July-August issue of the *Spirit*, editors charged that the PTA was a socialistic organization that was "hiding" its political motives "under the caption of 'child welfare.'"[125] In the spring of 1966, National PTA president Moorhead bewailed a loss of 339,887 PTA memberships over the past three years. She placed the influence of the "radical right" at the top of her list of reasons for the decline. Officials agreed that extremist-caused confusion was a leading factor in the dissolving of ninety-seven PTA units in California. When surveyed to find out why units disbanded or experienced "takeovers," a representative from one unit responded, "Three women, extremists, on executive board. Man president didn't know how to handle them."[126]

Right-wing groups had been linking the PTA with communism for many years, as seen in "How Pink Is the PTA?" an article in Frances Bartlett's *Facts in Education* in 1957. A poem, "The Little Red Hens," printed in the Minute Women's July-August 1958 newsletter charges that PTA women sought "One World under Moscow."[127] In an article in the September 7, 1965, issue of *Look* magazine author Ernest Dunbar reported on a "plot to take over the PTA," describing how rightist housewives, teachers, principals, school board members, and others were participating in assaults on the PTA. Dunbar charged that Mrs. Ordeen Knight had manipulated her way into the presidency of the PTA in Upper Saddle River, New Jersey, a well-to-do suburb of New York City. Following tradition, the nominating committee for the Edith Bogert School PTA had proposed Vice President Jerry Schlossberg to succeed the outgoing president. Soon a telephone campaign began to spread word that Schlossberg, a member of a local fair-housing group, had plans to bring some black families into the all-white community. A few days prior to the election, Knight hosted a meeting in her home, whereupon Schlossberg's name was mysteriously withdrawn and Knight's name placed at head of the slate of PTA nominees. After Knight's election came the revelation that both she and the new PTA vice president were members of the John Birch Society.[128]

While men made up the majority of the leadership of the John Birch Society, women were also active within the organization. In the fall of 1960, a listing of the Society's "Committee of Endorsers" revealed a significant percentage of women supporters in some states. Of the seven endorsers from Florida, three were women, and in two states, Hawaii and Oregon, women were the sole endorsers. Lucille Cardin Crain was one of the two female endorsers out of the thirteen listed for New York State. Three of the four endorsers from Wisconsin and two of five from Montana were women.[129] Nevertheless, in 1965, a JBS pamphlet showing the "top advisory body in matters of organization and policy" revealed that the twenty-five members of that body were all male.[130] But, the organization did expand the political worlds of right-wing women. Historian Jonathan Schoenwald found that although few women held positions in the upper echelons of the JBS, they made up a majority of chapter leaders and members in a number of regions. Most of the women were housewives who became devoted volunteers for the organization. Schoenwald noted that the women gained self-confidence as a result of their experience working for the Society.[131] In her investigation into right-wing women of suburban Los Angeles, historian Michelle M. Nickerson found that women frequently hosted the JBS meetings. She suggests that this arrangement may have made the gatherings more comfortable for female attendees who might not have been eager to participate in meetings led solely by men.[132]

The John Birch Society was receiving attention in the classrooms of America's schools. It was not only right-wing groups, the PTA, and parents embroiled in controversy. Students became involved as well, debating the merits of the JBS on buses and in informal social groups, and some teachers included discussion about the organization in their lesson plans. For example, in 1963, Crain's step-granddaughter, Betsy, wrote to say that she had participated in a debate at her high school regarding the John Birch Society. Betsy had come across Crain's name as an endorser of the organization and decided to write her for information about the group. Unfortunately, Betsy did not state her position on the topic, and Crain's manuscripts do not contain a reply to Betsy's request.[133]

Although the majority of the nation's school districts were spared aggressive attacks from the far right, one source reports that the National Education Association found that, in 1964, one in every thirty school districts was forced to contend with extremist attacks and that in five states the radical right was threatening to take over the PTAs.[134]

Conclusion

From the time that Lucille Cardin Crain and William F. Buckley Sr. formulated plans for the Educational Reviewer, through the mid-1960s when the PTA came under attack from right-wing extremists, the issues drawing the attention of the right changed very little. Fears of students becoming imbued with socialistic or communistic ideology continued well into the 1960s. Other issues, such as sex education and desegregation, which will be examined in later chapters, were on the rise by the mid-1950s but were in a large sense viewed as a product of collectivism. The right held that progressive education, federal aid to education, desegregation, and a loosening of moral codes were all part of the same package.

The matter of what was to be taught in the nation's public schools was one which rightist women believed they were capable of addressing on a level equal to, if not higher than, men. Often individual rightist women and women's organizations called upon others of their gender to join the fight "as women." It was their responsibility to see that American children received a proper education, and many believed that they could have a greater impact on public opinion if they mobilized, as women, as a force. Networking served them well; nevertheless, there were times when they turned to men who shared their concerns about school textbooks and curricula. Such men as William F. Buckley Sr. and John T. Flynn provided both moral and financial support. Some rightist women chose to join male-dominated organizations, often in addition to their participation in female-led associations. For most of these women, the driving force in their activism was the need to properly educate the country's youth. Crain and others who organized women around the censorship issue, were also seeking to enhance the power of women for the betterment of society. However, they allowed the empowerment of women to become a secondary goal. It was secondary, but still important.

The postwar boom in marriages and babies took women back into their homes, with a focus on family.[135] Yet, similar to circumstances leading to women's involvement in social reform movements of the nineteenth century and early twentieth century, the issue of public education gave women opportunities to extend their moral authority beyond their house-holds and into the community. By the 1950s women had been voting for more than three decades. Still, outside of local communities they held few positions of leadership in government. The education issue provided impetus for women on the right—a group of women that, more often than others, is thought of as being linked to the home—to become politi-cally active. Anticommunism played an important role in motivating the women to activism as did their anxieties over the younger generation's growing up without a solid knowledge of the foundations upon which America was built.[136]

The period following World War II was a time of adjustment for these women as they joined in the right wing's attempts to return the country to an idealized pre–New Deal America while dealing with the changes that the war and the postwar upheaval had wrought. As a result, the women on the right were dealing with much larger and complex issues than had rightists of the past. The women studied here saw education as being in-timately connected with all of these issues. As women and as American citizens, they believed they had important roles to play in the shaping of American institutions and society.

Not all historians agree as to the impact of this right-wing campaign. Jonathan Zimmerman points out that the *Educational Reviewer* could claim only about 2,000 subscribers, and that other right-wing publica-tions fared similarly.[137] Other historians, however, emphasize the num-bers of teacher and school administrators who were fired, forced to resign, or left their positions because they were uncomfortable with the thought that they were being watched for signs of having leftist sympathies. Da-vid Caute estimates that during the Truman-Eisenhower era at least 600 teachers and professors lost their jobs as a result of purges, about 380 in New York City alone. Julia L. Mickenberg includes in her estimate those teachers who left their employment because they refused to take loyalty oaths and writes that thousands were pushed out of the schools.[138] Just how many jobs were lost, how many teachers carefully avoided poten-tially controversial topics, and how many librarians refrained from order-ing controversial books as a direct result of right-wing women's activism will likely never be known; for it was not only right-wing women who were putting pressures on public school systems. Americans, parents in particular, with views ranging from one end of the political spectrum to the other were wary of "un-American" ideas making their way into the country's schools. Mickenberg, for example, found that in the immediate aftermath of World War II American leftists were seeing schools as "training grounds for fascism." Some on the left viewed the efforts to keep communist ideology out of the schools as rightist attempts to convert children into nonthinking Nazi-like robots.[139] Fears brought on by the Cold War, postwar conspiracy trials, and McCarthyism served to enhance the effectiveness of the right's campaigns against modern education, and rightist women took advantage of this opportunity. They played major roles in campaigns that resulted in teachers and administrators losing their jobs in at least several locales, Pasadena, Sarasota, and Houston among them. The experiences of Dorothy Frank, who stood up in opposition to the right in Los Angeles, reveal that some people even feared physical harm at the hands of some of these right-wing activists.

Right-wing women made a difference as to what textbooks students were reading in various school districts around the country. As a result of these women's campaigns, many thousands of students learned from books that left out materials that were objectionable to the right. Whether done deliberately or not, students were often prevented from gaining access to a variety of perspectives on issues and thus grew up with fewer analytic skills than they might otherwise have acquired.

Often baby boomers, including those interviewed for this book, recalled that what they learned in school about political issues sometimes motivated them to become politically active in the future.[140] Sociologist Rebecca E. Klatch, who interviewed more than seventy former young activists in her study of the rightist Young Americans for Freedom (YAF) and the leftist Students for a Democratic Society (SDS), discovered that activists on both left and right had teachers who introduced new ideas and inspired them to think in new ways.[141] Thus, the more rightist teachers there were in the classroom, the more likely it would be that students would leave school with a right-wing point of view.

Books, too, influenced activists on both the right and the left. Although it is not clear whether the upcoming activists chose books based upon their existing political inclinations or if the books caused them to move their political thought to the right or the left, both former SDSers and YAFers listed books that they had read in high school and found influential in their thinking. According to Klatch, a significant number of YAF members recalled that former Communist Whitaker Chambers's autobiography *Witness* (1952) swayed their political outlooks. Right-wing youth reported that libertarian Ayn Rand's *The Fountainhead* (1943) and *Atlas Shrugged* (1957) and rightist Phyllis Schlafly's *A Choice Not an Echo* (1964), in support of presidential candidate Barry Goldwater, were other influential works. Many YAF activists were introduced to the right-wing magazines *Human Events* and *National Review* through their parents making them available in their homes.[142] Whether read at school or in their homes, students' access to rightist thinking frequently influenced their outlook.

Censorship of books continued into the 1970s. One baby boomer from Virginia recalls "a mandate by local school boards to publicize the books being checked out of the public libraries by general citizens." She remembers that a local librarian risked jail time when she "refused to give out the names of patrons" checking out controversial books.[143] At times book censorship backfired: several baby boomers recalled that publicity about books such as J. D. Salinger's *Catcher in the Rye* (1951) being banned from school curricula and libraries raised their interest and led them to seek out the books from other sources. Some look back to their elementary and high school years with a feeling that they did not receive a balanced look at their nation's history and believe the right was at least partially responsible. It was usually suggestions of sexual content that led young people to seek out banned novels. Young people paid considerably less attention to what might be missing from their history or economics textbooks. Students usually did not bother to look into varying points of view on those subjects.[144] Thus, it was on those topics that rightist women's campaigns for censorship likely had the greatest impact.

Despite the harm resulting from their efforts to stifle ideas and cause job losses for those who did not view the world as they did, rightist women did help to bring into open debate important questions about the roles that public schools should play in advancing specific political and social ideologies. The raising of issues surrounding the education of youth revealed to parents just how important it was to know what their children were learning in the classroom.

Crain, Bartlett, and other leaders, along with such groups as Pro America and the Minute Women, helped to keep the right wing alive in the United States. Although the *Educational Reviewer* failed, Crain continued to be consulted about the quality of textbooks well into the 1960s.[145] She and other rightists received notice in national magazines and on radio broadcasts, enabling their message to reach a broad segment of the American population, even though some of the publicity was hostile. Millions of Americans had concerns about the quality and direction of American education and paid close attention to the debate over modern education. Thus right-wing women had a large audience to listen to their claims of education being a part of a deep and widespread conspiracy that involved many facets of American life. Although they failed to provide sufficient evidence to support such claims, a significant number of school boards and parents, as well as some prominent people, were paying close attention to their concerns and ideas. Listeners included men like William F. Buckley Jr., political theorist Russell Kirk, and educator E. Merrill Root who would become leaders among the right for decades to come.[146]

While the education of America's youth was of great importance to rightist women, there were other issues that drew them to become active in the public sphere. As will be seen in the next chapter, public health was a topic that led many of the women who were engaged in campaigns over education to also join in debates over health matters. Indeed, many of the women found both modern education and newer developments in public health to be part of a pattern that suggested a large conspiracy to undermine American values, health, and overall way of life.

⚙ 2

PUBLIC HEALTH

In our fight here on "fluoridation" the damage to brain and nervous system kept cropping up. At the same time the Alaska Mental Health [Act of 1956] went through. It's impossible not to put 2 + 2 together. Am about convinced that this "Mental Health" is pretty close to Orwell's 1984 nightmare.

Beverly Chase Perroni, ca. November 1956

During the late nineteenth century, with the population of the United States burgeoning and cities becoming crowded, many Americans looked to local governments to take steps to create sanitary and healthful environments. Meanwhile, scientists were making discoveries about the causes and prevention of diseases. Scientific findings that diseases had specific causes, and were preventable, gave government authorities reason to oversee the establishment of health agencies, laboratories, and institutions. Public health quickly became a scientific enterprise, administered under the guidance of experts in communities throughout the United States. In the years that followed, the federal government increasingly became involved in public health. Congress took a major step in 1906 with its passage of the Food and Drug Act; another milestone came in 1912 when the Marine Hospital Service received a new name and became the U.S. Public Health Service. As time passed, local, state, and federal responsibilities expanded, and from the time of Franklin Roosevelt's New Deal through President Lyndon B. Johnson's Great Society, the federal government's participation in public health became well established.[1] For such Americans as those right-wing women who resented government interference in personal matters, this was not a welcome development.

The fluoridation of public water systems, mental health, and polio vaccines were public health topics that were of particular interest to the right wing during the 1950s and 1960s. Although Americans of varied political persuasions found reasons to question the implementation of public health programs, it was the right that stirred the most controversy. Right-wing women, anxious about the future of America, were often at the center of the disputes. Of great concern to the right was that government—local, state, and federal—played prominent roles in administering public health programs. Thus, for those on the right, the issues involved not only health but also liberty and individualism. In the eyes of those on the far right, the issue of conspiracy was present as well. New Mexico Women Speak!, an anticommunist right-wing organization of the 1950s, combined the three public health issues, perceiving them as part of a pattern that was aiming the United States in the direction of communism.[2]

While not all right-wing women's organizations consciously combined the three public health issues, most agreed that they all were part of a larger government plan to usurp the liberties of individuals. Fears of inherent dangers in these government-backed health programs led concerned women to organize on a grassroots level to fight to protect their own health and that of their friends, families, and future generations. Rightist campaigns were effective, and women's prominence in many of the local campaigns was important to their effectiveness. An important factor was the long-held tradition that women, particularly mothers, were the family nurturers. Thus, Americans were inclined to listen when women actively campaigned regarding local, state, and federal government policies that would affect their health and that of their families.

Fluoridation

Considerable controversies erupted during the 1950s and 1960s when state and local governments announced that, for purposes of preventing tooth decay, they planned to fluoridate their public water systems. At that time right-wing women made up a vociferous segment of the antifluoridation side of the argument. Many of those on the far right considered the chemical additive to be part of a plot to weaken Americans, both physically and mentally. They took it upon themselves to voice charges that scientists and government officials were attempting to poison the public, and the women warned Americans of potential dangers. Other rightist women, whose politics were closer to the mainstream, were milder in their accusations. They argued that fluoridation was experimental, unreliable, and being forced upon the American public, and saw it as further indication of unwarranted government interference in their lives.

The antifluoridation campaigns proved to be among the right-wing women's most successful crusades. Although they eventually lost most of their fights to halt fluoridation, their tactics raised questions within the general community and caused delays in the implementation of fluoridation programs. In fact, some areas of the country continue to have nonfluoridated public water systems. Because the majority of people in the United States were not drinking fluoridated water until most baby boomers were adults, it can be argued that rightist women's campaigns had a significant effect on the dental health of that generation.

The addition of the element fluorine to drinking water—called "fluoride" in its ionized form—was designed to help prevent tooth decay. Experimentation with fluoride was under way in Europe by the mid-nineteenth century, with studies on both animals and humans. The concept of fluoridating drinking water came under serious consideration in the United States in the middle of the twentieth century. In 1901, Colorado dentist Frederick McKay noticed that many of his patients had mottled teeth. Staining ranged in color from yellow to brown and black; a few patients also had pitting on their enamel. Curious as to the cause of the staining, McKay spent the next three decades investigating the phenomena. He found that people who had lived in a particular community all their lives had the stains on their teeth, but those who had moved into that community later did not. Further investigation led him to the conclusion that ingredients in the water were responsible. By the mid-1930s, several additional studies confirmed McKay's hypothesis and determined that fluoride was the active ingredient. During the process of his study, McKay observed that those patients with stained teeth had less tooth decay than those who were stain free. The fluoride connection led the U.S. Public Health Service (USPHS) to research the matter. Trials were expected to last ten to fifteen years. However, after only a few years, communities that were being tested with fluoridated waters revealed obvious reductions in tooth decay. Proponents of fluoridation began to pressure the USPHS to begin treating the nation's water systems. Encouraged by preliminary findings, both the American Dental Association and the American Medical Association gave their support.[3]

In the United States such decisions are made on the local level, meaning that changes often move very slowly. But, due to scientists' and doctors' claims that fluoridation of the water could reduce tooth decay as much as 50 to 60 percent[4] and at little cost to local communities, by the early 1950s many citizens sought to have fluoride added to their communities' water systems. In June 1951, the *New York Times* reported that eighty-eight cities had adopted the service, including three—Grand Rapids, Michigan; Charlotte, North Carolina; and Corpus Christi, Texas—with populations of more than 100,000. Wisconsin led the way, with forty-six communities in that state already adding fluorides to their water supplies.[5]

Yet almost as soon as the push for fluoridation began, opponents were organizing to prevent it. Often standing out among the opponents of fluoridation were right-wing men and women. Skepticism regarding water fluoridation was based upon a number of factors, ranging from medical to economic to political issues. For example, in 1953, when the New York state legislature held hearings on a bill to fluoridate all public water intended for human consumption, Chester A. Smith, a representative of a Peekskill citizen's committee, voiced one of the right's most extreme points of view. In his appearance before the legislature's Conservation Committee he charged that the fluoridation plan was "un-American" and that the chemical industry was promoting it due to profits it could derive through disposal of fluoridation's waste products.[6] Smith warned, "You can call this forced mass medication, but it might turn out to be mass liquidation. . . . This is something that the Russians might well consider."[7]

A dentist argued in favor of fluoridation, declaring that the results of an experiment on the citizens of Newburgh, New York, were very encouraging, and that there had been no ill effects on the fish in the town's water supply reservoirs. Other speakers did not accept those findings. They took the rightist position, claiming that sodium fluoride was responsible for such medical problems as kidney disease, heart trouble, brain lesions, and cancer.[8]

Additional objections to fluoridation, coming mostly from the right, included arguments that the forceful medicating of public water supplies violated religious freedom. Although not generally aligned with the right, Christian Scientists were among those crying foul because their religion forbade the use of medication. In the early 1950s, plaintiffs filed lawsuits in five American cities, charging that fluoridation of municipal water supplies violated the Fourteenth Amendment to the Constitution which, plaintiffs claimed, indirectly protected citizens from invasion of their religious freedom. The courts rejected the arguments of religious freedom in all of the cases.[9]

The idea that Americans were being *forced* to drink fluoridated water appears to have been the impetus for much of this outrage. Maintaining this point of view was Charlotte Koch, who wrote the *New York Times* of her concern that "the proposed fluoridation of the New York water supply [would] make 'captive consumers' of those of us who do not approve of the addition of yet another chemical to our diet."[10] Eva L. Collins expressed similar concerns, and argued that "Doctors and scientists of impressive background tell us there are other ways of giving fluoride to children (if their parents want them to have it) than by mixing this chemical with the public water supply."[11]

While the majority of dentists and physicians favored the addition of the substance to drinking water, a small minority of medical people suggested possible harmful side effects for persons with such ailments as diabetes and kidney disease. Such suggestions created propaganda for the right and added fuel to the controversy. As a result, both rightist and nonrightist individuals and groups sought to slow the pace of water fluoridation. The Woman's Club of Westfield, New Jersey, appears to have been typical of "mainstream" groups with concerns about the chemical's side effects. Announcing that the club was opposed to any fluoridation program until all facts were in, it also favored a referendum to resolve the question.[12] In 1955, Emily Mehr, who chaired the Nassau County (New York) Committee Opposed to Fluoridation, raised the wider question as to the general importance of preventing tooth decay. Although prevalent, tooth decay was not a contagious disease. Mehr, who would become a local leader among right-wing antifluoridation groups, pointed out that even those who advocated water fluoridation "admitted that it would only affect those from infancy to the age of 10." Why, then, should older people drink the added chemical?[13]

Throughout the 1950s, when the public voted on the question of adding fluoride to public water systems, the measure met with more defeats than victories. Reasons for the public's opposition ranged from concerns that such a chemical additive would change water's taste to fears that it would lead to death. In the spring of 1955 journalist Murray Illson of the *New York Times* investigated the controversy and found that while eighty-five communities had passed referendums in favor of fluoridation, similar propositions had failed in 105 communities.[14] As time passed, opponents were continually finding additional reasons to fight fluoridation. Fluorides were poisons that were used to kill rats. Fluoridation was a plot by certain "big business" interests. Some believed that aluminum companies would profit from selling fluorine waste. They believed, too, that the sugar industry was promoting the use of fluoride so that it would not lose sales from anxious parents who feared sugar would cause decay in their children's teeth. One of the more extreme assertions, usually emanating from the far right, was the claim that fluoridated water had a harmful effect upon the human nervous system. These opponents alleged the Russians had used such devices to their advantage on their slave laborers and prisoners to rob them of their will to resist. The campaign for fluoridation, then, was the work of communists, desiring to brainwash Americans. Rumors abounded.[15]

Although rightists took advantage of almost all of the suggestions that pointed to dangers in fluoridation, what differentiated the far right from the mainstream to the greatest extent was their belief that there was a conspiracy behind the program. Members of the general public might question the chemical's taste or even its safety and desire further testing. The right, however, especially the far right, was not willing to accept the findings of scientists, no matter how vast or well controlled the research might be.

"They say if you repeat propaganda loudly and often enough, people will believe it," wrote Emily Mehr. "But as far as fluoridation is concerned, the Public Health groups after ten years of promotion, haven't impressed the public, who have an inherent sense of self-protection."[16] Mehr and other antifluoridation crusaders took the idea of repeating propaganda to heart, for the tactic of continually raising the issue of possible dangers was proving quite successful. Movements do not become forceful if they are ahead of their time; they draw masses of participants when they tap into concerns that people are already mulling over.

The antifluoridationists' tactics drew the attention of groups not ordinarily associated with the right, including the New York City Federation of

Women's Clubs. The Federation joined the opposition in May 1955, when it adopted a resolution to oppose the fluoridation of the city's public water system. The group voiced the usual arguments, coming mostly from the right, that forced fluoridation violated liberty and that even in greatly diluted form, fluoride could be harmful. It raised an additional fear: that accepting the fluoride additive might create a precedent whereby another "like authority" might decide to treat other diseases through the public water system. The group's resolution was not unanimous, but the majority was able to prevent dissenters from presenting an amendment or substitute resolution.[17] Eight months later the Long Island Federation of Women's Clubs, which was under the umbrella of the General Federation of Women's Clubs (GFWC), unanimously approved a similar resolution.[18] The GFWC was founded in 1890 when diverse local women's groups united to increase club women's influence over local affairs.[19] It is usually considered a conservative organization of middle-class women, resting within the mainstream of American politics. Indeed, right-wing women often criticized the organization, believing it too sympathetic to leftist ideas. Now, however, local affiliates were voicing some of the fears that the far right was pushing in its opposition to fluoridation. This was the mid-1950s, a time when the Cold War and McCarthyism were still in the minds of tens of millions of Americans. Who was to know to what extent communists—both foreign and domestic—might go to hinder Americans' freedom?

Overall, those opposing fluoridation were better organized than their foes. Hearings on the matter frequently brought out significantly more critics than defenders. At a hearing in Albany, New York, in March 1956, state officials clearly favored water fluoridation, but most of the citizens present opposed the project.[20] Such opposition could be very effective, as evidenced by an early attempt to fluoridate the local water supply of Cambridge, Massachusetts. In the fall of 1950, the local health department conducted a poll of dentists, asking if they would support fluoridation of the community's drinking water. Thirty-six of the thirty-nine respondents answered in the affirmative; the remaining three expressed no opposition to a fluoridation program. After the positive response from Cambridge dentists, the City Council held several discussions concerning the project, and in mid-May 1951, in a unanimous nine to zero vote, approved the installation of the required fluoridation equipment. The process proceeded quietly until late February 1952, when a Boston newspaper published an article announcing that Cambridge would be the first large New England city to put fluoride in its public water system. Within a month, letters opposing fluoridation were arriving at the Cambridge Health Department, newspaper editors' offices, and the mailboxes of city councilors. Some were from local leaders, others from antifluoridation groups based around the United States. Boston and local Cambridge newspapers both carried stories about the fluoridation fight. The pressure became so strong that the City Council voted six to two to rescind its earlier decision to proceed. On November 3, 1953, the city held a referendum, which resulted in a 20,194 to 13,935 vote against fluoridation.[21]

In an article for the summer 1959 issue of *Public Opinion Quarterly*, social scientist Thomas F. A. Plaut discussed findings from his study of the fluoridation referendum in Cambridge. He found that once a person well known in local political affairs made fluoridation a prominent issue, the already existing political and social alignment of political forces quickly weighed in on the topic. The loudest voices invariably came from those who opposed fluoridation. The issue had suddenly gone from one that was unknown to most of the community to one hotly debated throughout the region.[22] A similar situation arose in Cincinnati, where voters rejected a fluoridation referendum on the very day as that held in Cambridge. Although all three of Cincinnati's daily newspapers, many dentists and physicians, and the Public Health Federation had campaigned for approval of fluoridation, voters defeated the referendum by an approximate six to four margin. At least some of the credit for the outcome went to Cincinnati radio news commentator Tom McCarthy, a leader of the opposition.[23] But while prominent men often led the opposition, women, too, played large roles in influencing public opinion.

By the mid-1950s the Massachusetts Women's Political Club was charging that state and local officials were employing "Gestapo methods" to force people to drink fluoridated water. The club, which described itself as "Non-partisan, non-sectarian," advanced a variety of rightist arguments, including the claim that government health officials were brainwashing the American people. Florence Birmingham, the group's president, wrote the Massachusetts legislature, enclosing statements from religious leaders that asserted that fluoridation was a moral issue. In addition, she cited such figures as Abraham Lincoln and "the Patriots of 1776," concluding a letter of protest with a quote from political theorist Thomas Paine, "These are the times that try men's souls. . . . Tyranny, like hell, is not easily conquered."[24] As will be seen, invoking patriotism was a tactic that rightists frequently used in campaigns, on this and on other issues. Indeed, at times their adherence to their interpretations of the words of the country's founders appears to be on an equal level with their devotion to God.

Religion, too, became an issue, and some Christian fundamentalist groups entered into the fluoridation controversy. Unlike the Christian Scientists, whose main argument was that medicated water violated their religious beliefs, Ann and Russell Ackley, in their monthly religious tract, *Portions in Due Season*, took the far right position that local governments were poisoning their constituents. The Ackleys published a photograph of a person in a head-to-ankle protective suit, looking as though he was about to pour something from a large rectangular bag. The caption described the scary scene as "an actual photograph of a man placing fluorine in the water supply of some unsuspecting community. Fluorine is such a deadly poison that it would be fatal to come in contact with it."[25]

While antifluoridationists painted some grim pictures in regard to the chemical's effects, there was a movement in favor of the additive. Generally less well organized than the opposition, proponents of fluoridation drew upon some prominent supporters. In March 1957, noted pediatrician Dr. Benjamin Spock, chairman of the Committee to Protect Our Children's Teeth, Inc., spoke in favor of fluoridation before a crowd of hundreds of people gathered in New York's City Hall to hear testimony on its effects.[26] In 1953, *Better Homes and Gardens*, a magazine with a mostly middle-class female readership, included an article that offered hope for the use of a new substance, an enzyme inhibitor that could be added to toothpaste or mouthwash to control tooth decay. However, the new enzyme inhibitor would be in addition to fluorides, either in the drinking water or painted on the teeth.[27] Thus, it did not offer an alternative for those who were fearful of the effects of fluoride, but was yet another chemical for suspicious people to worry about.

As long as there were some doctors and scientists who disputed the value of fluoridated water, or who raised questions, many people were unwilling to accept arguments in its favor. On March 3, 1957, the *New York Times* published an article by Wisconsin historian Donald R. McNeil, "Fluoridation, Pro and Con," which presented an objective account of the history of fluoridation in the United States. The article drew varying responses from the public. A mother of two small children wrote that she was "deeply concerned about the physical well-being" of her family. She was particularly worried about "the problem of controlling the toxicity of fluorides," fearing that there was "no guarantee that a safe balance" would be "maintained at all points of distribution." "Tooth decay is far from being one of our most pressing problems," argued another woman. "No one has died of it yet!" A New Jersey woman claimed, "[T]hose of us who are opposed to fluoridation on the ground that it is a vicious and subtle infringement on individual rights are far from radical people," adding that asking the minority to give way to allow fluoridation "is pure socialism."[28]

Americans' almost innate attachment to the idea of personal liberty, combined with the country's movement to the left that had occurred during the Roosevelt era, gave the right opportunities to spread its message that fluoridation was another step toward communism. As will be shown in later chapters of this book, rightists frequently campaigned with an emphasis on the idea of an individual's freedom to make his or her own decisions on issues. However, in some instances, such as in regard to a woman's right to choose whether to have an abortion, the right's position reversed.

Donald McNeil noted in his report for the *New York Times* that there were some agitators who made some extreme statements. Among them was San Francisco housewife Golda Franzen, who claimed that fluoridation would produce "moronic, atheistic slaves" and would "weaken the minds of the people and make them prey to the Communists." She charged that communists were planning to "'rape' the people through fluoridation," but admitted that she lacked proof, the reason being that "Those who have informed me cannot testify—they would be liquidated if they did."[29] Franzen was a leading activist against fluoridation in California. In 1951 she led the fight that defeated fluoridation in San Francisco, then continued the fight in other parts of the Bay Area. She threatened lawsuits, helped in a futile attempt to push a bill prohibiting fluoridation through the California legislature, and circulated her information through privately published pamphlets and numerous letters to other opponents who often cited Franzen as an authority on the subject of fluoridation and frequently quoted her arguments.[30]

Franzen was one of many who linked the fluoridation of drinking water to communism. Leona Scannell, a leader of the right-wing American

Woman's Party, did not directly accuse the communists of wanting to poison America's public water systems; however, she considered fluoridation one of the nation's "present day evils" that fostered communism and socialism. Expressing concern for the baby boom generation, Scannell maintained, "This is a conspiracy against the health of our innocent children, a danger as great as Communism." She continued, "We are becoming our own worst enemy and will destroy ourselves within, just what Joe Stalin is looking forward to. It is time for the women to act."[31]

For some among the far right, one's position on the fluoridation issue was a litmus test of one's "Americanism." Editors of the San Francisco-based right-wing newsletter *Right* considered guest columnist Mrs. Herman J. Kuppers to have passed the "Americanism" test, praising her success in her efforts to retain the purity of the water of her hometown of Lakeland, Florida, and her continuation of the fight in other communities. In "The Fluoridation Lie," published in June 1957, Kuppers was another among those who believed that fluoridation was a communist conspiracy to socialize and possibly poison Americans.[32] This was a fight not only against plots to weaken Americans by poisoning their drinking water but also to prevent Americans from gradually accepting more government interference in their lives. As Taylor Caldwell argued in *The Devil's Advocate*, a resulting consequence could well be that future generations would find that individual rights had all but disappeared.

While conspiracy theories were among the far right's main arguments against fluoridation, few openly charged that Jews were major participants in such plots. In contrast to right-wing allegations during the 1930s and 1940s that Jews were leaders in a major conspiracy to take the United States into war, such blatant anti-Semitism had diminished during the postwar era. Nevertheless, there were some among the far right who did proclaim fluoridation to be a Jewish attempt to weaken the Aryan race, both mentally and spiritually. Among these was the National Blue Star Mothers of America, a right-wing women's group that had espoused anti-Semitism during its antiwar campaigns both before and after Pearl Harbor. They now linked Jews with what they thought was a conspiracy to poison community water systems.[33]

A much milder complaint about fluoridation concerned its cost to the taxpayer. The expense of fluoridation was quite small, especially when the savings for consumers for dental work were taken into consideration.

Thus, cost was not high on the list of the negatives. An estimate of the annual cost of fluoridating the public water systems in the United States, in 1952, put the price between five and fourteen cents per person,[34] a miniscule amount even if one did not receive the benefits of lower dental bills for their children. Nevertheless, a financially conservative woman from Larchmont Manor, New York, was not alone when she complained, in 1959, that she saw no reason for New York City to "incur the tremendous expense of fluoridating water which will be used by the Fire Department, the street cleaning department, laundries, etc., and thus literally be poured down the drain." The money could be "used to better advantage for the benefit of the city and for all of its inhabitants," not just for those under the age of thirteen.[35]

Women opposing fluoridation used a variety of tactics to promote their campaigns. In addition to writing to newspaper editors and appearing at local and regional hearings, they distributed newsletters and pamphlets and organized local citizens to join the opposition. Some were successful fund-raisers. One was Mrs. Peder Schmidt, a middle-class woman of Minneapolis, who was able to raise enough money from local fluoridation opponents to travel to Washington, D.C., to lobby for a bill that would outlaw the additive. Others paid their own way across the country for the opportunity to personally lobby Congress. Golda Franzen of San Francisco appeared before the House Committee on Interstate and Foreign Commerce hearings on a bill to protect the public health from the dangers of fluorination of water, May 25–27, 1954, as did Aileen Robinson of Seattle. Robinson, a Christian Scientist and a woman Donald McNeil found to be "one of the nation's most diligent workers against fluoridation," taught like-minded people how to embark on whispering campaigns. She also prepared and loaned tape recordings for radio broadcasts.[36] Robinson kept close account of "wins" for the anti groups, and her statistical compilations surfaced in pamphlets distributed in an antifluoridation campaign in her state.[37]

In April 1958, at their national convention in Washington, D.C., the DAR revealed what was perhaps a sign of weakening in favor of fluoridation. Although a resolution to oppose water fluoridation eventually passed, it was only after considerable debate, and it did not pass unanimously. A Florida member pointed out that water fluoridation was part of a program of the World Health Organization which, in turn, was an agency of the United Nations, an organization that the DAR had always opposed. Another member argued the far rightist position that it was part of a master plan constructed by those desiring to dominate the world.[38] Keeping watch for news of activities of other rightist organizations, the Pasadena Anti-Communist League, had nothing but praise for the DAR's successful passage of their resolution.[39] Nevertheless, the fact that a small minority of DAR delegates opposed the fluoridation resolution reveals a crack in the armor of a conservative group, especially when compared with the unanimous decision of the Long Island Federation of Women's Clubs just two years earlier. It also reveals that DAR members, as with members of other women's organizations, did not all share the same opinions on issues.

Women entered the debate on both sides of the issue. In 1956, in Montclair, New Jersey, Edna Troisi, a housewife who had been active among those opposed to water fluoridation since 1954, presided over both the New Jersey Council Opposed to Fluoridation and the Montclair Committee Against Fluoridation. Leading the local pro-fluoridation organization was another housewife, Sally Huffaker, founder of the Montclair Committee to Protect Our Children's Teeth. Among those aligned with Huffaker were Montclair's Health Department and 95 percent of the region's doctors and dentists—200 of them—who had signed pro-fluoridation petitions.[40] From appearances, this was a formidable group; but it did not deter Edna Troisi.

Gerald Walker, a freelance reporter who did a case study of Montclair's fluoridation debate, described Troisi as "an energetic woman in her thirties," a college graduate, and a mother of six children. She claimed to have started studying about fluoridation to protect her children. Although she seldom read scientific journals, she became convinced that water fluoridation was dangerous. Troisi soon began working to defeat fluoridation by organizing, recruiting, and mailing "information" propaganda. Zelma Pack Cordwell from nearby Glen Ridge, who Walker described as "a distinguished-looking matron," joined her campaign, as did Dr. A. Allen London, a dentist from Boonton, New Jersey. Cordwell was associate editor of the monthly newsletter the *National Fluoridation News*, and wrote nineteen articles rebutting a pro-fluoridation series that Huffaker had written for the *Montclair Times*. London was an active speaker for the few among the medical community who opposed fluoridation.[41]

The debate over fluoridation of the Montclair public water system typified arguments around the country on the question. Those who favored fluoridation based their arguments upon decade-long tests in Grand Rapids, Michigan, and Newburgh, New York, that showed reductions in tooth decay among children who had been drinking fluoridated water. Proponents also pointed to positive reports concerning twenty-two major American cities that were fluoridating their waters, including Chicago, San Francisco, and Philadelphia. Nevertheless, Montclair's fluoridation foes maintained it was an "unproven experiment," with Cordwell declaring it "a Left-Wing bureaucratic plot that may lead to socialized medicine or worse." The Montclair antis carried out an extensive telephone, letter-writing, and doorbell-ringing campaign, and circulated flyers featuring a skull-and-crossbones over "Do You Want Rat Poison in Your Drinking Water?"[42] The antis called upon so-called experts who supported their views. One who did was Dr. George L. Waldbott, an allergist and researcher whose wife was editor of the *National Fluoridation News*. Waldbott, who one researcher described as "the most prestigious opponent" of fluoridation in the United States, campaigned against fluoridation from the mid-1950s until his death in 1982. The Montclair opponents relied heavily upon such reports as those alleging "chronic fluoride poisoning."[43]

In Montclair, as in other communities where fluoridation was debated, the strength of the fluoridation opponents' attacks, combined with the fears they were able to raise among the populace, kept the proponents in a defensive position. Helping the opponents' cause was the proponents' tendency to use scientific detail in their rebuttals, language that the average citizen could not always comprehend.[44] Such language could only add to the distrust many Americans had of the scientific elite. On the other side, antifluoridation groups were more likely to use plain language and simple diagrams. The Salem (Oregon) Pure Water Committee, for instance, arguing that "over 99% of the water in any city is used for non-drinking purposes," presented a diagram of a dump truck dumping fluoride in a city reservoir, followed by drawings of ten uses for city water—washing dishes, toilets, bathing, laundry, watering gardens, washing cars, washing floors, street cleaning, radiators, and the final drawing was of a child pouring himself a glass of drinking water.[45] The visuals made a point that almost anyone could understand.

Figure 2. Antifluoridation diagram circulated by the Salem (Oregon) Pure Water Committee, 1953. Courtesy of Oregon Historical Society Research Library, Politics Collection, MSS 1513, sLibrarycop13032023380_0001.

The outcome of the Montclair controversy revealed the power of fluoridation opponents. After hearing arguments from both sides in an open town meeting in February 1957, and two months later in private, the Town Commission tabled the matter pending the receipt of a statement from the American Medical Association regarding its re-evaluation of fluoridation, which was scheduled to be released to the public in December 1957. On February 27, 1958, approximately two months after the AMA's House of Delegates reaffirmed its pro-fluoridation stance, Montclair's Town Commission issued a statement. They concluded that fluoridation would not cause physical harm, could be easily controlled, and would significantly reduce tooth decay in children. They decided, however, not to adopt fluoridation "at the present time."[46]

Observers offered various interpretations of the commissioners' decision. Some claimed that the commissioners were reacting to "public

WHY *Fluoridation*

SALEM PURE WATER COMMITTEE

P. O. Box 652 - Salem, Oregon

What Does This Mean?

Only children 9 years old and under benefit from fluoridated water. Only one tenth of 1% of the water they drink helps prevent tooth decay. Let's put this into figures.

In a city of 15,000 population, cost of erecting and equipping a building for fluoridation totals $80,000. Maintenance and fluorides each year cost another $5,000.

Of a total investment of $85,000, therefore, over $84,150 goes down the sewer for non-drinking uses. Of the 1% or $850, only $85 worth benefits the children who drink it. Is this a wise investment of public funds?

Fluoridating 100% of the water supply of any city is costly, wasteful, and possibly harmful, in view of

OTHER FACTS

The sodium fluoride used in fluoridating water is a deadly poison never found as such in nature. It is made from waste products chiefly of the fertilizer and aluminum industries.

Artificial fluoridation prevents tooth decay in 50% of the children by hardening the enamel. What else does it harden? What of arteries, kidneys, brain, heart, eyes or nerves?

One part per million of fluorides are recommended. Yet .8 parts per million of artificial fluorides cause fluorosis—ugly mottling of children's teeth, and breakdown of teeth in teen-agers, adults and oldsters.

Natural fluorides exist in many common foods—wheat, apples, cheese, fish. Why add artificial fluorides to our drinking water at such huge cost and waste?

Only dentists and doctors should prescribe a drug so powerful and dangerous as the fluorides used for fluoridation.

Are There Better Ways?

There are several better, safer, cheaper ways to do the job.

WHAT TO DO

First, in no case use raw, inorganic fluorides for human consumption. They are deadly, violent poisons. Beware!

Second, under supervision of federal, state or local health officers, fluoride compounds derived from living foods can be

  a. Bottled as medicine and prescribed by dentist or doctor.

  b. Made into tablets and sold by prescription in drug stores.

  c. Added to table salt and used on recommendation of dentist or doctor.

  d. Added to milk, plainly labeled, and distributed in grammar schools.

WHAT CAUSES TOOTH DECAY?

Reports in the official journal of the American Dental Association say: tooth decay is the result of bad nutrition—too many refined sweets and starches, candy and soft drinks. The addition of one element, like fluorine, will not stop tooth decay.

Calcium, not fluorine, is the main element in tooth formation and dental health. Other food factors are Vitamins A and D. No one element can do the job. Food and soils hold most of the answer.

Preventing tooth decay, then, adds up to this: cut out most of the refined, starchy foods, sweets and soft drinks; eat more fresh fruits, vegetables; get plenty of sunshine, fresh air, pure water and rest. See your dentist twice a year.

THINK BEFORE YOU LEAP! Fluoride poison in drinking water is no substitute for good food and clean living habits.

180 *The CHALLENGE Magazine — Medford, Oregon*

Figure 3. Antifluoridation pamphlet "Why Fluoridation?" circulated by the Salem (Oregon) Pure Water Committee, 1953. Courtesy of Oregon Historical Society Research Library, Politics Collection, MSS 1513, sLibrary-cop1303202380_0002.

apathy." While the fight raged between groups of proponents and opponents, most individuals within the community appeared indifferent. Out of 25,000 registered voters, only 2,100 signed petitions on the issue—1,500 in favor of fluoridation and 600 opposed. Others asserted that the commission did not want to take the chance of splitting the town. One Montclair resident, a former mayor of a Pennsylvania community that had adopted fluoridation, called the Town Commissioners "spineless" and "remiss in their duties." Still others pointed to proponents' failure to successfully communicate to the citizenry. For instance, many citizens considered doctors' and dentists' attitudes to be paternalistic, hindering efforts to convince the community of the positive aspects of fluoridation.[47]

Citizen apathy was apparent in other communities, including Cambridge, Massachusetts. There, a study concluded that while both sides of the issue had a small number of individuals who were enthusiastic campaigners, the majority of the community displayed little excitement. Several respected associations that might have influenced voters did not take a stand on fluoridation, including the League of Women Voters, the Cambridge Chamber of Commerce, and the Parent-Teacher organizations.[48]

Nor was Montclair the only community to back out of a fluoridation plan. In the Westchester, New York, village of Mt. Kisco, the trustees voted four to one, in October 1956, to go forward with a fluoridation plan. More than two years later, after lengthy debate, the trustees voted three to two to abandon it. Mayor Betty Potter, who cast the sole dissenting vote in 1956, announced in 1958 that the Village Board sought advice during the interim from experts and was now better aware of the dangers that might result from excessive fluoridation.[49] On this rare occasion wherein a woman held a prominent role in local government, Mayor Potter had some considerable influence.

Right-wing fluoridation foes monitored news of scientists, medical people, and communities taking stands against fluoridation. The various organizations then spread this information via their newsletters, encouraging their readers to pass on the information. In addition to their campaigns to influence public school textbooks and curricula, the Minute Women of the U.S.A. adopted the rightist position on fluoridation and made it one of their many issues. Members received information as to where they could obtain a list of doctors opposed to fluoridation. A leader noted, "It can be helpful in having others take the same position."[50]

Minute Woman Lucille Cardin Crain joined the antifluoridation cause. As a member of the New York Citizens Committee Opposing Fluoridation, she kept a close watch on the communities who discontinued adding the chemical.[51]

In the 1950s and 1960s some psychological and sociological studies focused on the controversy. In 1955, social psychologist Bernard Mausner and his wife, Judith, a physician, surveyed the backgrounds and attitudes of almost 400 persons living in Northampton, Massachusetts, a few days prior to its referendum on fluoridation. They found that those favoring fluoridation were more likely to have young children, were usually more highly educated, earned more money, and held more prestigious occupations than the antis. Ninety-five percent of the proponents considered scientific organizations reliable sources of information, while the opponents were more likely to reject such authority. The Mausners found the antis more impressed with the few deviant scientists than with professional associations and were suspicious of intellectuals in general, fearing that they were conspiring against the average American.[52] Such suspicion was similar to the right's position on education, wherein it distrusted most of the intellectuals who were writing textbooks and administering the public schools.

Other studies revealed results similar to those of the Mausners. For example, Thomas F. A. Plaut, in his examination of the Cambridge referendum, found that in the seven precincts voting in favor of fluoridation, almost all adults had high school diplomas. Conversely, in the thirteen opposing precincts, eight possessed a large proportion of adults who lacked high school diplomas. Precincts favoring fluoridation tended to be upper middle class, included many elderly residents, and had few foreign-born residents. Most of those on the opposing side lived in poor housing, included only a small proportion of aged people, but had a large proportion of residents who were not born in the United States.[53] Similarly, a mid-1950s study of a California community found that the better educated and wealthier people tended to endorse fluoridation, as did those who supported racial integration. "Conservative" Cambridge Democrats were more likely to oppose fluoridation than "liberal" New Deal Democrats. Plaut defined conservative Democrats as those Democrats who voted for Republican Dwight Eisenhower and liberal Democrats as those who voted for Democrat Adlai Stevenson in the 1956 presidential election.[54]

Stevenson was an outspoken supporter of both the New Deal and the Fair Deal well into the 1950s.[55] In general, Cambridge precincts that supported a liberal position on other issues were most likely to favor fluoridation. Both the California and Cambridge studies found that, overall, Republicans were more likely than Democrats to vote in favor of fluoridation.[56] A pattern, it seems, was developing of working classes being more likely to oppose fluoridation than the middle class. However, the leaders of the antifluoridation movement, whether male or female, were frequently of the middle class.

As historian Gretchen Ann Reilly and other researchers into the issue note, defining the typical antifluoridationist is practically impossible.[57] However, questions over the seemingly obsessive behavior of some of fluoridation's opponents led some social scientists to analyze the thought processes of the leaders. One hypothesis centers on "alienation," a quite popular term during the 1960s.[58] In a collaborative effort during the late 1960s, sociologist Robert L. Crain, social psychologist Elihu Katz, and political scientist Donald B. Rosenthal found that a "tiny but strident" minority, claiming to be "protecting the majority against an infringement of their liberty," spearheaded the opposition. Due to the vagueness of the antifluoridationists' charges, their perceptions of conspiracy, and some of their illogical statements, some might label these leaders "extremist." Yet they successfully influenced public attitudes. When citizens voted on fluoridation, they revealed the power of the antifluoridationists' campaigns. Robert Crain and his associates could not classify the leaders' behavior as "alienated" because of the tremendous numbers of people who accepted their ideas. In some communities three-quarters of the voters turned fluoridation referenda down. Nevertheless, they found it difficult to believe that most Americans accepted all of the charges the leaders were leveling against fluoridation. Instead, much like Plaut in his Cambridge study, Crain, Katz, and Rosenthal placed blame upon the failure of community leaders to lead the efforts in favor of fluoridation.[59]

Although there were many setbacks, throughout the 1950s the fluoridation movement made slow, but steady progress. While only a decade earlier just a handful of communities had fluoridated their public water systems, John Knutson of the U.S. Public Health Service reported that as of August 1959, 35,738,842 Americans in 1,830 communities were drinking fluoridated water.[60] In an editorial entitled "Fluoridation Is Here to Stay," published in the November 1962 issue of the *Journal of the American Dental Association*, the editor expressed confidence in the future of fluoridation, tempered by frustration over the continuing opposition. The article sought to educate the public on the benefits of fluoridation, but the opening editorial revealed a condescending attitude toward those opposed, which could only have widened the gap between scientific elites and the less educated skeptic. For example, the author ridiculed the skeptics with the remark that, throughout history, there have been people opposed to change, including such inventions as the wheel and the automobile.[61]

Despite the antis' gradual losses, in 1960, there still remained well over 100 million Americans who were not receiving water with the fluoride additive. Opponents of fluoridation did not give up, but continued their fight through the 1960s. Among them was Emily Mehr, who had chaired the Nassau County (New York) Committee Opposed to Fluoridation in the mid-1950s and was presiding over the Association for the Protection of Our Water Supply in 1961.[62]

During the mid-1960s, following President Lyndon Johnson's endorsement of fluoridation, mail flowed into the White House from those opposed. In 1965, Hazel Kramer, treasurer of the Flint (Michigan) Civic and Health Committee, wrote, "We cannot believe that you endorse compulsory mass medication of the entire population for lifetime duration with a highly toxic, protoplasmic poison." Referring to the war in Vietnam, she added, "We cannot believe that while you commit our sons' lives and our country's resources to protect the freedom of people in distant lands to choose their own destiny, you endorse the denial of freedom of choice in health matters to your own countrymen."[63] The Flint group was made up of both sexes. It appears, however, that women dominated that organization, holding the offices of president, secretary, and treasurer.[64] Although it is not clear if the committee was a rightist organization, it did employ some of the long-standing rightist rhetoric.

While the president received letters filled with the right-wing's charges of "poison," complaints also came from nonrightists. For example, Mary DeRemer of Williamsport, Pennsylvania, an admirer of President Johnson who was apparently unaware of his position on the fluoridation issue, asked him to endorse a local citizens' campaign to fight fluoridation. One of many Americans who feared that "pure" water was becoming polluted through fluoridation, she wrote, "You know about our mountains and the wonderful spring water we have here. . . . I dare say there is no purer water anywhere in these United States."[65] Although she leaned to the liberal side in politics, right-wing antifluoridation campaigns appear to have influenced her thinking on the matter. The idea of maintaining pure and pleasant-tasting drinking water was important to people regardless of their politics. It became a task for proponents to convince Americans that the taste would not be affected by adding small amounts of fluoride. A baby boomer who was raised in Fayetteville, North Carolina, remembers the debate over fluoridation, recalling that as an adolescent she adopted her mother's position and opposed the additive because she feared that fluorides would spoil her drinking water's flavor. Only later, after her own children had reached puberty with little tooth decay, did she realize the benefits of fluorides.[66] With Americans with political views ranging across the political spectrum voicing concern over the purity or flavor of water, the right had an abundance of opportunities to plant seeds creating even greater anxieties over the possible presence of poison.

Yet amid the ongoing controversy, the number of communities adding fluorides to their water continued to increase. New York City began adding fluorides to its water supply in 1965, more than a decade after the City Council first introduced a resolution calling for fluoridation.[67] Neighboring New Jersey was slower to act than the Empire State, with state health officials reporting in 1972 that only about 12 percent of its population was using fluoridated water. This was at a time when 75 percent of the people of New York State and 50 percent of Pennsylvanians were receiving such water. Still leading New Jersey's fluoridation opponents was Edna Troisi, president of the New Jersey Council Opposing Fluoridation, Inc., and, together with other rightists, was proving to be a formidable force in that state.[68]

In February 1974, state officials held another hearing on the issue. On this occasion, opponents outnumbered advocates by an estimated twenty to one. Journalist Walter H. Waggoner estimated that about 200 people attended the hearing, many of them carrying homemade antifluoridation placards. Despite the high emotion of the crowd, he noted that fluoridation opponents' tactics appeared to have moderated in recent years. No longer were opponents charging that the fluoridation program was a "Communist plot" to undermine the health and resistance of the American people.[69] More than a decade had passed since the communist threat

was at a height. Most Americans, including the right, were no longer placing great emphasis on the idea of the United States being infiltrated by
communists. Only one person used a "scare tactic," a woman from Jersey
City, who he described as "friendly" and "elderly." She distributed flyers
headed, "Do you want rat poison in your drinking water?" Otherwise, the
opposition assailed the scientific findings and argued that mandatory
fluoridation was, at best, the introduction of a "prescription drug" into
the public water supply without popular consent.[70]

As time passed, further progress of scientific evidence and changing
political and social conditions, including the ending of the Cold War,
would impact the fate of fluoridation. By the end of the twentieth century, statistics would show that fluoridation had a positive effect on baby
boomers' teeth and that scientists had produced something positive. At
the beginning of the twenty-first century, only six of the nation's fifty
largest cities did not have fluoride in their drinking water. Although water
fluoridation continues to have its opponents, for the general population,
fluoridation became more of a practical than an ideological issue.[71]

Mental Health

Right-wing activist Ida Darden once proclaimed, "If You're a Good Conservative American Patriot—Let's Face It—You're Nuts."[72] Her comment
reflected rightist fears in the 1950s and 1960s, a time when communities
were beginning to promote mental health programs. Mental health was
an issue of great importance for women of the right, with three major
themes resonating among right-wing women in regard to the matter. One
fear centered on the idea that people whose beliefs and ideas lay outside of
the mainstream, and particularly if they were on the far right, were being
stereotyped as mentally unstable, and indeed were in danger of being sent
off to mental institutions. A second anxiety concerned their belief that the
increasing use of intelligence and personality tests in the schools was dangerous, as they were a means for brainwashing American youth. Another
concern was over the use of drugs and therapies to treat mental health
problems. Many rightists worried that such treatments were for purposes
of manipulating the minds of mental health patients. Combined, the three
themes provided evidence that the new public health programs were but
another aspect within a larger plan to create a new world order.

The mid-1950s was a time when new types of therapies and drugs were coming into use for the treatment of psychological problems. In 1953, American psychologist B. F. Skinner published *Science and Human Behavior*, describing his theory of conditioning. His work, which was important for those searching to understand human behavior, received considerable publicity. At about the same time, drugs were becoming available to treat psychoses. In 1954, chlorpromazine (marketed under the brand name Thorazine) was the first of the phenothiazines, a tranquilizing drug with antipsychotic actions, to become available in the United States. During the mid-1950s, such ongoing changes in psychiatry, in addition to a great increase in the numbers of patients being admitted to psychiatric hospitals,[73] brought enhanced attention from American rightists when Congress began discussing a mental health bill that contained some rather ambiguous statements.

The first cry of alarm came in late 1955 from the Burbank, California–based American Public Relations Forum, an organization of about one hundred housewives, following the introduction of the Alaska Mental Health Bill, H.R. 6376.[74] The bill's purpose was to transfer basic responsibility and authority for the hospitalization, care, and treatment of Alaska's mentally ill from the federal government to the territory of Alaska. The federal government was to provide the territory with funding to construct facilities to treat Alaska's mentally ill. The bill passed the U.S. House of Representatives by voice vote on January 18, 1956, and then went before the Senate. Women testified on both sides of the issue. Political lines were already drawn when a representative of the General Federation of Women's Clubs spoke in favor of the bill, while a woman of the 30th Women's Patriotic Conference on National Defense, representing the political right, opposed it.[75] Many right-wing women came to consider the Alaska Mental Health Bill as part of a broader plan of the more liberal majority to weaken the opposition. For example, in March 1956, Florence Walker of Auburn, New York, wrote that she was "almost certain that some red anti-American wrote this Bill. If the U.S.P.H.S. [United States Public Health Service] is tied up with this in any way, it should be investigated by the F.B.I. It almost seems that the fluoridation, mental health pressure groups are all one."[76]

Recent governmental policies no doubt contributed to the right's unease in regard to the Alaska bill. Historically, the care and institutionalization of mental patients was left to the states. In 1946, with the passage of the National Mental Health Act, the government became more involved in psychiatric programs. This act authorized the nation's Surgeon General to aim to improve the mental health of Americans through research into the causes, diagnoses, and treatment of psychiatric disorders. It also provided for the funding of psychiatric education and research, training for mental health workers, and grants to the states for mental health services. The act called for the establishment of the National Institute of Mental Health, which was accomplished in 1949.[77] The Alaska bill, later known as the Alaska Mental Health Enabling Act, appeared straightforward. Its purpose was "to transfer from the Federal Government to the Territory of Alaska basic responsibility and authority for the hospitalization, care and treatment of the mentally ill of Alaska."[78] There were, however, additional provisions that caused some unease among the American public and led to outrage among many on the right.

There was little complaint over the act's intent. Most among the right seem to have agreed with longtime rightist W. Henry MacFarland Jr., of the American Flag Committee, who noted that the territory of Alaska lacked facilities to care for its mentally ill. "Since 1910," MacFarland wrote, "these unfortunate folks have been sent to Morningside Hospital, a private institution in Portland, Oregon," with which the federal government maintained a contract for their treatment. Thus, ailing Alaskans were required to travel over a thousand miles south to Oregon, a trip that often caused high anxiety for the mentally impaired. It appears that most rightists agreed with MacFarland that Alaskans should have their own facility.[79] But the bill did not stop there. There were provisions in the bill that had the potential to affect mental patients in all of the forty-eight states.

Texas Women for Constitutional Government, a rightist group based in Houston, recognized that the bill would not pertain only to Alaska and Oregon, and found a variety of reasons to oppose it. They distributed a lengthy flyer, outlining their rationale for opposing the bill. The women considered three provisions of the bill as the most dangerous. Topping their list was Section 119(c), which authorized the governor of Alaska to "enter into a reciprocal agreement with any State providing for the care and treatment of mentally ill residents of Alaska by such State, and for the care and treatment of mentally ill residents of such State by Alaska, each on a reimbursable basis." They noted that since Alaska was a territory, and not yet a state, the governor was a presidential appointee. The people did not elect him. The Texas Women were hinting at possible corruption on the part of a leader who was not answerable to the people. Further, they interpreted the language about reciprocity as meaning that a disproportionately large number of Americans from the forty-eight contiguous states would be more likely to be sent to Alaska rather than the reverse. "Can anyone think of any good reason why an ill person should be sent to the frigid climate of Alaska? Surely all the careful wording of 'receiving' and 'sending' states is not meant to apply merely to a tourist in Alaska who suddenly goes mad and would naturally be sent to the place of his legal residence."[80]

Although not listed in the Texas Women's documentation of grievances, Section 202 of the act added to rightist fears. It granted the territory "one million acres from the public lands of the United States in Alaska," with the authority to "lease and make conditional sales of such selected lands."[81] It was not long before word began spreading among the right that the million acres of public lands were destined to become an "American Siberia."[82] The Texas Women's May 1956 news bulletin supports this perception. The group linked a possible government authorization of petroleum exploration on approximately 1.1 million acres of land in Alaska to both mental health and Russia. Noting the opening of a development contract "under which Colorado Oil and Gas Corporation would search for petroleum at Icy Bay," they asked if officials had "gone over the heads of the American people again and are transferring the land FROM THE FEDERAL GOVERNMENT to the mental health plotters without even asking consent of the ELECTED REPRESENTATIVES of the American people." A Mrs. Helen Walton had supposedly revealed that Russia owned more than "72 million shares of stock in our finest companies in this country. Just because the oil companies carry an American name does not necessarily mean that they are purely American."[83] The author failed to offer a coherent argument regarding how the development of oil fields, Russian ownership of American stock, and the "mental health plotters" were working together in this instance, but her linking the three topics undoubtedly added fuel to the idea of an "American Siberia." The author was probably suggesting, as another group had done, that the Colorado firm was part of a plot to transfer sections of land, a million acres at a time, to Russia.[84]

Also linking the Alaska bill to Soviet-style communism was the rightist

Pasadena Anti-Communist League. It argued that in a society where government leaders achieved their positions as a result of violence and had established a nation ruled by a dictatorship of the minority, "as in Russia," there was "little need for health legislation." In a Communist country mental illness was considered "simply a political deviation," a crime that could be punished. But, in a country not yet Communist, if the majority could be turned toward communism (in the League's words "coerced"), there would be no need for such techniques.[85] In the eyes of the League, the United States was taking the latter road to communism—with communists and conspirators in government gradually manipulating Americans until they found themselves in a situation from which they could not escape.

Other researchers point to evidence that anti-Semitism entered the picture too. They note that some on the far right charged that the Alaska bill was part of a Zionist conspiracy to spread communism throughout the world, or that Jewish psychiatrists were plotting to brainwash Americans.[86] Although there is little evidence in the written materials examined for this book that rightist women blamed Jews outright for those mental health programs they so despised, Jews were prominent in the psychiatric movement.[87]

The Texas Women voiced further concerns. They feared that under the Alaska Mental Health Enabling Act protection regarding commitment of the mentally ill, or those persons suspected to be mentally ill, would be "drastically lowered." As evidence, they pointed to Section 103, which included the statement, "Any individual may be admitted for care and treatment in a hospital upon written application by an *interested party* [Texas Women's emphasis, noting the ambiguity of the designation], by a health or welfare officer, by the Governor or by the head of *any* [Texas Women's emphasis] institution in which the individual may be, if the application is accompanied by a certificate of *a* licensed physician."[88]

The women looked to Section 105 for yet more evidence of loss of patient rights. That section provided that the head of the admitting hospital arrange for an examination of the patient within a period not to exceed five days. Exclaiming, "A lot can happen in 5 days!" the women referred to a recent article by Beverly Hills psychiatrist Dr. Nichols A. Bercel that discussed the use of injecting Lysergic Acid Diethylamide (LSD) into "normal" people so as to induce "mental illness." Scientists then would study the results. The Texas Women wrote that the study represented "the first time that human beings can be used for testing methods determining drugs which have an effect on mental illness."[89] They implied that any person who sought to have another person "out of the way" could apply to have that person committed. During the brief waiting period, anything could happen to the patient, including being administered drugs that could cause a mentally healthy person to become mentally ill. The patient could then be sent to a mental institution in "frigid" Alaska, away from friends, family, and any hope of returning to one's home state in the fore-seeable future.

The third controversial section of the act was near the beginning. The territorial government (which the women translated as the "governor") was authorized "to enact such laws" as it deemed appropriate "relating to the hospitalization, care and treatment of residents of or persons in Alaska who are mentally ill, and such legislation may supersede any of the provisions of Title 1 of this act."[90] Again the women emphasized words that pointed to the possibility of involuntary confinement. People's futures appeared to be arbitrarily placed in the hands of a governor who was conceivably completely apathetic in regard to their cases.

From Ithaca, New York, Gladice Woolf wrote that "Siberia, U.S.A.," a title that Mrs. Leigh F. Burkeland of Van Nuys, California, gave the bill in January 1956, and which quickly became a catchphrase for the right, was an apt description of the Alaska Mental Health plan. It bothered her that a doctor promoting the bill belonged to the World Health Organization that, she wrote, was "a consultative agency for UNESCO." She also feared that the legislation placed "every resident of the United States at the mercy of the fancies of any person with whom they might have disagreed." They could be assessed as mentally ill and then be faced "with immediate deportation to Siberia, U.S.A."[91]

Some rightists feared that mental health programs might be used specifically against them because of their ideology. In February 1956, editors of the newsletter New Mexico Women Speak! observed that people opposing fluoridation were frequently referred to as "Emotionalists, Fanatics, Crackpots, Fascists, Out of Their Minds . . . Pamphleteers, etc." The editors saw a pattern there, one by which those favoring fluoridation and mental health programs were finding means to eliminate their opponents. One way to purge objectors was to rule that they were mentally ill or had a mental deficiency and send them to an institution that might be thousands of miles away from family and friends who might have been able to come to their rescue.[92]

As evidence of the threat to the right, the article refers to remarks by historian Richard Hofstadter, who described "pseudo-conservatives" as having a tendency toward paranoia. The author recognized herself and her associates in Hofstadter's description: someone who opposed the United Nations, disapproved of the appointment of Justice Earl Warren to the Supreme Court, was opposed to foreign aid and the income tax, worried about subversion in the United States, and might have been a member of an "old family" American group that feared losing status.[93] No doubt those rightists were referring to Hofstadter's essay on "The Pseudo-Conservative Revolt" (1954), in which he includes Roosevelt-haters as an attribute of pseudo-conservative thinking.[94] Many women examined here would fit Hofstadter's description, as did a number of rightist men. In April 1956, a male correspondent thanked right-wing activist Lucille Cardin Crain for information about the Alaska Mental Health Bill: "It strikes me as a very dangerous piece of business. After looking at the quotations you gave, I conclude that I and a lot of others would be fit subjects for a mental institution."[95]

The numbers of Americans institutionalized in mental hospitals were at a peak in the mid-1950s as more types of behavior were being diagnosed as mental disorders. During the years 1880 to 1955, the numbers of inpatients increased from approximately 30,000 to 560,000, a rate significantly greater than the overall growth of the American populace.[96] The majority of patients in state institutions were female, of whom many had been diagnosed with schizophrenia when they were merely unhappy in their marriages or in their roles as housewives.[97] Since the mid-1940s, the public was aware of deplorable conditions in many mental hospitals—overcrowding, wards filled with naked patients, and attendants beating defenseless patients. At the same time, doctors were making liberal use of electroconvulsive therapy (ECT), which was used on women about twice as frequently as it was on men.[98] The thought of being confined in such a place, particularly for those who considered themselves to be mentally healthy but fearful that others were conspiring against them, was frightening.

In the mid-1950s, the California Minute Women brought up the important issue of how the psychiatric community was defining mental illness, or what they often termed "psychiatric defects." They wrote that the term was defined to "include behavior and emotional problems, addictions, perversions, mental deficiencies, [and] psychosomatic ailments. Thus, you see, *almost anyone might be included*" (Minute Women's emphasis).[99]

Philosopher and historian Michel Foucault points out that the definition of what connotes insanity varies as to time and place in history. While one culture might deem the poor as deviant and asocial, another might so characterize homosexuals or the political opposition.[100] Many among the right were uneasy that it was their time to be classified as "deviant" or mentally unbalanced. Post–World War II studies, often written by psychologists and social scientists attempting to psychoanalyze persons whose outlooks bore some resemblance to fascism, were drawing the attention of the far right. *The Authoritarian Personality* (1950) by behavioral scientists Theodor W. Adorno, Else Frenkel-Brunswik, Daniel Levinson, and Nevitt Sanford introduced the term "pseudo-conservative," and *Prophets of Deceit: A Study of the Techniques of the American Agitator* (1949) by Leo Lowenthal and Norbert Guterman, employed psychoanalytical concepts to define the far right. Most women of the far right could recognize themselves as agitators against "New Dealism," communism, and liberalism, and perhaps as being obsessed by conspiracy theories, behaviors that these scholars were defining as "paranoiac delusions."[101]

Adorno specifically pointed to "organized war mothers," alluding to right-wing women's campaigns during World War II, as belonging to the "lunatic fringe." He admitted that the latter was an often abused term, but believed it held some validity with regard to those women.[102] The war had been over for more than a decade in the mid-1950s, when mental health became such a large issue for the right. Yet it is very likely that many of these women had either participated in organized mothers' movements against the war or had friends who had done so. News of such studies, combined with analyses of antifluoridationists, as noted, understandably caused some uneasiness among many of the right-wing women's groups. The fact that women were more likely than men to be confined to a mental institution would have added to their feelings of vulnerability.

The December 1955 issue of the right-wing newsletter *New Mexico*

Women Speak! listed two people who had been placed in St. Elizabeth's Mental Hospital (the federal government's only civilian psychiatric hospital) in Washington, D.C. The editors wrote that they respected both people and felt their confinement was a great miscarriage of justice. One was a woman, proof to rightist women that it was not only right-wing men who were being watched. She was Lucille Miller, a person the New Mexico women described as "an out-spoken anti-communist" who "was railroaded" into the hospital. The second was poet, anti-Semite, and supporter of Italian fascists, Ezra Pound. Pound was "a brilliant man of letters," they wrote, "an ardent ANTI-COMMUNIST who opposed World War II," yet had been in the mental hospital since 1946.[103]

In June 1956, *New Mexico Women Speak!* reported of further injustices that they believed had resulted from mental health programs. Under the headline "Children Seized to Silence Anti-Communists," the newsletter reported on Kathryn Kingsley Deats, a single mother of four children who, the editors claimed, had been unjustly confined to a mental institution. This case hit home for middle-aged right-wing mothers on the lookout for threats against their ties to their children. According to the article, the institutionalization resulted from Deats's appeal to a children's court in New York State for a judgment that would compel her ex-husband (who had allegedly deserted her) to pay for her and her children's support. When the judge ruled against her, Deats appealed to the governor to remove the judge and the sheriff. Reading between the lines, it appears that she made some derogatory remarks regarding the judge, for she was ordered to retract the statements. Deats refused, was "kidnapped" from her home, and placed in Binghamton's Insane Asylum. These events occurred sometime in 1948, and she was released at the end of that year.

The article continued with the report that several years later, after a move to California, Deats began "exposing the NAACP and Urban League [organizations that many among the right considered to be overrun with communists] connections of some members on the San Diego school board." It appears that she also planned to testify before a congressional committee against the Alaska Mental Health Bill. According to the story, in order to prevent Deats from going to Washington, local authorities "seized" two of her children, threatening to hold them in custody unless Deats submitted to psychiatric treatment. This she refused to do after her seventeen-year-old son insisted that his mother needed to be at home with his fourteen-year-old sister. The boy was still in juvenile detention at the time the story was released.[104] For the New Mexico women, the Deats story was proof that the vendetta against the right was well under way.

A young Connecticut mother, Beverly Chase Perroni, wrote both Lucille Cardin Crain and Lucille Miller, expressing her fears of the impact of the Alaska Mental Health Bill. Perroni, who was in the midst of a local fight against fluoridation, wrote that it was "impossible not to put 2 + 2 together." She was convinced that her politics were causing her to become a target of the government, noting that, for causes unknown, her mail had not been delivered for three weeks during the previous summer, but had somehow landed in General Delivery.[105]

The rightist Minute Women, too, offered evidence that supporters of mental health programs had a hidden agenda: removing "patriots" such as themselves from the political scene. Their newsletter of May-June 1956 included excerpts from a paper written a decade earlier by psychiatrist Julius Schreiber of Washington, D.C., in which he warned of "super-patriots" who were "suspicious of all whose notions of what is loosely called 'Americanism' happen to differ from their own." The Minute Women pointed to a second article, one that linked anti-Semitism to a person's "feeling of rejection," and to a diagnosis of mental illness.[106] Such a thought caused unease among many on the right. Because of their belief that Jews dominated the field of psychology, many feared their anti-Semitism might result in their being defined as mentally ill.[107]

Shortly after the passage of the Alaska Mental Health Enabling Act, the Texas Women for Constitutional Government circulated a paper titled "Who Is Mentally Ill?" In it they cited some comments of prominent people about the mental health of those displaying a right-wing point of view. In one example, the Texas Women asked the reader, "Are you *for* the Bricker Amendment? If so, President Eisenhower probably thinks you are a little off. In January 1954, speaking to some of the Vigilant Women for the Bricker Amendment in Washington, D.C., he pounded his fist on his desk and yelled that the Bricker Amendment was backed by '*nuts*.'"[108] (This amendment was highly favored by the right because it would have required that all treaties be reviewed as to their compatibility with the United States Constitution and that the Congress enact legislation before the treaty could become law. Opponents argued that measures in the amendment would severely restrict a president's ability to conduct foreign policy.)

For the next several years, right-wing women continued to question how mental illness was being defined. In 1960, Elizabeth Chesnut Barnes, national chairman of the National Defense Committee of the DAR, wrote, "If you believe in the principles and ideals of the Founding Fathers, the mental experts will accuse you of being 'rigid.' They will say you have 'constellations of prejudice' areas if you are opposed to foreign aid, public housing, public ownership of utilities, liberalization of the immigration laws, or any other schemes of the socialist planners which you believe will tend to push this country farther along the road to its destruction." Barnes called the mental health movement a "Marxist weapon in the ideological war being waged for the minds of free men, a technique to compel conformity in an individual's political beliefs."[109]

Within two years after its signing, controversy over the Alaska Mental Health Enabling Act had died down. In the spring of 1956, popular columnist Drew Pearson credited rightist organizations, including the American Legion, the Minute Women, and other women's organizations, with raising such a ruckus over the issue that Congress reconsidered and made changes to the bill. He named Mrs. Leigh F. Burkeland, the woman who coined the phrase "Siberia, U.S.A.," as the person most responsible for kicking off the letter-writing campaign that instigated the tremendous controversy over what had been thought of as a simple, straightforward bill.[110]

When the results of the campaign were in, the right could claim at least a partial victory. Right-wing activist Anne Smart noted that "thanks to the efforts of alerted citizens across the country [the Alaska Mental Health Enabling Act] is not quite as bad as was originally drawn up." She then warned her audience of new dangers, rooted in the fact that states were enacting rules of their own.[111] Most rightists were satisfied with changes to the Alaska act that eliminated some ambiguities. New provisions more clearly defined under what circumstances a person had a right to a jury trial and what situations might lead to the transfer of mental patients from the lower forty-eight states.[112] Such successes provided lessons for organizing campaigns as well as incentives for activists to continue to pursue their causes. The Alaska campaign marked the beginning of a rightist mental health lobby, which looked at broader issues in mental health. They began to ask questions as to who was behind the emerging community health programs; and why the sudden need?

Psychiatrists, and others working in mental health programs during the height of the attacks from the right, feared that the anti–mental health movement was having too much success. From all across the country, but particularly in the West and South, came reports of public officials and state legislators voting against funding for much-needed mental health facilities. In Southern California, a stronghold of the right, citizens witnessed the elimination of some valuable mental health programs.[113] Psychiatrists blamed the far right for the situation. There were some reports that the anti–mental health program so frightened some people that they committed suicide rather than accept help from any psychiatrist.[114] Via their telephoning and letter-writing campaigns, pamphleteering, and vociferous rallies at public meetings, the right scored some significant victories. This was despite the fact that much of the information they espoused had very little evidence to support it.

The California State Bulletin of the Minute Women of the U.S.A., Inc., presented an organizational chart that supposedly illustrated the manner in which mental health was being administered. Topping the chart was the United Nations General Assembly, followed by the Economic and Social Council, Commissions, and Specialized Agencies. Then the chart branched out, with the World Federation of Mental Health, UNESCO, and the World Health Organization in the middle. Below them were voluntary agencies and such government agencies as Health, Education, and Welfare, the U.S. Public Health Service, and the National Institute of Mental Health.[115] The chart was claiming that world organizations, most of which these women had criticized for years, were directing the mental health movement in the United States. Despite the chart's inaccuracies, the Minute Women were raising the question of who was setting the standards for determining what types of behavior were normal and what were not.

New Mexico Women Speak! leaders warned of brainwashing techniques; and it was not only federal government initiatives that caused their anxiety. They warned that following the passage of mental health bills in state legislatures, clinics were opening up across the country. Some bills, they charged, put clinics under the control of "civic minded citizens, plus a director who need not be resident of CITY, COUNTY OR STATE, and who need have no requirements for citizenship."[116] For these "patriotic" women, for whom lack of citizenship was practically equivalent to "un-Americanism," the loose residential requirements were outrageous.[117]

California Minute Women brought up similar concerns, usually quoting the same sources. Additionally, they mentioned their fear of "maternal separation," the thought that mental health treatment might necessitate mothers losing close contact with their infants or very young children. Such an event would negatively impact the bond between mother and child.[118] In her study of San Francisco Bay area women confined during the 1950s, sociologist Carol A. B. Warren found that a mother's institutionalization did often hurt the mother's relationship with her children. Guilt and stress over the separation, and believing that she was not fulfilling her responsibilities as a mother, frequently led to an uncomfortable relationship once she returned home.[119]

In 1957, Texas rightist Ida Darden, in her newspaper, the *Southern Conservative*, dated the mental health issue back to the International Congress on Mental Health, held in London in 1948. She accused those gathering at the conference of ignoring mental health. Instead, she argued, they focused on "the framework of a new social structure." She believed it was largely due to that conference that recent movements to eliminate racial prejudice were put in force, movements that Darden mostly disdained. The new social structure, she complained, also intended that citizens of the world be "released from 'unhealthy family relationships'; unrestricted by 'pre-conceived notions of morality'; unhampered by 'narrow nationalism'; released from 'unwholesome parental influence'; and 'free from outmoded ideas of loyalty to Country or Flag.'"[120] Darden and others on the far right often created charts or "frameworks" to convince people of the veracity of their claims. With little or no evidence, they established links, moving from one factor to another, making larger leaps with each progression. Just as the California Minute Women gave no details as to how the United Nations and the various health agencies in the United States were connected—particularly on the matter of mental health—Darden provided no evidence as to how the London Conference could affect such matters as racial prejudices, family relationships, and patriotism.

In addition, Darden castigated women who, "without knowing where they are going," had recently "taken up the challenge [to improve mental health programs] and are out in full cry."[121] She was likely referring to such mainstream women's groups as the West Virginia Federation of Women's Clubs, which had taken on a seven-point program "to promote the mental health of every individual in every community."[122]

As far as these rightist women were concerned, they had more than sufficient evidence to make a case for a conspiracy on the part of communists, liberals, socialists, and "one-worlders." They believed there were plans afoot to eliminate those to the right of the mainstream who dared raise their voices to protest the direction the United States was taking, politically, socially, culturally, and morally. Adults could be railroaded into mental institutions, but could it happen to youth? In the eyes of the right, measures were already under way to manipulate the minds of the baby boom generation so as to make them into clone-like followers of a liberal agenda. As shown in chapter 1, the right fought to block what they considered leftist elements in school textbooks and curricula. But they also saw other issues connected to education, including personality and intelligence testing, that they feared would be used to manipulate the minds of American youth.

During the summer of 1955, several months before the Alaska Mental Health Bill passed through Congress, rightist Frances Bartlett addressed the mental health issue as it pertained to children. Bartlett was publisher of FACTS in Education and had been a leader in the campaign against progressive education in Pasadena, California, several years earlier. Although she agreed with a report in the conservative weekly Human Events that progressive education had recently died, she noticed that some of progressive education's supporters were pushing for more psychiatrists in the schools. As she saw the situation, it was these progressive educators who had caused behavioral problems in the schools in the first place![123] Over the next few years, other rightist women voiced similar concerns.

Writing for the right-wing publication the Education Signpost, Helen Hayne praised Lewis A. Alesen's book Mental Robots (1957). Alesen was a past president of the Los Angeles County Medical Association and California Medical Association, and quite popular with right-wing women. He spoke before such groups as Pro America, warning that "world planners see in mental health a wonderful new field for exploitation and indoctrination for the international slave state and world citizenship."[124] In Mental Robots, Alesen claimed that collectivists and "their education cohorts" had "all but completely destroyed the individual's understanding of and his will to defend his God-given rights as guaranteed under our Constitution." Now impatient, they looked to the field of mental health to "effect the *coup de grace*."[125] Hayne, who agreed with those who maintained that mental health was a serious problem, praised Alesen's work for having looked "analytically and critically beneath the surface" of health programs and disclosing "their subversive, sinister pattern." Instead of mental health programs, she believed more attention should be paid to educators' indifference to moral belief and religion and to the teaching of Americanism and individual responsibility. Such teaching, Hayne argued, would alleviate mental and social problems among children.[126]

To such rightists some of the ideas of "progressive education" may have fallen aside, but a new trend, that of giving students tests to determine intelligence and personality, was on the increase. Right-wing activist Jo Hindman, who like Ida Darden dated the mental health issue to the 1948 London Conference, expressed concern for the health of the next generation. In an article, "The Fight for Your Child's Mind," in the November 1957 issue of *American Mercury*, she wrote, "Mental undressing and inoculation of children's minds is being carried out in the schools, generally without the knowledge or consent of the parents."[127] The idea that students were filling out questionnaires that apparently had nothing to do with academic achievement led Hindman and others to cry foul, for schools were administering most of their tests without parental approval. Hindman and others, including Elizabeth Barnes of the DAR, referred to the testing related to children's mental health as "brainpicking tests." Barnes considered certain questions "abhorrent," particularly those asking children their views on sex and religion. Both Hindman and Barnes believed that questions such as these were invasions of privacy. For the same reason, they denounced questions that referred to a child's family's financial means, including those that asked about the size of a child's home and whether the family owned an electric refrigerator.[128]

What Barnes and Hindman were witnessing was an unprecedented growth in educational testing. Standardized testing first appeared in schools shortly after World War I and quickly caught on with educators as a way to solve a variety of problems in American schools. In December 1960, the *New York Times* reported that almost 130,000,000 tests were administered that year, enough for nearly every child in the first grade through college. Some schools with nursery programs were giving psychological tests to three-year-olds. While some Americans hailed the tests as important tools for the education of the country's youth, others saw them as potentially dangerous.[129]

In Northern California, right-wing activist Anne Smart spoke in 1958 of dangers present in Marin County, where plans existed to establish a local mental health clinic with services tied to public school programs. Like Hindman and Barnes, Smart focused on invasion of privacy, warning that there were teachers' guides being promoted throughout the United States that offered suggestions as to how to obtain family information from students. Teachers could keep charts showing a child's popularity, and they could keep logs in which they would evaluate the data they had gathered. As with others on the right, including the Minute Women, Smart suggested that the new programs were communist-inspired, with the aim of manipulating young minds so as to eliminate independent thinking.[130]

In 1961, Frances Bartlett wrote in *FACTS in Education* that "school children are the captive audience of their mentors" and accused school administrators of "bootlegging test materials into the schools for the illegal 'search and seizure' of the minds of our youth." School boards were derelict in their duty to monitor educational materials, and administrators were deliberately keeping secret the tests that were being given to the students. All over the country, she wrote, "Pseudo Psychos—the quacks of the profession—with the cooperation of the schools, continue to exploit youth for dubious purposes." She maintained that instructions to the students to carefully follow directions and to answer all of the questions, conditioned children to avoid questioning the propriety of a particular test.[131] It would likely follow that a student would be conditioned to conform to the ideas of the majority, one of the right's main arguments against progressive education.

Most rightist critics of mental health programs in education provided little evidence to support their charges, offering only a few examples of test questions. Bartlett was more specific, naming the California Test of Personality (1953 Revision—Form AA) and the Minnesota Multiphasic Personality Inventory (MMPI). She found them too intrusive and psychologically disturbing for adolescents. Bartlett objected to such questions on the California test as "Have you often wished you had different parents than you have?" or "Do you often have to fight or quarrel in order to get your rights?" She believed that some questions on the MMPI could induce abnormal concern, if not a state of hypochondria itself. She maintained that other questions ran "the entire range of mental symptoms characteristic of schizophrenia, paranoia, anxiety neurosis, et al." Certain true/false questions involved "delusions," such as "Evil spirits possess me at times." The tests also addressed sexual matters and home relationships. Bartlett questioned the accuracy of the test, believing that youth would answer the questions in accordance with how they believed their peers would answer them. "What teenager wants to be different from other teenagers?" she asked.[132]

The MMPI, which first appeared in 1940, was a psychiatric tool, used to detect such psychological problems as hypochondriasis, schizophrenia, and paranoia. It was designed to be a clinical instrument, not another test to be used in the public schools. Indeed, educators now warn that "perhaps more than any other self-report personality test, the MMPI should not be used by school personnel." This warning comes as a result of ethical issues, particularly the matter of invasion of privacy.[133]

Those who found tests intrusive had legitimate concerns, as many social scientists were indeed using tests like the MMPI to determine socioeconomic status. During the 1960s both the political right and the political left mounted attacks against the overuse of the MMPI. At the top of most opponents' concerns was the charge that the MMPI and other personality tests invaded students' privacy. Worrisome, too, was the matter of credentialing the teachers who were administering and analyzing the tests; and there was the danger that many children might mistakenly be branded "abnormal." Once such a designation reached the child's records, it was likely to follow the student throughout his or her academic career.[134] Schools now have the right to ask students about their families, emotions, and social lives only if the information will result in the betterment of their education.[135] Ironically, one study found that students taking the MMPI objected more to the length of the exam and the repetitiveness of the questions than they did to their alleged sensitivity. Despite the controversy surrounding the exam, the test did not undergo a major revision until 1990. The MMPI-2 is lengthier, but is less repetitive, and no longer contains items with "objectionable" content.[136]

Many American parents, on both the right and the left, complained that they were not allowed to view their children's student records; some went so far as to sue school districts—and at least some won. Some parents and educators advocated the idea of a reciprocal arrangement between parents and teachers, thinking that sharing their knowledge would aid them in guiding the child in a positive direction. Nevertheless, many schools continued to closely guard access to student records, knowing that teachers would refrain from adding comments to students' files that might offend the parents, or that the parents might misinterpret.[137] Yet unlike Frances Bartlett and others on the far right, most parents did not interpret their lack of access to those records as a sign of conspiracy.

Not all of the right's fears were products of their imagination. Historian Michelle Nickerson found in her research into rightist reactions to the Alaska Mental Health legislation that the right's concerns over the misuse of the act were not "paranoiac fantasy."[138] Rightist women examined here looked and saw how governments sometimes took actions to manipulate majority opinion and to persecute minorities who opposed them. One had only to look at the history of persecutions under the Third Reich or the purges in the Soviet Union under leader Josef Stalin to see atrocities committed with what seemed to be majority consent, or at the very least public apathy. Or they could look to the early decades of the twentieth century when the IQ test was being used in the United States for conservative purposes, including the tightening of immigration laws to favor English-speaking Northern Europeans. In the area of mental health, particularly when psychologists and social scientists were applying labels like "alienated," "lunatic fringe," and "paranoid" for their ideas and behaviors, these women had some legitimate reasons for their concerns.

The same is true in regard to many of the other questions that the right raised regarding mental health issues. In the early 1960s, members of the psychiatric profession were themselves beginning to raise questions about the legitimacy of diagnoses and treatments. Based upon his observations as a worker within a mental institution, prominent sociologist Erving Goffman criticized mental hospitals in *Asylums: Essays on the Social Situation of Mental Patients and Other Inmates* (1961). Also receiving attention was Ken Kesey's critical satire of asylums, *One Flew Over the Cuckoo's Nest* (1962), which was based on his experience with LSD trials and employment in a veterans' hospital.[139] Although criticism of mental health programs, tests, and procedures came from both the right and the left, their solutions to the problems differed. Rightists tended to advocate for a return to the old ways of dealing with mental illness, while those whose cultural views were farther to the left were more open-minded. The latter recognized that there were problems with methods and diagnoses within the world of psychiatry, but believed in fixing the problems and moving forward. They might consider that some of the tests were not administered fairly, or that some elites in mental health institutions were abusing their power to the detriment of their patients, and urge changes. Unlike the right, they were willing to search for remedies to the problems that might include more government regulation, for they did not consider government to be the enemy.

The Polio Vaccine

The polio vaccine, created to combat the dreaded disease poliomyelitis, was a major breakthrough in disease control. Yet, like fluoride, it was a substance that drew suspicion from the right and, at times, from a considerable number of other Americans. The idea of the government becoming involved in yet another health issue, particularly one that would compel Americans to have another drug forced into their bodies, led some to challenge claims by Jonas Salk, Albert Sabin, and other scientists as to the vaccine's effectiveness in polio prevention. Although there is little evidence of massive right-wing resistance on this particular issue, some rightist women did protest against what they regarded as yet another intrusion by government and scientific elites into their personal lives. Indeed, some raised the possibility that the vaccines were endangering the lives of children.

Criticism of vaccination has existed almost as long as vaccination itself, but organized opposition did not arrive in the United States until smallpox epidemics toward the end of the nineteenth century and the spread of diphtheria in the early twentieth century led to mandatory vaccination laws in cities and states around the country.[140] Court battles ensued. In 1905, in the case of *Jacobson v. Massachusetts*, the Supreme Court affirmed the right of local and state governments to use compulsory measures to enforce vaccination. Protests did not end there, however. Researchers studying the politics of vaccination in the early twentieth century have found that protests centered on the following: the increasing reach of the state into private affairs that emerged with the reforms of the Progressive Era; concerns over the growing spread of biologic products being used for the treatment and prevention of illness; and suspicions that some health officials, vaccine manufacturers, and physicians were conspiring to make huge profits from the vaccines.[141] Distrust of scientific elites and anger over government intrusion into one's private life did not end, but became major themes in right-wing protests of the 1950s and beyond. As with other issues, arguments of the far right about conspiracies, particularly those that involved communists or Jews, are what clearly separated their claims from those of other rightists.

Men led most of the Progressive Era antivaccination campaigns, but there were exceptions. For instance, in 1901, Mary Baker Eddy, founder of the Church of Christian Science, told her followers to allow their children to be vaccinated, but "see that your mind is in such a state that by your prayers vaccination will do the children no harm."[142] Believing that people should be free to make their own decisions regarding their medical care, Lora C. W. Little was a prominent leader of antivaccination campaigns in Portland, Oregon, from 1911 to 1918. She later organized the Chicago-based American Medical Liberty League.[143]

Poliomyelitis, popularly shortened to "polio," was most of all a disease of the twentieth century. There were minor outbreaks of the disease in the late nineteenth century, but not in sufficient numbers to attract special attention from either the general public or from the medical profession. But in the early twentieth century the numbers of cases began rising. Outbreaks in New York City, with 2,000 cases reported, as well as in Massachusetts, Minnesota, Ohio, Vermont, Nebraska, and Wisconsin between 1907 and 1914, caught the public's attention.[144] Then, suddenly, in 1916, a massive epidemic of poliomyelitis broke out in the United States, with 27,000 cases leaving over 6,000 dead. As in the case of President Franklin Roosevelt who contracted polio in 1921, many survivors were paralyzed for the remainder of their lives. Making the disease more terrifying was its tendency to attack children, especially those under the age of five. This circumstance led to the disease often being titled "infantile paralysis."[145] But, with these cases mostly confined to the states of New York, New Jersey, Connecticut, and Pennsylvania, this outbreak of polio did not lead to an immediate great movement to research and cure the disease. Only when the severity of outbreaks increased during the 1930s and 1940s did people intensify their demand for a search for a cure.[146]

Scientists responded to the demand and used their experimental vaccines on monkeys and on children. Tragically, during the 1930s, some vaccine trials on children resulted in several deaths and left several others paralyzed.[147] Research continued through the 1940s and into the 1950s. A typing program, lasting from 1949 to 1951, revealed there were three distinct types of polio viruses. Therefore, the vaccine needed to protect people against all three.[148] Meanwhile, cases of poliomyelitis continued to rise from an average of 6,400 cases a year during the period 1938–1942 to an average of 34,000 in the years 1947–1951. The worst of those years was 1949, with 42,000 cases, but the peak of the polio epidemic came in 1952 with 57,000 cases recorded in the United States.[149] That this was happening at the height of the baby boom in America created a greater sense of urgency to find a cure than ever before. Researchers were finding, too, that increasing numbers of adults were contracting the disease. It was, therefore, welcome news in late 1951 and 1952 that field trials of immune gamma globulin (IGG) were being conducted on American children, with some encouraging results. Only one case of polio occurred in the group receiving the IGG, while several cases occurred in the group receiving a placebo. Immune gamma globulin was a refined human serum, containing billions of polio antibodies. Its purpose was to protect those who had contacts with polio patients.[150] Meanwhile, Jonas Salk quietly conducted his research on a killed virus polio vaccine while others experimented with a live virus. Once news of the success of Salk's field tests reached the public, demand for his vaccine began.[151]

In the late spring of 1954, within a period of two months, 441,131 children received the Salk vaccine. During the same period, 201,229 children received a placebo, and 1,063,951 were the control group, receiving nothing. The young participants were called "pioneers," although they were in fact trial subjects. But their parents volunteered them because their fear of polio was so great that they overlooked the potential risk from the vaccine. The trial proved to be successful, and in 1955 people anxiously awaited release of the vaccine. But, as the vaccine was being administered during 1955, problems emerged. Some children who had been immunized were coming down with polio within a week or ten days following the first of their three shots. In every one of these cases the vaccine had been prepared by one pharmaceutical company, the Cutter Company. Within hours of news of the problem, the United States Surgeon-General ordered the vaccine withdrawn from the market. The faulty vaccine affected as many as 460 children, including 150 cases that involved paralysis and eleven resulting in death.[152] This was a small number considering five million people had received the vaccine, but many parents were alarmed.[153]

While most communities continued to administer the Salk vaccine, by May 1955, reports of parents withdrawing children from polio vaccination programs were on the increase. These parents had good cause because later investigation revealed that testing on the early lots of the vaccine in 1955 was practically nonexistent.[154] One community with a significant decrease (20 percent) in parents signing consent forms was Pasadena, California, a town that appears to have had an above average number of right-wing activists. Nearly 20 percent of parents in Chicago withdrew their children from the program, although some requested reinstatement. One mother sued the city of New York for $500,000 after her son received an injection despite her written instructions opposing the vaccination. Despite such skepticism, most parents believed immunization against such a horrible disease was worth the risk.[155] A year later, following an outbreak of new cases of poliomyelitis in Chicago, adults and children jammed the city's free inoculation centers. News that twenty-five cases were reported within a twenty-four-hour period ending at midnight July 16, 1956, caused the rush for the Salk anti-polio vaccine. Only thirty-five cases had been reported in Chicago for the entire year of 1955.[156] Such reactions to news reports reveal how quickly people often panic and make snap decisions, particularly in matters pertaining to defending their families.

Many on the right were not convinced of the vaccine's effectiveness. In the summer of 1957, right-wing Christian fundamentalists Ann and Russell Ackley who were also active in the right's campaigns to shape American education and to halt fluoridation, joined the fray. They attempted to cast doubt in the minds of the readers of their newsletter, *Portions in Due Season*, that the Salk polio vaccine was truly responsible for the approximate 48 percent reduction in polio cases for that year. The Ackleys argued that incidences of polio in children under the age of fifteen had been on the decline since 1915 because children were "developing a natural immunity to polio," and for a time incidences of polio were becoming rare.

They attributed the tremendous rise in cases during the late 1940s and early 1950s to the excessive use of sugar and the drinking of soft drinks. Overlooking the fact that people were continuing to consume such beverages, they doubted whether the Salk vaccine really deserved any credit for the recent reduction in diagnoses of polio. The Ackleys concluded their editorial with verses from Deuteronomy, proclaiming that if people kept God's commandments, "the Lord will take away from thee all sickness."[157] The Ackleys' information on polio was incorrect. Scientific evidence shows that babies are born with a temporary "natural immunity" against polio. In years prior to the late nineteenth century, disease-causing organisms in the environment soon enhanced this immunity. This "natural immunity" decreased in the United States at the end of the nineteenth century and the beginning of the twentieth century due to the greater attention paid to sanitation and hygiene. Children, therefore, were unable to fight the virus when they were exposed to the disease at a later age.[158]

Others on the right agreed that one's diet was a factor in contracting polio. One Santa Fe mother suggested in *New Mexico Women Speak!* that symptoms of polio resembled those of a vitamin C deficiency and advised mothers to make sure their children be fed an adequate diet, rich in vitamins and minerals. The newsletter's editors suggested that nutritional deprivation should be researched further, rather than submitting children to forced vaccinations. They hinted that much of the vaccine could be contaminated, citing alleged instances of the substances being "hoarded" or stealthily "slipped" from one state to another.[159] Writer Jeffrey Kluger notes in his biography of Salk that the scientist received a large number of letters from the right, including one from Duon Miller of Coral Gables, Florida. Miller, who was wealthy, a racist, and a marketer of nonprescription pills, also promoted the idea that polio's cause was malnutrition. He referred to Salk's vaccine as "monkey juice," and questioned whether the vaccines came from whites, blacks, or "a Jap."[160]

In the vaccine controversy, the Minute Women found yet another issue that combined the futures of the baby boom generation with the future of the nation. They raised concerns similar to problems they had with fluoridation, particularly the issue of freedom of choice. When the Virginia General Assembly considered a bill requiring all Virginia public school children to undergo vaccinations, the organization protested that such laws violated the Constitution by infringing on people's right to do what they wanted with their and their children's bodies. As in the case of fluoridation, the Minute Women, along with others on the right, found a medical expert to back their point of view. In their February 1960 newsletter they quoted Fred S. Klenner, M.D., who said, "No one has the authority to compel a person to submit to surgical procedure, or force him to take any given type of medication. This applies to indirect persuasion such as is being used in getting parents to give their children 'polio shots.'"[161]

Citing Gordon B. Leitch, a medical doctor and editor of *Northwest Medicine*, the rightist group New Mexico Women Speak! argued that the Salk vaccine was a program designed to prepare the American people for socialized medicine. An article in the organization's newsletter quoted Leitch's comparison of the Salk vaccinations with the medical experiments performed at a Nazi concentration camp. "At Buchenwald it was physical force," Leitch declared. "In America it was mental pressure—brainwashing—playing on the fear of one of the most spectacular and dread diseases, one which creates terror out of all proportion to its incidence and to its actual seriousness."[162] Leitch claimed that the U.S. Public Health Service, an organization that many rightists believed to be ridden with conspirators and communist sympathizers, required the assistance of practicing physicians in the testing of the vaccine. That government agency, he maintained, "strongly hinted" that doctors who refused to cooperate would find that they would be shunned. Linking the vaccination program with that of fluoridation, *New Mexico Women Speak!*'s editors proclaimed, "DENTISTS HAVE BEEN TREATED IN SIMILAR FASHION WHEN THEY OBJECT TO FLUORIDATION." They argued that the fluoridation, the mental health, and the Salk vaccine issues were not purely medical issues, but also political, declaring, "A precinct committeeman may soon be the socialized doctor who orders the pills en masse for the family! The pattern is forming rapidly."[163]

Rightist Phoebe Courtney was another who detected common threads connecting government-sponsored medical programs. In 1955, her newspaper *Free Men Speak* (later the *Independent American*) carried an article on fluoride and related "plots," such as conspiracies involving the Salk vaccine. At one point focusing on the polio vaccine's effects upon America's children, the author noted that parents had been warned to keep their children away from the vaccine, yet few heeded the warnings. The problem, she wrote, was that parents did not realize "that the school children of today represent our Army and Navy ten years from now"; yet millions of children were being inoculated with a substance that could cause cancer in a few years. As a consequence, in another ten years "communists could walk in and take over our nation."[164] Similar to far right-wing predictions regarding conspiracy plots associated with fluoridation and mental health programs, this author was picturing a weakened America, ripe for communist takeover.

Some right-wing women accused Jews of involvement in the "conspiracy." One was Lyrl Clark Van Hyning of Chicago, who since the beginning of World War II was preaching anti-Semitism in her newspaper, *Women's Voice*. An article in her June 1955 issue had the headline, "Jews Mass Poison American Children." Belittling Jonas Salk as the "Yiddish inventor of a so-called polio vaccine," author Eustace Mullins charged that Salk was "directing the inoculation of millions of American children" with a "sinister concoction of live polio germs." Its effectiveness in preventing polio, Mullins maintained, "is a myth of Jewish propaganda."[165] Thus, for some on the right the polio vaccination program was a part of the old Jewish-communist-government conspiracy that they had been warning of since the 1930s.

Although most of their theories regarding polio lacked scientific evidence, the right did have reasonable cause to question the massive dosing of America's children. Most parents were unaware that the vaccine lacked adequate preliminary testing. Throughout the mid-1950s, when millions of baby boomers were lining up for vaccinations, Dr. Albert Sabin, who was researching a live-virus vaccine, publicly criticized Salk's vaccine as being unsafe; but many considered Sabin's argument to be a case of "sour grapes." After all, he was testing a competing vaccine.[166] During the early 1960s, questions associated with the Salk vaccine continued as reports emerged of children becoming paralyzed or dying, but these numbers were few when compared to the tens of thousands who were contracting the disease only a decade earlier.[167]

With the Salk vaccine being administered in the United States, during the years 1957–1959 Albert Sabin took his vaccine to the Soviet Union, Poland, Czechoslovakia, Singapore, and Mexico, where a combined total of 4.5 million people swallowed his oral vaccine, allegedly with no ill effects. By July 1960, Sabin was reporting that fifteen million people had received his vaccine. While some Americans were suspicious of the positive news due to its link to the Soviet Union, Sabin's oral vaccine was soon accepted as safe for use in the United States.[168] Years later, Soviet scientists admitted that claims of a perfect safety record with Sabin's oral vaccine were false. They recalled that Sabin talked them out of revealing this information at the time.[169]

In 1961, the year before the Sabin polio vaccine began to be administered in the United States, the number of new polio cases dropped below one thousand for the first time in decades. By 1980, natural cases of polio were no longer developing in the United States. The eight to ten cases that arose during following years were due to the vaccine. Evidence pointed to Sabin's vaccine as the cause and, in 1996, after pressure from antivaccination groups and from Congress, the Centers for Disease Control began phasing it out. On January 1, 2000, the CDC abandoned its use altogether. The Salk vaccine is the only one currently being administered in the United States;[170] however, debate continues as to whether Salk or Sabin should receive the greatest credit for the virtual elimination of polio in the developed world.

During the period 1955 to the early 1960s, when tens of millions of Americans received the polio vaccines, those opposing the vaccinations were mostly a small minority. However, when problems arose, such as that which occurred in the case of the Cutter Company's batches of the vaccine, wider sections of the public became anxious as the right's warnings appeared to be justified. Nevertheless, once problems were solved, the public, en masse, again welcomed the vaccine, and the right's warnings were virtually unheeded. It was not because the right did not want a cure for polio that they raised alarm over the vaccine, it was due to their lack of trust in the safety of the vaccine and their fear of a government and scientific conspiracy to gain control of their lives and the lives of their children.

Despite the positive outcome from the polio vaccine, some scientists are raising the issue of a potential dark side to the vaccine. Some recent studies note that, during the 1960s, researchers found that a cancer-causing monkey, or simian, virus contaminated much of the polio vaccines administered between 1954 and 1962. In 1963, after finding no evidence that the virus, known as SV40, was causing cancer in humans, the federal government decided to keep the information quiet. But some scientists are linking the more than 30 percent increase in brain and central nervous system disorders occurring from the mid-1970s to the mid-1990s to the virus. Bone tumors and non-Hodgkin's lymphoma are also on the rise, and some scientists believe that fact, too, may be the result of contaminated vaccines.[171]

The government admits that "contaminated vaccine lots were inadvertently used for the first few years" of the polio vaccination program. However, National Institutes of Health investigations into the issue note no apparent links between the SV40 virus and human cancer. The study continues.[172] Evidence is sketchy, but if these allegations are true, the vast majority of baby boomers may be at risk. Nearly 100 million Americans received the Salk and Sabin vaccines before producers had to certify their products free of SV40 in 1963. A cancer link would certainly justify right-wing women's questioning of just what substances the government was encouraging Americans to ingest.

Conclusion

These three public health issues that were, in varying degrees, of concern to right-wing women—fluoridation, mental health, and polio vaccinations—affected baby boomers for years to come. The issue of experimentation, using youngsters as "guinea pigs," did not go away. By the early 1970s, news of schoolchildren receiving prescribed "behavioral modification" drugs, such as Ritalin, began to frighten some parents, including rightist women.[173] During the 1970s and beyond, baby boomers, now with children of their own, frequently made the difficult decisions as to whether their children would benefit from such drugs. Thus, amid their alarmist protests against the way authorities in government were administering health programs, right-wing women among the older generation raised some important questions. How safe were the chemicals that Americans were sometimes forced to ingest? How much power should government have in making decisions affecting the health of individuals? How was mental health being defined? Who was doing the defining?

At times, Americans, particularly parents concerned about their children's safety, did take a second look at the experimental nature of some of the health programs being directed at their children. Most, however, sooner or later accepted their local, state, or the federal government's assurances that the programs were well supervised. More Americans might have listened more closely to the right's questions if so many of them were not also making some outrageous claims about conspiracies. As it was, with the exception of the matter of fluoridation, few outside of their circles paid much attention to their, at times, legitimate questions.

As such right-wing groups as the Texas Women for Constitutional Government pointed out in regard to the Alaska bill, due process protections for mental health patients were weak during the 1950s. That situation has improved significantly since that time, making it much less likely that a person can be involuntarily committed to an institution without a thorough psychiatric evaluation. Mental health patients also have the right to defense counsel in all judicial hearings.[174]

The right's fears of being a target group were reasonable. Americans represent diverse cultural backgrounds. At first glance, one might assume that this diversity would make it difficult for subgroups to form a majority and dominate a single minority group. But such universal domination does occur in the United States, as with the cases of white domination over African Americans for centuries and the internment of Japanese Americans after Pearl Harbor. Such cases reveal that government can take actions, with a large degree of public approval, which later prove to be both extreme and unnecessary. Minority domination of the majority is also possible. Modern social theory reveals the deeper structure of social interaction, approaching this from different perspectives. In the early twentieth century, Antonio Gramsci, Vilfredo Pareto, and Sigmund Freud, among others, revealed how people of one specific political, social class, religious, or other orientation can gain control of society. These right-wing women feared that a group of liberal reformers, intellectuals, and government bureaucrats were aiming to take control at all costs. At times they saw those groups as joining together and forming a conspiracy. Even if they were not conspirators, the appearance that they were all aiming at the same goals was sufficient evidence for rightists to take action.

The right's protests raise the fundamental issue as to how government bureaucracies and scientific communities relate to other parts of American society. Problems with communication between these groups sometimes created difficulties in reaching a consensus. In the case of some on the right, the lack of rapport, combined with the fear of being manipulated might have contributed to their suspicion. It is, however, difficult to imagine that better communication could have changed many minds, given the rigidity of their thinking.

During the 1950s there was cause for questioning the actions of scientists and government officials, as both communities did hide tests and potential dangers from the public. During 1950–1951, for example, one scientist tested his polio vaccine on mentally ill children in a New York state institution. He referred to these recipients as "volunteers," but later examination of his research papers cast doubt upon his claim.[175] Also, the federal government hid dangers from the public, including threats to the public's safety caused by the Atomic Energy Commission's dumping of radioactively contaminated waste, contained in cardboard boxes, in an Idaho landfill during the years 1952–1959.[176] Such secrecy reveals that it is important that citizens attempt to keep authorities honest by raising issues of concern.

However, when citizens make repeated irrational charges in attempts to block a variety of programs, they create more problems rather than help resolve them. For instance, the right's attempts to block public health programs led to delays in some important programs, most notably in mental health. Some rightists remained rigid in their opposition to new health programs even after many years of successful trials. They would not accept the word of scientists and government employees as long as a few rightward-leaning authorities questioned the programs. While conservatives might gradually accept the changes, the farther to the right the women were on the issues, the less likely they were to accept such policies as public water fluoridation and polio vaccination. Distinguishing women of the far right from those who were more moderate was the fact that the far right saw the new programs as part of a larger conspiracy.

As in the issue of education, right-wing women who concerned themselves with public health matters communicated with rightist men, read their literature, and worked with them in various campaigns. But the women believed that, as women, they had special contributions to make to rightist causes, especially when they identified issues that they believed directly impacted their roles as mothers of the upcoming generation. Perceived threats against their children's health, safety, the nuclear family, morality, or the utopian America that they had long envisioned, drew them together as a unified force. At times, they led the activism on public health issues in a number of American communities. In doing so, they recognized that it was not only right-wing men who were having run-ins with government. The Lucille Miller and Kathryn Deats cases were but two examples. Through use of their organizations and their networking, they quickly spread the alarm and offered each other support when they encountered such threats.

Unlike the right, liberals did not look upon government as a threat, but as an aid in improving conditions in society and allowing Americans, no matter their social status, to have greater opportunities. The right saw the government as an intrusion. They believed that American freedom was innate, a basic God-given right, confirmed under the Constitution. Rightists felt threatened by the new roles of government, and believed it their duty to defend their country against such changes. Social change was becoming increasingly rapid during the 1950s and 1960s, causing more unease on the right and, as will be seen in the next chapter, at times leading rightist women and men to take to the streets to fight against it.

⚙ 3

RIGHT-WING WOMEN AND DESEGREGATION OF THE PUBLIC SCHOOLS

How would Mr. Eisenhower like to have his son's children mixing in school (little children would know no better), intermarry, and have negro [sic] children for his grandchildren?

Mrs. J. M. Burke Sr., December 7, 1958

As an institution bridging the public and private spheres, public schools have frequently been a flashpoint for regulating rights, privileges, and status in the United States, particularly around the categories of race and gender. Despite the developing concept in the latter part of the nineteenth century that public education should be accessible to every child, irrespective of race, gender, or economic status, it would take a long time to come to fruition. This is particularly true in regard to African Americans.[1] After the Civil War, during Reconstruction, coalitions of black and white Republicans in southern state legislatures passed laws that established public education. Nevertheless, most of the schools of the South were racially segregated.

In 1896, the Supreme Court, in the case of *Plessy v. Ferguson*, upheld challenges to racial segregation, including segregation in public schools, as long as the facilities were of equal quality. Few black students in the southern states received an education equal to that of whites. Schools for African Americans usually emphasized vocational rather than intellectual training, and the facilities were likely to be dilapidated buildings, with little heat during winter. In the North, de facto segregation due to African Americans usually living in neighborhoods separate from whites, often resulted in blacks receiving an inferior education. For decades, black students suffered as a result of these inequities.[2] While during the 1940s, the federal government had, via Executive Order, the Supreme Court, and other means, made some inroads into the granting of civil rights to blacks, it was not until the 1950s that the schools became the center of the movement toward full rights for African Americans.

On May 17, 1954, in a unanimous decision in *Brown v. Board of Education of Topeka*, the Supreme Court ruled that it was unconstitutional to separate educational facilities based upon race. Many Americans were appalled by the ruling. In the South, *Brown* threatened the whole of the region's distinctive culture. This was not so in the North, but many feared potential social, political, and economic consequences of the court's decision. Overall, the right wing, which was found throughout America, was intensely upset over the ruling.

Although not always for the same reasons, most rightist women, whether they resided in the South or in the North, joined racists in denouncing *Brown* and sought to do all they could to obstruct the implementation of the Supreme Court order. Three themes dominated rightist opposition to desegregation: their racism, their claims of "communist conspiracy" (particularly among the far right), and their objection to federal intervention into local affairs. As they saw the situation, the government, this time in the form of the federal Supreme Court, was again interfering in affairs that should remain in the hands of individuals and the states in which they lived. Most rightists believed that if they did not want to mix socially with those of other races, they should not be forced to do so. But despite their efforts and the efforts of tens of thousands of southern segregationists, there was no holding back the movement for black civil rights. Following the passage of Title IV of the Civil Rights Act of 1964, which gave the government the authority to enforce desegregation of public schools, the situation looked even bleaker for anti-integrationists. As a result of Title IV, the busing of schoolchildren soon became mandatory. This new development drew a heated response from the right, as it did from many other Americans. The issue of forced busing proved to be one over which many Americans all along the political spectrum shared concern.

Responses among right-wing women to the ruling on *Brown*, and to the civil rights movement that followed, took a variety of forms, ranging from letter writing and pamphleteering to rallies and school boycotts. While many of the women had already been involved in other right-wing crusades, some new names and faces emerged to join the battle. At the same time, many rightists and southern segregationists shared similar beliefs about the separation of races. Thus, the conflict over the desegregation of public schools offered women of the right the opportunity to enlist thousands of like-minded southern white women to this and other rightist causes. As they had with such matters as educational techniques and mental health, these women feared for future generations. Many rightist and southern segregationist women saw the court's decision as meaning much more than whites and blacks sharing the same classrooms. For them it was a tremendous blow against southern culture—and especially a giant step toward racial mixing and literally changing the complexions of future generations of Americans. In the minds of many, it was a violation of God's plan for the world. The far right believed that the *Brown* decision just had to be another part of a great conspiracy.

To clearly explain rightist women's actions in respect to school desegregation and their attempts to shape the ideology of the baby boom generation, this chapter is structured to begin with a look into southern culture, followed by an examination of rightist women's racial views and attitudes toward the civil rights movement overall. Next is a look at the attitudes and actions of rightist women as they sought to prevent the mixing of races in the nation's schools. The chapter also explores the changing attitudes of American youth regarding school integration, revealing that rightists were facing obstacles in their attempts to have the younger generation see the world their way. Because busing of children for integration purposes became an important issue in the North as well as in the South during the late 1960s and early 1970s, a separate "Busing" section comes in the latter part of the chapter.

Historian Joseph Crespino, in his study of links between Mississippians of the civil rights era and the rise of conservatism, notes how many of those fighting to preserve segregation shared commonalities with the right. Mississippi segregationists' outlooks and those of the right inter-twined on a variety of issues, including race, religion, education, and fears of communism. Crespino points out, too, that the relationship between conservative Mississippians and the conservatives of the national Repub-lican Party was complex. They did not share the same points of view on all levels, so it took time for leaders on both sides to make accommodations.[3] Evidence uncovered in this study supports Crespino's conclusions. It re-veals that conservative white women of the South and rightist women, living in both the North and the South, shared similar points of view on a number of issues. They had much in common, from their agreement regarding separation of the races to their fears of communist influences and their emphasis on patriotism. Historian Nancy MacLean notes that although the right wing had disagreements among themselves on other matters, "defense of white rule in the South" was a unifying force.[4] Just as thousands of southerners had called out for "states' rights" in support of slavery prior to the Civil War, the outcry for "states' rights" was now prevalent among southern segregationists who opposed integrated educa-tion. It was a demand similar to rightists' anger over government inter-vention into local affairs. As a result, it was easy for northerners on the right to become attached to the southern cause. The focus on "govern-ment" reframed the issue and, in many instances, allowed them to hide their racism behind ideological rhetoric.

The *Brown* decision challenged white southern culture's fundamental assumption that God intended that whites were superior to blacks just as males were superior to females. Most white southerners believed it neces-sary that a racially segregated social, economic, and political power struc-ture be maintained at all cost. In the fall of 1958, southern conservative writer Christine Benagh defended the South's racial order. She insisted that the South's agrarian economy, primarily fundamentalist religious turn of thought, devotion to states' rights, and emphasis upon maintain-ing a social equilibrium lay at the base of conflicts with reformers over such issues as desegregation. Benagh argued that those who dreamed "of a 'homogeny' of men and women" without such distinctions as "race, re-ligion, color, tradition, and the like," did not have a vision that was com-patible with Southern culture.[5] For Benagh, as it was for millions of white southerners, the civil rights movement aimed at disrupting a hierarchical culture that served the best interest of all levels of society. The South, they maintained, was a special place in the world, yet it was facing threats of being torn asunder.

Southern writer Lillian Smith opposed white supremacy, believing it was as totalitarian as communism or fascism. Yet she explained the reasons behind white southerners' fight to retain segregation, even as she condemned it. White southern children, she wrote in *Killers of the Dream* (1949), grew up with a loyalty to the region and defended their culture against all outside criticism. Her mother taught her tenderness and love, but also the rituals of keeping Africans in their "place." Southern mothers, Smith observed, instructed their children to "love God, to love our white skin, and to believe in the sanctity of both." In keeping with southern tradition, white mothers taught their children that disaster would befall the South if a child treated a black person as a social equal. Once children stepped outside of their homes, church and custom took charge of their education. Signs designating separation of the races were everywhere— "white" . . . "colored" . . . "white" . . . "colored."[6]

The actions of Mississippi journalist Florence Sillers Ogden provide an example of women seeking to emphasize the mother's role in maintaining the racial status quo. Ogden, a leading anti-integration activist during the civil rights movement, urged women to closely monitor their children's education, both at home and in school. Ogden stressed that it was the duty of southern mothers to teach their children the lessons of white supremacy. Historian Elizabeth Gillespie McRae maintains that this responsibility of preserving southern culture gave white women a sense of empowerment.[7] Such a function was in keeping with the tradition, in many societies around the world, of women taking on the responsibility of maintaining folk culture.

The threat of change to their culture and society was something that linked southern women who tended toward the right with nonsouthern rightist women. Both were clinging to an idealized past. For southerners such change was particularly upsetting if initiated by "outsiders." When so threatened, wrote Lillian Smith, suddenly the entire white South manifested a "collective fear and fury that wipe our minds clear of reason and we are blocked from sensible contact with the world we live in." Her explanation for such reaction was that "We Southerners had identified with the long sorrowful past on such deep levels of love and hate and guilt that we did not know how to break old bonds without pulling our lives down."[8]

Psychologist Deborah Atkinson, a baby boomer who grew up in a white, middle-class neighborhood in Fayetteville, North Carolina, largely agrees with Smith's perception of southern attitudes regarding blacks. She recalls that as a child during the 1950s and 1960s, there was a "tug and pull" in the South as to what black-white relationships were and remembers some interracial bonds. Her grandmother bonded closely with several black women, even taking food to them, yet her grandparents always mistrusted African Americans. Looking back she recalls, "We were so young. . . . For me growing up in the South, you grow up in a really conservative environment, and there is a lot of need to not look closely at your place in the universe. At the time, you incorporate those prejudices. . . . You were part of that oppression of keeping blacks and women down, yet it's a part of who you are."[9] As she matured and struggled to establish her own identity, Atkinson came to realize that women like her, as well as blacks, were under the domination of men who controlled the power structure—political, familial, and religious. Despite her conservative upbringing, Atkinson and millions of others of her generation grew to accept the change in racial dynamics that resulted from the civil rights movement.

The specter of communism within the black civil rights movement was another argument that segregationists, right-wing women included, used to support their point of view. During the late 1920s and early 1930s, the Communist Party, claiming to champion the oppressed and, in this case, black Americans, did attempt to exploit social unrest in the United States. In 1928, the Moscow-based Comintern surprised the Communist Party in America when it called for self-determination in regions of the South possessing a black majority. Few American Communists, white or black, welcomed the resolution, which only served to enrage southern whites. The unpopular idea was virtually dead by the 1950s.[10]

The Communist Party gained considerably more credibility within the black community as a result of what became known as the Scottsboro case. In 1931, two white girls who had hopped a freight train in Alabama, told police that nine black males, ages thirteen to twenty, had raped them. The NAACP and various liberal groups came to the defense of the accused, but Communists won control of the boys' legal defense.[11] Although the number of black members in the party remained low, anti-communist racists later pointed to the self-determination resolution and the Scottsboro case as evidence that Communists surreptitiously led the civil rights movement. The Communist Party did draw in a few prominent blacks, including the intellectual W.E.B. DuBois and athlete, actor, and singer Paul Robeson, which gave racists further evidence to support their arguments.[12]

The right seized on whatever evidence they could obtain that might link the black civil rights movement to communist conspiracies. From her early days of activism in the 1930s Elizabeth Dilling, a longtime campaigner to expose "reds" in government and elsewhere, maintained that African Americans were tools of the Communist Party. Other rightists and southern segregationists agreed.[13] During the 1950s, Marilyn R. Allen of Salt Lake City carried on campaigns similar to Dilling's, denouncing Jews, communists, and liberals.[14] In the June 1954 issue of her pamphlet series *I Love America*, she called the day of the *Brown* decision "a black day of infamy." She blamed the Supreme Court's ruling on Chief Justice Earl Warren, claiming he "used his influence and pressure to secure complete agreement." In fact, Allen was one of many rightists who contended that the Fourteenth Amendment to the Constitution, which granted full citizenship to blacks, had been "illegally railroaded" through Congress and the states.

Allen considered the *Brown* decision a victory for the Communist Party, predicting the ruling would "have wide adverse ramifications and repercussions against the prestige and rights of the White Race all over the world." She maintained that the ruling was a "typical Communist trick" to divide the nation, and an example of "the Soviet doctrine of 'catching the children young'—while their minds and opinions are malleable and unformed—and teaching them the forbidden doctrine of miscegenation."[15] What she was describing was a mirror image of what these rightist women were doing to their own children in inculcating racism into them.

Allen contended that blacks were indeed inferior and that *Brown* benefitted the nation's black children at the expense of the white majority. Similar to the issues of public health, wherein the right feared they would come under the control of minority groups, Allen suspected black/communist domination. "Does not this biased ruling prove that today we have Minority Rule in the United States? And does not Minority Rule of this type—the lower over the higher, and the few over the many—usually lead to dictatorship?" It was all part of a plot. Not only communists, but liberals, "minority-lovers," Jews, and the National Association for the

Advancement of Colored People (NAACP), which Allen referred to as the "Negro Gestapo," were involved in a conspiracy to destroy the white race.[16] While Allen's comments were extreme, her pamphlets were widely read among rightists.[17]

Other rightists sought further "evidence" for an African American–communist link. The *White Sentinel*, which carried the slogan "Racial Integrity—Not Amalgamation," and was edited by a rightist woman, Helen Wolf, charged that Eleanor Roosevelt was a part of the conspiracy. In June 1958, the *Sentinel* published an article titled "Eleanor Joins Communist Plot to Integrate South," announcing that the former first lady was scheduled to speak at a "communist training school." Roosevelt was speaking at the Highlander Folk School in Grundy County, Tennessee, a controversial school that promoted labor and civil rights activism. Calling Roosevelt "an officer of the Communist-dominated NAACP" and one "notorious for her race mixing," the article in the *White Sentinel* alleged that she was part of a "red" plan to fight segregation.[18] From early in her husband's presidency in the 1930s, the right was charging that Roosevelt was, at the very least, a communist sympathizer. Her association with Highlander would only add to such suspicions.

As part of their traditionalist and patriotic agenda, the Daughters of the American Revolution (DAR) extended their fight against communism to join with those opposed to integration of the races. Throughout the 1950s, it retained its desire for separation of the races. Although a national organization with chapters throughout both northern and southern states, its August 1958 statement on "Racial Integrity" manifested the traditional southern point of view, "that God created all the races . . . each separate, distinctive, and individual—and that the destruction of such distinctions constitutes the maximum degree of race hatred and prejudice." Therefore, the DAR resolved to "condemn the Communist objective of miscegenation, and declare racial integrity to be a fundamental Christian principle."[19] Just as it had in regard to education, the DAR accepted the "communist plot" theory then popular among the far right and many segregationists. That theory remained intact throughout the 1960s, with such prominent segregationists as Georgia governor Lester Maddox blaming the communists for school integration and busing.[20]

From New Orleans, outspoken segregationist Phoebe Courtney who was copublisher of the right-wing *Independent American*, claimed to have evidence of civil rights leader Martin Luther King's affiliation with the Communist Party.[21] In a 1963 editorial, she explained, "When Martin Luther King draws a parallel between the situation of the American Negro and 'oppressed peoples' rights against 'colonialism' and 'imperialism,' he is following exactly, to the word, the Communist line."[22] King's assassination in 1968 did not put an end to such attacks. Some saw his murder as part of the larger "conspiracy" to create a communistic United States. Sociologist Susan L. M. Huck, a ubiquitous voice for the right, wrote that "the fiction of 'non-violence' had served its purpose; Martin Luther King was phased out by assassination and a big funeral." King's murder, she hinted, was part of a larger desegregationist conspiracy, writing, "America was provided, by Government and mass media, with another secular politician-saint to worship en masse, often by public decree." As a result, "the whites of America were thumped into submission by phony accusations of collective guilt . . . [while] leadership of the radicalized young Negroes was solidified in the hands of open Marxist revolutionaries."[23]

Despite the DAR's anti-integrationist stance, on July 9, 1963, the organization's president, Marion Moneure Duncan, was one of approximately 300 women who, at the invitation of President Kennedy, assembled in the White House's East Room to discuss civil rights. The president requested the women's cooperation in supporting proposed legislation on civil rights and in opening women's organizations to all races. Following the meeting Duncan wrote Kennedy, stating that DAR members would continue to act "on an individual basis as good American citizens, in their respective communities." The DAR, she maintained, had "no policy on integration or segregation, as such," but for many years had "through pursuit of its educational activities—especially with youth—encouraged, recognized, and assisted students of various nationalities, race having had no bearing."[24] When a reporter raised the issue of integrating the DAR, a spokeswoman explained that "it would be rather difficult for a Negro to trace her ancestry back to the Revolutionary War because no records were kept on Negroes at that time."[25]

In addition to right-wing women in leadership positions, thousands of segregationist women of the grassroots South found the alleged African American–Communist connection to be one of many arguments for keeping blacks separate from whites. One was Mrs. P. D. Williams of Tyler, Texas, who ignored the reality of the inferior school facilities available to blacks and insisted that the "old stinking, nasty, negro race" had good colleges and schools. She charged that blacks did not really want to attend school with whites, but wanted to "stick their selves on the whites." Integrationist blacks and whites, she argued, were misusing the Constitution and using "dirty tricks, such as the communists all use." She attempted to portray herself as open-minded, writing, "I treat them nice . . . and these older ones, are as good as gold, when you do find a good one." Nevertheless, she did not want her children or grandchildren to have blacks "forced on them, in school."[26] Like Marilyn Allen, she believed that African Americans were inferior and that the Supreme Court was not abiding by the intent of the composers of the Constitution. Williams was also expressing another frequent complaint of the right, that of government forcing programs on the American people, taking away the rights of individuals.

The arguments of Mrs. Albert Davis of Port Neches, Texas, provide yet another example of grassroots agreement with the outlooks of right-wing organizations and their leaders. Davis opposed integration on the basis of states' rights, but also suggested that a larger conspiracy was involved. "When any one state has its duly constituted law struck down by pressure from an outside element, not only has *that* state been weakened, but *all* the sister states also." She claimed that the South protected the United States Constitution, exclaiming, "It is up to Us to *save* the nation!" Like Allen, Davis interpreted school desegregation as evidence that the white race was losing its dominance, contending that "Reds and Negroes [were] placed above and at the expense of average citizens."[27] Both Williams and Davis went beyond the traditional southern segregationist arguments of states' rights and black inferiority. They saw the situation from the far rightist point of view that the white majority and the nation as a whole were under attack.

Their attitudes contrast with more moderate thoughts regarding race, such as those of another Texas woman, Ella Ellisar. Writing Senator Lyndon B. Johnson in 1954, Ellisar declared that he was doing wonderful work in Washington, but added, "We trust you are not in favor of mixing the negroes and white people in the schools. We think most of the negroes had rather maintain separate schools."[28] While Ellisar upheld the traditional southern attitude about separation of the races, her statements do not reveal her to be on the political right. Williams and Davis, however, were pessimistic in their outlook, picturing an upheaval in the nation's racial structure that would destroy the country. Such fears of racial chaos offered southern right-wing activists an opportunity to attract new followers. Rightist women of the South, such as journalists Phoebe Courtney and Florence Sillers Ogden, promoted a cause that appealed to hundreds of thousands of prosegregationist southern women. Just how much of the broader rightist agenda the average southern woman would adopt was open to question.

Intermarriage between black and white was of primary concern for many anti-integrationists. Many women drew upon that possibility when presenting their cases against school desegregation. They were fearful of racial mixing among future generations of Americans. In the epigraph at the beginning of this chapter, Mrs. Burke asked how President Eisenhower would like to have his son's children producing black offspring. Scores, if not hundreds, of women wrote Lyndon Johnson with similar questions during his Senate and presidential years. Investigation into White House files on civil rights reveals that this was not an issue that inspired men to write the president. The vast majority of such letters came from women who were concerned about children and grandchildren.[29] Often more moderate Americans feared the social difficulties resulting from intermarriage. As a result, the matter gave rightist women, with their antimiscegenation message, opportunities to have greater influence than their numbers would normally allow.

Historian Jane Dailey, in her study of southern resistance to the *Brown* decision, notes a strong connection between sex, segregation, and religion. Dailey maintains that "the language of miscegenation," when linked with a theology that emphasized the Divine Order, became a powerful argument against desegregation of the public schools.[30] Indeed, evidence examined for this book reveals that religion was an aspect of many women's arguments against integration. For example, Mrs. L. H. Chaney wrote, "If this trend [toward integration of the races] is allowed to continue, I feel sure when we greet our heavenly Father, He will wonder what became of the different races He put on this earth to begin with."[31] Many right-wing Christian fundamentalists concurred. Rightist women in particular used religion to argue against the integration of public schools, just as it was mostly women voicing concern over sexual relations between men and women of different races.[32] Patriotism too often became part of rightists' arguments. Mrs. Burke, who was eighty-four years old and from Tyler,

Texas, emphasized her patriotic roots as a daughter of a man who had fought for the Confederacy when she wrote Johnson with her arguments against school integration. Religion, too, was part of her reasoning when she declared that just as God gave the races a country of their own, southern culture should not be interfered with.[33]

Known as a relatively small player in right-wing circles, Katie Lou Brown wrote a rambling treatise in opposition to the *Brown* decision. In it she offered an example of rightist women who considered integration upsetting to the Divine Order. "There is nothing," she declared, "in the Bible, nor in the Constitution, that justifies the Supreme Court integration decision of 1954," she wrote, punctuating her arguments against integration with biblical verses. The court's ruling, she declared, was destined to "set race against race and religion against religion."[34] Brown was espousing outlooks that were not only in line with those of the Christian right but also were basic to the old southern order: because of human imperfection, God set up relationships among man and beast, and it was not up to humankind to upset the Divine Order.[35] Numerous women professed that point of view.[36] Margaret Black, for instance, argued that God created "five races of people" for a purpose, and one must not question His purpose. She also made a connection between segregation and sex when she added her belief that "the negro is not educated enough in sex to be put in school with whites." White youth, she thought, might be able to resist the temptation of becoming sexually involved with blacks, but blacks could physically overpower them.[37]

Religion, sex, and patriotism were important themes among women opposed to integration. Although in their letters to Lyndon Johnson some women revealed themselves to be politically moderate, they also displayed aspects of the rightist point of view on this major issue in American culture. Each had her own values, and she expected others to live within the framework of those values. Amidst the world of change around them none of these women were willing to step outside of their zones of comfort to look at human relations from a different point of view.

In addition to moral values, many right-wing women also addressed economic issues that they saw as pertaining to school desegregation. Mrs. Burke was among many who complained that Americans were being taxed to pay for black schools. Admitting that most Africans did not come to the United States of their own accord, she added, "Of course we survived when we brought them here, but we have been taxed to build schools and colleges for them."[38] Ida Darden, editor of the *Southern Conservative* and a spokesperson for many right-wing causes, shared Burke's views on taxation for integration purposes. In an article titled, "More Than 88 Billion Dollars Are Required to Educate Texas Negroes," she claimed "it cost American taxpayers $410,333.33 per Negro for the nine colored students to attend Little Rock high school during the term of 1957–1958, including armed escorts." Based upon the Little Rock figures and the assumption that Texas citizens would also resist the "bayonet-in-the-back type of education" that was attempted in Arkansas, she calculated that it would cost more than $88 billion to educate the 215,465 black schoolchildren of her home state. Her adding machine, she wrote, was not large enough to calculate the costs to the "seven or eight other Southern States" where "race mixing" would meet opposition.[39] She did not calculate the cost of educating black children if desegregation came about peaceably.

But it did not come about peaceably. Several decades after the *Brown* decision, Frances Pauley, a political and civil rights activist in Georgia, recalled some of her encounters with the right, and how she came to realize what it felt like to have people hate her. She particularly remembered an experience in Baker County, where she encountered a woman who "cussed" her out. It was not the genteel behavior often associated with ladies of the South. As Pauley described the experience, "You never saw anybody hate anybody like she hated me. She just—it just looked like fire coming out of her mouth, almost. And all the mean things, nasty, filthy things that she could think of, she said to me, this white lady."[40]

Racist organizations frequently stressed the theme of physical safety, which served to attract anxious mothers to their segregationist cause. In 1958, the white supremacist National Citizens Protective Association included in its newsletter a letter from a concerned mother from Indiana who wrote that five black girls, "razor blades taped to their fingers," had attacked an innocent white girl who attended their school. The woman reported that there was no indication of the girls being expelled and complained of hypocrisy in favor of blacks.[41] Also warning of threats to children was Texan Ida Darden. In 1958 and 1959, she wrote of alleged instances of black students threatening violence, and in one issue of her newspaper she reported on "sex orgies between White girls and Negro boys." Such events, she maintained, were occurring throughout the United States.[42]

Such reports would surely worry mothers already fearful of physical and moral dangers for their children.

Darden's anxieties about the safety of white children apparently led to her entry into a debate over the appropriateness of some white mother's behavior during antidesegregation rallies. In January 1961, Darden lambasted newspaper columnist Inez Robb for her lack of understanding for "harassed and desperate mothers of New Orleans who are protesting the integration of the schools." Robb had found herself "sickened" by the behavior of the white women.[43] She was commenting on the unruly behavior of white New Orleans mothers who, late in 1960, had led demonstrations against the school district's attempts to desegregate two local elementary institutions. On November 14, when deputy U.S. Marshals escorted three black first grade girls into one of the schools, an estimated 150 protesters, mostly women and teenagers, were waiting outside. The following day, two women were among the eleven white "jeering demonstrators" arrested on charges ranging from disturbing the peace to insulting police patrolmen. The *New York Times* reported that a procession of mothers entered the schools to gather belongings of their children, many vowing that they would not allow their children to return as long "as Negroes were enrolled."[44]

In early December 1960, a group of women (whom reporters dubbed "the Cheerleaders") led demonstrations at the second New Orleans school to attempt desegregation. Novelist John Steinbeck, who personally witnessed the demonstrations, commented on how the women thrived on the publicity they were receiving. He reported that the women shouted words that were "bestial, and filthy, and degenerate," and the women's screams filled him "with a shocked and sickened sorrow." The words he heard there were "far worse . . . than dirt, a kind of frightening witches' Sabbath." As they screamed, the women passed newspaper clippings amongst the crowd, containing reports of their earlier demonstrations. "They simpered in happy, almost innocent triumph when they were applauded. Theirs was the demented cruelty of egocentric children, and somehow this made their insensate beastliness much more heartbreaking. These were not mothers, not even women. They were crazy actors playing to a crazy audience."[45]

Darden, who was a mother, viewed the situation differently. She wrote that reporter Inez Robb, "not having any children of her own, cannot be expected to understand or have any sympathy for the impulse which impels a mother to protect her young from harm even at the cost of her own life." But child safety was not Darden's only concern. She gave an indication of the extent of her racism when she added that Robb probably approved of a "sickening" incident, in which "a Negro man married one white female and publicly embraced and kissed another one."[46] A year later, following reports that newly integrated schools in Atlanta, Dallas, and New Orleans had opened in September "without incident," Darden derided what she called the "liberal press" for making no mention that police were stationed at the schools "with guns and blackjacks handy and with U.S. Marshals standing by ready to go into action."[47]

While many of the rightist complaints regarding desegregation of the schools came from the grassroots, leaders in local government also revealed their rightist leanings on the issue. Because of their strong identification with children, women were successfully running for positions on school boards in many cities. Right-wing women often found that holding these elective positions allowed them opportunities to push their points of view. Such was the case in Houston, Texas. Barely recovered from the rightist-led fight against progressive education during the 1950s, the 1960s saw trouble brewing once again in the Houston Independent School District. In 1963, Hattie Mae (Mrs. Charles) White, the school board's sole African American and the only liberal, drew the ire of many Houstonians when she criticized fellow board members.[48] Indeed, as an African American, White had a list of complaints. She charged that most members of the board were giving "protection to the use of the Confederate flag at a time when it is being used in Mississippi and other parts of the country as a symbol of defiance to the federal government." In addition, the board was refusing to accept food for hungry children because it came from the federal government. Moreover, there was a "continued effort to sabotage the Bill of Rights as applied to Negro children in the Houston Independent School District."[49]

Other board members disagreed, and one, Lois (Mrs. H. W.) Cullen, called for White's resignation. White refused.[50] Cullen, who was white, a native Houstonian, and mother of two had, like White, been elected to the school board in 1958. Even before her election Cullen was active in rightist community organizations, including the DAR and the Minute Women. While campaigning for the board, Cullen publicly opposed the Supreme

Court's *Brown* ruling, arguing that desegregation was illegal.[51] After 1957, when Houston schools received a court order to desegregate within three years, tensions rose, and conservative forces, including the Minute Women, once again took control. White pushed for rapid desegregation while such rightists as Cullen employed delaying tactics.[52] When a leader of the Houston NAACP defended White, Mrs. W. B. Zedler of Houston responded with a letter to President Johnson, stating that White's "actions and attitude have created ill feelings" among white people, including Johnson's friends and supporters.[53] White, who was only the second African American to hold political office in the state of Texas since Reconstruction, faced formidable odds. Even the *Houston Tribune*'s headlines pointed to White as needing to "explain" her "attitude."[54]

Despite continuing protests, the Office of Education of the U.S. Department of Health, Education, and Welfare reported in December 1966 that some desegregation progress had been made in the southern and border states. The southern states with the highest percentage of black students going to school with whites were Texas, Tennessee, and Virginia. Texas led the group with 34.6 percent of its black students attending schools in which they made up less than 95 percent of the enrollment. Comparable percentages in Tennessee and Virginia were, respectively, 21.9 and 20 percent. The greatest challenge lay in Alabama where only 2.4 percent of African American students attended schools in which they made up less than 95 percent of the student body.[55]

A letter to the White House from an Alabama woman gives an indication of obstacles that civil rights advocates had to overcome in that state. In 1967, she wrote that she had lived a "long, long time" and had seen the nation face "great problems" from "wars, depression, hurricanes, riots, etc." Now "the *very worst* thing this country has ever done is to *force* our fine white children to go to school to negro teachers." Enlarging on her lack of respect for black teachers and her fears for the future, she continued, "Next to the home, school has the greatest influence on the lives and character of our children. Small children usually learn to love and respect their teachers and this forced negro business will influence the young people for generations to come—and not for good."[56]

Not only desegregation, but other aspects of the civil rights movement drew controversy within school districts. For one, the movement brought a push for greater focus upon the teaching of black history. Blacks wanted to read about their own heroes, as well as the African American experience in general. However, as historian Jonathan Zimmerman shows, attempts to present a more balanced treatment in school texts met with frequent rightist resistance, not only in the South but also throughout the nation. Such emphasis on race, many on the right feared, would bias children, both black and white, against their country. A California mother complained about *Land of the Free: A History of the United States* (1966), charging that it emphasized America's history of prejudice, and thus played into the hands of communists and the "unpatriotic." One of the book's three authors was black historian and civil rights activist John Hope Franklin, whose contribution likely added to the controversy. During the 1960s, some Washington liberals sought to involve the federal government in getting multiracial and multiethnic books into the schools, and Congress did earmark $400 million for that purpose. But many school districts resisted.[57] For some on the right, such government involvement undoubtedly supplied further evidence of a conspiracy among communists, the government, blacks, and leftward leaning intellectuals.

Neither were racial tensions confined to the South. Historian Thomas J. Sugrue explored the struggle during the 1950s to desegregate schools in the largely affluent town of New Rochelle, New York. He found that while black protests and boycotts eventually brought about desegregation in that community, it would take government action to open all schools to blacks in some areas of the North.[58] In January 1970, Pasadena, California, became the first nonsouthern city to be ordered by the federal courts to desegregate its public schools. This was almost twenty years after rightists of that city succeeded in removing their progressive school superintendent and blocking educational reforms. Critics at the time pointed to racism as part of the right-wing's movement to prevent the mixing of races in Pasadena, though the opposition denied such accusations.[59] During the civil rights movement, the conservative communities of Pasadena were once again creating loud protests, this time against school integration and busing. As one historian notes, "One of their greatest fears was realized: The federal government stepped in to monitor the integration process."[60]

As racial tensions grew throughout the 1960s, the baby boom generation was growing up. By 1965 the eldest among the baby boomer youth were acquiring political and social awareness, and some were becoming involved in the civil rights movement—both for and against. Although most southern white children grew up with their mothers impressing upon them the idea of white superiority and the importance of separation of the races, it seems the lessons were not as deeply ingrained in their children as many parents supposed. As early as February 1956, some educators were reporting that the idea of sharing classrooms with children of another race troubled most children considerably less than it did their parents. At a conference of 350 educators from various regions, several delegates from the southern and border states reported that integration in their schools was usually going smoothly. Only when students' parents, or in some instances "outsiders . . . stirred them up" did problems arise.[61] One example of outside involvement causing an uproar occurred in Hoxie, Arkansas, where in late summer 1955, residents saw a flood of racist pamphlets and mimeographed materials pouring into town via the mail, under people's doors, and on automobile windshields. The right-wing women's organization Pro America was among the groups circulating the material. Some of Hoxie's teachers reported that this attention resulted in "signs of strain and restlessness among some of their pupils."[62]

Looking to the future, a New Jersey woman who favored integration asked parents to allow children to follow their own instincts rather than try to avoid the Supreme Court ruling. "This reaching out to the adults of tomorrow is the most important fact of all," she wrote.[63] Some students attending a special New York Times Youth Forum in May 1955, expressed similar sentiments. When discussing the integration issue, Juliann Bluitt, a sixteen-year-old from a Washington, D.C., high school, said, "Men are put on earth together. Now we have become mature enough to realize we must come together to work for the common good." Other students, including Celia Shapiro, also of Washington, D.C., blamed the older generation for problems surrounding desegregation. "If it weren't for the parents, we could have done a smoother job. . . . We all know these prejudices are inherited." The panel of six students all agreed that integration should come to pass. Yet, just as in regard to the issue of abolition a century earlier, there was some disagreement over whether integration should evolve over time or be immediate.[64]

By the 1960s, many among the boomer generation were voicing their concerns over the civil rights movement and the overall state of the nation. Some blamed the far right for causing the problems. In 1965 a fifteen-year-old girl wrote President Johnson concerning the Ku Klux Klan:

"What gives them the authority to judge and condemn another fellow human being?" She viewed the internal unrest in the United States as a sign of instability, wondering how the nation could set an example for other countries if there was no "just democracy" at home. "I'm only a teenager," she wrote. "Most of our crazy ways are just fads. These KKK members are adults who should know better."[65] This fifteen year old and other young people were coming to realize that the world around them was in the midst of change. They were seeing that many of the older generation were rigid, hanging onto their traditional mindsets, often to the detriment of American society. The new generation was testing the waters, assessing just how much change ought to be allowed.

More signs of a change of attitude among the younger generation of the South came in the spring of 1963, when white students from the University of North Carolina took to the streets of Chapel Hill to demand an end to racial inequality. North Carolina's General Assembly, believing that such student activism was linked to communism, passed a Speaker Ban Law. In keeping with the long-standing southern point of view that challenges to the existing social order were likely Communist-inspired, legislators thought that such a law would curb civil rights activity. But, as William J. Billingsley notes in his study of race and politics at the University of North Carolina during the 1960s, the activism of an increasing number of whites, especially students and intellectuals, led to the demise of segregation.[66] Thus, to at least some degree, the right's distrust of the intellectual elite was justified. Jim Crow needed near unanimity to survive, and partly as a result of the influence of educators, support for segregation was crumbling.

On July 2, 1964, President Lyndon Johnson signed the Civil Rights Bill into law, making segregation in public facilities and racial discrimination in employment and education illegal. At about the same time, the editors of the *Spirit*, a right-wing publication self-described as "The Woman's Magazine Men Read," were arguing against the new law. The *Spirit* was the voice of Woman's Right to Know, Inc., of Lakeland, Florida, and described itself as dedicated to the conviction that "American woman cherishes her Independence and her Liberty" and that "she will insist on preserving for her children the heritage of a FREE AMERICA." To support those claims its editors compared the views of a "naïve" twenty-year-old white woman with those of a "mature" black female. Two letters appeared side by side in the July-August 1964 issue under the title, "Two Letters—Two Views—Negro Maturity, White Immaturity."[67]

Because it challenged their racist point of view, the editors mocked the heartfelt letter of young, white Kathy Fentress of Ormond Beach, Florida, as "immature." Writing from the county jail in St. Augustine, Florida, following her arrest during a civil rights march, Fentress maintained that in joining the civil rights movement she was a recruit in a nonviolent army, and she was "concerned not only with the welfare of America's Negro citizens but with the spiritual well being of our whole country." She marched with "400 others through the streets of St. Augustine," because she opposed those who clung "to the immoral traditions of the past," and wanted the United States to live up to the principles on which it was founded, promoting "a spirit of love and brotherhood."[68]

The second letter writer, Jessie Gillespie, publisher of the *Mid-South Informer* of Walls, Mississippi, presented a contrasting view. She wished to maintain the status quo. Gillespie, an African American, asked if the majority of blacks were "thinking seriously of where our so-called leaders are attempting to lead us. When we clamor to patronize white establishments, we are saying that we are inferior to the white man. We are saying that we do not have the ability to build establishments for ourselves. . . . Perhaps the NAACP meant to help us at one time but someone got the idea that they could use the Negro as a political football to gain for themselves power and wealth."[69]

The magazine's editors responded to the two letters, remarking that Fentress's letter reminded them "of the impractical dreams of youth," adding that they were tempted to use the title that occurred to them first—"Sense and Nonsense."[70] Gillespie's letter makes some legitimate points, in regard to some of the leaders using the civil rights movement for personal gain, and particularly the idea of black-owned businesses being viewed as inferior to those of whites. However, she failed to see the broader picture, the idea that the movement sought to give African Americans the right of free access to public institutions and business establishments. Gillespie's remarks reveal pride of race, but also show how deeply embedded was the southern tradition of "knowing one's place" in nature's order. As Lillian Smith explains, numerous southerners believed that disaster would occur if society treated blacks and whites as social equals. Gillespie's point of view was useful as right-wing propaganda, as the publishers of the *Spirit* well knew. (The magazine would soon adopt the more patriotic-sounding name *American Spirit*.)

Despite continued protests, desegregation slowly proceeded in Florida and elsewhere. In 1963, because of her many years' experience teaching black children in public schools, the Sarasota County School District hired Barbara Needleman, an educator from Massachusetts, to teach at a newly integrated school in Nokomis, Florida. Many years later, the teacher recalled one little white girl who was determined to do her part for the integration process, saying, "I'm going to be so nice, Mrs. Needleman, and I ain't going to call them niggers." Overall, Needleman felt that integration had gone smoothly. The most positive aspect was that black and white children were showing the ability to get along with one another.[71] Some baby boomers growing up in the area recalled that during early stages of school integration, most white students viewed the few blacks assigned to white schools as a "novelty" and readily accepted them into the student body. However, as the ratio of black to white students rose, tensions did as well.[72]

As white resistance to school integration continued, some children took it upon themselves to attend mixed-race schools and to educate their parents about the benefits of integration. For example, ten-year-old Jerry Parker, a white boy of Anniston, Alabama, introduced his mother to an integrated school. Gertrude Parker, who had only a fourth-grade education, was the mother of nine children. Neither she nor her husband wanted their children to attend integrated schools. While the family was making plans to move to an area of town where the children could attend an all-white school, young Jerry disappeared one day. When his mother confronted him as to where he had been, he admitted that he had attended the integrated school. "I wanted to see how it was. My friends told me it was good."[73]

Gertrude Parker agreed to allow Jerry and his younger brother to attend, but only if she went with the boys and saw the school for herself. The black principal showed Parker around the school. She was impressed with the school's cleanliness, neatness, and examples of the young students' fine writing and immediately enrolled her sons. The experience led her to change her views regarding African Americans. She told a reporter, "I've never cared for them. I've never associated with them." Hesitating a little, she said, "I don't think the same way now, not really. Because they was too nice to Jerry." She admitted that she might find it difficult to accept the idea of a black family moving to a house next door, but left the thought open. "It'd take me awhile to really get used to the idea. I'm not like a child, they accepted it easier."[74] Largely as a result of her son's intervention, Parker's mind was now open to the possibility that the tradition of segregation, with which she had been so familiar in her forty-two years, was not the only way for blacks and whites to get along. Although there is no way of knowing where Parker stood on other matters, on the issue of integration she moved from a right-wing to a moderate position.

The Parker family was among many that sought means to avoid sending their children to integrated schools. A baby boomer who grew up in Manassas, Virginia, recalled that many white parents sent their children to private "segregation academies," often against the wishes of their children.[75] Rightists who established independent Christian schools for purposes of escaping desegregation soon discovered that the federal government was not going to let them off so easily. During the 1970s, the Internal Revenue Service denied tax exemptions to private religious schools that failed to admit sufficient numbers of blacks. This new act of government interference created considerable anger among the Christian right.[76]

Whether for or against the civil rights movement, whether on the right or on the left, women—mothers in particular—faced the question of just how active they should become in promoting their causes. In 1965, the *Ladies Home Journal* drew responses from women of varying political and social persuasions when it asked whether or not a mother should leave her family to become a civil rights activist. The question became more urgent following the murder of a white woman, Viola Liuzzo, a Detroit mother of five, who was killed in Alabama on March 25, while participating in a civil-rights protest march from Selma to Montgomery. In addition to sponsoring a survey on the issue, the *Journal* covered a meeting of eighteen white, middle-class women held in an unidentified medium-sized northern city. Both the survey and the meeting's moderator asked if Liuzzo, "as a mother of five, had a right to leave home and risk her life for a social cause."[77]

Among the women surveyed, only 15.6 percent of southern women answered "yes," while 61.2 percent said "no," and 23.2 percent had no opinion. Eastern women answered in the affirmative at the rate of 35.5 percent, while women from the western and central states answered "yes" at the rate of 33.7 percent and 27.5 percent, respectively. Overall, the response was 26.4 percent "yes," 55.2 percent "no," and 18.4 percent "no opinion." Unfortunately, the article did not indicate the number of women surveyed. However, the eighteen women who met with the moderator agreed that there were causes for which they would take risks, particularly if they involved ways to protect their children. One said, "I'd march in the street to campaign for a traffic light because I'd rather take a chance on my getting hit than my child getting hit on the way to school. But if my children weren't involved—no." Others said that they would be willing to fight for their country or for religious freedom.[78]

Although the survey was not scientific, the results do suggest several factors. Most women believed their responsibilities to their children were more important than their participation in any social cause, and they would be willing to risk their lives to protect their children. Despite the researcher's asking that the respondents put aside their own opinions on the question of civil rights, reasons behind southern women's exceptionally low number of "yes" responses may relate to the nature of the cause in which Liuzzo was participating. In 1965, tensions over civil rights were high, and southern women were perhaps objecting to northerners, mothers or not, entering their region to join the civil rights movement. Among the many flaws in the survey, at least as it was reported in *Ladies Home Journal*, is the lack of information as to race, social class, or marital status of the women surveyed. A disproportionate number of white, middle-class women (the *Journal's* readership) might skew the survey's results. Perhaps the results would have been somewhat different if the survey concerned a southern prosegregationist woman who put her life on the line in support of that cause. While right-wing activists often verbally attacked their opponents, none of the women studied here indicated a willingness to risk their lives for their causes.

For African American women living with segregation, whether in the South or in the North, the question of desegregation was much more personal and immediate. Their political consciousness developed out of the discrimination they faced in their own life experiences. The chance to desegregate the schools and open the way for their children to have an education equal to that of white children was a vital part of their civil rights struggle. From 1957, when civil rights activist Daisy Lee Gatson Bates mentored nine Little Rock, Arkansas, children in becoming the first

African American students to integrate the city's schools, black women showed their willingness to risk their livelihoods, and sometimes their lives, to work for a cause they believed in. Indeed, black women's activism over education predated the *Brown* decision. For example, African American women actively challenged inferior education in Chicago's schools from the early 1930s.[79]

White rightist women, including mothers and grandmothers, were active in almost all aspects of the antidesegregation movement. Some were widely read among rightist circles, including Phoebe Courtney and Ida Darden. Others rallied for their causes in spontaneous gatherings and as members of organizations. At times, husbands and wives could be found working together in prominent roles. The racist monthly newsletters, the *White Sentinel* and the *White American News Service*, products of the National Citizens Protective Association, had Forest W. Wolf serving as president and Helen M. Wolf as the paper's editor. Serving on the organization's Executive Board were Anna Marie Ammann and William Ammann. Sharing the same last names, these were likely two married couples. Until their divorce, Phoebe and her husband, Kent Courtney, together published the *Independent American* which, in addition to supporting other right-wing causes, was prosegregation. After their divorce, Phoebe became the sole publisher.[80]

White men dominated the largest white supremacist organizations, including such groups as the Ku Klux Klan and Citizens' Councils, and most news accounts focused on male leaders. Although some professional women of the South, including journalists Phoebe Courtney, Ida Darden, and Florence Sillers Ogden, achieved recognition for their activism, most appeared to be satisfied with their subordinate roles. Many agreed with Christine Benagh and Ogden that women had specific roles within the southern hierarchy, and the important thing was to perform those roles well. Nevertheless, Ogden and other women were not shy about pushing such all-male organizations as Mississippi's Citizens' Council, to adopt women's ideas about education and youth activities into their campaigns.[81] Little by little women were developing their own consciousness and joining together more as women. Remaining fervent anti-integrationists, they were in fact themselves, as conservatives, starting to change the locus of power.

Sociologist Kathleen M. Blee's findings about women of the 1920s Ku

Klux Klan, reveal that their motives for activism differed to some extent from those of men.[82] The same was true for right-wing women campaigning against desegregation. They were more concerned with tradition, family, and future generations, while for the men it was more about power. Thus, many were more comfortable as members of women-only organizations. But whether it was behind the scenes or in the foreground, women did make a mark on the anti-integration movement.

Each faction in the debate over civil rights had an agenda. Ardent segregationists, including many on the right, wanted to turn the clock back to the idea of "separate but equal," despite the fact that "equal" was usually left out of the equation. Within this group were the right-wing religious fundamentalists who held up the Bible, considering their interpretation was the only legitimate one. There were also secular racists who hated blacks on both a physical and social basis. At the same time, ardent anti-segregationists worked for immediate desegregation and social equality. Then, there were those in the middle, people who were not segregationists but who were worried about the safety of students, particularly during the turmoil of the integration process. Also in the middle were people who sympathized with integration, but feared that a rapid change would disrupt the social order. At the same time, the younger generation, the baby boomers, were becoming politically aware and were starting to make decisions as to whether to join any of these factions or to develop new agendas of their own.

During the mid-1960s to mid-1970s, the topic of busing brought some new elements into the mix as the civil rights issue reached farther into the North than it had since the Civil War, and gave the right the opportunity to enlist thousands more to its cause.

Busing

Title IV of the Civil Rights Act of 1964 gave the U.S. Attorney General the authority to enforce desegregation. Opponents argued that the act would lead to mandatory busing, and indeed it did. Two years after its passage, the Department of Health, Education, and Welfare mandated that school districts incorporate busing in order to meet designated mathematical ratios of black and white students. Although challenged in the courts, the mandate was sustained in 1971 when the Supreme Court upheld its consti-tutionality in *Swann v. Charlotte-Mecklenburg Board of Education.*[83]

The practice of busing students was controversial, and remained so from the late 1960s through the mid-1970s. Again, white racists and the right wing protested the loudest against this latest example of govern-ment interference in local affairs; but there were signs of reluctance among other Americans as well. Although most African Americans believed that desegregation of schools was the only way their race would achieve an education on a level comparable to that of whites, some were reluctant to fully endorse busing. Not only was busing often inconvenient, requiring additional time for transporting students to and from school, but also, as with school desegregation, it brought anxieties for parents regarding the quality of education (a concern found mostly among white parents) and the safety of their children.

For those who believed in separation of the races, busing was a further step toward total social integration. Although racism was at the base of most antibusing campaigns, other factors led Americans who were not racists to protest school busing. Both black and white students often com-plained about being taken out of their neighborhoods, which commonly resulted in their being separated from their friends. In 1966–1967, the U.S. Commission on Civil Rights investigated the attitudes of some schoolchil-dren. It found that in Columbia, South Carolina, all of the white children surveyed, with one exception, preferred to attend their former all-white schools. At the same time, the vast majority of black children in the study chose to attend their former all-black schools.[84]

Due to the unpopularity of busing, rightist arguments on the issue, such as those of Phoebe Courtney, were often not far outside the main-stream. During the mid-1960s to early 1970s, Courtney's *Independent American* published several articles that voiced opposition to the practice. In 1966, her newspaper included an article designed to show that govern-ment leaders in support of busing were hypocrites. It charged that Harold Howe III, U.S. Commissioner of Education, wanted to bus schoolchildren to other neighborhoods; yet he sent his own son to a private school in Connecticut rather than to his local mixed-race public school in Washing-ton, D.C.[85] This complaint was similar to rightist charges during the 1950s that such prointegration senators as Lyndon B. Johnson were sending their own children to private schools. In addition to alleging hypocrisy on the part of politicians, the writers were pointing out the advantages of being of a wealthier social class.[86] As late as 1977, the concern was still appearing in Courtney's newspaper, with an article titled "How to Stop Forced Busing" calling for an amendment to the Constitution that would outlaw the practice. Courtney alleged that 70 to 75 percent of Americans supported such an amendment.[87] Although she tended to exaggerate her statistics, busing was not very popular.

Coming more than a decade after the *Brown* decision, busing created tense times not only for parents but also for baby boomers, black and white. For example, a black baby boomer who grew up in Manatee County, Florida, recalled that being bused to a white school was one aspect of integration that he disliked the most.[88] A white boomer recalls rioting in the public schools of Gainesville, Florida, during the early 1970s, when busing was still quite new in the region.[89] Such tensions existed in schools from coast to coast, and in both the North and the South. Parents' groups formed throughout the country to protest busing, offering numerous reasons why it was a poor policy. During Richard Nixon's presidency, as in the later years of Johnson's leadership, letters from busing opponents far outnumbered those in favor.[90]

Despite the broad distaste for school busing, there were arguments that separated the right wing from the mainstream on the issue. One example is a Louisiana mother who held a point of view that racists and the right wing often shared. The Louisiana woman wrote President Nixon in 1969, asking that he fulfill his campaign pledge to pursue a "choice of school plan." She reluctantly accepted the idea of black children being placed in her daughter's white school, but wrote that she would prefer that her daughter "be a drop out" than go to a "colored school." Revealing that far rightist attitudes about a black/communist conspiracy were still alive a decade-and-a-half after *Brown*, she predicted, "If things continue the way they are now, the colored people and communists will soon take over the country."[91] Yet her willingness to accept black children into her daughter's "white school" seems to reveal a recent transformation in her thinking. What for integrationists would be a small accommodation was for her a much larger acquiescence to a movement that she saw as progressing much too fast and leading the country in the wrong direction.

Figure 4. Demonstration against school busing for integration purposes in front of the Manatee County (Florida) School Administration Building, April 14, 1970. Courtesy of Manatee County Public Library Historical Image Digital Collection.

Some of the loudest arguments against busing came from rightist women in the North. Among those protesting in the late 1960s was a right-wing San Francisco group of women known as Mothers Support Neighborhood Schools, who argued that there was no need for busing. They pointed out that other racial groups also faced discrimination, including American Indians and Chinese. President Johnson and the U.S. Commission on Civil Rights, they argued, were taking racial balance as their goal when a more appropriate aim lay in an "excellent education for all children." Further, the women maintained that schools were not the only cause of blacks' poor performance; more weight should be given "to parental motivations, heredity and environment."[92] Earlier, in regard to textbooks, curricula, and teachers, the right had stressed the role of

Figure 5. African American children on their way to PS204, 82nd Street and 15th Avenue, Brooklyn, New York, pass mothers protesting the busing of children to achieve integration, September 13, 1965. Courtesy of Library of Congress Prints and Photographs Division, LC-USZ62-134434, New York World-Telegram and the Sun Newspaper Photograph Collection.

schools, for they thought they could maintain control over education. Now they were de-emphasizing the importance of the schools for black children, protesting what they saw as federal interference. However, outside of the busing issue—on such matters as sex education and intelligence and personality testing—they continued to stress the importance of what young people learned in school.

Northern rightists raised a variety of arguments in support of their antibusing campaigns, and some of their contentions hinted at racism, mirroring those being voiced in the South since the *Brown* decision. In the late 1960s and early 1970s, Parents of New York United (PONY-U), an organization with which Lucille Cardin Crain was associated, expressed concerns about the quality of education. They joined the antibusing protests, citing examples of black students physically assaulting whites. Adding fuel to their argument were allegations that Social Security funds were paying for busing.[93] Here again were the multiple issues of children's physical safety, government misuse of taxpayers' money, reduced quality of whites' education, and sheer racism.

Moderates, too, had concerns. Mrs. Thomas DeGeorge of Laurelton, Queens, New York, was one of many moderates who was apprehensive over her son being bused to a school in "a bad neighborhood." What would she do if her son became sick and had to leave school early, or if he missed the homeward bound bus?[94] As revealed in women's discussions about the murder of Viola Liuzzo, most mothers sought to keep their children out of danger whenever possible. Even families whose overall politics and social attitudes might be described as "liberal" often considered moving away from neighborhoods and cities if they thought the move would prevent their children from being physically hurt.[95]

In her studies of women associated with the Ku Klux Klan and other racist organizations, sociologist Kathleen Blee found that women were more likely to be drawn into such groups over fears for their children's physical safety than through appeals to pride of race.[96] For example, a group known as Restore Our Alienated Rights (ROAR) recruited white working-class Boston mothers into a campaign against school desegregation by suggesting that busing would jeopardize their children's safety and the quality of their education.[97] This study corroborates Blee's findings. In addition to fears that fights might erupt between black and white students, many of the women writing President Johnson revealed anxieties concerning the quality of education their children might receive as a result of the disruption brought on by busing. An Atlanta mother of four voiced such a concern, complaining that her children had been living amid the "turmoil of uncertainty in their schools for fourteen years," and school busing was an additional disruption. She felt powerless as the court system was making decisions that were "vitally important to the destiny of a minor child."[98]

A white Atlanta teacher, Helen P. Taylor, whose views on integration were moderate, agreed that the quality of education was bound to suffer if school districts instituted the wide-scale school desegregation plans associated with busing. In 1973, she wrote Lonnie King, president of the Atlanta Branch of the NAACP, that for nine years she participated in "a very orderly desegregation process at one Atlanta high school." At that school there were whites and blacks of several economic levels, as well as foreign-born students. While there were fewer honors classes and National Merit

Scholarship winners than in the past, and more need existed for remedial instruction, "spirit remained high, and students had an opportunity to learn to live and work together in a healthy kind of integrated society because they were not forced into it."[99] Now, Taylor wrote, there was a push by the federal courts, the NAACP, and others for rapid desegregation. This process, made possible by massive busing, would spell tragedy for the public school system. Planning school curricula and activities took time, energy, and a fairly stable faculty. Widespread relocation of students and faculty would make planning very difficult. Additional problems centered on individualized instruction and counseling in completely unfamiliar surroundings, and little would be known of students' previous records.[100]

Documents submitted during a push for integration in the Atlanta Schools in 1973 reveal differences in motivating factors behind various mothers' resistance to busing. Moderates mostly worried about disruption of their children's academic lives while the arguments of those on the racist/far rightist side agreed with the mother who wrote that Atlanta's children were "targets for the NAACP or any other *subversive* group."[101] Others, like Helen P. Taylor, were moderates or liberals, believing that the mixing of racial and ethnic groups could have positive results. Too much change, though, enabled through busing and happening too quickly, seemed bound to backfire.

Detroit, Michigan, housewife Irene McCabe was one of the first northern white women to gain publicity as a sole leader of an antibusing campaign. In 1971, after a federal judge ordered that thousands of Detroit schoolchildren be bused outside of their neighborhoods, thirty-six-year-old McCabe formed a group of her neighbors to join in protest. The group organized a boycott, keeping an estimated 35 percent of the white students at home when schools opened in September. They did not stop there. As one reporter described the events, after the boycotts came "frontal assaults on the school gates themselves, with Mrs. McCabe in T-shirt, gesticulating and shouting, leading the demonstrations."[102] In April 1972, McCabe led a group of her followers on a 620-mile walk to Washington, D.C., in a failed attempt to win support for a constitutional amendment to end school busing for purposes of integration. The boycotts and demonstrations soon ended, but McCabe began traveling around the country, expounding her views and calling for a grassroots movement. "Busing is not an educational tool, it is an integrational tool," she declared.

It was destroying neighborhood schools. Her loosely organized group became known as the National Action Group (NAG). It claimed seventy-one chapters in Michigan and elsewhere, boasting a total membership of 100,000.[103]

Divisions between those who campaigned against busing because of their far rightist and racist beliefs and those who were less radical are often blurry; however, McCabe tried to make the distinction obvious. She mandated that her followers only wear the NAG label if they vowed to focus their work solely on the issue of busing and to avoid association with white supremacist organizations. Following a Ku Klux Klan firebombing of ten buses in Pontiac, Michigan, in August 1971, McCabe announced that the KKK did *her* antibusing group a favor. It made NAG appear to be more moderate. Despite McCabe's denials, and her rhetoric differing from the extremism of such groups as the KKK, her arguments had a racist tone. While denying her racism, she said that she could not "see why blacks [had] to go to white schools for cultural reasons. There are other ways to improve their education."[104]

McCabe was one of many rightist women to encourage others of their sex to take a stand on busing. Another was television personality Martha Rountree who founded the Leadership Foundation to mobilize women to political action. She argued that the courts were wrong if they believed that "in order to achieve equal educational opportunity for all, bad schools require the presence of white children," and called upon women to work within their states and communities. "If WOMEN TAKE A STAND [Rountree's emphasis] right now, we can stop this lunacy once and for all, and concentrate on buying books for our children instead of buses."[105] As a woman working in television, Rountree was in a good position to realize that, more and more, women were receiving the attention of the media. She wanted to be sure that they stood up and spread the right message.

As the fight against busing continued, women were frequently found on the forefront of those campaigns. One of the largest antibusing drives in the nation was in Boston, where Louise Day Hicks, an Irish-Catholic Democrat, led the fight and was elected to Boston's School Committee as a result of her stance on busing. When she stood up to fight the state's Racial Imbalance Act, which mandated that no school could be more than half black, many whites considered her a heroine.[106] The act was a decade old on June 21, 1974, when Federal Judge W. Arthur Garrity ordered the

Boston School Committee to use busing to begin desegregation of the city's public schools. The court order came after Boston's black community spent many years struggling against discrimination in the schools. African American women often led those campaigns, but black students joined the fight in the late 1960s and early 1970s.[107]

Hicks possessed a law degree and thereby held the social status associated with the upper-middle class, but studies of the fight against busing in Boston found that the women involved were both middle- and working class.[108] In 1975, in the local communities of Charlestown, Southie, Hyde Park, West Roxbury, and Boston's North End, mothers held prayer marches to protest busing. On one occasion, estimates placed approximately five hundred women marching through Southie.[109] Some mothers involved in this march were older baby boomers who had seen televised reports of earlier protests. Charlestown mothers encouraged their boomer daughters to organize prayer marches. They were carrying on a local tradition. During World War II, the older generation of women acted similarly, praying for the safety of the town's men who were serving overseas. Now, in their fight against busing, mothers, grandmothers, and great-grandmothers all became involved in nighttime candlelit gatherings and prayer marches.[110]

Some white teenagers, particularly boys, resorted to more violent means of protest. A journalist for the *New York Times* reported that some African American parents so feared these assaults on their children that they often kept them out of school.[111] Teenage girls' participation in the antibusing movement was minimal. Sociologist Julia Wrigley's assertion that since the girls did not identify themselves as mothers, they felt no special connection with the busing issue, helps to explain their lack of involvement.[112] Furthermore, they might have placed more importance upon personal issues and relations with their peers than on community concerns during that transitional period of their lives.

There is considerable evidence that both mothers and fathers were willing to take action. In Boston, where mothers led the antibusing campaign, fathers often provided support, including performing such physical labor as setting up loudspeakers at rallies and fixing up storefronts for antibusing offices. If a man wanted to be a leader in Boston, he likely developed a special area of expertise in order to avoid encroaching on someone else's territory.[113] At the same time, most of those women who revealed their occupations described themselves as homemakers. Their more flexible schedules allowed them greater opportunities for campaign involvement.

Whites were not alone in protesting busing. While most African American parents supported the idea of school integration, some protested aspects of busing. For example, in Chicago, in 1973, there were reports of black parents protesting busing at Douglass High School.[114] They, too, were anxious over the disruption in their children's lives and worried about them being verbally, or even physically, assaulted. A study of Alabama schools in the early 1970s found black parents fearing that white teachers would discriminate against their children. As a result, many African American parents were concerned that their children might never fully engage in school activities.[115]

Black leaders, too, differed among themselves. In 1972, a cross section of prominent African Americans, representing a wide range of philosophies, gathered in Gary, Indiana, for the National Black Political Convention. Amid considerable disagreement, the majority of the 3,456 delegates passed a resolution condemning busing, though participants later qualified the resolution. The group eventually decided to oppose busing in communities where high quality schools already existed, but backed it when busing enabled their children to enjoy an education equal to that of whites.[116]

Despite their prominence in antibusing campaigns, most of the women involved returned to their homes once the controversy ended. Although this was the time of a movement for equal rights for women, studies show that most of the women involved in antibusing were traditionalists, believing that they were in a campaign that was appropriate to their gender.[117] Similar to the southern women who campaigned against school integration during the 1950s and 1960s, feminism was not on their agenda. These women were willing to push hard on issues that affected their families, but readily adhered to limits that society had long ago set for women.

In the early 1970s, amid all the controversy over busing, the moderate to leftward-leaning League of Women Voters voiced its opposition to antibusing legislation that was under consideration in the Senate. Lucy Wilson Benson, president of the 160,000 member LWV, pointed out that when busing, on occasion, was "used to continue illegal segregation," no one had campaigned against it. Only "when busing has been associated with integration . . . has it become a point of contention and an hysterical 'trigger' word."[118] To a great extent, Benson was right. In the 1960s and 1970s, all over the country, students who did not live within walking distance of their schools were relying on buses to take them there. Busing for integration purposes usually did take them farther away than the buses to the schools in their local district. However, parents' willingness to go to the expense and inconvenience of moving to a new neighborhood or to enroll their children in private schools, often requiring significant commuting time, reveals that busing was fundamentally a racial issue. Benson's outlook was liberal. Unlike the right, she believed it important for youth to learn to participate in a multicultural, multiracial society.[119]

By the end of the twentieth century the busing issue was practically moot. Due to the federal government's releasing school districts from mandatory busing for desegregation purposes, the practice had virtually ended. For a variety of reasons, millions of students continue to take buses to school. Many find that the closest school is too far away to walk to. Others choose to attend public magnet schools, with their specialized courses or curricula. Nevertheless, the legacy of busing for desegregation purposes is mixed. Schools have officially integrated, but in many cases the actual student ratio has changed very little. Many neighborhoods in which students live have not integrated, and with busing no longer mandatory, local schools usually reflect that reality.[120]

Conclusion

While by no means were all anti-integrationists and antibusers on the far right of the political spectrum, the desegregation issue drew women who were activists for other rightist causes. Outspoken on various issues in education, mental health, and morality, and warning of communist conspiracies within American institutions, such women as Ida Darden, Marilyn Allen, and Phoebe Courtney viewed school desegregation as part of an agenda that went beyond race. The same can be said of such organizations as Pro America and the Daughters of the American Revolution, and various local community organizations, including citizens' groups in Houston and Pasadena. These women and organizations were scattered around the country. What held them together was their ideology.

As discussed above, three themes dominated rightist opposition to desegregation: racism, claims of "communist conspiracy," and objections to government intervention in local affairs. Many politically and socially moderate parents shared a fourth theme with the right—fears for the immediate safety of their children. White racists objected to school integration due to their beliefs in the inferiority of African Americans and fears of racial mixing leading to an eventual "tan" America. Even nonracists often worried that an in-rush of students from poorer neighborhoods, often with inadequate educational background for the grades to which they were assigned, would lead to their children receiving a lower standard of education. The disruption upset some black families as well as white. Thus, while the right sometimes led the protests, it had little problem recruiting other whites, many of whom lacked right-wing credentials. The unpopularity of forced busing made the right wing more prominent, allowing it to draw more followers to its larger agenda.

In his study of the South covering the period 1932 through 1954, historian John Egerton maintains that most white southerners believed that any challenge to regional racial laws constituted an attack on the whole "Southern Way of Life." From there it was only a small step to being called either a "communist" or a "communist sympathizer."[121] Southerners' concern about outside challenges to their culture, combined with the far right's long-held linking of communism with African Americans' campaigns for civil rights, made it quite easy for the right to attract large numbers to their program. At the same time, as historian Nancy MacLean points out, many northern conservatives came to idealize the pre–Civil War South. In doing so, they joined southern racists in denouncing the Fourteenth and Fifteenth Amendments to the Constitution, which gave citizenship and voting rights to blacks.[122]

Many on the right claimed that government intervention in local matters was the major issue, though it seems that individuals often emphasized that argument to hide their racism. Racism, particularly among the far right, remained a prevalent theme. Indeed, in future decades, the right often continued to link matters dealing with the treatment of racial minorities to the question of states' rights. For instance, rightists returned to the argument of government intervention when they spoke out against affirmative action.[123]

Underlying much of this uneasiness was the matter of violence. Not only were their children threatened with physical violence but there also existed the fear that rapid changes could lead to continued chaos across

America. For many, recent history provided evidence that the mixing of peoples could lead to violence. The movement and mingling of people during World War II, for instance, led to racial confrontations over jobs and housing. During the 1960s and early 1970s, racial tensions were leading to riots throughout the United States. Apprehension over the spread of violence fueled the fears of many Americans, not just the right wing.

The younger generation was aware of the upheaval, and for many the 1960s and early 1970s was an unsettling time. As they approached adulthood, they realized that they were reaching the point in their lives when much of the responsibility for the fate of America would be on their shoulders. Thus, they needed to define their personal visions of the country's future. Race was one of the most important issues with which they were forced to deal. Millions of baby boomers grew up in the South with traditional southern values and many more grew up outside of the South with conservative backgrounds. Although large numbers of baby boomers joined with their mothers and fathers in the protests against integration and busing, as a whole they were more accepting of change. In fact, many were advocating it in both the North and South, rebelling against the establishment and questioning the older generation's rigidity.

One factor that enabled baby boomers to more easily accept integration was that they had been growing up during a time when numerous changes were taking place in a wide variety of areas. In addition to African Americans making some inroads in being granted civil rights—such as in the military, workplace, and sports world—scientific discoveries abounded. Students lined up for polio vaccines and, because of the Soviets' acquisition of an atomic bomb, America's youth had to adapt to "duck and cover" exercises in school. Their youth and the vast size of their cohort was another contributing factor. Boomers' youthful flexibility, as well as their greater access to the media via television and portable radios, allowed them to look at issues in new ways. What emerged from the tumultuous civil rights era was not a solution to all racial problems. Nevertheless, as a result of the broadening minds of a growing number of Americans, there was an enhanced opportunity for open discussion.

PROTESTING
THE PROTESTS

4

SEX, GOD, AND THE AMERICAN FLAG

Tradition and Change in Moral Values

We need to inform ourselves of how the communists are all doing their part to soften the younger generation to a point of "moral decay." With alcohol, narcotics, obscene literature available to our youth, and with much of our TV-fare featuring crime, violence and loose morality, it is time our homes, churches, schools, and government combine to convince youth that honesty and decent living represent the highest type of intelligence and patriotism.

Holly Holmes, May 1, 1961

In their campaigns to direct Americans to follow their ideas on politics, social behaviors, and culture, rightist women frequently employed the words "moral" or "morality." Indeed, their definition of morality lies at the heart of most issues examined in this book. Right-wing women considered their beliefs, positions on issues, and actions to be "moral," while those of the opposition were not. Those who were mothers took a particular interest in seeing that their children received an upbringing that maintained their moral codes. Their efforts to censor textbooks and to rid schools of teachers and administrators who did not subscribe to their way of thinking were largely due to fears that young minds would be corrupted by "un-American" ideals.

Similarly, rightist campaigns to block fluoridation, mental health programs, and polio vaccinations usually centered upon concerns that government, scientists, liberals, communists, and other "outsiders" were conspiring to use such devices as drugs to manipulate the thinking of all Americans—but particularly the country's youth. Right-wing women

Figure 6. Women from Boston and Charleston, West Virginia, in Washington, D.C., in March 1975. They are demonstrating against busing and are addressing several other issues, including prayer, morality, and censorship of textbooks. Courtesy of Library of Congress Prints and Photographs Division, LC-DIG-ds-00764, U.S. News & World Report Magazine Photograph Collection.

were especially disturbed over the desegregation of public schools. Besides their fear of social mixing of the races and declining standards of behavior, they foresaw integration reaching beyond the classroom and into the bedroom. Meanwhile, three additional struggles developed that brought moral standards and behavior into a sharp, central focus. These were the issues of sex education, school prayer, and patriotic behavior.

For generations, parents have voiced anxiety over the morals of youth. Parents of baby boomers were no different. Loretta Killian, a mother of a son and a daughter, expressed an anguish that many mothers were experiencing during the 1960s and early 1970s when she asked President Nixon, "Where has all the morality gone?" Girls were wearing too much makeup; both boys and girls were trying to be "sexy." Teenage pregnancy was the result. The youth of the time, she declared, were "not using the good Brains that the Good Lord gave them."[1]

The role of the American mother, since the time of what historian Linda Kerber calls "Republican motherhood" in the early years of the nation, was to care for, protect, and educate her children.[2] It was the mother's responsibility to instill strong moral values within the family unit. During the early nineteenth century, American mothers formed church and other associations to insure they were using the most effective methods to rear their children to fear God and to lead pure lives.[3] As the century progressed, women began to enlarge their influence to the public realm, often banding together to publicly oppose behaviors that they believed threatened American morality. An example is the Women's Christian Temperance Union, which organized in 1874 over the concern that alcoholism had a deleterious effect upon families.[4] While historian D'Ann Campbell maintains that by 1940 the distinctive link between morality and gender roles had largely dissolved,[5] that was not the case for right-wing women; nor was that totally true for other women. During the third quarter of the twentieth century many mothers, all over the country, responded to the real or imagined threats against the lives or sensibilities of their offspring. Some considered the burden of saving their children from moral decay to be solely the responsibility of women. Blanche Winters, one of the few rightists who identified herself as a feminist, was convinced of this. In the early 1950s, Winters, who led the right-wing American Woman's Party, announced that "youth problems and juvenile delinquency [are] strictly women's business."[6]

After a steady decline in crime during the aftermath of World War II and through the 1950s, a dramatic rise in serious crime, including murder, rape, and auto theft took place during the mid-1960s.[7] This surge in criminal activity, combined with premarital sex and the use of mind-altering drugs among the nation's youth, loomed large during the 1960s and into the 1970s. Right-wing women, as well as many men and women whose ideologies could be found all along the political and social spectrums, shared anxieties over what they saw as changing moral values of America's young.[8] Yet the right-wing women examined here held ideas about the origins of youthful morality that differed from most of the mainstream and the political left. That is, many of them detected conspiracies behind the moral choices that large numbers of the younger generation were making. Thus, in regard to moral issues, these right-wing women put a great amount of emphasis upon youthful behavior and what the young were learning—particularly in school—about sex, religion, and patriotism. They viewed those three issues as major factors in determining the moral direction the nation would take in the future; thus, they felt it their duty to actively promote their versions of morality.

Sex Education

Sex education in the public schools had been the subject of debate since early in the twentieth century when moral reformers emphasized "social hygiene," seeking to eliminate prostitution and sexually transmitted diseases. During the first half of the century, however, controversy was usually minimal and often local. The first recorded attempt to introduce sex education in a citywide public school system occurred in Chicago in 1913. It was part of Progressive reformers' crusade against prostitution and venereal diseases and focused on teaching personal purity and convincing youths of the dangers of illicit sex. Despite its moralistic purpose, a great number of Chicagoans disapproved of the program, including the city's religious leaders, and the experiment with sex education in Chicago was short-lived.[9] During the 1920s, more schools began to introduce sex education into their curricula, again with the idea of teaching youth to resist sexual urges.[10]

Roman Catholic leaders were frequently behind the opposition to sex education, although there was other organized opposition as well.[11] Popular dissent over sex education grew during the 1960s, and it was during that decade that the topic rose on the agenda of right-wing women, as they rallied to keep "sex education" and "family life education" (terms they often used interchangeably) off school curricula. These women had an attitude similar to that of Howard Whitman, a writer on human affairs, who theorized that the rise in sexual activity among youth in the postwar period was due to youth lacking direction as to traditional standards of morality. He placed the responsibility of teaching morality in the hands of parents, contending that youth had a "natural urge" in addition to the sexual urge, which was the urge to be good. What youth needed was direction.[12] Both Whitman and rightist women believed in parental direction, not sex instruction in schools.

As in Chicago in 1913, from the 1910s through most of the 1950s, abstinence from sexual activity was at the core of sex education.[13] However, by the 1960s, as the reality of youth's participation in premarital sex set in, some progressives sought to use the classroom to provide students with broader knowledge about their sexuality. The reformers believed that among other positive results, such knowledge could help prevent students from experimenting with sex.

Rightist Frances Bartlett, whose activism on behalf of the education of youth dated back well over a decade, did not agree. In the summer of 1963 she jumped into the sex education discussion with a series of articles in her *FACTS in Education* newsletter. An article in her May-June issue asked the question, "'Modern' Morality: Is It Moral?" If instruction on sex was put in the hands of schoolteachers, her answer to the question was—at least in most instances—no. Bartlett believed that sex education was primarily the responsibility of the parents, who were probably just as capable at providing sex instruction as the "untrained, irresponsible, and often neurotic teacher." Bartlett claimed to not disapprove of "the scientific and objective approach" provided in classes such as biology, life science, and physical education, including sex hygiene in the latter course, but she found sex education per se inappropriate. She argued that too much was being taught too early, and it was being taught without "regard to the spiritual aspects of marriage and family life."[14] Morality, she maintained, was missing from the school curriculum.

In the July-August 1963 issue of *FACTS*, Bartlett challenged those who had been claiming that exposing children "to a vast knowledge of sex information at an early age is the surest way to avoid problems." There were, she wrote, no facts to support the advocates' thesis, and she claimed that sex education programs had backfired in many schools. In New York City, for example, "in one year, the schools had to excuse 1,500 pregnant girls under 15 years of age." She added that there was news of a variety of agencies, including some within the federal government, that were providing hundreds of millions of dollars in assistance to children and unwed mothers. As Bartlett saw it, such intervention was damaging to American society overall, writing, "society in its culture of indulgence bends over backwards to eliminate any sense of guilt or stigma of embarrassment to the girl who gets into trouble. And it is just this cover-up policy that [FBI Director] J. Edgar Hoover says is encouraging all forms of juvenile delinquency."[15]

Bartlett made clear her beliefs that government agencies were contributing to the problem of unwed motherhood becoming too easy and that, in the end, it was the taxpayer who was stuck with the bill.[16] In addition to its potential of being a burden on American taxpayers, unwed mothers threatened Bartlett's values, as well as those of other conservative women. By virtue of raising a child in a fatherless household, an unmarried mother would not be living a lifestyle and caring for her child in a manner that traditionalists deemed appropriate. Thus, this mother was corrupting the iconic image of motherhood. Many males, too, disapproved of unwed motherhood, but they came from the viewpoint of inherent male dominance within the family unit.

Long attentive to what students' textbooks taught about American history and patriotism, in the 1960s the Daughters of the American Revolution took interest in textbooks' teachings regarding sexuality. In 1964, the Alabama Society of the DAR found the officially adopted state textbook *Personal Adjustment, Marriage and Family Life* (1960), by Judson and Mary Landis, to be unsatisfactory for use in public schools. Referring to a page in the book that mentioned "the 'educated' mother" relaxing her muscles during childbirth, the DAR's textbook reviewers complained that such a subject should not be raised in the readings of sixteen- and seventeen-year-old high school students. "Chastity and morals should be taught in high schools," not "the mechanics of child delivery." The DAR considered such teachings as part of a trend toward dilution and destruction of the moral standards of young Americans and suggested that communists might be involved in yet another matter affecting youth. The women protested further that the book called for the elimination of the requirement of paternity information on birth certificates, arguing that "nothing in the Alabama educational process should be taught or tolerated to erase the importance of marriage before parenthood."[17]

The Sex Information and Education Council of the United States (SIECUS), founded in 1964, became the focus of numerous attacks from the right throughout the remaining years of the 1960s. Its founders believed that youth who were ignorant about sexual matters, or those who learned about sex in bits and pieces from the streets, were prone to suffer from a variety of social problems. To counter such problems, SIECUS created a comprehensive sexuality education program. It claimed to teach age-appropriate information to students from kindergarten through high school, with subjects ranging from anatomy, physiology, and human reproduction to masturbation and sexually transmitted diseases. Promoters of SIECUS contended that students would be less likely to be ashamed of their sexuality if they had greater knowledge of the subject. They also believed that their program could help prevent students from experimenting with sex, thus avoiding unwanted pregnancies and the spread of sexually transmitted diseases. The program recommended abstinence for youth, although it did provide information about contraception and abortion. Founders of SIECUS discarded the older ideas that stressed the teaching of morality, contending that sex educators should respect young peoples' right to make their own decisions.[18]

The right objected to SIECUS's effort to adapt lessons in sex education to stages of a child's life. Rightists considered it a form of progressive education, aimed at meeting children's needs as they develop from childhood to adolescence. Even the organization's name was problematic. Although SIECUS was a private organization, the inclusion of "United States" at the end of its name led many parents to believe it was a government agency.[19] For those believing in the conspiracy theory, here lay added evidence.

From its beginning, SIECUS had close ties to religious groups. One of the group's five founders, William Genné, was a minister with the National Council of Churches.[20] Since leaders of the National Council of Churches often took moderate to liberal stances on political issues, such as criticizing Senator Joseph McCarthy's "witch hunt" during the 1950s and supporting the United States' participation in the United Nations, rightists frequently linked the council to "communist conspiracies."[21] Thus, the National Council of Churches connection would not help SIECUS's relations with the right.

During the spring of 1964, what was touted as the first extensive sex education program in the United States was launched in Anaheim, California. A little more than four years later, in the fall of 1968, the Anaheim school board was facing angry parents who charged that the board was ignoring their pleas to investigate complaints about sexually explicit materials in junior high and high school textbooks. Local woman Arlene Steinmeyer wrote to the *Anaheim Bulletin* that citizens saw no indication that SIECUS had helped uplift either their children or their community. From what she observed, sex education had not diminished the problem of sexually transmitted diseases nor of babies born out of wedlock. Indeed, she claimed that those problems were on the increase.[22] A mother's reading of a "vividly detailed" account of sexual intercourse from a district-approved eighth-grade textbook, *Attaining Manhood*, reportedly drew "gasps, giggles, and exclamations of amazement from a capacity crowd" attending a school board meeting. Some parents called for the firing of Anaheim's sex education coordinator.[23]

Many parents objected to their not being allowed in classrooms during the sex education classes. Board members explained parental exclusion, stating they believed the presence of parents during such courses would be distracting.[24] One mother, who claimed that she had been complacent on the issue, noted that her eyes were opened when she learned that her fourteen-year-old daughter "had been instructed in all details in sexual intercourse by a teacher at her junior high in a MIXED [the mother's emphasis] class" of girls and boys. "Lack of communication may be MY generation's problem, but it won't belong to our kids! They practically shout sex every other word." She removed her daughter from the class.[25]

In 1968, following the implementation of sex education in San Francisco schools and its endorsement by radio station KCBS, Margaret Scott, publicity chairman for Citizens for Parental Rights, presented an opposing view. Similar to Frances Bartlett, she did not object to those courses on hygiene and biology. However, "family life education," she said, was not in the same category. Rather, she called the program "psychological indoctrination in adult sexuality" and insisted that the program should "remain 'extracurricular' for the children of those parents who request it specifically." As an example of disreputable people teaching sex education to their students, she mentioned a teacher in Flint, Michigan, who was rumored to have completely disrobed for her sex education class.[26] This allegation, which became widespread among those opposing sex education courses, was found to have been greatly exaggerated.[27] As evidence of the immorality of sex education programs, the anti–sex education crusaders had a stock set of stories that were repeated to audiences, stories that were either exaggerated or untrue, but were sure to lead parents to fear for the innocence of their children.

During the 1960s, the sex education controversy became another issue to interest Phoebe Courtney. She printed two articles on the subject in her June-July-August 1969 *Independent American*, including one by former Alabama governor George C. Wallace, who complained about teachers' lack of training, explicit material, and that moral and spiritual factors were never mentioned. The second article, a reprint from the *Houston Tribune*, reported that parents were "waking up" to what their children were being taught in their schools—"the whole gamut of raw sex without any instruction in right and wrong." As a result, parents were turning against the program.[28]

In addition to addressing the subject in her newspaper, Courtney wrote and published *The Sex Education Racket* (1969), a chapter-by-chapter compilation of reports attacking sex education and SIECUS in particular. While claiming to have been objective as she approached her research into the matter, she noted in her introduction that she omitted a large amount of the teaching materials presented to America's children because it was "too disgusting to be reprinted" in her book. Courtney believed it was her duty to inform parents and grandparents of what American youth were truly learning in school. One of her greatest concerns was her belief that students accepted everything they were taught in the schoolroom as fact.[29] Three years later, rightist Gloria Lentz wrote a book, similar to Courtney's, with the provocative title, *Raping Our Children: The Sex Education Scandal* (1972).

In Pasadena, the rightist Patriotic Network of Letter Writers circulated a lively document titled "Sexploitation" that sums up many of the attitudes that right-wing women shared regarding school-sponsored sex education. Author Violet Hansen described the issue on a personal basis, while idealizing the older generation's experiences and satirizing the new sex education. She wrote that when her generation was young, their visions for the future "were 'hung-up' with dream houses and hope-chests and honeymoons and white satin dresses, church weddings and cuddly babies and living happily ever after." But, she implied, modern sex education was destroying all of that: "According to the sex education 'experts' of this Age, my generation got all their sex education behind the barn. Our pig pen was behind the barn, so it is possible that I could have received an education much like that being promoted in our schools. However, I had no teacher to tell me that the sex life of a pig and that of my fellowmen was the same."[30]

Hansen emphasized her belief that since the older generation had no need for sex education in school, neither did the younger generation. She argued that since the introduction of formal sex education, loose morals, including premarital sex, were on the increase. Hansen did not believe that there was an unbridgeable generation gap, but asked, "Have girls really changed so much that they enjoy being pawed and fondled by someone who has studied the art of love-making in school, but has all the morality and affection of an alley-cat and all the glamour of a 'Driver-Education' student?" She did not believe that they had. Rather, she was blaming the new methods of sex education, along with restrictions against biblical instruction, for leading the younger generation toward moral destruction. In her conclusion, she made clear her ideological alliance with the far right, arguing that educators who participated in sex education were aiding Communists' attempts to take over the United States by destroying the morality, faith, patriotism, and family life of a whole generation of Americans.[31]

Although some rightist women joined male-led organizations, including the John Birch Society–sponsored MOTOREDE (Movement to Restore Decency) committees in their campaign for moral purity, vast numbers enlisted in women's groups.[32] In keeping with their traditional roles as supervisors of American morality, women led or were prominent in numerous organizations that fought against sex education in the public schools. While such groups as the DAR and Network of Patriotic Letter Writers addressed a variety of rightist causes, there were some groups that focused on morality and some that centered on sex education alone. One vociferous female-led group was named Mothers for Moral Stability (MOMS).[33] Both Rosa Vellella, president of Concerned Parents of Livingston (New Jersey), Inc., and Edith Winter, president of Parents Against Unconstitutional Sex Education earned praise from the right for their leadership in campaigns against sex education.[34]

On the issues of sex education in schools, the line dividing the right wing from nonrightist Americans was permeable, for many among the general population had similar concerns. This gave the right wing increased access to the general population. One question that parents from both the mainstream and the right frequently raised was whether teachers possessed the credentials to teach such subjects. How many teachers were trained in Freudian psychology? This was a particularly important question for the right since many of the course guides included Freud's theories, and since the right considered Freud's theories on the human sex drive to be immoral.[35] In their January-February 1969 newsletter, the Minute Women of the U.S.A. combined questions about teachers' intentions with religion in their arguments against sex education, referring to verses of the Bible to support arguments about unqualified teachers. An Education Code, dating from 1873, they found, was more in line with their thinking. It required teachers to endeavor "to impress upon the minds of the pupils the principles of morality, truth, justice and patriotism, and a true comprehension of the rights, duties and dignity of American citizenship." Students were to be taught "kindness toward domestic pets, humane treatment of living creatures . . . [and] to avoid idleness, profanity, and falsehood." Instruction in "manners and morals and the principles of a free government" was another requirement.[36]

The Minute Women were clinging to tradition as their guide for teaching morality to students. They believed that contemporary educators were using children either as guinea pigs or as what the Minute Women called "objects of a subversive manipulation." At the same time, they maintained that producers of textbooks, films, and teaching aids were reaping extensive financial rewards at the expense of American youth. As proof, they included in their newsletter both a copy of a *Wall Street Journal* report on profits that publishing firms were poised to make and a news report of parents complaining about their children suffering from insomnia and hysteria after taking part in "sensitivity training" in high school.[37] Thus, they brought up the idea of corporate greed, particularly as it is linked to intellectual enterprises. As they saw it, capitalists willingly joined leftward leaning intellectuals in fomenting conspiracy. On this issue, they broadened their attack to include certain aspects of large-scale capitalism, a position that conflicted with the libertarian strain of conservatives, who opposed regulation of corporate profits.

While many women spoke through their organizations, much protest came from the American grassroots. In June 1969, fifteen women from Vernon, Texas, petitioned the White House, saying they were "opposed to any SIECUS-type philosophies . . . having anything whatsoever to do with instruction of sex, directly or indirectly," in their public schools.[38] These women, although not members of an official organization, came together as a group of like-minded citizens to defend the rights of parents and the morals of Texas youth. Similarly, a group of thirteen women from Ferndale, Washington, petitioned President Nixon, proclaiming "SCHOOL-HOUSE PORNOGRAPHY CAN BE STOPPED!" They shared the rightist opinion that there were forces in the country that were determined to destroy America by undermining the morality of its youth and blamed those parents who gave their approval for school-sponsored sex education for enabling the country's destruction.[39]

The women also drew upon language and anticommunist influences of the Cold War, writing, "Little do they know that there is sinister national direction behind the scenes—with objectives tied to 'sensitivity training'—a process similar to North Korean brainwashing." As "proof" that sex education was urgent to the left, they reported that the "Anti-Defamation League has come out into the open—and is sending out *its paid agent* [the petitioners' emphasis] to speak against the opponents of SIECUS."[40] Thus, anti-Semitism, too, entered into their argument.

The Ferndale women voiced support for Wisconsin representative Henry Schadenberg's bill, H.R. 8976, which sought to prohibit the dispensing of federal funds for sex education. They wrote, "Sex cannot be properly taught, apart from God's Word. Sex is only proper for married couples, anything else is regarded as Adultery or Fornication, in God's Holy Commandments."[41] In this one petition, the Ferndale women raised the major fears of many among the right—attacks on fundamentalist religion, the decline of morality, and conspiracy. The right wing's understanding of the connection between God and nature had already been shaken by Darwin's theories of man and of changes in nature throughout the ages. Now the connection between God and humans was being challenged in a social sphere.

Not only the right but also other parents had concerns about the morals their children were learning in the classroom. Gwen Mote, a teacher from Lookeba, Oklahoma, wrote President Johnson with a plan for a course on "family living." Family living courses often offered instruction not only about sexuality but also about human relationships, marriage, and family. However, the right joined other fearful parents in focusing on the human sexuality aspect of the course. Mote believed that her course would mitigate the fears of many parents over what was actually being taught to teenagers and who was doing the teaching. Judging from her letter, Mote appears to have been politically and socially moderate, but concerned about how youth were being taught the facts of life. Mote wrote that she did not believe that all parents and students understood what was meant by a course in "family living." To solve that problem, she suggested that parents be given complete summaries of each unit of the family living course.[42]

Ideally, the courses would cover human relations, including "plain old everyday manners," and provide means by which young people could improve themselves mentally, socially, and physically. Whenever possible, parents should be encouraged to involve themselves in the program and set examples to their children through the passing on of basic values and standards. At the same time, Mote believed it important that teachers be well trained, writing that increasingly more classes were being given in American colleges to prepare teachers to teach such courses.[43] Mote sought to satisfy parents who desired that both their feelings and interests and those of the students received consideration. Her ideas addressed some of the concerns among the right, particularly Mote's encouragement of parental involvement. However, she failed to address anxieties regarding communist conspiracies to undermine the morals of American youth. She might have resolved that problem by involving persons who were highly regarded in right-wing circles in the course planning.

The push for sex education in schools seemed to be successful when SIECUS was initially launched, with almost half of the nation's schools adding sex education courses to their curricula by 1965. Yet by late 1969, at least fifteen states were considering legislation to cut back or to abolish the courses. Other states passed laws that permitted parents to decide whether they wanted their children to participate.[44] The outcry spurred by propaganda from the right, especially from rightist women, was an important factor in the turnabout. If they doubted the consequences of introducing controversial material to their children, many mothers were inclined to adopt the conservative point of view. Many mothers believed youth were having more than enough exposure to information concerning sex. They did not need more from the schools.[45] "Happenings," such as Woodstock in 1969, where young people openly participated in sexual intercourse, served as proof that youth need not look far to learn all there was to know about sex. As to rightist women's reactions, writer and social critic Philip Wylie was very close to the truth when he wrote, "Those multitudes who are currently broadcasting hysterical and infamous lies in an effort to stop simple sex education in our schools . . . are not going to take a kindly view of public sex education by exhibition."[46]

Sex education in schools was part of a much larger morality issue. Crime, drug use, premarital sex, and interracial relations were also on the minds of many mothers. Although mothers with varying political points of view feared what their children were being taught about sex in the classroom, women on the right had complaints that others usually did not have. It was not only anxiety over what their children were learning about sex but also the fact that it appeared to be one more instance of the state's intrusion into their families' lives. Other than the government—in the form of schoolteachers and administrators—there was really no tangible enemy to fight against over sex education.

For some, their concerns about sex education went beyond anxieties over what young people were being taught in the classroom. Many women anxious about the morals of youth in the 1960s did not appreciate the news, reaching the public early in 1964, of President Johnson inviting male guests to "skinny dip" in the White House pool.[47] Here was a prime example of a government leader taking American morality in the wrong direction. One mother, who found Johnson's behavior distasteful, wrote that she was sure that the United States' economy was sufficient to allow the government to spend enough money "to provide our guests with at least a tank type suit." Others wrote to express their "shock" when learning of the president's "'skinny dipping' parties," asking how they could teach their children modesty when the president was setting such a poor example.[48] That was not the only incident to attract complaints about immoral behavior on the part of the Johnson administration. News that government leaders in Washington were enjoying late-night parties, dancing the Watusi, and that one female guest had shown up at an event in a transparent dress also drew criticism.[49]

World War II and the social changes that it brought about in America also played a role in producing the moral problems that the right and many others were concerned with. As a Kentucky mother expressed it, the "children born during World War II and since are victims of circumstances." She explained with an example: "Both parents in most families have had to work to provide good homes, schools, clothes, and luxuries due to continued rise in living costs. Security, love, understanding, and wisdom have become obsolete in this era." Thus, she concluded, American youth were seeking and finding substitutes to take the place of these needs. This mother found it inevitable that youth were committing crimes, using drugs, and openly having premarital sex relations.[50]

One baby boomer who grew up in a conservative household in the university town of Gainesville, Florida, recalls that both fears for their daughter's safety and their religious beliefs influenced her parents' attitudes about higher education. She recalls that, during her youth, the University of Florida was "a very wild place to be," and her parents did not want her to go anywhere near the campus. Her parents' perception of the university, she said, was of drugs and people going around without clothes. Also, her parents were Pentecostal. Members of that faith did not approve of higher education, fearing that more education would expose youth to ideas that did not conform to Pentecostal teachings. Her parents were especially fearful that if she went to college, she would become connected to a fanatical group. "I was easily led, so I could have gotten myself into a lot of trouble," she admitted.[51]

While more rigid than most, this boomer's parents, like millions of others, recognized that young people absorbed messages emanating from their social environments. Young American youths' ideas on morality and sexuality came not only from sex education classes but also from their relationships with friends and from their observations of the world around them. Parents realized that when their son or daughter left the home, parental authority receded. Government and progressive educators, and such groups as sociologists and practical-minded medical people, approached these problems differently. They stressed practical needs and the belief that individuals, including young people when properly informed, were capable of making moral decisions and acting in a responsible fashion.

Despite the right's frantic attempts to destroy it, SIECUS did survive.[52] The right lost on most of its points, and sex education turned out to be less than earth-shattering in its effects, but in the 1960s the right was convinced that modern sex education posed a serious threat. The introduction of modern sex education, based on a more objective, present-centered view of what youth needed to know and do, threatened their understanding that Americans' sexual ideals should come from tradition. Tradition, the right claimed, had been the good and necessary framework upon which American society was built and developed over the generations. The right struggled to keep new and outside elements from threatening and potentially ruining this structure. The rapid increase in the number of baby boomers—which became the largest new generation in American history—and the sudden rise of communism to world power, with its overwhelming threat to tradition, made the issue of moral training crucial. If the baby boom generation was lost, and they passed on their new morality to succeeding generations, could the America the right wing knew ever be revived?

School Prayer

Prayer and the teaching of religion in public schools has long been a contentious issue in the United States. During the mid-nineteenth century, when the Roman Catholic population in the United States was growing at a great rate, many Catholics began to complain about the Protestant bias. At the same time, Protestants considered the schools to be an effective vehicle to transform the children of Catholic and Jewish immigrants into loyal Americans. Thus, Protestant prayers were included in the curricula of many public schools.[53] During the late 1940s and the 1950s, with the rise in juvenile delinquency, and amidst the fear of communism, many Americans looked to religion as a part of the solution to these problems. Indeed, as historian Elaine Tyler May points out, membership in churches and synagogues reached new heights during the postwar years, and churches and synagogues expanded their functions to include youth programs and social events.[54] While such programs might enhance opportunities to influence moral values of churchgoing youth, those desiring to reach young people who were not associated with established religions needed to use other means.

From playing a central role in the growth of the Second Great Awakening of the early nineteenth century to striving to achieve positions of authority within the nation's churches, women have long sought to influence the shape of American religion. Despite continued male dominance in most churches, by the 1820s, the role of teaching children about religion, both at home and in Sunday schools, was largely in the hands of women.[55] During the 1950s and 1960s, the school prayer issue offered women of the grassroots, including those on the right, the opportunity to exert their moral authority.

Most rightist women of the post–World War II era continued to consider religious education to be of major importance in the building of American character. For them, the teaching of religion went hand in hand with lessons about the greatness of the nation's founders. It was, they believed, a weapon in the fight against the rapidly increasing secularism, and especially the ever-present threat of the spread of atheistic communism. In their eyes, anyone who sought to weaken or eliminate religion from public education was part of the "conspiracy" to undermine American freedom as well as the moral fiber of America. Although most rightist women studied here were long on the alert for signs of a slackening of instruction in the values that they held dear, it was the Supreme Court's rulings against school prayer in 1962 and 1963 that inspired them to rally their grassroots forces. They were ready to fight to restore prayer to the schools.

The school prayer controversy reflects the right's uneasiness over social and political changes that were disrupting their "traditional America." Many of the same women and their organizations involved in the prayer crusade were active in campaigns against school desegregation, fluoridation, and modern education. The Supreme Court's ruling was yet another sign that their cherished values were crumbling. No longer were they secure in the belief that their vision for future generations would come to fruition. So forceful was the school prayer issue that it played a large role in the development of the Christian Right, a major movement by the end of the twentieth century.[56]

Signs of what was to come from the right after the court's decision on school prayer came in the 1950s. In 1956, six years before the rulings on prayer, the DAR passed a resolution calling for a revitalization of religious teaching in the classroom.[57] Three years later, the California chapter of the rightist group Pro America addressed the consequences of that state's new restrictions on the teaching of religion in its public schools. In its "School Affairs Report," Pro America noted that California attorney general Edmund G. Brown had ruled the distribution of Gideon Bibles throughout the public school system unconstitutional. Pro America happily noted, however, that Brown had stated that it would be "unthinkable" to leave lessons about California's early Catholic missions out of school curricula and that the state would not attempt to eliminate religious symbols found in art, European history, and elsewhere.[58]

Nevertheless, the Pro America women believed that students needed more emphasis on religion, particularly as it pertained to American tradition. Schoolchildren should be reminded, they wrote, "that we are, and were, a nation founded under God." As evidence, they pointed to historic American documents that mentioned God, including the foreword of the Mayflower Compact, George Washington's order to staff the armed forces with chaplains, and the motto "In God We Trust" on the nation's coins. They emphasized the need to "preserve" those facts, as they would guarantee that God be mentioned in the public schools.[59]

That the United States was founded as a Christian nation is an argument of long-standing among the Christian Right. So adamant are they in their belief in the importance of the Christian tradition in America, that they often interpret that tradition to be law. The founding documents and practices had been around for so long, and had such universal acceptance, that to right-wing women they took on the force of common law. Because of the clear and direct mention of God, the Creator, within such documents as the Declaration of Independence, the women attributed that law to God. In their many examples of founders' emphasis upon the importance of God in American life, the women of Pro America failed to mention that Thomas Jefferson and James Madison, leading advocates for public education, were also major promoters of the separation of church and state.

Any complacency the Pro America and other women on the Christian right might have been feeling following the California ruling was soon dashed. In 1962 and 1963, amid considerable controversy, the United States Supreme Court issued two decisions that rendered prayer in school to be unconstitutional: *Engel v. Vitale* (6–1) followed by the combined cases of *School District of Abington Township Pennsylvania v. Schempp* and *Murray v. Curlett* (8–1).[60] The former case involved the reading of a New York Board of Regents–sanctioned nondenominational prayer in the Herricks School District on Long Island. In *Engel v. Vitale*, the Supreme Court ruled that just because a prayer is nondenominational and voluntary, it does not follow that it does not contravene the Establishment Clause of the First Amendment.[61] The question before the Supreme Court in the second case centered on whether school officials in Pennsylvania and in Baltimore, Maryland, could require students to participate in daily devotions that often included listening to Bible verses. Madalyn Murray (later

Madalyn Mays Murray O'Hair), the plaintiff in the *Murray v. Curlett* case, was an outspoken crusader for atheism and was committed, she said, "to the destruction of God and the Church." She had also worked briefly for the Communist Party.[62] In the eyes of the right, Murray's atheism and ties to communism made her a perfect example of a person out to destroy America.

Since more than two-thirds of the states either permitted or required Bible reading in public school classrooms, the court's decisions created an uproar throughout the country. Over the next several years, not only the right, but millions of other Americans backed proposals in Congress for a constitutional amendment that would allow school prayer.[63] For many, and particularly for religious conservatives, the Supreme Court's decision marked a giant step in the direction of producing an atheistic America. Bette Pforr of Redwood City, California, was typical of many women, maintaining that the ruling signified that atheists and agnostics were at the point of running the government.[64] Opponents wasted little time before moving to restore prayer to the schools. Women from throughout the United States and from all walks of life responded to the call. If one atheist mother, Madalyn Mays Murray O'Hair, could take the matter before the Supreme Court, surely Christian mothers, working together and with God on their side, could mount a campaign that would overturn the court's ruling.[65]

The right-wing women's Network of Patriotic Letter Writers maintained that there was a problem in the United States due to "our national fervor to insure the unquestioned rights of minority dissenters." Although it conceded that minorities possessed the right to protest the desires of the majority, it denied that the majority should be forced to "abdicate its duty to maintain this nation as a Christian Fortress, bulwarked by religious faith."[66] These rightist women, as well as many other Americans, both Protestants and Catholics, considered the Supreme Court's prayer decisions to be contrary to the American right to freedom of religion. To them the Court was favoring atheists at the expense of Christians.[67]

In 1963, Phoebe Courtney added the school prayer issue to her other right-wing causes when she addressed the issue in her pamphlet, "Let Our Children Pray!" She began with the familiar claim that America was founded as a Christian nation and then addressed other arguments popular among the right. She declared that the prayer ban violated the First

Amendment and asserted that the Supreme Court was procommunist and was discriminating against children. As evidence, she noted that when adults were involved—as in courts, where witnesses took oaths ending with the words "so help me God"—the Supreme Court had no problem with invoking God's name. Courtney reasoned that children were targeted because Communist leaders such as Vladimir Lenin and Nikita Khrushchev recognized that their minds were malleable. Children could easily be led to reject God and accept atheism and communism, and thus weaken "the national determination to withstand and defeat the atheistic International Communist Conspiracy."[68]

The Network of Patriotic Letter Writers took the position that school prayer did not challenge the nation's founders' intent to keep church and state separate. They maintained that few Americans would object to the "established principle of the complete separation of Church and State," because the "founding fathers" were determined that there be no state church, "no all-powerful ecclesiastical sword of Damocles suspended over the American people." Thus, unlike many nations of the world, the United States had no state church. Nevertheless, the Network of Patriotic Letter Writers insisted that the founding fathers were "deeply reverent, each in his own manner, and each according to the faith of his fathers" and described moments when George Washington and Abraham Lincoln turned to prayer.[69]

The Daughters of the American Revolution agreed with such sentiments. In addition, they argued that the school prayer issue involved states' rights, which the organization considered a founding principle of American political order. Thus, the organization sought to counter what it believed was the federal government's intrusion into those rights. In April 1962, it resolved to "exercise every effort for the retention of the Constitutional right of the States to control local educational requirements, and steadfastly oppose any effort by the courts, under the guise of enforcing the First Amendment, to suppress recognition of a reverence for God in our public schools." At the same time, the DAR stressed that American schoolchildren must be taught "to reverence God and His teachings during the formative period of their lives."[70]

Not only women's patriotic organizations but also individual women from grassroots America manifested their dismay over the Supreme Court's ruling on school prayer. While their expressions of anguish over the ruling shared similarities, their arguments varied. Some stressed the points popular with the right, while others centered more on their own personal experiences. Veronica Cassidy of Brooklyn, New York, found the decision "unbelievably shocking," writing that "it denies our American heritage."[71] Upon reading that leaders of government, business, and labor were praying at what was called a "Presidential Prayer Breakfast," one woman asked President Johnson why her children could not be afforded the same privilege in their public school. Considering the world situation, she believed that they needed to pray as much as the president did.[72] Mabel Hanlen of Marietta, Pennsylvania, pleaded with President Johnson to restore the Bible and the recitation of the Lord's Prayer in schools. Dealing with the recent loss of a brother-in-law and with the everyday challenges connected with the raising of a retarded son, she found comfort in her religious beliefs and thought that what was helpful for her would be of great value to the nation.[73] For these women, as it was for many, the issue was a personal one. The religious tradition was a part of the foundation upon which they raised their families.

For many rightist Christians, including the Network of Patriotic Letter Writers, the loss of prayer in schools was directly related to a decline in moral values. Leaders pointed to FBI director J. Edgar Hoover's multiple warnings about the "erosion of moral values among the youth of America" and the high crime rate among those under eighteen years of age as evidence that young Americans needed direction. They considered the Supreme Court decision as an "attempt to isolate children from the moral truths which are a part of every religion." Referring to the recent spread of communism in Eastern Europe, Asia, and elsewhere, they added, "We are passing through an era in which a Godless conspiracy against the rights of man has seized control of half a world."[74]

From all over the country, women wrote to express their displeasure. Helen Thornton, a Michigan housewife and mother of four, was one of many who considered the elimination of school prayer to be further evidence of communist infiltration into American institutions. Not only was prayer in school being abolished but also scientists were questioning Christian doctrine. In addition to her fears about what the American government and the Supreme Court were doing, Thornton shared the view of many on the right who saw scientists as contributors to the destruction of the moral order. Since the late nineteenth century, Christian fundamentalists in America had been voicing concern that science was replacing faith. Thornton found the school prayer situation appalling. "What are we leaving the coming generation to believe in?" she asked. "Frankly, I'm fast getting to the point where I regret ever bringing my children into the world."[75]

Considering it an obligation connected with their roles as guardians of moral values, many women took on leadership roles in the prayer crusade. Evelyn Wyatt, director of the "world wide" ministry Wings of Healing, held an American Heritage Rally to show support for "restoring the privilege of prayer and Bible reading" in the nation's public schools.[76] In October 1964, former screen star Mary Pickford, cochairman of Project Prayer, announced a rally to be held in Los Angeles to gain public support for an amendment to the Constitution that would allow for voluntary prayer in schools.[77] Project Prayer, backed by dozens of celebrity members and financial supporters, also held several petition drives. Among Project Prayer's members were such rightist film stars as John Wayne, Ronald Reagan, and Ginger Rogers.[78]

Although few women were church or political leaders during the 1960s, they played prominent roles in the movement to return prayer to the schools. Women-only organizations flourished, but women also worked effectively alongside men. In 1966, We, The People, a national conservative organization based in Phoenix, Arizona, that included both men and women, actively supported Illinois senator Everett Dirksen's proposal for a school prayer amendment. Paula Sherrod, who chaired the Yarnall, Arizona, branch, announced that in a local telephone poll, people voted seventy-two to three in favor of the amendment. Five others said they had no opinion.[79]

If the telephone poll was similar to the written form, it was not scientific. The poll's wording was biased in favor of school prayer, which would have skewed the results. For instance, on the written form, pollsters asked for opinions on Dirksen's wish that Congress "pass an amendment to the Constitution to allow voluntary prayer in our public schools—despite the Supreme Court Ruling." The statement continued, "But powerful pressure groups are working to keep all mention of God, the Bible, and even voluntary prayer out of our schools. They are opposing majority rule." Five questions on the issue, requiring "Yes" or "No" answers, followed.[80] We, The People members were encouraged to circulate the poll among their

friends, associates, and church members, which would also have contributed to the skewing of the results. Overall, headquarters reported that 97
percent of those polled favored prayer in schools, with an equal percentage believing that children should be taught that God was the source of
our rights, "as stated in the Declaration of Independence."[81]

Despite the apparent bias in We, The People's polling, evidence indi-
cates that the majority of Americans were unhappy with the Supreme
Court's rulings on school prayer. A Gallup poll, taken shortly after the
Engel decision, revealed that 85 percent of Americans disapproved of the
Supreme Court's ruling. Historian Bruce J. Dierenfield, in his study of the
court's decisions on school prayer, found that, of all religious organizations, the Roman Catholic Church was the most outspoken against the
ruling. He found that many mainline Protestant organizations and leaders supported the ruling and that most Jewish organizations stated their
approval. On Long Island (where the Engel case had originated) the local branch of the generally mainstream General Federation of Women's
Clubs, in an almost unanimous vote, resolved to support a constitutional
amendment that would permit voluntary nonsectarian devotions in the
public schools. That branch of the GFWC had taken a conservative position in the past on the debate over fluoridation.[82] The prevalence of those
opposing the Engel decision showed that lines were somewhat fuzzy as to
the positions of the right wing and those who were more socially and politically moderate. However, as with other issues of the time, the far right
sensed a plot afoot to undermine American values and institutions.

As the years passed, and the issue continued to be debated, the right
wing made up a large proportion of those who carried on with the fight
for a constitutional amendment. Mrs. Ben Ruhlin of Cuyahoga Falls, Ohio,
emerged as a heroine among those who persisted in the campaign. During the late 1960s and early 1970s, Ruhlin, a Protestant and the mother
of three, led a two-and-one-half-year crusade to amend the Constitution.
She later recalled that her son, Benjamin, then fourteen years old, inspired
her to action. Arriving home from school one day, he asked her why people
parked God outside of school. After she and Benjamin discussed the issue
of separation of church and state, and after he raised the point that both
houses of Congress opened their sessions with prayer, Ruhlin promised
her son that she would do something about it.[83]

Ruhlin kept her promise, founding the National Prayer Group, and pushing for a constitutional amendment that would permit school prayer. When House Judicial Committee chairman Emanuel Celler, a New York Democrat, blocked the proposed amendment's release for a full House vote, Ruhlin led thirty female volunteers in a campaign to influence House members to sign a petition to discharge the matter from committee and send it to the floor. Six months after the drive began, Ruhlin's Prayer Campaign Committee had the required 218 signatures. They did not accomplish the task alone, but had the assistance of Ohio Representative Chalmers Wylie and several other legislators. However, many of those involved in the effort gave Ruhlin most of the credit. Ruhlin declined such recognition, stating that it was the people who won. She had a lot of help, she said, from those who telephoned congressmen, wrote letters, and spread word about the campaign.[84]

The scores of failed efforts to pass an amendment supportive of school prayer frustrated the amendment's supporters. It was one of several issues that a group of more than thirty women believed Congress was mishandling. They wrote President Johnson in 1967 that the United States was "founded on a religious foundation which we seem to have thrown to the wind because one woman didn't want her son to pray." The women complained that instead of addressing important issues like racial unrest, draft card burners, and school prayer, Congress was discussing making changes to dates of national holidays so that people could have more three-day weekends.[85]

Some on the right blamed President Johnson for the trend away from religiosity, believing that he was showing favoritism to Catholic, Jewish, and left-wing Protestant clergy, while discriminating against fundamentalist clerics. Several women took exception to a resolution of the largely Democratic Pennsylvania General-Assembly that labeled far rightist Reverend Carl McIntire a danger to the country. Since the end of World War II, Christian fundamentalist McIntire had zealously preached about the threats of communism, often declaring that mainline churches, and particularly the National Council of Churches, were under the influence of communists. During the 1950s and 1960s, he joined other rightists in opposing the civil rights movement and fluoridation in public water systems. During the 1960s, McIntire was at the height of his fame.[86] The women pointed out that the General-Assembly's censure was a violation of religious freedom. A woman from St. Cloud, Minnesota, saw in the incident evidence of a "trend of intolerance in our country toward those termed fundamentalists, conservatives, 'right wingers' and extremists." Another woman inquired, "Haven't we had enough young people charging 'God is Dead,' without persecuting Christian American people [meaning Reverend McIntire] who believes that 'God is living?'"[87]

Many women hoped that if school prayer could not be restored to the schools, other ways might be found to instill religion and strong moral values into young Americans. Some offered their ideas to the president. Although she did not address the school prayer issue per se, Emma Timerman, a retired rural schoolteacher, wanted religion to retain a strong presence in schools. Worried about the decline in morality among youth, in 1965, she sent a plea to the White House that children be compelled to participate in a character-building program in their schools. She maintained, "If children get a purpose in life to make the world better by their influence and see how to do it, I'm sure that there will be less and less . . . crime. Furthermore, no book or library book that even suggests religion as a myth should be allowed in school libraries."[88] A North Carolina woman, who worked as a buyer for children's clothing and also was a youth counselor and Sunday school teacher, telegraphed the White House in 1966, to say that she had a plan for a prayer room in every shopping center in the United States.[89]

Some women expected President Johnson to become a righteous role model for Americans. Mrs. Margaret Blake of Georgia chastised Johnson for not referring to Jesus Christ when offering aid to the needy. "I have heard you say, 'I pray thus and so.' That is as far as I have heard you go." At the same time, she registered her complaint that prayer was no longer a part of the public school curriculum.[90] Marjorie Maloy, a mother and minister's wife from Hamden, Ohio, asked the president to seek national repentance. She was confident that if the American people returned to God, many of the country's problems would be solved. The Pilgrims "prayed, believed, had faith, and it was done. . . . Our Nation was always a Christian Nation. Let's get back that way."[91]

President Johnson did receive several letters from women who supported the separation of church and state; however, few called upon the separation of church and state line of reasoning to express agreement with the Supreme Court's decision on school prayer. Rather, many of the women who advocated separation were protesting federal aid to Catholic schools under the Economic Opportunity Act, or "anti-poverty crusade," of 1964.[92] As taxpayers, they did not want to help finance parochial schools.

Because moral issues were very important to women, and to mothers in particular,[93] the school prayer issue sometimes found women of varying religious and political backgrounds taking similar stands on the matter. The issue gave women, who mostly held subordinate roles in the realms of church and politics, an opportunity to step out of the shadows to influence public policy, and many responded to it. Yet the far right, with its continuing charge of government, liberal, and communist conspiracy, could clearly be singled out from the crowd. Although it was voicing fears and beliefs that, at times, much larger numbers of Americans shared, the world was changing. The majority of Americans, including more moderate conservatives, accepted that change existed and tried to influence the direction it was taking. The far right resisted change, seeking to turn back the clock. As years passed, and the New Right replaced the old, there was some hope among the right that Congress might yet pass a school prayer amendment. The ruling may have lost its political relevance, but there continues to be the unresolved issue of what influence, if any, should personal and group morality have in American political, economic, and social life.

Patriotism

"In recent years I've become increasingly aware that Americans have lost Americanism," wrote a middle-aged Pennsylvania woman in 1967. "No one sings the National Anthem at sports events or salutes the flag when it passes at a parade; and when another human being needs aid, we stand around and look."[94] This woman was not alone in her perceptions. Many among the younger generation were also concerned. In 1967, a high school student from Spencerville, Indiana, wrote President Johnson that "this country has a lack of patriotism." She noticed that at high school basketball games few people bothered to sing the "Star Spangled Banner" and men did not remove their hats when the flag passed by in a parade. She observed that no one seemed to care about the freedom that the national anthem and flag symbolized.[95]

During the 1960s, the seeming disappearance of patriotism in America emerged as a significant concern among adult rightist women; and, as they entered their teenage years, a number of baby boomers also expressed alarm over the direction the nation seemed to be taking. Representatives of both generations of Americans sought ways to inspire the young to focus greater attention upon their allegiance to their country and all that it stood for. In the process, rightist women strove to guide young people to join them in the fight against those who were supposedly dedicated to destroying the America the women so revered.

As early as 1955, right-wing activist Ida Darden was issuing warnings that conservative values were in danger of becoming extinct in America. The issue came up after the University of Texas's student newspaper, the *Daily Texan*, denounced her *Southern Conservative* as a "reactionary" paper. Concluding that the editors were "poor little brain-washed, deluded and mind-controlled youngsters," Darden blamed their professors. She found it a shame that "the majority of university students today have never had a ghost of a chance to think for themselves, arrive at sound and fundamental conclusions or to acquire the faintest understanding of the basic principles on which the economy and governing processes of their country are founded." Much of the problem lay in the fact that the curriculum included "few subjects dealing with Americanism, and the history and traditions of the Republic [were] as strange to them as the philosophy of the Taoists or the priestly rituals of the Tibetan lamas." Darden was particularly fearful that many students of these universities would themselves become educators and begin to "perpetuate the vicious circle by infiltrating the immature minds of another generation of students with Marxist theories."[96]

To defend America from such grim prospects, the right sought to create conservative leaders for the future. A major move in that direction occurred in September 1960, with the founding of Young Americans for Freedom (YAF). The group's first meeting, which came to be known as the Sharon Conference, was held in the Sharon, Connecticut, home of rightist William F. Buckley Jr., a leading YAF supporter. At least initially, most right-wing women looked upon YAF with favor. The group's beginnings were part of an effort of conservatives within the Republican Party to develop a new core of leaders, capture control of the party, and take it in a rightward direction, a sentiment with which most rightist women agreed. Having "Young" in the organization's title was appropriate, for while the majority of YAF activists joined the organization during their college years, a large minority enlisted during high school. What also would have appealed to the women was that from the time of the organization's founding, YAF members indicated a willingness to accept advice and assistance from the older generation.[97] This proved to be true for other young rightists and was consistent with their political philosophy, which was based upon their respect for the past.[98]

Lucille Cardin Crain, with her long-standing interest in youth, as well as her association with the Buckley family, was invited to the Sharon Conference. In August 1960, just prior to the event, she was designated one of the "120 outstanding youth leaders across the Nation—known to be active and influential Conservatives." It is not known whether she accepted the invitation.[99] Her name was not listed on the National Advisory Board for the group, although author Taylor Caldwell, former Communist Bella Dodd, and radio commentator Irene Corbally Kuhn were.[100] In March 1961, at its "Freedom Rally" in New York, Caldwell was among those receiving awards from the YAF, honoring their support for conservative causes.[101]

The formation of the YAF was a positive initial step for rightists desiring to influence youth. Rebecca E. Klatch, in her study of YAF and SDS activists, found that the older generation often influenced the youths' decisions to join those organizations. Relatives, family friends, and activists within the community frequently served as role models. For example, one YAF member recalled that her father's stepmother, a devout anticommunist, taught her about the dangers of communism, inspiring the young woman to involve herself in politics.[102] Editors of the YAF magazine, the New Guard, displayed an awareness of parental influence on their offspring's politics when, in September 1965, they printed an article about "second-generation radicals." "The Red Diaper Babies Grow Up" focused upon the left wing, reporting that many of the radicals of the 1960s were children of American leftists of the 1940s.[103] Both the right and the left passed at least some of their political views on to their children.

Throughout the 1960s, emphasis upon educating the young to adopt a rightist outlook remained an important part of right-wing women's agendas. On the West Coast, Mrs. Leslie Fleming, the wife of Oregon's state coordinator of the John Birch Society, sought to do her part to lead students in a rightist direction. In 1961, she established the Freedom Forum Book Store in downtown Eugene, near the University of Oregon, explaining that her store would provide people with "the responsible libertarian materials that are so hard to obtain." It would give students ammunition if they wished to fight the "communist conspiracy." Meanwhile, she was giving evidence as to just where her political convictions lay by charging that the university's president, Arthur S. Flemming, a Republican whom Franklin Roosevelt had appointed to the Civil Service Commission in 1939, was responsible for putting known communists in Civil Service jobs.[104] Just how popular the bookstore became, in a region usually associated with liberalism rather than conservatism, is not known.

It was not only the influence of liberal educators that disturbed rightist women. Some considered the media to be playing an equally important role in shaping the minds of youth. In the mid-1960s, Susan Vance, a native Californian, the mother of a teenage daughter, and a self-described Libertarian, wrote *Youth on a Pendulum*, in which she warned of the susceptibility of youth to brainwashing by both the media and their schools. A flyer advertising her book described how Vance proved that young people were "being led to believe that Americanism and patriotism are outmoded words. Instead of pride in Capitalism, they are being taught that Socialism under such names as the New Deal, Modern Republicanism, and the New Frontier is the only answer." It warned that along with young people becoming "convinced that the UN, disarmament, summit meetings, and foreign aid are the keys to survival," some were even mouthing "the disgusting phrase, 'Better Red than dead.'" Through *Youth on a Pendulum*, Vance intended to open the public's eyes to the problem. The book was aimed at the youth themselves, particularly high school and college students, but was also designed to be useful for "inarticulate parents."[105]

Scholars of right-wing politics have found that southern California had a larger than average conservative population during the 1950s through 1970s.[106] Studying the right wing in Orange County, historian Lisa McGirr found that the prevalence of residents aligning with the right was due to the combination of several factors. Prior to World War II, many of the county's residents had long traditions of conservative values. Then, in the postwar years, there was an economic boom in the region, at which time businesses and entrepreneurs flourished and tended to join the Republican Party.[107] Historian James Gregory, in his study of the migration of the "Okies" to California from the southern plains Dust Bowl during the 1930s, and historian Darren Dochuk, in his examination of the rise of evangelical conservatism, point out that millions of southerners moved to the Golden State between 1930 and 1970.[108] Thus, many of the people attracted to Los Angeles, San Bernardino, and Orange counties came from areas that held deep religious, moral, and nationalistic values. And, as Mc-Girr points out, they enhanced the rightist tendencies already present in those areas.[109]

Some of the Southern California Republican women's clubs, including the East Pasadena-Sierra Madre Republican Women's Club and the Arcadia Republican Women's Club, were among those that contemporary investigators deemed part of the far right.[110] Anticommunism was a major focus of the two groups, with both frequently hosting lectures by persons who spoke on communist conspiracies. Often the speakers were male, such as Lieutenant Gordon Browning of the Los Angeles Police Department, who was described in the *Arcadia Tribune* as "an authority on communism."[111] Another was Dr. William E. Fort Jr., director of the Americanism Educational League at Knott's Berry Farm, the California theme park owned by rightist Walter Knott. In a speech before the Arcadia women in June 1964, Fort said that while most teachers and educators were upright and dedicated to their profession, there were those who were among the "elite" of the Communist Party and were following orders to subvert students. Fort claimed that these party faithful were undermining the morality of America's youth by destroying both their faith in God and their respect for their parents. Warning that time to save the country was running out, he urged Republican women to "adopt the tactics of Paul Revere and Joan of Arc and point out the true spiritual values on which our country was founded."[112]

The president of the Arcadia [California] Republican Women's Club was already taking action to direct young people away from any leftist ideas that they might encounter in their schools. In the June 1964 club bulletin, President Mrs. E. C. Rhodes announced that in an effort to combat "the Socialist trend of today," she was proposing the creation of a High School Republican Club. She noted that "these students are the citizens and voters of tomorrow," and she wanted the older women of the Arcadia Republican Women's Club to sponsor them, assist, and guide them. The club did launch the high school group and held a variety of events for them.[113]

The Los Angeles chapter of the Women's Division of Freedom's Foundation at Valley Forge invited a military officer who defected from the

Soviet Union to speak to members and guests. Captain Nicholas Arta-manov urged parents to teach children not only about freedom but also about protecting it. "Women," he said, "are a strong force in this country. They can do more with children than men."[114] Over and over, both rightist women and men emphasized the importance of women's influence over the youth of America. Women, they believed, and most particularly moth-ers, were the first line of defense when it came to saving America from outside threats.

In the January 1965 issue of *American Spirit*, editor Sarah Watson Em-ery presented a structured outline of what the right was fighting. She warned that identical programs of subversion were occurring in both public and private institutions of higher education throughout America and listed a step-by-step process that such subversive groups used to en-tice a young person to the communist point of view. The first step was to "'alienate' young people from family ties, religious faith, moral ideals, and national loyalty," because such estrangement softens young intellectuals into joining the "'disaffiliates,' the 'beats.'" From there, the communist sympathizer exploits the youth's natural curiosities about sex and drugs. "Once seduced to this point," she warned, "his alienation from conven-tional society is usually complete."[115]

After becoming a "Beat," the young person goes on to join "the new community," which Emery described as either the Communist Party or one of its fronts. At that point the new recruit is alienated from "the God of his fathers, from the human decency and morality of everyday Ameri-can society at its best," and becomes committed to a new credo with a special lingo. "He will tell you that American society is so diseased that it deserves to die." He will also call for a new kind of religion, one that would replace traditional Christianity. Instead of Christianity, the "young convert will borrow the terminology of the Communist existentialist—'integrity,' 'guilt,' 'choice,' 'death'; but with a new meaning." Emery pre-dicted extreme consequences, writing, "For the Communist existentialist 'integrity' is shown in performing one's duty as a Communist—killing one's father, if the Party orders." During summer breaks from college and after graduation, the youth might "go underground" to work in new lo-cales and take part in demonstrations aimed at disturbing the peace so as to interfere with "the normal course of justice."[116]

Emery maintained that no matter that the youth once had ambitions to be a physician, a priest, a businessman, or lawyer, the son or daughter would likely return home with plans for a new career. She believed that careers in philosophy, psychology, sociology, history, political science, and religion were those most attractive to young Communists, for these subjects were the most important for molding minds. Parents, Emery predicted, would no longer recognize their children, for they will be merely cogs "in the relentless machinery of the Communist Revolution."[117] Her prognosis was in many ways similar to that of novelist Taylor Caldwell in *The Devil's Advocate*, which showed dire consequences once the Americans lost their connection with the conservative tradition. Both women's predictions could have powerful effect because they express highly organized versions of man's descent into a hell-like environment. Emery's structure is very clear, detailing how the youth might pass downward from step to step, until reaching the very depths. The most sinister element at the bottom is communism—or the devil.

Joyce Zuck, president of the East Pasadena-Sierra Madre Republican Women's Club, believed that the older generation of women, if they acted quickly, could still have an influence upon America's youth. In March 1965, she railed against the student demonstrations at the University of California at Berkeley, asking that members of her club "push for the Board of Regents at Cal to clean up the so-called 'free speech movement.'" She also called for the expulsion of students who were "responsible for these reprehensible actions on campus." Mediation was not the answer, she declared. It was "time for action."[118] She did not dislike young people, but wanted them to show their patriotism and to adopt conservative views. As a way to achieve those objectives, Zuck's group sponsored a Teen Republican Club, the Pasadena Young Republicans.[119] Historian Mary C. Brennan points out that it was at about this time that the Republican National Committee was exploiting the Young Republicans, the College Republicans, and the Teenage Republicans in its attempts to rebuild the party after the failed Goldwater presidential campaign.[120] Zuck was among the rightist women revealing a willingness to help out.

So many cultural changes were occurring during the 1960s that many women with traditional values were feeling overwhelmed. Among them were the editors of *American Spirit* magazine, based in Lakeland, Florida. In the spring of 1965, these right-wing women were discouraged because they believed the country was becoming increasingly liberal. As noted in chapter 3, racial integration was one of their concerns; the lack of patriotism and leftist influences were others. The women noted that while they were dedicated to the American tradition, they were starting to wonder if other Americans "will make every effort to 'turn the tide' which seeks to engulf us." In particular, they wrote, "We wonder if the American woman cherishes her independence and her liberty. We wonder if she will insist on preserving for her children the heritage of a FREE AMERICA."[121]

Two news items appearing in *American Spirit* that month contributed to their anxiety. One reported on "Communist folk singer" Pete Seeger's scheduled appearance before the youth organization of the Lutheran Church, Missouri Synod (one of the more conservative branches of the Lutheran Church). The other item told of students donating to a fund to bring civil rights leader Martin Luther King Jr., to the historically Lutheran Valparaiso University.[122] It was unsettling to these women that Lutheran youth, with their Christian backgrounds, would willingly listen to such radicals as Seeger and King.

While numerous American parents worried about their children listening to rock 'n' roll music that might have pornographic lyrics—such as in the case of The Kingsmen's "Louie Louie" (1963), with its unintelligible words[123]—rightist women appeared more concerned about communist influences within the music scene. Music is often a major factor in defining a generation, and actions of the older generation of right-wing women indicate that they recognized this. As early as the 1950s, some alarmists had branded teenagers' music another tool in a conspiracy to ruin the morals of the upcoming generation.[124]

The popularity of folk music raised anxiety among the right, particularly due to the antiestablishment views of many songwriters. The Network of Patriotic Letter Writers circulated a document titled "Folk Songs Push Communist Line," which included articles written by conservatives who found the lyrics of some popular folk songs disturbing. Rightist Lawrence Cott, in his article, "Subversion by Hootenanny Is Revealed as No Myth," objected to Pete Seeger's song "Who Killed Norma Jean?" (1962) (that is, Marilyn Monroe) because the lyrics in the song answered the question—American society killed her. From the lyrics of the song came the interpretation that it was the "demanding public, harassing press, greedy agents and impresarios" who killed her. Seeger's "Who Killed Davey Moore?" (1963) gave a similar answer.[125]

Also included in the Patriotic Letter Writers' document was a reprint of Edith Kermit Roosevelt's article "Mass Media Subversion," originally written for the January 9, 1963, issue of the *Freedom Press*. Roosevelt, granddaughter of President Theodore Roosevelt, argued that the American mass media was unwittingly transmitting communist propaganda. An example was a songbook, *The Fireside Book of Folk Music*, which she claimed was "used in schools throughout this country." She noted that the book contained the song "Moscow," which glorified "dear Moscow's land" and also included the battle hymn sung by "American communists who fought for Spain in the Abraham Lincoln Brigade," and "the Red Chinese Workers song." Also objectionable to Roosevelt was a picture in the songbook "of an American soldier, unshaven, arm in arm with a Nazi and a British soldier, singing the song of the German prostitute, 'Lili Marlene.'" She found this particularly offensive because she believed there was a significant contrast between that picture and the "vibrant, heroic picture given of the communist military" in the book. Then there were songs that spoke of loose morals and one with lyrics that glorified a labor organizer. As far as Roosevelt was concerned, this songbook and similar materials had no place in the schools.[126] Young people, she and other rightists believed, were too easily led astray.

Rightist women worried that youth were hearing the wrong messages from many sources and did whatever they could to fight that trend. In July 1967, twenty-seven members of the executive board of the Arcadia Republican Women's Club wrote the president of the Pasadena Junior College board of trustees, expressing regret over the governing board's newly adopted policy of allowing controversial speakers to address students. They complained that some recent speakers included an admitted communist, a draft counselor who offered information on how to avoid conscription, and an educator who used vulgar language. Such speakers "poison the minds of our young people, and even though attendance at such speeches is not compulsory, young people will attend them out of curiosity and are bound to be influenced to some degree." The women charged that by providing a platform for these speakers, the board of trustees gave them credence and an opportunity to acquire more disciples.[127]

Some familiar rightist groups, including Pro America, focused upon directly influencing baby boomers to their point of view and became involved in a variety of projects designed to make the youth of America better citizens. In California, Mrs. D. J. Geary, president of Foothill Towns Unit, Pro America, gave a lecture on subversion in television and the motion picture industry. A Pro America branch in the Los Angeles area launched its 1967–1968 season with an informal dinner for members, guests, and families. Instead of its usual gathering of adults, the night's agenda "was designed with teenagers in mind" and included the showing of a film entitled *The Hippies*, which portrayed an unflattering depiction of the hippie lifestyle. A lieutenant from the Los Angeles Police Department was slated as the guest speaker.[128]

Although right-wing women at first welcomed the YAF as a bulwark against the rise of leftist youth, as time passed, concern developed among some right-wing women that the YAF might not be conservative enough. In September 1968, Mary Erb, a right-wing activist and a longtime friend and correspondent of Lucille Cardin Crain, expressed distress over a statement made on the radio by a young man who was introduced as a YAF member. Just returned from Czechoslovakia, he apparently mentioned that the YAF was planning to send materials to the young people there. Among the materials to be sent were recordings by Pete Seeger, Joan Baez, and Bob Dylan. Erb wrote, "As you know, all of these are supporting the Communist plan to use their 'beat of the jungle' music to help in the destruction of the standards and morals of our youth." In addition, she heard over the radio that a YAF member intensely and bitterly criticized the action of the Chicago police during the Democratic Convention. "What's happened to the YAF?" Erb asked.[129]

Helen M. Peters, who led the far right organization Defenders of the USA Republic, went even farther than Erb in her criticism of the YAF, calling it a "Red Front" group. She warned that the youth of America believed the YAF to be a patriotic organization and thus were unaware that, by joining the YAF, they were "working for the overthrow of the government of the United States." William F. Buckley Jr., she maintained, only posed as a conservative. Her charge was largely based upon a report of Buckley's support for such treaty organizations as NATO and SEATO in the fight against the spread of communism. Like Erb, and most right-wing women leaders, Peters vehemently opposed the idea of the United States entering into any international alliances.[130]

These traditionalist rightist women had cause for concern about the YAF. From the time of the Sharon Conference, there existed a libertarian strain within the organization, so much so that by the late 1960s and early 1970s there was a growing rift between libertarians and traditionalists. Controversy surrounding the Vietnam War was a catalyst for the heightening of tension between the two factions. Throughout the 1960s the organization officially supported the war. Some members, particularly those who feared the spread of communism, said they chose to join the YAF because of its pro-war position. Others, mostly libertarians, joined despite the organization's official stance, as many of them considered the war both illegal and immoral. At a convention of the California YAF in 1969, one self-declared Libertarian member set fire to his draft card. Although he was subsequently expelled from the organization, his action revealed the measures some members would take in order to express their dissatisfaction with the YAF's official position on the war. Also opposing the war was a minority faction of YAFers who adopted an Ayn Rand style of "objectivist" libertarianism and its ethic of self-sufficiency and individual achievement. These young people opposed the draft, censorship, anti-abortion laws, the illegality of drug use, and state authority in general. Admitted one Rand follower, their intentions were to transform the YAF into an objectivist-oriented political institution.[131] Most women studied here, with their emphasis on "traditional" morality, would find such beliefs reprehensible.

The divisions within the YAF reflected a lack of unity within the conservative movement as a whole. During the late 1950s, and well into the 1960s, conservative intellectuals such as Buckley and Russell Kirk sought, often unsuccessfully, to find a common ground to hold the differing factions together. The major division was between the libertarians and traditionalists, but the objectivist theories of Rand fractured the movement even more. Yet despite the factionalism within the YAF, in 1970, the group claimed more than 50,000 members, more than any other nonpartisan political action organization in the nation.[132]

Another youth group that right-wing women hoped to influence was Teen Age Republicans (TARS). However, that group did not function in a manner that pleased all rightist women. In August 1968, Lucille Cardin Crain wrote Donald E. Lukens, a young Ohio congressman and a supporter of TARS. Although active within the Republican Party herself, she told him that she could not in good conscience contribute money to TARS because Lukens supported the Atlantic Union. "How can you lead young Americans while supporting a proposal which would tatter their unmatched Constitution and deny them their American citizenship?" she asked. The Atlantic Union was another example of an internationalist organization which the right felt impelled to denounce. Many Democrats, including Presidents John F. Kennedy and Lyndon Johnson and moderate Republicans, including Senator Mark Hatfield of Oregon and New York governor Nelson Rockefeller, supported the idea of a partnership of free states that would include the United States and Western Europe. The Atlantic Union was a part of a movement for free trade as well as a defensive move in the face of the growth in power of the Soviet Union. Some supporters—and Governor Rockefeller was one—promoted the creation of a federal union of free nations that would be similar to that of the thirteen American colonies.[133] Although Lukens is known for helping to push the Republican Party to the right from the time that he was an active leader of the Young Republicans during the 1960s, from Crain's point of view his right-wing credentials were lacking.[134]

While rightist women had some success with recruiting youth into rightward leaning political groups, they often decided that a more effective option was to promote respect for the United States and its history in the schools. For example, when they detected a decline in patriotism among Americans, the conservative Long Island Federation of Women's Clubs passed a resolution in May 1968, urging that American patriotism be taught in all grades from kindergarten through high school and college. This, they believed, could be accomplished not only in history courses but also by means of references to patriotism in such subjects as English and sociology. The women contended that college admission should require applicants to have completed at least one high school course in American History and that all college students pass American History prior to graduation.[135] In addition to building patriotism in youth, such knowledge prepared them for the future, when they would become part of the electorate.

As it was for many Americans, politically right-wing women believed voting to be an important part of citizenship. But for many rightist women, voting was a right that should not be conferred upon just anyone. They preferred that voters be those who saw the world as they did. When the issue of lowering the national voting age from twenty-one to eighteen emerged during the 1960s, a number of rightist men and women were prepared to debate the issue. In particular, their fears of communist influences on youth affected right-wing women's stance. The issue of the adoption of a Constitutional amendment to lower the voting age was not altogether new. It had emerged in Congress in 1943, and again in 1953, when it was discussed in Senate Committee hearings. Not until the mid-1960s, however, when hundreds of thousands of American men were being deployed to Vietnam and student movements were under way, did the lowering of the voting age become a large issue. Nevertheless, as early as 1959, rightist writer and publisher Alice Widener included an article, "Let's Not Have Infant Suffrage," in her magazine *USA* ("An American Magazine of Fact and Opinion"). The article's author, Homer Joseph Dodge, charged that "leftist advocates of social change and a new social order have always sought infant suffrage," and wrote of his belief that "boys and girls" of eighteen through twenty years of age would be "swayed almost wholly by emotions and by youthful Utopian ideals." He disagreed with President Dwight Eisenhower that eighteen-year-olds' service to their country in time of war justified the granting of the vote to youth under the age of twenty-one.[136]

Lucille Cardin Crain was another who voiced her opposition to the lowering of the voting age. When the proposal was under consideration in New York in 1966, she wrote State Assemblyman J. Mercorella to protest. She wrote of a decline in the quality of education during recent decades and claimed that students were continuing to receive "slanted indoctrination" in their textbooks and from their teachers. She noted that the Communist Party had endorsed the idea of expanding the electorate by lowering the voting age. "The fact that this is advocated by the Communists should put an end to anyone proposing it."[137] From Crain's point of view, the world was divided into black and white, or "good" and "bad," and any idea that the Communist Party advocated had to be bad.

In 1967, the issue came under serious discussion at the New York State Constitutional Convention. An attempt by some delegates to lower New York's voting age to eighteen failed, but the issue remained active over the next several years. The Republican Committee of One Hundred, Inc., a right-wing women's group of which Crain was vice president, wrote to the state legislature to protest the idea of lowering the state voting age to eighteen. "Uppermost in the minds of our members," wrote President Julia B. Steiner, "is the knowledge that this proposal is a long-sought objective of the Communist Party." Lowering the voting age would be allowing Communists to score yet another victory in their nefarious schemes to lead high school and college students to revolt against authority. People under age twenty-one lacked the maturity to vote, Steiner maintained; and numerous reports of teens dropping out of high school, bearing children out of wedlock, and using illegal drugs proved their immaturity.[138] If the majority of teens had revealed themselves to be politically right of center, these women's positions on the issue might have been different. But such was not the case.

The Nixon administration investigated youths' overall political outlook prior to taking a stand on the matter. It looked closely at surveys of the political stances of eighteen- to twenty-year-olds, paying attention to a 1970 California poll that revealed that this cohort considered itself much more liberal than the present voting population. Of the eighteen- to twenty-year-olds, 50 percent considered themselves Democrats, while only 21 percent called themselves Republicans. At the same time the percentage of Californians already registered as Democrats was 55 percent while 40 percent were registered as Republicans.[139] Nevertheless, in April 1971, Anne Armstrong, cochair of the Republican National Committee in charge of women's and youth activities, told an audience that included young people, that she hoped the Twenty-Sixth Amendment, lowering the voting age, would win approval. When a college student asked what the GOP planned to do to overcome its poor image with many youths, because of the war in Vietnam and other issues, Armstrong replied that the party was not inclined to change its views to make a bloc appeal to youth or any other group. However, she indicated that an effort was under way to give eighteen-year-olds a greater voice in the nominating process at the 1972 Republican National Convention, and was optimistic that the GOP could win more youth support by Election Day in 1972.[140]

Unlike Widener and Crain, the more moderate Armstrong was reaching out to youth who did not necessarily have a political outlook similar to hers. She sought to win their confidence by offering them hope that their government would give consideration to their opinions. Armstrong likely recognized that the late 1960s and early 1970s was an important transition period. The first of the baby boomers were teenagers; some were entering their twenties. Young people were beginning to give an indication of the directions they would be taking, both politically and socially.

Youth Respond to Moral Issues

Most youth of the 1960s were well aware of the older generation's concerns for their morality. Some of the more conservative youth voiced their own worries that Americans were no longer placing sufficient value on patriotism and morality and took it upon themselves to publicly express their support for God and country. Among the latter was a group of three hundred teenagers who gathered at a Seventh-Day Adventist camp in Michigan. During the summer of 1967, they held a week-long "Prayer-In" to show their support for President Lyndon Johnson and to thank God for giving them the privilege of living in "the greatest nation, where we are blessed with freedom of speech and religion."[141] Yet, despite that group's enthusiasm for God and country, rightist women would probably not have been satisfied, for, unlike the right, the teenagers did not mention the need to fight off threats to the nation.

Rightist women would, however, have been more pleased with the views of teenager Joyce McLewin, who had spent most of her life with her missionary parents in South Africa. Upon her return to the United States in January 1968, she was impressed with the "potential and power" of the country but expressed disappointment with the "lack of national spirit." Even more disturbing was "the lack of interest in God." Ignoring God could very well lead the nation to destruction, "not by outside forces but our inside forces and factions."[142] She did not give specifics as to what forces she feared, but revealed that she shared anxieties similar to those that rightist women were expressing.

Also concerned about the morals of her generation was Debra Clement, a sixteen-year-old girl from Erie, Pennsylvania. She was one of several girls to write President Johnson about teenagers who were involving themselves in a conservative movement known as "Moral Re-Armament (MRA)." In 1967, Clement wrote that she had recently joined an offshoot of the MRA, Sing-Out Erie, Pa., one of 270 such groups across the United States. She explained that the Sing-Out groups were comprised of teenagers who used their singing performances to show people "that there are still many, many of today's young people who do care about the situation of the world and are working hard to do something about it." They sought to live up to the MRA's "four absolute standards of Love, Honesty, Purity, and Unselfishness," and saw themselves as patriots, wrote Clement, and "an expeditionary force from all races engaged in a race with time to modernize the character and purpose of men." She added that the organization intended to secure freedom for the entire world by raising the moral standards of all people. Clement also mentioned Sing-Out performing the song "Up With People,"[143] a song that proved to be very popular. The group soon changed its name to match the song title.

Despite its positive outlook, focus on morality, messages of hope and goodwill, and its members being of clean-cut appearance, at least some right-wing women viewed the group with suspicion.[144] Documents uncovered in this study do not state the reasons for their distrust of Up With People, but right-wing women likely objected to the group's associations with persons on the liberal side of the social and political spectrum. Examples include performances in the Watts neighborhood of Los Angeles following the race riots there in 1965, and their being invited to help facilitate desegregation of the Boston public schools.[145] Nor would right-wing women have approved of the worldview of the Moral Re-Armament movement. While the teenagers in the MRA and in Up With People were referring to themselves as "patriotic," they were also proposing to work with people of other races, cultures, and social classes. The MRA was more in line with the ideology of Christian evangelicals than with fundamentalists who, as historian Andrew Preston points out, did not share evangelicals' promotion of human rights and international engagement.[146] Also, with their standards of "Love, Honesty, Purity, and Unselfishness," MRA leaders were striving to establish a firm basis for society. Those four virtues, however, were too abstract for many rightist women. Sarah Watson Emery, with her step-by-step path to the abyss of communism, could not relate to the MRA's agenda. Nor could traditionalist right-wing women who relied upon their own interpretations of America's founding documents to define their versions of a "true American."

What these right-wing women may not have known at the time was that the wholesome songs and clean-cut look of Up With People's members had also drawn the attention of conservative corporate America. Recent investigations into Up With People's financial backing found that Patrick Frawley Jr., a right-wing evangelist and owner of Schick, was a major supporter. He and others on the right apparently found the group useful as a means to contravene the hippie counterculture. Others donating to the nonprofit entity included companies like Coca Cola, Coors, Halliburton, and General Electric. Altogether, donations of tens of millions of dollars kept the group singing until the early twenty-first century.[147] Even if they had known of such support, it is unlikely that those rigid-thinking, suspicious women would have changed their minds.

Pamela Jones, a teenager whose outlook was more in line with that of the right, was a high school student from Arkansas, who had attended an American Citizen Seminar at Harding College, a conservative college in Searcy, Arkansas. This young woman wrote that the week-long seminar had taught her about "the many threats facing the United States today," threats of which she had not been aware. She had not known "of the immediate dangers posed by socialistic and communistic forces working within this great capitalistic nation to destroy its government and morals" nor of the apathy of the American people over what was taking place. Jones reported that the 335 students who attended the seminar had become so concerned that she and several others formed a committee to draw up a letter stating their views on various issues. They sent the letter to government leaders, including the president. Jones surmised that if three-quarters of American youth could learn what she had learned during the seminar, "we could change our country's disastrous course and insure future freedom for the nation." Reminiscent of the forces driving older right-wing activists, but focusing on age rather than gender as the uniting factor, she exclaimed, "The people must be awakened. I have often heard that the youth of today can preserve our country and its freedom. Let's prove it!"[148]

By 1968, letters from teenagers were pouring into the White House, as many felt overwhelmed by the turmoil that was spreading throughout the country. Not only their elders, but young people, too, expressed concern as individuals over what it meant to be patriotic during the Cold War. In August 1967, a thirteen-year-old girl wrote that her family often discussed current world affairs and that she was worried about the spread of communism. She asked what she could do to support her country "to make it more of a *United* States."[149] Another example of the concerns of youth came from a fifteen-year-old Memphis boy who wrote the president that he was expressing the views of many. He maintained that he was but one of 95 percent of teenagers who were "very proud to be American citizens." It was the minority, he wrote, who were behind such behavior as the burning of draft cards and protests against the Vietnam War, "the ungrateful 5% who will gladly take all that America offers but yet are not willing enough to defend her in such a time as this." He wanted Johnson to know that there were vast numbers of youth who loved the United States and were "willing to defend her and stand up for her at all times."[150]

Most of the teens writing the White House were from the mainstream. Like the rightist women, they recognized that their country was experiencing challenging times. Unlike the right, and particularly the far right, the teenage correspondents had faith that their generation could help move the nation in a positive direction. Right-wing women presented a much more pessimistic outlook for America.

In addition to writing letters and joining such conservative groups as Up With People, teens found ways to express their concerns over the direction the country was taking. An event that won the approval of at least some rightists was a teen decency rally held in Miami. Seventeen-year-old Mike Levesque and several of his high school friends planned the rally following the now infamous incident wherein Jim Morrison, lead singer of The Doors, exposed himself before 12,000 youth during a concert in Miami on March 1, 1969. The teens' idea took off. An estimated 35,000 teens gathered at the Orange Bowl to show their support for a movement for decency in entertainment and their love for God and country. Many waved American flags, and some carried signs reading "Down with Obscenity." One reporter described the rally as being "like the Newport Jazz Festival, a Fourth of July rally and a Billy Graham crusade rolled into one big protest demonstration."[151] Had the teens not had the assistance of adults, it is unlikely that such an event could have taken place. But they had the support of the clergy of many faiths and some celebrity participants. One celebrity supporter was singer Anita Bryant. The mother of four, Bryant was an activist for the Christian Right. A few years later, she would be leading the first religious crusade in America against gay rights.[152]

Despite such positive reports of teenagers' quest for a moral America, a 1970–1971 poll of college-age Americans gave conservative mothers reasons to worry. The poll revealed that one-third of the respondents believed marriage to be obsolete. At the same time, nearly one-half of them believed America to be a "sick society."[153]

Conclusion

The three major issues discussed in this chapter—sex education, school prayer, and patriotism—are bridge issues between the Old Right and the New Right. The Old Right, examined here, put considerable emphasis on moral issues. In recent decades, the New Right has continued that theme with its emphasis on "family values" and concentration on such issues as abortion and homosexuality.[154] During the 1950s, 1960s, and early 1970s, grassroots activists throughout the country were pushing their concerns about morality. As shown here, women often joined together to bring attention to their concerns, while many wrote to the president of their distress. Though many of their organizations were not permanent, the women were showing a growing social and political awareness. The women were identifying what they believed to be the core problems and were presenting ideas as to how to deal with these problems. From their point of view, American society had lost its core unity; and its growing amoral approach to sex, secularism, and the decline of patriotism were key reasons for this development. And, again, Communists, government, and intellectual elites were at the base of the problem. The women's uneasiness over what they saw as changes in American values helps to explain the rapid and widespread rise of the New Right in the years that followed and the continuance of the right's stress upon questions of morality. Specific emphases differ, but the basic moral themes remain.

Moral issues are becoming increasingly prominent because of the many challenges to the old ways society has dealt with them. Gays demand equal rights, women demand control of their own bodies, and so forth. At the same time, sex education (stressing abstinence-only), the push for voluntary prayer in schools, and crusades in support of patriotism remain on the rightist agenda. Both the earlier rightist Christian fundamentalists and those of recent decades refer to both the Bible and the nation's founders to support their arguments. Writing of the New Religious Right, religious scholar and politician Walter H. Capps pointed out that they looked to the past with a longing for a time "when shared religious and patriotic ideals were one and the same."[155] For many of the rightist women discussed in this chapter, so closely was God tied to America's founding that they believed that the nation's founders worked side by side with their Creator.

At the core of morality are decisions on how people should act. This centering on behavior provided the right wing with an organized framework for furthering their beliefs. They believed that having a strong and sharply defined moral character would help keep away outside threats. Especially, they feared forces and institutions coming at them from a distance. Thus, they favored parental, church, community, and state authority as opposed to the growing power of the federal government and of the scientific and liberal elites. As the latter forces grew, rightist women clung to the security of their traditional beliefs.

While right-wing women were often extreme in their investigations and critiques of what the youth of America were learning in their public schools, they did raise some important questions as to what roles those schools should play in advancing particular religious, social, and political ideologies. What rights do parents have in determining how their children are taught and what their children learn? Where should children be taught moral values? In school? At home? Or both? How do Americans define patriotism? Is it possible for a person to be patriotic if that person does not salute the flag or wear one on their jacket lapel? Such questions need to be raised so that issues can be discussed in open forums, allowing parents and other interested persons to know what might be expected of future generations. Nevertheless, by pushing their rigid agendas, the right was attempting to impede opportunities for others to make their own moral choices.

During the 1960s, anticommunism was a stronger theme than in recent years, making it easier for the right to link it with morality. One right-wing writer of the time maintained that while the Communist Party might not be the instigators of the hippie movement, they were reaping the rewards of an American youth culture that had become debased as a result of pornography, drugs, and propaganda in their music.[156] American women with political outlooks ranging across the spectrum worried about the direction youth were taking. Yet for many among the right, the seed of the problem was planted during the late 1940s and early 1950s, when what they saw as communist influences were becoming predominant in the public schools. Nor did they believe that such influences were confined to education. Many rightists saw signs of communism in other areas, such as in the counterculture, popular music, and in youth groups. Some of the women on the far right suspected that the YAF, a group that was founded on conservative principles, had leftward-leaning inclinations. As these rightists saw the world, such destructive forces were not about to subside. The struggle would have to go on. Indeed, with the coming of the Vietnam War and the widespread student unrest, the challenges of defeating communism and asserting American values would become burning issues.

5

THE VIETNAM WAR
AND STUDENT REBELLION

Fellow Americans. . . . Is it true? Are we civilians so sick with subversion that the only nationwide organized home-front we can produce in the American scene in this Viet Nam War is the beatnik, Vietnik, churchnik, peacenik front?
Alice Widener, March 19, 1966

Americans' uneasiness over the Vietnam War and the student rebellion that coincided with it brought many of right-wing women's anxieties to a peak. Unrest on college campuses throughout the nation, along with reports of actions of leftward-leaning students and other young insurgents, led rightist women to believe that their dire predictions about the decline of civic virtue and personal morality were fast becoming reality. Student strikes, antiwar demonstrations, the rise of "Black Power," protests against the "establishment," and the wearing of "peace symbols" were all proof of the general decay of older values. To them, it seemed that a communist-inspired conspiracy was now reaching fruition. To make matters worse, an amendment to the Constitution giving eighteen-year-olds the vote would soon be ratified. Yet while many rightist Americans believed that the situation was getting out of control and that radicals within the baby boom generation were destroying American values as the right understood them, a considerable number of youth were eager to prove that this was a misconception. Though rebellious youth often made the newspaper and television headlines, as shown here and in the previous chapter, thousands of young people actively sought to communicate their respect for American tradition. This was particularly true for socially and politically conservative youth, such as those in the Young Americans for Freedom (YAF), but others, too, attempted to communicate with the more conservative element of the older generation. They thought they could prove that all was not lost if only their elders and people in power would listen.

To explain the various reactions of the population to the war in Vietnam, this chapter first takes a brief look at the stages of development of the war itself. Next, it stresses right-wing women's reactions to the war and their tremendous concern about the future of the younger generation. Youth's reaction to the war is examined here, too, because they were the generation being called to fight for their country. By virtue of its vast numbers, these young adults had the potential for a great impact on the country's future. Right-wing women saw a close connection between the war that American soldiers were fighting in Southeast Asia and the social unrest on the home front. For them, the youthful rebellion of the 1960s and early 1970s was the United States' version of the war overseas.

The Vietnam War

In the summer of 1965, Lucille Cardin Crain wrote that her main preoccupation at the time was the Vietnam War.[1] She was not alone. From the summer of 1964 onward, Vietnam was increasingly on the minds of most Americans. There was an American presence in Vietnam since shortly after participants in the Geneva Conference of 1954 divided Vietnam at the 17th parallel—into Communist North Vietnam and noncommunist South Vietnam. Concerned that communism would spread throughout Southeast Asia, the Eisenhower administration soon began dispatching American military advisers to train a South Vietnamese army. In 1961, President John F. Kennedy sent more advisers, and by the time of Kennedy's assassination in November 1963, there were more than 16,000 military advisers in South Vietnam.

Kennedy's successor, Lyndon Johnson, committed the United States fully into the war. In early August 1964, North Vietnamese patrol boats allegedly clashed with two American destroyers in the Gulf of Tonkin. Although evidence of an attack on the U.S. ships was sparse, Johnson portrayed the Americans as victims and convinced Congress to pass what became known as the Gulf of Tonkin Resolution. The resolution gave the president the authority to take "all necessary measures to repel any armed attacks against the forces of the United States and to prevent further aggression." Soon after, the United States was fully engaged in the war. Meanwhile, coups—and attempted coups—led to several changes in South Vietnam's government. Buddhist monks, students, and others were demonstrating for a negotiated peace; and the military situation became worse as the U.S.-backed government in Saigon lost more and more territory to the Communist North. At the end of July 1965, Johnson announced that the United States would increase its strength in Vietnam to 125,000, adding that he was ready to send more troops if needed. On the home front, a movement against the Vietnam War was taking shape.[2]

In general, the right, both men and women, supported strong military action in the fight against Communist North Vietnam and frequently worked together to promote their ideas as to how to win the war. Rightist women, however, often joined women's groups, especially "mothers" groups, as they believed that the "mother" status gave them more incentive as well as greater legitimacy as persons truly concerned for the soldiers involved in the fight. Crain, for example, responded to the Vietnam crisis by involving herself with a number of rightist organizations. A major argument of these organizations was that the Johnson administration was not conducting the war properly. In addition to her work with adult groups, Crain sought to guide the younger generation into adopting her point of view. In August 1965, she wrote a leader of the Young Americans for Freedom that she was proud of that organization, but suggested that the YAF could "add to its stature" by insisting that the conflict must be won, and quickly. Like many other rightists, Crain mistakenly assumed that the UN was involved in directing American actions in Vietnam. There was no need for ground troops, she believed; the war could be won with naval and air power and with the "unleashing" of Chiang Kai-shek, the anticommunist Chinese leader of Taiwan.[3] Never one to sit quietly when she saw American policy taking the country in the wrong direction, in 1965, she joined a new right-wing organization, the Mothers' Crusade for Victory over Communism;[4] and sometime during the late 1960s, she became an officer and member of the advisory committee for the New York City branch of the Victory in Vietnam Committee.[5]

During the mid-1960s, most women on the right, along with millions of other Americans, believed the war in Vietnam to be necessary in the fight to prevent the further spread of communism. As the years passed with no sign of victory, many Americans were bothered that, from all appearances, the United States was not fighting the war to win it. This was the belief of Ada B. Gourdin, an officer of the South Carolina chapter of the rightist Daughters of the American Revolution. Gourdin was leery, she wrote, of another "'Bay of Pigs' fiasco," referring to the unsuccessful attempt of U.S.-backed Cuban exiles to overthrow the government of Cuba's Communist dictator Fidel Castro in April 1961. She did not want a similar outcome in Vietnam. "If it means an all out war," she wrote, "let's get on with it and stop sacrificing our boys needlessly."[6]

Meanwhile, some rightist men took advantage of mothers' worries about their sons being called upon to fight in Vietnam. Edwin A. Walker, for example, directed his article, "To Mothers: Why Viet Nam?" at such women in the September 1965 issue of *American Mercury*. The burning, looting, and destruction that occurred during the Watts riots, he wrote, were "part of the world revolution—proclaimed by Johnson, the Kennedy brothers . . . Martin Luther King." He maintained that race riots "cannot be separated from Selma marches, Berkeley sit-ins, demonstrations against troop trains . . . and escalating warfare in South Viet Nam." He asked again, "Why are your sons in South Viet Nam?" and answered his own question, "Because you have voted for a One-World Government, the UN, which is a World Police-State, which is Communism."[7] With most mothers considering it their moral duty to protect their children from danger, Walker's accusations were brutally harsh. Telling mothers that they had only themselves to blame for their sons' sacrifices put a tremendous load of guilt on mothers, whether or not they had voted for the current political leaders. However, for right-wing mothers, who were already making connections between international agreements, the civil rights movement, youthful rebellion, and government interference in lives of individuals, Walker's statements would only have confirmed their suspicions.

As the war accelerated, many Americans, including both rightists and antiwar demonstrators, came to view the war in Vietnam as a moral issue. However, there were differences as to what they defined as "immoral." Antiwar demonstrators frequently condemned America's breach of the Geneva Accords of 1954, charging that American policy did not adhere to several articles in the United Nations Charter and violated the United States Constitution. They denounced as immoral the military's use of

Figure 7. Flyer, Mothers' Crusade for Victory over Communism, ca. 1966. Lucille Cardin Crain papers, Coll. 95, box 84. Courtesy of Special Collections and University Archives, University of Oregon Libraries, Eugene, Oregon.

cluster bombs and chemical and biological weapons, emphasizing their effects upon innocent civilians. In addition, they stressed the moral cost to the American people, arguing that the continuous fighting and killing could dull Americans' moral sensibilities.[8]

Most of the right-wing women examined here saw the moral issue differently. They perceived the Vietnam War as a test of American morality in the fight against communism. In a March 1966 press release, Mrs. Jess Conant Jr., president of the Mesa, Arizona–based Mothers' Crusade for Victory over Communism, expressed this point of view, while announcing that the newly created group was not a pacifist organization. "We know with an enemy like Russia or any other communist government, military action is necessary. In any dealings with atheistic, immoral people, as all communists are, meaningful negotiations are impossible."[9] The group circulated a flyer, picturing a serpent and a dragon, with the word "communism" emblazoned across their bodies. The serpent is devouring bags of American money and wheat and boxes of "taxes," guns, and ammunition, while the dragon is killing American men. In the background are cemeteries designated as "Korea" and "Vietnam," and the dragon's tail encircles the Earth. In the foreground, a group of mothers shed tears and kiss their men as they march off to war. One raises an American flag and others carry Bibles under the banner "Mothers' Crusade for Victory."[10]

The Mothers' Crusaders were arguing that any aid to a Communist nation, whether food or ammunition, only helped make Communist nations stronger. The stronger nations would aid the weaker. Of immediate concern was the thought that the powerful Soviet Union was aiding North Vietnam. Rightist Phyllis Schlafly, in *A Choice Not an Echo* (1964), made a similar argument, maintaining that there was a "simple solution" to ridding Southeast Asia and the rest of the world of communism—"just stop helping the communists." She wrote that if the United States would refrain from sending aid, such as "64 million bushels of American wheat," the "Soviet empire . . . would die of its own economic anemia."[11] Schlafly and other rightist women were seeking ways to defeat communism without the loss of more American lives.

During the spring and summer of 1966, the Mothers' Crusaders worked to recruit members from across the United States. With the help of like-minded supporters, they placed advertisements in newspapers in Los Angeles and San Diego, California, Louisville, Kentucky, and other cities. News of Mothers' Crusade–sponsored parades reached rightist women in other areas of the country, including a Mrs. Mitchell in Houston, Texas, who was the wife of an attorney. A crusade leader described Mitchell as "a real ball of fire" after Mitchell embarked on a campaign to obtain financial help for the organization from local businessmen. The movement was growing.[12]

Lucille Cardin Crain contributed money to the Mothers' Crusade, and said she intended to spread word of their cause to others. On July 31, 1966, Ethel Johnson, a leader of the Mothers' Crusade, wrote Crain a letter of thanks. At the same time, she warned of the need to only recruit women who would adhere to the right-wing point of view, suggesting that Crain find a way "to coordinate just the various constitutional conservative women's groups." They all would then "concentrate their efforts on just several basic issues, and then demand in every way possible that those issues be accepted by our Congress." Johnson was optimistic that women's groups might, "just because we are women and mothers, get better and fairer treatment from the Press." She expressed no desire to enlist men in the cause, writing, "I feel so strongly that it is definitely going to have to be the women who are going to have to take whatever action is necessary to save our nation. Most of the men just seem to talk, but seem immobilized as far as any positive action is concerned." Also, Johnson perceived male-run organizations as being unwilling to cooperate with one another, writing that, unlike men, women were more "willing to swallow our pride" for the good of the overall cause. She added that she realized that "we women can get away with more in the way of action than the men could." For that reason, she organized parades of modestly dressed women—no pants or jeans allowed. The "mothers," she wrote, received "fine treatment from all news men. Of course, we conducted ourselves like ladies and dressed like ladies."[13] Their dress and demeanor represented their middle-class social status and traditional upbringing. As such, not only in the streets but also in the media's photographs, they stood in stark contrast to the young and vociferous antiwar demonstrators, who wore T-shirts and jeans.

These rightist women's special attention to how they were being portrayed in the media, and pointing to differences in the dress and behavior of their group and the youthful antiwar demonstrators, marks their recognition of the fact that the older cohort of the baby boom generation had grown up. No longer could the right try to influence them by focusing upon what they were learning in their schools and textbooks. The situation had reached a point where, via the media, women on the right were now recognized as being in conflict with young antiwar activists.

Crain became a spokesperson for the Mothers' Crusade, twice representing the organization on a Sag Harbor, New York, radio talk show. In August 1966, she explained the objectives of the Mothers' Crusaders and asked for signatures on a petition to support legislation that would prohibit trade with Communist nations. A month later she reported that the rightist Mothers of Servicemen of South Pasadena, California, was performing equally important work. She reported on research that group had done to determine what types of products were being shipped to Communist nations, noting that many of the chemicals, goods, and technical data licensed for export to those nations could easily be used to produce weapons.

Crain claimed that the trade with Communist nations would not help the American economy, citing a Moral Rearmament pamphlet that quoted former Soviet foreign minister Vyacheslav Molotov. In 1946 Molotov allegedly stated, "We are not fighting America as yet. But once we have deprived her of her markets, crisis will follow. . . . She will curtail her production, and then will follow unemployment." The statement does not specifically address the topic of American trade with Communist nations, but it does illustrate the Soviets' willingness to use trade as a weapon. More direct in supporting Crain's assertions was a statement of Tim Buck, who she described as "a Canadian former communist." She quoted Buck: "For the communists, trade is an ideological weapon. If you deliver even ten percent of your national trade to the communist world, you give them the perfect chance to create a crisis in your country any time they wish to pull the economic rug from under you."[14]

In the summer and fall of 1966, the Mothers' Crusade for Victory over Communism and Mothers of Servicemen of South Pasadena held petition drives, urging the ending of trade and aid to Communist countries. Mothers' Crusade leader Ethel Johnson claimed that many other women and their organizations were participating in the petition drives, including Republican women's clubs, the Gold Star Mothers, many American Legion women, and members of the Daughters of the American Revolution. She noted, however, that the support from the DAR was on an individual basis. Johnson, who was a DAR member and national defense chairman of her local chapter, attempted to acquire full support from the national organization. Receiving no response, she surmised that, for fear of losing its tax-exempt status, the national DAR was afraid to openly back any political action group.[15]

The Mothers' Crusade circulated a brochure, "Why Should We Help Communists to Kill Our Sons?" that described their organization as a "little group of average housewives or mothers of boys who have been or may be drafted for service in Vietnam." They claimed that "hundreds of thousands of Americans" had signed their petitions, but noted that while everyone seemed to believe as they did, the trouble was that "the average person just can't believe that we are aiding communist countries that are helping our enemies in Vietnam to kill our boys!"[16]

Right-wing women faced the dilemma of wanting to defeat communism, but not wanting their boys killed. They eased that dilemma by blaming the U.S. government and the United Nations for making boys fight a lengthy war. Once drafted, their sons could not refuse to serve and "fight in UN wars." Thus Mothers' Crusaders argued that they were taking on the responsibility of letting "their leaders know in no uncertain terms that they [were] violently opposed to their sons being sent to fight in any more" such wars.[17]

In September 1966, Mothers' Crusaders in Alabama organized a march in Birmingham with the intent of increasing public awareness of the dangers of communism, to demonstrate support for America's fighting men, and to show "the power of women in influencing public opinion." The following spring, the Mothers' Crusade and the South Pasadena–based Mothers of Servicemen, groups with similar agendas, planned a joint rally in the place they believed their voices would have the greatest effect, the nation's capital. In May 1967, members of the two groups traveled to Washington, D.C., where approximately one thousand women, carrying flags and dressed in red, white, and blue, demonstrated against aid for and trade with Communist nations.[18] They claimed to be carrying petitions with a total of more than 100,000 signatures that they would be presenting to sympathetic members of Congress. In preparation for the event, the women had the help of three Arizona congressmen sympathetic to the "mothers'" cause, Senator Paul Fannin and Representatives John Jacob Rhodes and Sam Steiger, who arranged for the petitions' delivery.[19]

Prior to the journey to the Capitol, crusade leaders issued strict rules of conduct for the rally participants. All women were to be "modestly attired," and the only signs permitted were those that the Mothers' Crusade furnished. Participants were to obey instructions of rally directors as well as all laws and police regulations and were not to talk unless "absolutely necessary." They were to display attitudes of "seriousness and solemnity," so as to show their "concern for the injustice being perpetrated against U.S. Servicemen by government leaders, of both parties, who are promoting Trade with the Enemy." The women were told to refrain from speaking to bystanders, and only Mothers' Crusade officers had the authority to speak to the press.[20] The leaders were very much concerned with their image, including how they might be presented in the media. They were drawing clear distinctions between their manner of demonstration and those of leftist youth. At the same time, they revealed their fear that rank-and-file members might express an opinion that could cause trouble for their crusade.

Mothers' Crusade leaders believed that if they avoided verbal attacks on government, individuals, or specific organizations, and focused only upon the issue of trading with Communist nations, most Americans would support their cause. Founding leaders of the crusade were convinced that the cause of unrest and trouble in the world was "atheistic communism and the one-world socialists who are using the Communists to foment revolution" for the purpose of setting up a "one-world government under the United Nations." However, they feared that if they expressed their true beliefs about the war and the world situation, they would be labeled "crackpots."[21] As seen in chapter 2, the thought of being deemed mentally unstable caused anxiety among many right-wing women. They believed that their politics could cause them trouble.

While the women hoped to meet face-to-face with President Johnson, they reluctantly accepted, in his stead, a meeting with Nathaniel Davis, senior staff member of the National Security Council. Ethel Johnson, executive vice president of the crusade, presented Davis with an open letter to the president. The letter stated that American women were "fed up" with the country's trade policy and that morale among American soldiers in Vietnam was terrible because "the boys over there realize they are giving their lives for nothing."[22] This statement is reminiscent of the antiwar propaganda that right-wing women's groups such as the National Blue Star Mothers (initially known as the Crusading Mothers of Pennsylvania) and We, the Mothers Mobilize for America distributed during World War II. Those "mothers" contended that World War II was being fought for the benefit of Jews, the British, and the rich, and that the United States had been duped into participating. In March 1941, nine months prior to the Japanese bombing of Pearl Harbor, these groups joined Elizabeth Dilling and other rightist women in a five-hundred-strong Mothers' Crusade to Washington, D.C., in opposition to the Lend Lease bill.[23] Although the earlier women's groups failed to sway government policy, the rightist Mothers' organizations of the Vietnam War era hoped for a better outcome.

Upon meeting this new generation of rightist women crusaders, Nathaniel Davis reportedly told them that President Johnson was "deeply interested" in their views. However, he also attempted to convince them that trade did not constitute aid to Communist nations, but was a part of the president's plan for world peace. He noted too that "many of our boys have fine morale in Vietnam."[24] This was not what the women had traveled to Washington to hear.

The Mothers groups returned home dissatisfied because of their failure to speak directly with Lyndon Johnson. A Houston crusader noted that this was not the first time that the women had been denied an audience with the president. They had attempted to meet with him in September 1966, but failed. She wondered "why a dozen beatniks who sat on the steps of the Pentagon received national attention" while women who spent their own money to travel to Washington "to uphold American traditions were ignored."[25] Ethel Johnson displayed particular upset, vowing that the crusaders "shall continue to ask why President Johnson refuses to talk with the Mothers of America and explain to them why our government feels it is in the best interest of our Nation and our suffering and dying servicemen to be trading with Russia and her slave states."[26] Johnson was likely posturing. A year earlier, when the women were vainly trying to arrange a meeting with the president, crusade leader Johnson wrote Lucille Cardin Crain that her organization did not really care too much if he could not see them. "If he does not see us," she wrote, "we can use his refusal for a real emotional campaign issue.... [I]f a number of women will get to their TV newsman with a press release saying that the President has not granted us the Mothers of America an interview, it can start some sleeping Americans to thinking."[27]

The Mothers' Crusade for Victory over Communism did not limit their agenda to the issues of the war in Vietnam and trade with Communist nations. They shared with other rightist women some core beliefs, which explains why Crain and others with similar political and social outlooks enlisted in the Mothers' Crusade. In addition to their hatred of communism, they criticized the direction the Supreme Court seemed to be taking, promoted a strict interpretation of the Constitution, and campaigned for the return of voluntary prayer and Bible reading to the nation's schools.[28] To a much larger extent than Mothers' Crusaders, Mothers of Servicemen sought to establish relationships with military men and women serving in Vietnam. Thus, their program went beyond that of the Mothers' Crusade to include extending aid to and attempting to boost the morale of those serving their country.[29]

As leaders described the organization, it was made up of mothers, wives, other relatives and friends of servicemen, who supported American service personnel "in all parts of the world." Because of the major fight in Vietnam, their focus was on that conflict, and they encouraged their members to visit the Vietnam wounded. In their flyer, "This Nation Under God," they not only offered suggestions for visiting and helping those who were hospitalized, but recommended that people who shared their rightist opinions on the war involve themselves in "spontaneous letter writing." They gave the following example: "The government sends up a trial balloon concerning a future truce in Viet Nam. When this appears in the news . . . Spontaneously, from all over the country, letters protesting the truce should pour into Washington, D.C." The Mothers pointed out that servicemen, too, appreciated letters, and suggested that potential correspondents send the usual types of packages to service personnel—various foods, Bibles, "magazines, hometown newspapers, church bulletins and any other publications that will help the serviceman keep in touch." At the same time, they sought to censor reading materials, asking people to not send the popular James Bond books, for the reason that the soldiers had seen enough fighting.[30] While showing support for the young American military personnel, through the reading material, the women were subtly attempting to influence their thinking.

In her study of Americans who backed the war in Vietnam, historian Sandra Scanlon found that many Americans, including women's groups, were more willing to join in conservative patriotic campaigns when the focus was on "supporting the troops," rather than committing to a prowar stance. Aiding the troops with blood drives and gift-giving campaigns offered women opportunities to show their patriotism without committing themselves to a prowar political position.[31] Such outlooks likely helped Mothers of Servicemen grow their membership.

The organization's leaders offered advice regarding the establishment of local groups of Mothers of Servicemen, stating they had received many requests to do so. There were no dues associated with the "national organization," but they suggested that the new members order and distribute the organization's publications. The Mothers of Servicemen posted their address at the bottom of their flyer, as well as that of the right-wing Network of Patriotic Letter Writers, and suggested that potential members write to the Patriotic Letter Writers for two publications that would help them write effective letters.[32] Both groups being from the rightward leaning Pasadena area, it is likely that their memberships overlapped.

Although only some DAR members participated in rightist mothers' groups' activities, the organization gave wholehearted support to the American armed forces. It praised the soldiers for their valiant efforts in Vietnam "to aid free nations from oppressors which have marked this century," but criticized what they saw as "American military subordination to United Nations limitations." Limited war objectives, the DAR maintained, should be replaced with the goal of victory.[33] Like other rightist groups, the DAR was supportive of the war, but believed that changes, including banning trade with Communist nations, needed to be made in the way the Johnson administration directed the war and the nation's foreign policy.

Their misconception about the United Nations' involvement in the war resulted in President Johnson receiving numerous letters from the grassroots right who wanted the United States out of that organization. Some of the misunderstanding regarding the UN and the war in Vietnam might have been due to memories of the Korean War of the early 1950s, which was technically a police action fought under UN auspices. Although regarding the war in Vietnam UN secretary general U Thant repeatedly stated that the United Nations was powerless to take action, his words did not convince the right wing. In addition to their longtime distrust of American involvement in international alliances and their conviction that its UN membership meant the loss of American independence, the right's awareness that the Soviet Union held one of the five seats in the body's Security Council was disturbing. Also troubling was the fact that, by 1967, U Thant was suggesting that the United States declare a unilateral cease fire of its bombing of North Vietnam in order to create conditions that might allow the initiation of peace talks.[34]

For some among the religious right, the war was a battle for Christianity, and the UN seemed to serve as an impediment to fighting for that cause. For example, Mrs. Dennis Lorance's religious beliefs became a part of her argument when she wrote that "the only possible way for victory . . . is to withdraw from the United Nations and fight this war alone in the name of our God." In a letter to President Johnson, she suggested he study the Bible "and see what God says about national associations with the wrong people and what God has decreed will happen to such associations." Lorance, who along with her husband, was a fan of Christian fundamentalist Reverend Carl McIntire (see chapter 4), saw UN membership as associating with the "wrong people."[35] Lorance's was one of a series of letters that

Lyndon Johnson received from women who voiced support for McIntire while offering ideas on how the war in Vietnam could be won.[36] Although they did not directly credit the reverend for their positions on the war, he likely had some influence as both evangelical and fundamentalist Christians distrusted international organizations, including the UN.[37]

As events in Vietnam caused Americans to newly assess its progress in the war, right-wing women faced greater challenges to their position regarding the conflict. On January 30, 1968, during Tet (the celebration of the Vietnamese New Year), Communist commandos took the American forces by surprise when they blasted a hole in the wall surrounding the United States embassy in Saigon. For the next six hours guerrillas fired mortars into the building. There were simultaneous assaults in every major region in South Vietnam. Television cameras captured the story, revealing, in living color, the strength of the enemy and the vulnerability of the United States embassy. The result was that many Americans changed their minds regarding the war.[38] According to a Gallup poll taken just prior to what became known as the Tet Offensive, 58 percent of Americans said they supported the war. A month later, support had dropped to 40 percent. Opposition rose from 28 percent to 40 percent in the same brief time span.[39] But even while the idea of seeking peace in Vietnam was becoming widespread, some rightists brought up a new issue.

During the 1960s and early 1970s, many youth who opposed the Vietnam War were wearing a "peace symbol" that was designed in 1958 by the Direct Action Committee Against Nuclear War. It was a graphic merging of the semaphore signals for the letters N and D, representing the words "nuclear disarmament." A decade later, the Network of Patriotic Letter Writers began circulating an article that contended the peace symbol was in fact an emblem of the anti-Christ, known as "the Broken Cross," and other rightist groups spread similar allegations. For these women, the fact that American youth were wearing this "symbol of atheists" as necklaces and on their clothing was yet another sign of communist infiltration in the United States. The Patriotic Letter Writers asked that a copy of the article be given to anyone spotted wearing the symbol, as well as to local merchants who might be selling the item. For, as the article's author stated, "every symbol of the Broken Cross that is publicly displayed is noted gleefully by the godless Communists, who can see how thoughtless and vulnerable the Americans really are."[40]

Because of their limited understanding of the outside world, these right-wing women were interpreting the peace symbol from their own narrow perspective. Indeed, for those who viewed the Vietnam War as a Christian crusade there was, they believed, an actual symbol—of the "anti-Christ"—that women on the home front could seek to destroy. By the summer of 1970, the flyers opposing the peace symbol were causing anxiety among many religious people. While most mainline Christians recognized the Patriotic Letter Writers' flyers as far rightist propaganda, a leader of the Anti-Defamation League found it "easy to pick out anti-Semitic inferences" in the material.[41] The right wing, with its baseless charges, was not only drawing a line between Christians and non-Christians but also between the older and younger generations, since it was usually the young who wore the peace symbols.

From 1968 through the early 1970s, numerous letters poured into the White House from Americans distressed over unrest in the nation, whether it be over Vietnam, civil rights, or other matters. Women, in particular, wrote President Lyndon Johnson and, beginning in 1969, President Richard Nixon. Much of the concern, coming from women whose politics spanned the political spectrum, was over what the soldiers fighting for their country in Vietnam would think of the unrest at home.[42]

Student rebellion reached a peak in the spring of 1970, following President Nixon's unexpected announcement on April 30 that he had ordered American troops to invade Cambodia. This action shocked most Americans, but students and other young people were particularly stunned because they had been lulled into thinking that the war was winding down. Nixon's 1968 election campaign had included hints of a "secret plan" for ending the war. Since his election, there were periodic announcements of troop withdrawals from Vietnam and much fanfare about "Vietnamization," the effort to gradually place responsibility for the war in the hands of the South Vietnamese. All this seemed to indicate that the war was winding down. But now, hundreds of thousands of American youth were infuriated, believing they had been betrayed. In May 1970 alone, there were protests at more than thirteen hundred colleges and universities.[43] In the minds of many on the right, however, the invasion of Cambodia was a welcome signal that the government was intent upon winning the war.[44]

Although for many rightists Richard Nixon's domestic and foreign policies were not much more to their liking than those of Lyndon Johnson, some announcements from the White House in May 1972 brought hope to some right-wing women. Responding to a massive offensive by North Vietnam into South Vietnam and Cambodia, Nixon launched an aerial attack on North Vietnam. The retaliation included a massive and awe-inspiring attack on fuel depots in the Hanoi-Haiphong region.[45] Eleanor Spicer, president general of the DAR, wrote the president that the organization "wholeheartedly" supported his "decisive action, which seeks an honorable end to the Vietnam War and which aims also at the release of the American prisoners of war." Unlike President Johnson, Nixon, it appeared, was conducting the war in an "appropriate" manner.[46] But Spicer and many others on the right would soon be disappointed.

In January 1973, President Nixon and Secretary of State Henry Kissinger, announced that the United States and North and South Vietnam had achieved "peace with honor" in their agreement to end the war, but few Americans were satisfied. Although many conservatives accepted the peace, those on the right who wanted to fight to win the fight against communism were sorely disappointed in the outcome. Many saw it as a betrayal of American ideals and a sign of national weakness.[47] The war was finally over, but at a steep price. Throughout most of American history, the country's leaders and citizens had been accustomed to tense situations eventually being resolved in their favor. But the outcome of the Vietnam War was different. The right was correct, it seemed—the communist threat may have been much larger than most Americans realized. Yet, as time passed through the late 1970s and the 1980s, not only did communist expansion slow down but also American presidents, including the conservative Ronald Reagan, were forging treaties with Communist China and the Soviet Union. By the late 1980s, the Soviet Union was beginning to crumble, and many Eastern European nations were rejecting communism in favor of democracy and capitalism. Such changes made it difficult for those believing in foreign-based communist conspiracies and allowed for the growth of the New Right and an emphasis on other issues.

The Vietnam War was unlike most other issues of concern to right-wing women in that the war erupted outside the United States, yet it involved the country directly. For many of these women, the solution to the war seemed simple—stop all trade with Communist nations and go in and blast North Vietnam. In this case they wanted the government to do more, not less. They also expected the government to do more to stop student demonstrations, whether through the passage of laws that would restrict protesters and draft dodgers from attending college or through greater presence of the National Guard and police force at such demonstrations.

Initially, the far right had considerable company in its support for the war. Most moderate conservatives from both the Republican and Democratic parties sanctioned the war, as did many liberal Democrats who saw communism as a continuing threat. As time passed, and American losses grew and received greater media coverage, many of the American people who had earlier supported the war increasingly turned against it. Had the situation been different, rightist women's idea to ban trade with Communist nations might have appealed to Americans in the midst of the Cold War. But, so many people approved of the government's efforts to contain communism and were optimistic about the military's success in Vietnam during the war's early years, that the rightist women's campaigns received little notice. At the same time, their mostly hidden agenda, based on charges of a general conspiracy to create a one-world government under the control of the UN, failed to garner much support.

On the left were growing numbers of people opposed to the war. Youth, the leading force in the antiwar movement, had a tremendous advantage in being able to rally others to their cause by virtue of being in institutions of education, whether in high school or in college. They were associating with hundreds and thousands of their peers and were among intellectuals who often taught students to question authority and come to their own conclusions.

Student Unrest

Although the baby boom generation was the one most affected by the war in Vietnam, unrest among youth went well beyond that issue. Black civil rights, women's rights, the way colleges were being run, alternative lifestyles, and the spread of recreational drug usage, were among the many topics that sometimes led youth to reveal their discontent over the status quo. As the war progressed, increasing numbers of baby boomers were reaching their late teenage and young adult years, and they were discovering that they did not always see the world in the same way as their parents did. At the same time, the sheer size of the baby boom generation made it a huge factor in American life. Whatever they did could not be ignored—neither by their peers nor the older generations.

In the fall of 1964, just as the Vietnam War was accelerating, that and other issues began driving young people to openly display their discontent. They were especially unhappy over the direction the establishment, particularly authorities in government and public institutions, such as universities, were taking. Over the next several years, college campuses became the central forums for demonstrating their dissatisfaction.

The first major sign of student discontent emerged in the "free speech movement," which began at the University of California at Berkeley. The movement started when the university banned civil rights activists from setting up tables for raising funds and soliciting recruits near the campus gate. An area near the gate to the campus was traditionally open to such political activities. However, at the urging of local conservatives, the university discontinued the practice. In response, a coalition of student groups demanded the right to carry on political activity on campus. The dispute soon erupted into student demonstrations, student occupation of the university's administration building, and the arrest of more than seven hundred. Before the conflict ended, almost 70 percent of the student body had participated in at least one strike.[48] The movement spread to hundreds of college and university campuses across the country. Over the next six years, hundreds of thousands of students voiced their discontent on numerous topics. What began with complaints about their lack of influence in respect to college curricula and the strict rules and regulations—including dress codes and curfews—erupted into protests against racism, the military draft, and the war.[49]

Almost from its beginning, some rightist women took it upon themselves to try to end the student rebellion. Joyce Zuck of the East Pasadena-Sierra Madre Republican Women's Club, a right-wing group that sponsored a Republican club for teenagers, was one who denounced the students' actions. "Mobocracy on the campus is inexcusable," she wrote in the Republican women's March 1965 bulletin. "Let us push for the Board of Regents at Cal to clean up the so-called 'free speech movement,' subsequently followed by the 'filthy word-magazine and play movement.' Extremist students responsible for these reprehensible actions on campus should be expelled."[50] Zuck's wishes were partially fulfilled. By the end of

March, the student newspaper, which some university officials said contained language that was offensive to good taste, was suspended. In April, the university dismissed one student, and three others were suspended for shouting vulgarisms over loudspeakers.[51]

In 1965, libertarian and best-selling novelist Ayn Rand entered the discussion. As biographer Jennifer Burns writes, Rand had a great interest in youth and wanted to build a cadre of young activists who would influence the country's political future. She visited and spoke at college campuses nationwide. Those students who were attracted to her ideas usually gravitated toward conservative student groups.[52] Regarding student rebellion on college campuses, Rand contended, "What we are witnessing today is an acceleration of the attempts to cash-in on the ideological implications of welfare statism and to push beyond it. The college rebels are merely the commandos, charged with the task of establishing ideological beachheads for a full-scale advance of all the statist-collectivist forces against the remnants of capitalism in America; and part of their task is the takeover of the ideological control of America's universities." She considered the battle to be useless, writing, "If the collectivists succeed, the terrible historical irony will lie in the fact that what looks like a noisy, reckless, belligerent confidence is, in fact, a hysterical bluff. . . . Collectivism has lost the battle for men's minds."[53]

Rand, who at the time was at the height of her influence on college campuses, did not recommend that "rational students" enter debates with student rebels or try to convert them. She believed that the first goal of the battle should be "to wrest from a handful of beatniks the title of 'spokesmen for American youth,' which the press is so anxious to grant them."[54] Like other right-wing women, Rand and Zuck recognized the importance of the media. They realized that students had a significant advantage in delivering their messages, whether it be via student publications, local newspapers, or national television.

Writing for the rightist *Independent American*, Edith Kermit Roosevelt had a more dismal outlook on the situation on college campuses than did Rand. Roosevelt's commentary reflected the fears of many others on the right. She predicted that many of the youthful activists of the 1960s would become professional insurgents. Roosevelt had briefly been married to a former Soviet diplomat, Alexander Barmine, who had defected to the West in 1937.[55] Her former husband's rejection of life in the Soviet Union probably influenced her belief that an American version of Leon Trotsky's "permanent revolution" was on the horizon. The fact that many liberal arts college professors were among the campus activists was all the evidence she needed to support her contention that a communist conspiracy was afoot. She warned that as part of the plot, Marxist professors would select college students with leadership qualities, who would then take time off from school to work and train with left-wing groups. Organizations such as Students for a Democratic Society (SDS) and the Student Nonviolent Coordinating Committee (SNCC), she believed, would be prime organizations for training more potential leftists.[56]

Roosevelt was correct in her assumption that most of the campus activists were left of center. Conservative groups soon dropped out of the free speech demonstrations at Berkeley. For the most part, Young Americans for Freedom supported military action in the war, although many individuals within the organization opposed the draft. In 1968, some YAF members established the national Student Committee for Victory in Vietnam, which distributed literature and countered campus peace vigils, as did the YAF itself.[57] In November 1969, the YAF and other conservative youth organizations rallied alongside such traditional groups as the Veterans of Foreign Wars and the American Legion, in a weeklong series of demonstrations in support of President Nixon's policies. A reporter for the *New York Times* noted that the YAF wanted to go beyond the current strategies for winning the war and pursue enemy forces into Cambodia, Laos, and North Vietnam in a "declared-win policy," a plan that generally appealed to the right.[58] The YAF and other conservative groups for young people, including the Youth Committee for Peace with Freedom, did receive some media attention, but the numbers of rightist youthful activists paled in comparison to those to their left.

Roosevelt warned of campus insurgents who were not students, but who were under the direction of the Communist Party to create student uprisings. Many of the insurgents, she maintained, had parents who were communist and socialist revolutionaries. These parents, Roosevelt insisted, had been teaching their children to become revolutionaries from the time their sons and daughters were in baby clothes.[59]

Student revolts, she wrote, had become professionalized. Participants had developed sophisticated internal communication systems as well as effective ways to distribute propaganda. In addition, these leftist groups were able to raise money from those she referred to as "pliable groups in the community that don't want any trouble." Recognizing the importance of the media, the agitators skillfully created the illusion that the "enemy"—police and college administrators—were in the wrong. They knew how to go limp when arrested, she wrote, giving the impression of police brutality. Roosevelt continued her scenario of conspiracy, predicting that once the insurgents reached middle age, they would be able to rely on a number of respectable "cover jobs." The occupations most likely to be available to them would be as university professors, employees of tax-exempt foundations, or as workers within the federal bureaucracy.[60]

Americans, Roosevelt asserted, had only themselves to blame for the present and future rise of insurgency. That included authorities who allowed the staged "teach-ins," mass demonstrations, and other nonviolent techniques to continue. Roosevelt believed that once youth experienced the thrills that accompanied their crusades, they were not about to give them up. The government, she charged, was paying too much attention to students and professors involved in the campus movements, and consequently allowing them too much power.[61] Roosevelt thought she had a clear vision of America's future. In 1965, when she wrote her essay, the first of the baby boomers had not yet reached voting age. But already she could see that change was coming to America. If the government was paying too much attention to them now, matters would be much worse once they were the voting majority.

Most adults combined all the rebels, whether their rebellion was in terms of protest demonstrations, drugs, colorful and outlandish clothes, long hair, open sexual activity, or alternative lifestyle, into what they loosely defined as a "counterculture." As historian Mark Hamilton Lytle points out, "In a society where children were supposed to improve on the status of their parents, these young people had chosen to be downwardly mobile."[62] Such behavior on the part of their children caused many adults to worry about the nation's future. This was particularly the case for social conservatives who worried about moral decay, and for those on the right who envisioned the work of a communist-backed conspiracy behind the youthful rebellion.

The National Student Association (NSA), with chapters on more than 300 college campuses, received frequent criticism from the right as being too liberal. It is not surprising, therefore, that rightist detractors were shocked when, in February 1967, the NSA admitted it had been receiving funds from the CIA since 1952. Soon after the disclosure, the White House released a report indicating that the subsidies to the NSA, as high as $200,000 annually for several years, were part of a government plan to discourage the growth of communistic elements in educational and labor organizations. Following a tremendous outcry from the left as well as the right, President Johnson announced that attempts by the CIA or any other government agencies to influence education would no longer be permitted. The disclosure of its history of association with the CIA did not end the right's criticism of the NSA. In 1969, Young Americans for Freedom asked Congress to remove the NSA's tax exempt status, contending that the group was fomenting campus disorders.[63]

Although he was far from being rightist on most issues, President Lyndon Johnson did nothing to quell fears of communist conspiracy. In 1968, CIA director Richard Helms reported that his agency had found no convincing evidence of Communist Party influences behind the student protests. Nevertheless, the president nurtured a conspiracy theory, suggesting that the dissenters had links to Moscow or to the Communist Party.[64] The Nixon administration, too, believed that foreign communists were aiding the antiwar movement. In June 1969, Nixon directed the FBI to investigate and prepare a report on communist subversion in the United States. When the FBI reported that it found no evidence of foreign intervention, Nixon concluded that American intelligence was impaired.[65]

As happened on hundreds of other campuses, student protest erupted at Kent State University following Nixon's announcement on April 30, 1970, that he had ordered the invasion of Cambodia. Following a campus demonstration on May 1, Ohio governor James Rhodes ordered some three thousand National Guardsmen into the town of Kent. On May 4, what began as a peaceful demonstration turned to chaos and tragedy when authorities ordered the crowd to disperse. Amidst the turmoil, four students were shot and killed by guardsmen.[66] Students, parents, and others were horrified throughout the nation. But many Americans, and especially those on the right, blamed the victims for the events at Kent State, believing that campus protesters brought the violence of the National Guard and police upon themselves.

Numerous petitions, carrying names of concerned citizens from all regions of the United States, poured into the White House. Some denounced the guardsmen's actions, but more believed them to be justified in their reactions to the demonstrators.[67] An Ohio woman gathered signatures of her friends and neighbors for a letter she wrote the president, stating that they were "upset, very upset" over the campus uprisings. She was angry that "not a word" was spoken "in behalf of the guardsmen who went to Kent at the risk of their own lives." Her anger was particularly directed at the radicals who threw rocks and damaged property. She asked a question common among the right, "Since when does the minority rule?" Taxpayers should not be paying to educate "punks" and "parasites." Such "trouble-makers" should be expelled.[68]

Muriel Roberts, who described herself as a "disturbed Orange County [California] Republican," wrote the president that she opposed the stu-dents' behavior and was 100 percent behind his policies. She also praised Governor Ronald Reagan for his strong stand against student violence in California. Living in a region long associated with right-wing activism, Roberts revealed that her outlook was in line with that of many other local residents when she contended that college students' antiwar demonstra-tions were "part of a plot to destroy our country." Money, she wrote, was coming from Cuba and Red China, "so why is not something done about it?" Roberts wrote that her husband, an attorney, called her a "rabble rouser," and she admitted that she was, although she did not believe in violent action. She did, however, believe that politicians should pay more attention to women's opinions, writing, "maybe it will take the women to save the country."[69]

Doing her part to change the direction the country appeared to be tak-ing, much of Roberts's "rabble rousing" was accomplished through her letters. She wrote the presidents of eight major universities in various re-gions of the country, stating her views regarding antiwar demonstrators. She charged that while activist students and professors were demanding free speech, they really only wanted free speech for themselves, but not for those who disagreed with them. Blaming college students as a whole for the acts of violence that often accompanied campus protest rallies, she believed student activism to be an example of why eighteen-year-olds should not be given the vote.[70]

Many other women agreed with Roberts, taking the rightist position that the campus protests were communist inspired. Among them were six Cincinnati, Ohio, women, who wrote that, "if the issue was not Cambodia, it would be something else . . . what they are looking for is confrontation."[71] But other women took more moderate points of view. An example is Mrs. William T. Wilkerson of West Virginia, who blamed the campus uprisings on "the failing few who are looking for a cause or someone to blame for their lazy, dirty, drug-filled minds." She acknowledged that there were thousands of young people who were upstanding citizens and criticized the "T.V. cameramen and news media who play up the dissenters continually."[72]

Letters continued to pour into the White House as men and women wanted to express their concerns about problems on college campuses. Signatures of women outnumbered those of men in a letter to President Nixon that more than fifty people signed to say that they praised God that they now had a "praying president" who would try to "save our country and protect our children." They wanted to see communists out of the nation's public schools and university systems. "Our country was founded on the principles in the Holy Bible, but we sit back allowing a few Godless people to use our freedoms for their own advantage and ruin our great Heritage," they wrote. Overall, the Christian right had greater confidence in Nixon than they had in Johnson.[73]

Conservative and moderate-minded young people too voiced their frustrations over the turmoil on college campuses.[74] In May 1970, with student protests headlining the news, the majority of the students at C. F. Brewer High School in Fort Worth, Texas, signed a resolution, stating that they did not "condone the irrational and sickening behavior of any student deliberately destroying public property, forcefully occupying campus buildings, or terrorizing fellow students." Students who participated in violence should be expelled from college and any college draft deferment that had been granted to them should be revoked.[75] These students, who were approaching the time when they would be making decisions in regard to furthering their education at colleges and universities, had reason to be uneasy as to what might await them if they entered those institutions. In the best of times, the move from the more structured high school environment to the less structured college campus, with its wide range of choices about lifestyle and curriculum, often causes anxiety among youth. News of recent uprisings made the prospect much more daunting.

Young people's increased use of drugs during the 1960s and early 1970s was another matter of concern to youth as well as to their parents. In

1969, the National Teen Age Republicans, a group that often received encouragement from rightist women, chose to take action against youthful drug use by circulating "The Drug Society." This flyer was a printed version of remarks that television personality Art Linkletter gave in October before a White House–sponsored bipartisan leadership discussion on the narcotic problem. Linkletter's twenty-year-old daughter had recently leapt to her death from her apartment, a suicide that was believed to have resulted from her experimentation with LSD several months earlier. The Republican teenagers were passing on the message that tragedies associated with drug usage could happen in any family.[76]

There was reason for concern. A 1971 report on marijuana usage estimated that Americans were spending nearly $100,000,000 on the illegal drug. Somewhere between 35 and 50 percent of high school and college students had tried it, and there were indications that marijuana use was spreading to younger children and to large numbers of adults. Several estimates showed that, at the end of 1970, about one of every seven college students was using it at least weekly.[77] In 1972, there were an estimated 400,000 to 500,000 heroin addicts in the United States, and in New York City drug abuse was the single largest cause of death among people between the ages of fifteen and thirty-five. In 1971 alone, 1,250 people of that city died as a result of drug usage.[78]

The use of marijuana and mind-altering drugs such as LSD was associated with the large counterculture that developed within the youthful community at that time. Most obvious participants in the counterculture were the "hippies," whose colorful styles of dress, flowers in their hair, experimentation with drugs, and expressions of "Make love, not war," were direct challenges to the establishment. Other aspects of the counterculture were young people's challenges to racial segregation and America's military actions in Vietnam, their promotion of women's and gay and lesbian rights, and their new ways of artistic and spiritual expression.[79] Although the counterculture was the most colorful, and often the most radical, a broad spectrum of youth opposed the war and wanted a more liberal society. Many adults, especially those with moderate or liberal political outlooks, agreed with the counterculture youth on a number of the issues—civil rights for blacks and ending the war in Vietnam, in particular. But the youthful counterculture was similar to the far right in that they often acted in the extreme. Their radical forms of behavior and dress separated them from the larger consensus. Such a variety of challenges to the status quo caused considerable apprehension among many older adults, especially among those on the right.

Both Johnson and Nixon received letters from adults—from women more than men—and from youth, that indicated that there truly was a generation gap. Youthful challenges to the establishment, and particularly their choice of taking to the streets to raise their voices, got the attention of the government as well as that of ordinary citizens. At times, parents and government officials took extra steps so as to avoid trouble. An example of this occurred in Oregon during the summer of 1970. Kent State and its repercussions—including a campus uprising in Portland—were still in the news. As a result, federal and state government officials became anxious over the prediction that young antiwar and other protesters would descend on Portland during an American Legion convention to be held there in August. To avoid potential problems, officials arranged a Woodstock-style rock festival in a state park outside the city. Most officials deemed it a success as thousands of young people attended the festival, while only about one thousand antiwar protesters rallied in Portland.[80]

Under the Nixon administration, in particular, the goals of government and those of young people appeared to be polar opposites, officials within

Figure 8. Portland State University student protest, May 11, 1970. Courtesy of City of Portland Archives, A2004-005.2364.

Figure 9. "Fort Tricia Nixon," named for President Nixon's eldest daughter, constructed on Portland State University campus, Portland, Oregon, ca. May 1970. Courtesy of City of Portland Archives, A2004-005.2528.

the administration frequently fretting over Nixon's inability to develop rapport with youth. Many among the American public, too, were concerned. In May 1970, Joan Levine, director of the Nassau Long Island district of the New York State Congress of Parents and Teachers, wrote that members of that organization were deeply concerned about disillusionment among youth over the present processes of American governmental and educational institutions. This politically moderate organization suggested that the federal government pursue greater efforts to reach out to young people who were searching for solutions to the nation's problems.[81]

A survey of attitudes of college students, commissioned by the American Council on Education in the late spring of 1970, confirmed the New York State group's concerns. The survey found that there was a genuine feeling among college students that they had new priorities and lifestyles that needed to be understood by the older generation. The survey found, too, that among students who considered themselves conservative or far right, 60 percent believed that communism remained the nation's biggest threat. In agreement were 42 percent of those who considered themselves centrist, while only 22 percent of liberal or far leftist students considered communism their greatest fear. Altogether, 71 percent believed that their parents saw communism as the major threat,[82] revealing that college students of varying political outlooks recognized that they viewed the communist threat differently than did their elders. Among conservatives, it was a sign that the next generation of right-wing leaders might remove the fight against communism from the top of their agenda.

In December 1970, the John D. Rockefeller 3rd Task Force on Youth concluded a study that found that the vast majority of college students were politically moderate, antiviolent, and desirous of working within the system. Nevertheless, the task force found that over the period of only one year—during which time American forces had invaded Cambodia and students had found themselves battling police and National Guardsmen on college campuses—student criticism of government and society had increased significantly. For instance, the rate of those who were strongly critical of the nation's foreign policy had increased from 31 percent in 1969 to 48 percent in 1970; and strong criticism of racism in the United States had risen from 38 percent in 1969 to 53 percent in 1970. Students cited the Vietnam War as their major concern, but poverty, racism, pollution, and drug addiction also ranked high on their list of problems needing to be addressed.[83]

Overall, the task force concluded that student rebellion was not a transient phenomenon, but a signal of vast changes in American culture. The investigators predicted that the revolution in student values "was destined to spread its influence from the campus throughout the full breadth of the society."[84] Thus, much of the task force's findings confirmed right-wing women's fears that the white-dominated utopian America that they visualized in their fight against change was moving farther and farther away from becoming reality.

A Gallup poll of 1,063 full-time college students, representing sixty-one campuses and conducted at about the same time as the Rockefeller Task Force investigation, found that liberals or leftists outnumbered their right-wing or conservative counterparts by a ratio of more than two to one. In the poll, 41 percent declared themselves "middle-of-road," while 37 percent considered themselves left of center, and 17 percent to the right. Graduate students were more likely than undergraduates to consider themselves on the left or the far left.[85] This latter finding coincides with a Louis Harris and Associates survey in June 1970, which found that as they matriculated through college, students' political philosophies were

inclined to move leftward. At the time of the survey, 56 percent of ju-
niors and seniors considered themselves liberal or far left; although when
they entered college, only 27 percent of that cohort had placed themselves
in left-leaning categories. Surveyors also noted that incoming freshmen
were more likely to be to the left of center than were students who entered
college two to three years ahead of them. Thus, if the trend was to continue, college campuses would eventually be leaning heavily to the left. If
this was the case, it was thought that the potential for activism would be
greater since most of the overt activism of the past few years had come
from the left.[86] These studies validate Edith Roosevelt's anxieties about
the leftward trend. Indications were that, as the war expanded and they
became more aware of the world around them, baby boomers—including
many with conservative or rightist backgrounds—were ignoring earlier
influences and were adopting leftward-leaning attitudes that they encountered in college.

The Republican White House, too, was concerned that most youth
would be lost to the mostly more liberal Democrats, and made efforts to
win the hearts of America's youth. Early in 1970, First Lady Pat Nixon
went on a tour of American colleges. The positive responses that emerged
from the tour impressed some of the president's advisers, who were eager
to capitalize on the rapport she appeared to have developed with the students. One adviser suggested that Pat Nixon write an article for a magazine such as Readers Digest that would present an accurate description of
the First Lady's tour and would show the positive works of some young
people whom she might choose to recognize. More college tours could create more visible evidence of the Nixon administration's interest in youth.[87]
However, White House advisers believed that the president needed to become personally involved in winning young people's approval. One adviser, Coral Schmid, wrote, "We (the Administration) are alienating our
Youth. Those of the silent student majority have no . . . spokesman in this
Administration. The old and middle folk have Spiro Agnew, but who does
Youth have?"[88]

There were numerous young people who were eager to communicate
their ideas to the president. For example, Jean Strauss, a high school
sophomore, wrote Nixon that she and other students had ideas that
they wished to convey to the president, believing that they might help
put an end to the "generation gap." Gayle Goolsby of Galesburg, Illinois,

president of Teenagers Helping in Society, was another correspondent. She described her organization as being an interracial group of high school students who wanted to promote better communication among the people of their community. Overall, there are several boxes among Nixon's presidential papers that contain letters from teenagers desiring to work with the government and others to solve the "communication gap" dividing the older and the younger generations.[89] Rightist women likely would not have condoned Goolsby's interracial group of teenagers, but they might have been relieved had they realized that millions of baby boomers shared at least some of their unease concerning the direction the country was taking.

In the fall of 1971, Anne Armstrong, cochairman of the Republican National Committee, was working tirelessly to recruit women and youth into the Republican Party. Part of her job was to encourage party leaders to start registering voters aged eighteen to twenty-one, who had recently become eligible to vote, and would be voting in a presidential election for the first time. With a recent Gallup poll showing that 42 percent of the nation's youth considered themselves Democrats, another 42 percent called themselves Independents, and only 16 percent Republican, she was not optimistic about President Nixon and his party winning the youth vote in 1972. But she believed that a good number of the Independents could be won over, since their registration as such was likely a temporary way to show their disillusionment with what was happening in the country.[90]

Armstrong's analysis of the situation had merit, for as they entered their twenties, many baby boomers were yet undecided about where their political allegiances lay. For example, one boomer, who would later be elected to Florida's state legislature, was uncertain as to whether to become a Republican, like her father, or join the Democratic Party, as her mother had done. It was not until she opened her own business that she realized that the Republican Party's agenda most closely matched her own.[91]

Conclusion

Amidst all the other issues of the 1960s and early 1970s, the Vietnam War stands out as the most complex. Presidents Eisenhower, Kennedy, and Johnson all believed in the "domino theory": If South Vietnam fell to the Communists, other nations of Southeast Asia would soon follow. Although he was not a strong subscriber to the theory, Nixon made use of it to buy time before making the final push of his plan for "peace with honor."[92] The generations of Americans who were in their late teens or were adults during the late 1940s and early 1950s, were well aware of how quickly nations could fall to communism. World War II was hardly over before the Soviet Union was in control in Eastern Europe; Nationalist China fell to the Communists in 1949; and Communist North Korea threatened to overpower South Korea during the Korean War in the early 1950s. Then in 1959, Fidel Castro's victory in Cuba brought communism within ninety miles of American borders. The Cold War was not abating, and many saw the conflict in Vietnam to be a key test of the West's ability to contain communism. It is therefore not surprising that most Americans initially supported the idea of aiding the South Vietnamese in their fight against communism.

As the war expanded, with more and more American troops being deployed to Vietnam and increasing numbers returning as wounded veterans—or not returning at all—some Americans began to question the United States government's and military's strategy in the war. The 1968 Tet Offensive, which led Americans to realize that the war was not progressing as well as the government claimed, was a turning point. From that time forward, increasingly large numbers of Americans began to turn against the war. Among those questioning and criticizing the country's strategies and policies were right-wing women. Like most Americans, they wanted the war to end quickly—and in victory. Nevertheless, there were several aspects of these women's campaign for victory that were unique.

These rightist women believed that as largely middle class, morally upright, and openly patriotic women, their public campaigns should receive greater respect than those of others. The dress codes and strict rules and regulations their leaders imposed upon women marchers were signs of their rigidity. They also made use of their roles as mothers, as well as the services they provided to enlisted men and returning veterans, to draw attention to their agenda. The Vietnam War was overseas, but the threat of Communists taking over all of Vietnam and, subsequently Southeast Asia was, in their minds, similar to what was happening in America. Rightist women considered the spread of communism in Southeast Asia as a threat to the position of the United States in the world, but they also believed communism was spreading within America itself.

The baby boom generation was the generation most directly affected by the war, and its overall antiwar stance contributed to right-wing women's fears of conspiracy. It must have been particularly disturbing to these women that most of those opposing the war purported to be doing so on moral grounds. This position challenged rightist women's claim to be the moral force. As rightist women saw the situation, whether student protesters were true communists or merely idealistic kids following the "peacenik" line, their antiwar campaigns were aiding the enemy.

Perhaps more than any other group, rightist women found youthful rebellion horrifying. College students' demands for reforms, the end to the war, and their protests against the establishment disturbed many older Americans, regardless of their political outlook, particularly when demonstrations erupted into violence. However, for rightist women, almost everything the younger generation enjoyed or promoted, from their music and dress to the loosening of sexual mores to calls for a negotiated peace in Vietnam, directly challenged the values these women held dear. While many of the more moderate American mothers attempted to understand and relate to their baby boomer children's new ways of looking at the world, most women on the far right of the political spectrum saw the youth of America as becoming puppets of communist conspirators. Some tried to influence youth by working with youth groups that were aligned with the Republican Party; most turned to the government with their arguments. Many sought the attention of the news media to get their messages out to the public and to political leaders.

Despite their great efforts, rightist women's attempts to shape government policy on Vietnam and to quell youthful rebellion met with little success. Nevertheless, the women's activism helped build their confidence and their awareness that they could be most effective if they fought for measures that could attract the sympathies of a large portion of the American public. At the same time, they developed a greater awareness of ways to manipulate the media, which would serve them well in future campaigns.

For youthful activists of the 1960s and early 1970s, much of what they saw in American politics and culture was not to their liking. Their ideas were in many ways polar opposites to those of the rightist women examined here. At times, the generally leftward leaning youth and right-wing women argued in the streets, but mostly their disagreements raged separately, in issue-based rallies, marches, and other demonstrations, or in written material. Both sides were aware of each other, but there was little attempt to gather together to discuss differences. Judging from the correspondence in presidential archives, young people tried more often than their elders to establish a dialogue between generations.

There were some who blamed American women for much of the disorder. Writer and social critic Philip Wylie, who criticized women as, among other things, an "idle, spending class" and coined the term "Momism" to describe what he believed to be the overprotective and destructive powers of mothers, in his 1942 work *Generation of Vipers*, continued to have few positive comments regarding women. In *Sons and Daughters of Mom* (1971) he attempted to diagnose the causes of student rebellion in the 1960s and beyond. Wylie blamed parents to a great degree, contending that during the postwar period parents were spoiling their children. Young people, Wylie wrote, were raised to believe that there was no punishment for wrongdoing, but rewards for doing what was right. In addition, youth so enjoyed all the consumer goods their parents bestowed upon them that they chose to remain in "a category of immaturity" until they reached the age of thirty. Wylie criticized mothers in particular, since he found that women were not only the nation's major consumers but also as mothers they had the most influence upon their children and, thus, the American culture as a whole.[93]

Both Wylie and rightist women stressed the importance of women's role in raising children and in shaping America's future. They agreed, too, that American culture overall was becoming too permissive and that there needed to be a central core of strong values that could hold society together. Rightist women, however, did not see mothers as the major problem. Rather, they believed that in order to achieve the necessary moral structure, conservative women should extend their influence beyond the home and into the political and social realms.

Because the Korean War occurred when they were small children, or even before they were born, the war in Vietnam was the first such conflict of which most boomers were aware. The federal government, parents, liberals, rightists, and other adults made attempts to control the thinking and the behavior of the younger generation during the 1960s and 1970s, but most boomers found other influences at least equally persuasive. Whether it was due to images of death in the newspapers or on television, from personal experiences in the war, or from the influences of their peers, millions of baby boomers were making decisions as to where they stood on the issue. With the baby boom generation being the largest generation in American history, the country's youth had more peers than ever before. Their sheer numbers allowed them greater opportunities to influence one another on such issues as the draft and bringing peace to Vietnam.

Television brought the war home, and the conflict in Vietnam proved shocking to some.[94] Having a close friend or a family member in the military also made a difference to the way they looked at the war. Many could have identified with a Portland boomer whose brother served in the Marine Corps. Although she did not believe the war to be a good war, nor that the United States had good cause to be in Vietnam, she was proud of her brother for serving his country and was supportive of all American troops.[95] What was in the past solely a political issue was suddenly personal. In such instances, all the circumstances connected with the Vietnam War became even more complicated.

The 1960s and early 1970s were challenging times for baby boomers. They came from diverse backgrounds and grew up in different regions of the country, but most, in one way or another, became caught up in the turmoil and complexities of the era. At the same time, they recognized that they were a new generation with new ideas, and they wanted their elders to make room for them. As time passed, it appeared that the youthful reformers were getting their way. America was moving farther to the left.

Although Republican Richard Nixon defeated the liberal George McGovern in the presidential election of 1972, there was no rejoicing for the right. Nixon had visited China earlier that year, beginning the process of establishing diplomatic relations with that Communist nation. The Vietnam War ended in January 1973, not in victory, but with "peace with honor," which in the end turned out to be neither when Saigon fell to the Communists in 1975. But all was not lost for rightist American women. As bleak as matters looked, there were some baby boomers who sided with the right on the Vietnam issue. In addition, there remained more battles to be fought. A significant battle, and one in which they would score a major success, was one with members of their own sex. It was a battle in which Americans were deciding the question: Just what were the rights and roles of women?

☼ 6

"WOMEN'S LIBERATION" AND THE EQUAL RIGHTS AMENDMENT

As long as there's the girl back home, mom's apple pie and the Kodak camera, there will be no ERA. When the girl back home becomes a woman, and mom is remembered for more than apple pie, and Kodak reflects the future and not the past, then and only then will women be equal and free.

Cathy Pitts, November 12, 1975

In the epigraph above, Cathy Pitts writes of a substantial obstacle that she and other women's rights advocates faced in their quest for ratification of the Equal Rights Amendment (ERA) to the United States Constitution. "The girl back home," "Mom and apple pie," and the Kodak camera are all American cultural icons. Thoughts of "the girl back home," as well as the linking of "Mom" with "apple pie" placed women firmly in the domestic sphere. By the 1960s and 1970s, the Kodak camera, invented late in the nineteenth century, was an object of Americana. Pitts recognized that the ERA represented deep cultural changes for those Americans inclined to attach themselves to tradition. The Kodak symbolized that tradition, for the photographs being developed from the film in the camera were pictures of the past. Pitts believed that only when Americans were willing to lay tradition aside and look to the future, would they be ready to take the necessary steps to enable women to have rights equal to those of men. Once Americans release themselves from those chains to the past, the Kodak will capture the new freedoms on film. Pitts imagined that the result would be new traditions, offering equality to all. However, right-wing women proved to be a force determined to maintain traditional gender roles, one that would prevent the passage of the amendment that Pitts and women's rights activists were eager to obtain.

This chapter begins with a brief history of the movement, then, on the basis of archival and published sources, it looks at women's responses to the equal rights issue. Most of the women examined here opposed the ERA, but some supporters are included here as well. Some of the women are well known and others, like Pitts, are from the grassroots. Their own words are important for understanding what leads women to engage in such movements. They are speaking for themselves as individuals, rather than being discussed in abstract terms. The chapter ends with a sampling of baby boomers' reflections on what the conflict over the ERA meant for them.

After a long struggle for recognition as competent political players, women won suffrage in 1920. However, many gender-based inequalities persisted. Over the following decades, many women sought further reforms. Among them were former suffragist Alice Paul, leader of the National Woman's Party. In 1921, she wrote the Equal Rights Amendment, which was first introduced in Congress in 1923.[1] Although the amendment was introduced in every subsequent session of Congress for the next twenty years, it met with repeated defeat. During that time, many influential women, including Eleanor Roosevelt and Frances Perkins, opposed the amendment. They saw it as a threat to the "protective" laws to safeguard women's health, particularly that of women workers. Progressives had fought for that protective legislation during the 1890s and early twentieth century, and many disagreed with Alice Paul and the National Woman's Party, who believed in equal treatment of the sexes.[2] During the 1950s, the amendment received some life, with the United States Senate passing it in 1950 and 1953, but it included the "Hayden rider," which allowed for special exemptions, rights, and benefits for "persons of the female sex." The House of Representatives did not vote on the amendment during those years, and pro-ERA women's organizations did not approve of the Hayden rider because they did not want women to receive special benefits, only equal rights.[3]

A great step toward receiving equal rights for women came with the passage of Title VII of the Civil Rights Act of 1964, which prohibited job discrimination on the basis of sex. Labor unions initially opposed Title VII because they believed it would nullify "protective" legislation already in place. However, over the next several years, the federal courts and the Equal Employment Opportunity Commission (EEOC) decided that although Title VII invalidated protective legislation, it extended most of those protections to men, rather than eliminating them for women. Because the protection issue had long been an important factor in unions' disapproval of the ERA, their opposition to the amendment began to decline.[4]

By the mid-1970s, feminists seemed to be on the verge of achieving their most lofty dreams. It did not appear to matter if they were Republican or Democrat, many prominent members of both parties were voicing support for equal rights for women. Feminists within the Republican Party formed an official organization, the Republican Women's Task Force, which was dedicated to supporting women's causes. Betty Ford, wife of Republican president Gerald Ford, toured the United States, voicing her support for the Equal Rights Amendment (ERA).[5] Feminists believed it likely that the United States Constitution would soon mandate that American women have the same rights as men. Millions of women welcomed the change.

But there existed a growing number of women, mostly on the social and political right, who did not share feminist sympathies. They feared that if the ERA were enacted, it would lead to many very undesirable consequences. For them, the Supreme Court's ruling in *Roe v. Wade* (1973), which gave women the right to have abortions, was a prime example of such consequences. To the right, the fight over the ERA was a moral issue on which they needed to take a strong stand. Some of these women were veterans of other right-wing crusades, while new voices rose from the grassroots. Many of the older guard saw the women's rights movement to be a part of the "conspiracy" they had been warning of throughout the Cold War. Such notions as sexual freedom and attacks on accepted middle-class norms of social behavior angered the right wing—rightist women in particular. Some of the issues with which the right had long been struggling now became interwoven with the ERA. The debate over who should control textbooks is one example. Some school texts explained the ERA in favorable terms, which the right, of course, opposed; and just as they did on the issue of school prayer, women of the religious right played prominent roles in the fight against the amendment.[6] Again, it was a question of morality.

As with so many of their earlier crusades, right-wing women's battle against the ratification of the ERA lasted several years. For them it was a battle over how future generations would define "women." Although both sides of the issue, both pro- and anti-ERA, enlisted multiple generations of women to their causes, it was baby boomer women and those a few years older who constituted the majority of those favoring the amendment.

The Immediate Postwar Years

Throughout the post–World War II era, right-wing women's identification of the home as the center of a mother's place in the world affected their outlook regarding women in the workforce. For example, in an open letter to their members in July 1954, the president of the New York State Minute Women of the U.S.A. stressed the importance of a mother being home for her children. President Anna O. Nisbet pointed to statistics that revealed that juvenile delinquency increases in a strife-ridden world, and argued that working mothers, who often are not at home when their children need them, contribute to the problem. She claimed that without the all-important parental guidance, the spiritual structure of the child suffers, and the child can easily slip into criminal activity.[7]

This negative assessment of the side effects of the growing trend of middle-class mothers participating in the workforce remained troublesome for mothers for years to come. Yet, these women need not have worried as much as they did about the issue. Reports in the early to mid-1950s of working mothers contributing to juvenile delinquency had multiple flaws, and by the latter part of the 1950s, researchers were beginning to challenge such conclusions. Some tightly controlled studies of children of both employed and nonemployed mothers found that whether or not a mother was employed outside of the home, there was little or no difference in the likelihood of her child becoming involved in criminal activity.[8]

As time passed, the right continued to speak out regarding the roles of women. But while they wanted mothers to stay at home with their children, when it came to working for their own aims, many rightist women stepped out into the world of politics. As Kathleen M. Blee revealed in her study of Women of the Ku Klux Klan during the 1920s, hundreds of thousands of right-wing women joined the Klan, many of whom spent considerable time away from their homes involved in WKKK activities.[9] Again, in late 1939, upon the onset of World War II in Europe, rightist women's antiwar organizations (which tended to exaggerate their numbers) were claiming up to a million members. Thousands left their homes to gather for protest rallies;[10] and, as the present study shows, during the 1950s and 1960s rightist women left home to campaign on a variety of issues. When they believed in a cause, they were willing to put aside domestic responsibilities to participate in political activity.

Under the leadership of Blanche Winters, the right-wing American Woman's Party pushed the notion of women replacing men in the political world. Although Winters was an activist for right-wing causes during the 1940s and early 1950s, she was also a feminist, having joined Alice Paul's National Woman's Party in 1938 in its struggle for the ERA.[11] In a pamphlet prepared for the 1952 presidential election, Winters wrote, "The political conduct of male politicians has forced women to come to the rescue of our country, our homes and our children." Men, she believed, had failed to protect American institutions and way of life. "It is our last opportunity to save constitutional government to pass on to our children to enjoy. Women cannot stand idly by and forsake their duty any longer." Men have had their chance, she maintained; it was time for women to take control—for "women power is mother power."[12]

While Winters promoted the idea that women were perfectly capable of being the nation's rulers, she also supported the idea of women as nurturers. But the time had come for them to expand their roles. Women, she wrote, were better equipped to ensure that Americans could afford life's necessities. "Food is woman's business, as a finished product," Winters argued. "God made it so. We feed the generation in its babyhood." She also believed that women could bring an end to the Korean War, predicting that "in the 1952 elections the woman viewpoint will stand out as a beacon light from an entirely new angle, and the mother viewpoint on war as a means of settling disputes among nations will be the issue."[13]

Here was a right-wing woman who promoted states' rights, complained that the government was "toadying to the communists within our Country," and demanded that the United States pull out of the United Nations. Yet she broke away from American tradition with her conviction that women could rule.[14] Women, she believed, needed to be more than part-time political activists; they needed to become regular players in the world of politics. Yet it was precisely women's qualities as mothers and homemakers that prepared them for new political roles. Thus, her attitude about women's qualifications differed from that of most ERA activists of the late 1960s and the 1970s, who emphasized qualifications that placed them on a level equal to men. Most of these later feminists believed that, mothers or not, women, as *women,* needed to be recognized as being equal to men in all spheres of life, including politics, the business world, and the professions.

During the immediate post–World War II years and through the early 1960s, discussion about the rights of women normally focused on the choice between protection, equality, and the status quo.[15] Few women were as outspoken as Winters, and debate during the early 1950s, when she was politically active, was mild in comparison to what would materialize during the late 1960s. Signs of right-wing women's opposition to the federal government's involvement in the issue of rights for women came in a March 1962 Minute Women newsletter, in which they warned that President Kennedy's Executive Order to establish the President's Commission on the Status of Women was part of a United Nations and leftist plot. They objected to the president's statement that he hoped the commission's report would "indicate what needs to be done to demolish prejudices and outmoded customs which act as barriers to the full partnership of women in our democracy," writing that they saw no barriers, and were "perfectly happy to be left entirely alone." Noting that Eleanor Roosevelt was named chairman of the commission, they saw that as further evidence of it being part of a left-wing conspiracy: "That's the deal—Eleanor is going to send us out to work just like the Russian women."[16]

Although they were wrong about the President's Commission on the Status of Women being a leftist plot to force them to work, the Minute Women were correct in foreseeing that the commission's report would lead to change. Following the 1963 report of the commission, which found that women suffered occupational inequities similar to those endured by minority groups, some older, professional women sought to remedy the problem. They successfully lobbied Congress to include the prohibition of sexual as well as racial discrimination in employment in the Civil Rights Act of 1964.[17] But soon, a new generation of young women—those choosing to enter college, to begin careers, to join the counterculture, or

to explore paths that in many ways differed from those of their mothers—
became part of the movement to establish equal rights for all Americans,
regardless of one's gender.

The Late Sixties and Beyond

During the late 1960s, as the earliest of the baby boom generation was entering adulthood, some women—frequently those moderate to leftward-
leaning on the political spectrum—envisioned a future wherein women
would enjoy equal rights with men. They were aware that to reach such
a goal, numerous obstacles needed to be overcome. Myths that claimed
that women were passive and basically defined by their maternal instincts
needed to be defeated, as did stereotypical ideas as to what was masculine
and what was feminine. These feminist women were dissatisfied with arguments that in the 1960s a "New Woman" was emerging, one who was
middle class and liberated from much of the drudgery so often associated
with housework. Because of labor-saving devices, she could have both a
family and the leisure time to participate in self-fulfilling activities. But
feminists wanted much more than just an easier home life. They especially desired the opportunity to compete on an equal basis with men in
the business and political worlds and wanted to be judged as human beings rather than be stereotyped to occupy limited gender roles. Thus, they
called upon like-minded women of America to join in a movement to address the political and social roots of discrimination and to seek changes
to social and political institutions where necessary.[18]

The 1960s found more women employed in the labor force than ever
before, yet many occupations remained closed to women, or at the very
least were difficult for women to break into; thus, the vast majority of
women held low paying, service jobs. In 1968, full-time white male workers earned an average annual income of approximately $8,000, while full-
time white women received only $4,700.[19] Along with their recognition of
the vast earnings differential between the sexes, many women believed
they were being exploited in a variety of ways. Young, white, college-aged
women who had rallied in support of such campaigns as those for black
civil rights and against the war in Vietnam, discovered that sexism prevailed within the New Left, just as it did throughout the broader American
society. Within such organizations as Students for a Democratic Society

(SDS) and the Student Nonviolent Coordinating Committee (SNCC), they realized that they were being relegated to inferior roles such as secretaries and coffee preparers, while males held the leadership positions. No longer did these young women want to be dependent upon men and defined in sexual rather than human terms. These leftist women, largely among the eldest of the baby boomers, began making their own demands and articulating their own interests. Often referring to themselves as "radical" feminists, they helped launch the "women's liberation" movement.[20]

Significantly, while a large proportion of the women of the leftist SDS believed they were being exploited, sociologist Rebecca Klatch found a much different situation in the conservative Young Americans for Freedom (YAF). From interviews with female former members of both groups, Klatch heard only a few YAF women complain about men viewing them as sex objects or of not being respected as intelligent human beings. Investigating further, she found that mothers of SDS women frequently worked outside of the home while their children were growing up, and those who had working mothers were more likely than others to recognize sexism. At the same time, few mothers of the YAF women she interviewed had paid employment outside of the home.[21] It therefore appears that their mothers' actions and attitudes had considerable impact upon baby boomer women, both left and right. However, not all of the younger generation chose the same paths as their mothers. For example, Klatch interviewed two YAF women who became leaders of the rightist "pro-family" movement during the 1970s while their mothers were feminists.[22]

Meanwhile, some older, less radical women were also mobilizing on the issue of women's legal equality. They were demanding legislation to address issues of women's legal equality, job discrimination, and inadequate child care. Under the leadership of Betty Friedan, author of *The Feminine Mystique* (1963), a number of these women formed the National Organization for Women (NOW) in 1966. Both the older and the younger groups of feminists believed that the existing system perpetuated artificial and invidious gender distinctions that needed to be eliminated, but the two groups differed over specific demands as well as methods of achieving those goals. For example, historian Alison Lefkovitz points out that both groups found marriage laws that defined males as the breadwinner and head of household to be major obstacles to achieving gender equality; however, the more radical feminists disagreed with the more moderate

feminists who believed that the issue could be resolved simply by reform-
ing the current marriage laws.[23] The young, New Left women did not build
a large organization, but mostly banded together in small groups in their
push for women's liberation and an end to "male chauvinism." (These
younger women were the most colorful of the two branches of the movement, drawing the media's attention in such activities as burning their
bras and protesting the 1968 Miss America Pageant.) As the 1960s ended
and the 1970s began, the movement grew to include previously nonpoliti-
cal housewives as well as college and high school students.[24]

Some conservative women, too, were encouraging others of their sex to
push for more power. They wanted women to become leaders in promoting a rightist agenda. As their activism on such issues as education, public
health, school desegregation, morality, and the war in Vietnam shows,
rightward-leaning women were not averse to involving themselves in politics. In the early 1970s, veteran television personality Martha Rountree, of
Washington, D.C., was eager for women to become politically involved and
founded the Leadership Foundation, Inc. Rountree believed it important
for women to hold more power in the nation's capital. As the situation
now stood, "Washington doesn't give, it takes," she said. "Congress is no
longer representative of the people. . . . It's time for a change and women
must take a stand." Conservative on the issue of school prayer, remarking that the Bill of Rights guaranteed freedom of religion, "not freedom
from worship," her opinions on "women's liberation" came from a similar
side of the political spectrum when she charged that "Women's lib has
set womanhood back." The movement was too radical for Rountree, as it
was for most other rightist women who sought greater political influence
for women.[25] Despite the reluctance of Rountree and like-minded politically oriented women to join the campaign for equal rights, for a while it
seemed that the ERA movement was unstoppable.

The text of the Equal Rights Amendment is brief, and the wording dif-
fers only slightly from the amendment presented to Congress in 1923.
Section 1 reads, "Equality of rights under the law shall not be denied
or abridged by the United States or by any state on account of sex." The
remaining two sections, the enabling clauses, give Congress the power,
through appropriate legislation, to enforce the provisions of the law, and
state that the amendment will take effect two years following the date
of ratification. The House of Representatives passed the ERA in October

1971, and the Senate followed in March of the following year. The amendment was next sent to the states for ratification. Then, on January 22, 1973, the United States Supreme Court legalized abortion in the case of *Roe v. Wade*, a ruling that was a victory for those feminists who were demanding that women be allowed to make their own decisions about their bodies. Within a year of the Senate's passage of the ERA, thirty states ratified the amendment. For American feminists, it seemed it would be only a matter of time before the necessary thirty-eight states would ratify the ERA.

The outlook for women in politics appeared bright as well. At the 1968 Democratic and Republican national conventions female delegates had held only 13 percent and 17 percent of the seats, respectively. But in 1972, women filled 40 percent of the delegate seats at the Democratic convention and 30 percent at the Republican convention. Meanwhile, women's share of offices in local government more than doubled in just a few years, and they were beginning to win seats in Congress in their own right, not merely as successors to their husbands.[26]

The climax for feminist morale came on September 20, 1973, when in the "Battle of the Sexes," one of the world's top-ranked women's tennis players, Billie Jean King, defeated fifty-five-year-old Bobby Riggs, a former Wimbledon champion. King had been struggling for years to bring gender equality to tennis, and Riggs had been taunting her, saying that female athletes were inferior and did not deserve equal prize money. He had bragged that even an old man could defeat the best of the women's tennis players. King proved him wrong, and their match came to symbolize the women's movement for equality.[27]

The feminist celebration was short-lived. The Equal Rights Amendment met a roadblock—right-wing women. While most rightist women had long sought greater political power, few extended their desire to include a constitutional amendment granting full equality with men. For them, a much more important cause was the protection of their families. It had been at or near the core of their agenda for decades. Now they were ready to mount a grassroots campaign that would bring about a major defeat to feminism.

At first, ratification of the ERA progressed at a rapid pace, with state after state passing the amendment. But suddenly the rapid progression came to a halt. The last state to ratify the amendment was Indiana in 1975, and as of July 1976, thirty-four states had ratified the amendment. But the deadline for ratification by the states of March 1979 was fast approaching, and the process had bogged down. A sign of what was to come emerged in New York and New Jersey. The two states' legislatures had already ratified the national amendment when both states held referenda on November 4, 1975, to add an equal rights amendment to their state constitutions. Voters in both states rejected the measures.

Postelection analysts found that many women who had originally supported the idea of equal rights had suddenly developed second thoughts on the issue. Among the greatest concerns these women raised were questions about unisex toilets, the military draft, and women's right to financial support from their husbands.[28] There was also the fear that the ERA would promote promiscuity, as men and women would be brought together "unnaturally," not only in the military but also in prisons, on sports teams, and in close quarters on the job, such as in police cars.[29] These second thoughts were largely the product of successful campaigns of right-wing women. While others, including the male-led John Birch Society, actively fought the amendment, it was right-wing women who led the opposition.[30] It was the presence of *women* campaigning against an amendment that supposedly was designed to uplift women that led many Americans to rethink the issue. The battle developed into one of women against women, yet it was also often seen as a generational fight of young women versus the middle-aged.[31]

Middle-aged Illinois resident Phyllis Schlafly, long active in right-wing Republican circles, became a household name during the mid-1970s, when she became the recognized leader of the anti-ERA campaign. Schlafly had been active in rightist causes for a number of years, including campaigns on education, Vietnam, and moral issues. In support of Barry Goldwater's run for president in 1964, she wrote *A Choice Not An Echo*, and in 1967, she began publishing a newsletter, *The Phyllis Schlafly Report*. But it was not until December 1971, when she was forty-seven years old, that she developed an interest in feminism, an ideology that she opposed. She launched her antifeminist crusade in February 1972 with the article, "What's Wrong with 'Equal Rights' for Women?" in the *Phyllis Schlafly Report*. In September 1972, approximately six months after the United States Senate passed the ERA amendment by a vote of eighty-four to eight, Schlafly organized the STOP ERA movement.[32]

She began her campaign against the amendment with arguments supporting the stereotypical role of women as mothers, wives, and homemakers but soon she was addressing a moral issue: connecting the ERA with abortion. She explained why the two issues are so closely linked in a flyer, "ERA's Assist to Abortion," written in late 1974 or early 1975. Schlafly stated that "the very language of ERA" opens the door for abortion. After quoting section 1 of the amendment, she wrote, "Since a man obviously has the right NOT to be pregnant, the women's libbers argue that no Federal or State law against abortion would be able to deny a woman the 'equal right' NOT to be pregnant." Raising another moral issue, Schlafly argued that the ERA would not only "invalidate all Congressional and State law prohibiting or regulating abortion," but "the best legal opinion is that ERA will legalize homosexual 'marriages' and grant them the legal rights of husbands and wives." The legalization of abortion and homosexuality, she contended, were the driving forces behind the amendment.[33] Her focus on homosexuality, and abortion in particular, had a huge impact on the women's movement. Abortion was a hot issue during the early 1970s, both before and after the *Roe v. Wade* decision. Historian Stephanie Gilmore's study of NOW reveals that in 1968, when the national organization took a stand in support of abortion, it lost a large number of members, including some of its founders.[34] During the years 1970 through 1972, scores of petitions signed by thousands and letters from young and old poured into the White House. They represented both sides of the issue.[35]

In addition to struggles between the left and the right, the abortion issue sometimes caused conflicts within families and challenged religious teachings. At times the conflict was between generations. In August 1972, the *Washington Post* related the story of baby boomer Barbara Roberts who made the difficult decision to resist the teachings of her parents and her church, and to follow the path she believed was right. Roberts, a medical doctor, and a volunteer at an abortion clinic, grew up in a conservative Catholic family. The eldest of ten children, she realized the sacrifices that her parents made to feed, clothe, care, and pay for a Catholic education for each of the children. She also realized that, as a female, she had more obstacles to face than did males of her circumstances. Because she was born female, her early ambition of becoming a priest was quickly laid to rest. Her quest to become a doctor ran into traditionalists' attitudes regarding "women's place" as well. For example, following the birth of her first child, a pediatrics professor told her that her place was at home with her daughter, not in medical school.[36]

Despite such obstacles, Roberts was determined to "prove you could be a great doctor and a great wife and mother at the same time." What she described as a formative experience in her life came while she was a medical student and observed a woman in the hospital emergency room who almost died as a result of an illegal abortion. Notwithstanding her Catholic upbringing, this and other incidents of women's lives being endangered due to antiabortion laws and attitudes, led Roberts to evolve into an active proponent of both abortion rights and of women's liberation.[37]

Not all young people saw abortion as Roberts did. Two weeks after publication of the Roberts article, the *Washington Post* reported on a rally of the National Youth Pro-Life Coalition being held in the nation's capital. Although organizers had predicted a crowd of 25,000 to 50,000, only about 200 young people participated. Representing a variety of religious faiths, the demonstrators voiced opposition to abortion, euthanasia, and federal aid to Planned Parenthood. A young male doctor, a resident in obstetrics and gynecology, had similar experiences as a medical intern as those of Barbara Roberts, but he emerged with a completely different outlook. "I got sick of seeing women psychologically torn, or with perforated uteruses, post-abortion hemorrhages, infections, tubal pregnancies, being sterile," he said, and he joined the pro-life movement.[38] Whereas Roberts blamed the mutilation of women's bodies, and their near-death experiences on *illegal* abortions, this doctor blamed the problem on abortion itself.

The male doctor and the other young demonstrators at the rally were not "right-wing" on all issues, however. Although they were pro-life, most of the crowd voiced opposition to President Nixon's policies in Southeast Asia. They believed that Senator and presidential candidate George McGovern's antiwar views best represented their opinions on that issue. Torn between the two issues, many faced a dilemma as the 1972 national election approached.[39] With the voting age now lowered to eighteen, millions of baby boomers had important decisions to make.

A Gallup poll taken during the summer of 1972 revealed that age made little difference in the opinions of Americans over age eighteen on the issue of abortion. Sixty-four percent of those under age thirty agreed that the decision to have an abortion should be made solely by a woman and her physician, while 63 percent of those thirty and older took the same position.[40] So while young people were seemingly becoming more liberal than their elders on some matters, abortion does not appear to have been one of them. However, studies show that a woman's age apparently did make a difference as to her stand on an issue that rightists came to link with abortion—the Equal Rights Amendment. In this case, young, single women were considerably more likely to support the amendment than older, married women who did not work outside of the home.[41] Nevertheless, as women's personal circumstances changed, so might their positions on women's rights.

On the surface, Phyllis Schlafly's STOP ERA campaign pitted homemakers against professional and other women employed outside of the home. Yet not all homemakers shared her point of view. In the spring of 1973, the Chicago-based Housewives for ERA was actively countering Schlafly's arguments, noting their particular annoyance over her argument that she was representing all Illinois housewives. These women believed the amendment would improve their lives.[42] In her study of homemakers and the ERA campaign, historian Lisa Levenstein found that during the early years of the movement, some feminists within the National Organization for Women successfully campaigned to convince federal and state governments to pass legislation that would recognize the economic value of household labor. However, when NOW's leaders narrowed its agenda to focus more strictly upon winning the ERA, Phyllis Schlafly succeeded in co-opting and misrepresenting the feminists' position with her message that ERA supporters were anti-homemaker.[43]

Schlafly also attracted some young baby boomers to her cause, including several female members of Young Americans for Freedom, who later recalled that she played a crucial role in raising their consciousness. The STOP ERA leader personally convinced one young YAF member to testify against the amendment at hearings before the Virginia legislature.[44] Noticeable numbers of baby boomer women also joined in demonstrations opposing the amendment. For example, of the approximately thirty-five women picketing the White House in February 1975, protesting Betty Ford's pro-ERA position, a reporter noted that many were "young and wearing blue jeans."[45] Unlike leaders of the right-wing Mothers' Crusade, which maintained a dress code during their Vietnam War rallies, the anti-ERA leaders had reason to celebrate members in blue jeans. Their youthful dress gave the impression that women of all ages and social circumstances had reason to protest the amendment.

At the same time, many middle-aged women who favored the ERA took offense when the media stereotyped them as "pro" or "con" based upon age. Olga Coren of Bronx, New York, took umbrage upon reading an article in the *New York Times Magazine* in April 1976 describing a photograph of a middle-aged woman as "American woman (nonlibber)." Coren wrote, "What shocks and offends me is the implication that women of a certain age and appearance are as a matter of course opposed to the ideas and principles of the women's liberation movement and to the Equal Rights Amendment." As a fifty-seven-year-old mother of two adult children, who had been working as an editor for twenty years (since her sons began attending school full time), she argued that her outlook on life had much in common with women's liberation. Other women, both white and black, expressed similar views.[46]

On the other side of the issue was Annette Stern of Rye, New York, president of Women United to Defend Existing Rights (WUNDER) and founder of Operation Wake-Up. She, too, objected to stereotypes and wanted it known that it was not only middle-aged women who believed as she did. Like right-wing women who feared fluoridation and polio vaccination, Stern was worried about the outcome of the ERA. It was an unproven remedy to eliminate what she thought was, at most, a minor handicap for women. Stern maintained that she and others opposing the amendment did so because of the vagueness of the wording and "its uncertain consequences"[47] and argued that the majority of American women were happy and fulfilled in their present roles as homemakers.[48]

Stern did, however, propose a new title for women whose lives were centered on their responsibilities in the home: "home executives."[49] She and many other rightist women sought greater recognition for women who carried on "traditional" domestic roles. One way to achieve this was by defining homemaking as a profession. Both the right and the left courted homemakers, but the rightist anti-ERA forces had the greatest success. As Levenstein points out, it is the anti-ERA group that people remember as campaigning for the rights of housewives, not the pro-ERA forces.[50]

While Schlafly's STOP (Stop Taking Our Privileges) ERA was the leading group opposing the amendment, Stern's WUNDER was one of many other anti-ERA organizations with attention-getting acronyms. Schlafly was also a founder of Memphis-based AWARE (American Women Are Richly Endowed, alternatively, American Women Against Ratification of ERA), a group that served as an instrument for writing letters to legislators in states that had not yet ratified the amendment. Stephanie Gilmore notes that AWARE members were willing to work with politicians for small pieces of legislation that could alleviate some of the problems that women faced. For example, the Memphis branch of AWARE supported national bills that would make it easier to obtain credit in their own names. The Memphis branch of NOW, however, did not endorse the bills, as the group was focused upon the goal of winning the ERA.[51] With similar situations occurring on both local and national issues, it becomes easier to understand why the anti-ERA movement might be better remembered than ERA proponents for aiding homemakers.

The anticommunist John Birch Society actively opposed the ERA, and some of its members founded HOT DOG (Humanitarians Opposed to Degrading Our Girls). This Utah-based organization's objectives were in line with those of the Mormon Church, which also opposed the ERA.[52] Other groups forming in the 1970s were HOW (Happiness of Womanhood), FOE (Females Opposed to Equality), Ha! (Home Administrators, Inc.), HAM (Housewives and Motherhood Anti-Lib Movement), and W.W.W.W. (Women Who Want to be Women). Among the few groups that avoided the acronym trend were the Right to be a Woman Organization, Women for Maintaining the Difference Between the Sexes and Against the Equal Rights Amendment, the Committee for the Retention and Protection of Women's Rights, and Viva La Difference Committee.[53]

The titles of these organizations suggest that most of these women accepted Phyllis Schlafly's emphasis upon women's role within the home and her argument that God created women and men with not only physical differences but also designed them to assume different roles and responsibilities. Not unlike the Christian right's claims of a Divine plan that included a racial hierarchy, Schlafly and other rightist women believed in a gender-based hierarchy. Schlafly claimed that American women were a privileged group because they lived in a society that respected the family unit. As a result, the nation's laws and customs were based upon the fact that "women have babies and men don't." She wrote that those laws and customs assured women "the most precious and important right of all—the right to keep her own baby and to be supported and protected in the enjoyment of watching her baby grow and develop." While "a man may search 30 to 40 years for accomplishment in his profession," a young woman, by having a baby, "can have the satisfaction of doing a job well— and being recognized for it." The Equal Rights Amendment, she argued, would destroy all of that. Not only would it relieve men of the responsibility of providing financial support for their wives but also it would remove the woman's right to her children—"her best guarantee of social benefits such as old age pension, unemployment compensation, workman's compensation, and sick leave. The family," she wrote, "gives a woman the physical, financial and emotional security of the home—for all her life."[54]

While Schlafly's arguments convinced women with traditionalist leanings, many pro-ERA women could not comprehend why all women could not support the amendment. Patricia S. Caplan of the Committee to Ratify the Massachusetts State Equal Rights Amendment was one woman who attempted to understand the opposition's thinking. Caplan decided that the ERA controversy had arisen over a "clash of all-American ideals: Mom and apple pie versus equality, democracy." Schlafly, she wrote, "claims to speak for women who got their act together under the old rules and fear a change because they're not equipped for and not interested in work outside the home."[55] Caplan was just one of numerous ERA supporters who considered the fear of change to be a major factor in the reluctance of so many women to endorse the Constitutional amendment.

Lila Anastas of East Greenbush, New York, a supporter of the ERA, believed that fear played an important role in the defeat of the amendment in her state: "Fear of the unknown can do a job on people. The opposition, with its money and grassroots rhetoric, was aware of this."[56] Law professor (later Supreme Court Justice) Ruth Bader Ginsburg recognized such fears, but wrote that those fears "must not deter us . . . for the ERA represents the highest American ideal: recognition of the value of each individual." She maintained that the ERA would not cause an "overnight change in the law," but simply provide a foundation upon which to build nondiscriminatory laws.[57]

As evidenced in earlier chapters, fear is one of the various forces that lead to human action or reaction. Nevertheless, people who do not perceive of issues in the same way as their neighbors often dismiss opposing points of view as being due to fear of change when, in fact, that is not the

Figure 10. Women's liberation march from Farrugut Square to Lafayette Park, Washington, D.C., August 26, 1970. Courtesy of Library of Congress Prints and Photographs Division, LC-DIG-ppmsca-03425, U.S. News & World Report Magazine Photograph Collection.

case. There are many instances when they like and want to keep what they have. Thus, it is not fear, but desire that moves them to act. Both sides wanted what has for centuries been important to Americans, "life, liberty, and the pursuit of happiness," but they disagreed on what stood in the way. For the right, apprehension over change was an issue, but that was by no means the only issue involved. There were others, including those of states' rights and individual rights. Annette Stern argued that the ERA "would open a Pandora's box of constitutional issues" that could result in "harsh and heartless rulings" in court cases. She contended that the ERA proponents were falsely accusing the opposition of using scare tactics and were discounting mounting evidence that states with equal rights amendments in their constitutions were facing difficult legal issues.[58]

Writer Jane Dedman was another among the ERA proponents, who tried to understand the thinking of anti-ERA activists. In an article for *Playgirl* in July 1976, she wrote of the successes of the amendment's opponents in saving America's "far right wing" from the obscurity that befell it after Barry Goldwater's resounding defeat in the 1964 presidential election. Dedman described the issues surrounding the ERA as "sexy"—unisex bathrooms, homosexual marriages, and women soldiers sharing foxholes with men. After decades of fears of communist conspiracies, which Dedman saw as boring, at last the right had an exciting cause to rally behind.[59] In the debate over the ERA, sex again emerged as an issue for the right,

Figure 11. Demonstrators opposed to the ERA in front of the White House, Washington, D.C., February 4, 1977. Courtesy of Library of Congress Prints and Photographs Division, LC-DIG-ppmsca-01952, U.S. News & World Report Magazine Photograph Collection.

just as it had in the matters of integration, busing, and sex education. It would soon show up again in the battle over the rights of homosexuals. Dedman failed to note, however, that many among the far right considered the rise of the "women's liberation" movement to be the fulfillment of a Communist Party goal to undermine the foundations of American culture—the family, morality, and religion. The Network of Patriotic Letter Writers, who were among the older rightist groups joining the anti-ERA campaign, perceived of such a catastrophe. One member wrote Betty Ford to protest the First Lady's outspoken support of the ERA, charging, "The ERA is being forced upon us by subversive organizations, subversive people, and now YOU."[60]

The allegation of communist conspiracy was at the base of many of right-wing women's arguments. Dorothy Frooks, attorney and publisher of New York City's the *Murray Hill News*, wrote in February 1975 that the "majority of women in the nation do not know that there is a subversive group that are bringing Russia to our nation." As proof of the Communist Party's link to feminism, Frooks and others gathered documents that cited equal rights for women in the Soviet Union.[61] Frooks and many other rightist women believed that communists planned to use the Equal Rights Amendment to destroy the American family. Not only would women be required to leave their homes to go to work but also their children would be required to enter government-run day-care centers; men would no longer be responsible for supporting wives and families; and homosexual marriages would become legal.

Although the right wing objected to government interference in individual affairs, they exhibited no qualms about leading potentially vulnerable homemakers to believe that the ERA might cause them to lose some government benefits. Allegations that Social Security benefits favoring women would be eliminated with the passage of the ERA and that women would lose protections under state laws, spread quickly.[62] Suggestions from the right that married women's Social Security benefits could be affected resonated among the population. Many years later, a homemaker who describes her politics as having always been moderate to liberal, recalled her concerns about the possible loss of such benefits. Although she supported equality for women during the 1970s, she did have some concerns about the consequences of the ERA. She also remembers that she and her baby boomer daughter, who was single and employed at the time, had some arguments because her daughter thought only those employed outside the home should receive Social Security benefits.[63] Such conversations likely added to this and other mothers' anxieties over the consequences should the ERA be ratified.

Historian Alison Lefkovitz's research into "the problem of marriage in the era of women's liberation" found that the right was expressing concerns over having to pay increased taxes should the ERA result in homemakers being financially compensated for their domestic labors, especially if these wives were to receive Social Security benefits on a level equal to their husbands.[64] While such rightist women as Annette Stern wanted to define homemaking as a profession, when the question arose as to financial compensation, they had second thoughts. Fears about their personal financial losses could explain the right's emphasis on the reverse circumstance—a wife's potential loss of Social Security benefits—in their propaganda.

Some rightists connected the school textbook issue, which had never really died, with the Equal Rights Amendment. Mary Margaret Hober, of

Operation Wake Up, complained in a letter to Dorothy Frooks that the government was pushing pro-ERA at taxpayers' expense. As evidence, she gave an example from a textbook that her teenage daughter was reading in her high school history class, which stated that, if ratified, the ERA would "prohibit both federal and state governments from denying equality to women on account of their sex." Virginia Lavan, also a member of Operation Wake Up, agreed that texts giving positive reviews of the ERA should not be used in classrooms. Mothers and fathers, she wrote, should demand that schools use textbooks that honor the family, woman's role as wife and mother, and man's role as provider and protector.[65]

The forces opposing the ERA were well organized. It did not take them long to establish well-coordinated state campaigns throughout the country. Anti-ERA crusaders employed rightist women's long-practiced tactics of massive literature blitzes and letter-writing efforts, invited like-minded "experts" to give testimony for their cause, and put pressure on lawmakers to adopt their point of view. Rallies too, including one on Wall Street in October 1974, drew attention to their cause. Although only about forty women arrived for this "Operation Wake-Up" rally, they represented several women's organizations, including WUNDER and HOW. The newest group, WUNDER, claimed a total membership of about 5,000. The hour-long rally attracted an audience of Wall Street workers and the press.[66] Although often appearing in small groups, the women were dedicated, well organized, and frequently represented regions throughout the nation. In early 1973, when the anti-ERA groups first surfaced, women working for ratification were unprepared for how quickly the rightist forces could strengthen and grow.[67]

Many of the female leaders of the anti-ERA crusade were experienced campaigners for right-wing causes. Phyllis Schlafly of Illinois, the foremost leader of the movement, had considerable political experience within the Republican Party, including unsuccessful runs for Congress in 1952 and 1970. Diane Edmondson, a rightist Oklahoman who organized anti-ERA campaigns in three states, had experience within the far right as a member of the John Birch Society.[68] Ann Patterson, another Oklahoma leader, had been, along with her husband, active in Republican politics since the late 1940s. A third Oklahoma leader, Beverly Findley, first revealed her rightist credentials when Oklahoma City established school busing. She removed her children from public schools and helped to found a private school in her fundamentalist church. Findley had also been a member of the John Birch Society, but left because its literature about the communist threat scared her.[69]

Kathryn Dunaway led the campaign against the Equal Rights Amendment in Georgia. Married to a lawyer and the mother of two sons, Dunaway had experience in the conservative political world as a member of the DAR and as an activist with the Republican Party. From the time of the United Nations' founding, Dunaway had opposed it. She also shared the right's position on fluoridation, joining the movement during the early 1960s to fight against the chemical being added to Atlanta's water supply. In 1964, she organized "Bake for Barry" cake sales to raise funds to support Senator Barry Goldwater's presidential campaign.[70]

Anti-ERA leaders often found the John Birch Society to be a good source for recruiting grassroots volunteers. Dorothy Malone Slade, who chaired North Carolina's STOP ERA, was a member of the society, and networked within that organization to enlist participants. Some northern women too, including leaders of the North Shore group of Boston's STOP ERA, recruited from the JBS.[71] For those ERA opponents who believed in the existence of an ongoing communist-backed conspiracy to undermine American morality, the JBS served as a fruitful source. The long-established rightist Daughters of the American Revolution and Pro America organizations also produced large contingents of anti-ERA activists.[72]

Christian fundamentalist churches also proved to be excellent sources for enlisting women to the anti-ERA cause. Political scientist Jane J. Mansbridge notes that the anti-ERA movement grew considerably when fundamentalist groups joined the protest. The women's church activities gave them experience in public speaking as well as reaching out to strangers to win converts to their viewpoints. Their evangelical enthusiasm, coupled with the opportunity to network within their already organized churches, were valuable assets in the anti-ERA fight.[73]

As other researchers into the movement have shown, and as the references to God by women examined here also indicate, religious tradition played a large role in the defeat of the ERA.[74] Nevertheless, as seen in historian Martha Sonntag Bradley's study of Mormon women and the ERA, one cannot draw assumptions about a woman's stand on the issue solely by knowing her religious affiliation. Bradley found that while the Mormon Church held conservative attitudes regarding women and was antifeminist, female members were split on the issue. Both those Mormon women who favored the ERA and those who opposed it looked back to nineteenth-century women of their faith as models. Conservatives focused on the earlier women's domesticity and satisfaction with their marriages, while pro-ERA Mormon women emphasized their ancestors' desire for personal and public power.[75] Thus, while one group found tradition to be an argument for maintaining the status quo, the other allowed it to become a vehicle for change.

Jewish women, too, were split over the ERA. Many Orthodox Jewish women expressed concern over the requirement that women be treated equally with men should the military draft be reinstated. Again, fear of the unknown and fear of change were important issues. They worried that young Orthodox Jewish girls, who were accustomed to separation of the sexes, including during religious services, would be exposed to a lifestyle antithetical to their religious and moral convictions.[76] Other Jewish women, including Eleanor R. Schwartz, executive director of the National Federation of Temple Sisterhoods, argued that the ERA did not threaten Orthodox traditions and should not pose problems for them.[77]

Phyllis Schlafly mostly stayed out of the religious aspects of the debate over the amendment, but after many years in politics, she considered the ERA to be an issue that could rally the grassroots right.[78] A contemporary observer suggested that Schlafly saw it as a potential winner for the far right in that it could be defined as an "anti-family" issue because it was one that could be exploited as a serious threat to the traditional and moral values of less sophisticated homemakers.[79] Indeed, the influence of right-wing women expanded rapidly when they developed the term "pro-family" to describe their cause. This term was short, powerful, and broadly appealing. It proved to be an excellent propaganda tool. Historian Marisa Chappell points out that the proliferation of feminists alarmed many Americans who saw the "traditional family" as an "ideological and economic haven in a heartless new world."[80] Also, the idea of defending the family helped considerably to define the emerging New Right and was part of a platform that would soon marginalize feminist Republicans.[81] But grassroots campaigns require considerable time; thus, homemakers, with their often flexible schedules, became a natural constituency for anti-ERA organizers.

At first glance, attorney and newspaper editor Dorothy Frooks's anti-ERA stance might have seemed surprising to those who knew her as a child and young adult. Frooks was in her seventies during the ERA movement, but she was a single woman with a profession outside of the home and had a long history of helping to create new opportunities for women. In 1912, at age eleven, she became known as the "child suffragette" when she spoke to crowds on Wall Street in support of woman's suffrage. She broke new ground for women when she became a chief petty officer in the United States Navy during World War I. After the war she attended New York University Law School, the only woman among 300 male classmates. Frooks was the first female attorney for the Salvation Army, and helped establish the Small Claims Court, then known as the "Poor Man's Court." In 1934, she became the youngest woman ever admitted to the United States Supreme Court Bar. Her sympathy for the poor did not lead her to support President Roosevelt's Depression-era welfare policies. A disenchanted Democrat, she published an anti–New Deal book, *Over the Heads of Congress* in 1935. After the United States entered World War II, Frooks enlisted in the military once again, serving in the U.S. Army's Judge Advocate's office.[82]

Frooks's rightist views became more apparent during the 1950s when she avidly supported Wisconsin senator Joseph McCarthy's hunt for communist conspirators. In her autobiography, *Lady Lawyer* (1975), she writes that when others were attempting to discredit the senator, she joined with those who organized "Fifty Million Americans: A Society of Patriotic Men and Women for McCarthy Against the Pack."[83] Later, when she was approaching age eighty, Frooks described herself as a proponent and defender of both veterans' and women's rights, and credited herself as responsible for many laws in their behalf. She was a self-identified conservative who vehemently opposed the Equal Rights Amendment.[84]

In 1970 Frooks told an interviewer that the feminists were destroying what she and others had worked for over many years. She claimed that women now had more rights than men. Despite her personal history as an independent woman, she declared that members of her sex have a "historic and genetic place in society" and need men's protection. "God didn't intend women to go into cellars to repair plumbing."[85] Much of her animosity toward the ERA was based on her ideas concerning male-female relationships and her negative views of homosexuality. In August 1975, she wrote, "The so-called Equal Rights Amendment is being confused with Equal Rights for Women." Frooks alleged that the elimination of the word "sex" from the Constitution would not only allow for homosexual marriage but also would "do away with rape laws [and] 'private toilet facilities,' [would] mix the sexes in jails [and] hospitals, eliminating all privacy and freedom of choice." Later, in a letter to philanthropist John D. Rockefeller III, she wrote that another reason she opposed the ERA was that it would allow gay couples to adopt children. Also, as a veteran, Frooks believed that if women wanted to serve in the military, they should volunteer, as she did. They should not be drafted, which she was certain would occur if the ERA was ratified.[86]

In December 1977, as a representative of Women World War Veterans, Inc., Frooks appeared at New York City Hall to present a statement on women's rights. Recounting her activism in favor of female suffrage during the 1910s and reminding her audience that she and hundreds of thousands of other women volunteered to serve in the two world wars, Frooks denounced "this new breed of women libbers." She charged that they were not only attempting to destroy American homes but also were "doing everything in their power to destroy womanhood." The ERA, she argued, "forces women to become men."[87] Like many other rightist women leading the campaign against the Equal Rights Amendment, Frooks believed that broad opportunities and power in the business and political world should be open to women, but she also believed in adherence to limits as defined by gender and American tradition.

At the time that the amendment's path to ratification was coming to a halt, researchers launched investigations to discover what attributes characterized anti-ERA activists. In April 1975, when approximately 2,500 women traveled to Austin, Texas, to lobby for the rescinding of the state legislature's vote to ratify the ERA, female students from the University of Houston, under the supervision of their professors, interviewed 154 of these women on-site. It was not a scientific sampling, although students had instructions to choose respondents in such a manner as to "'represent' the population in terms of age and style of dress."[88] All of the women interviewed were white, as were all but "a handful" of the more than two thousand women at the capital. They were of the middle and upper classes, and nearly all were described as being well-groomed. Most of the interviewees were married (84 percent reporting that they were either married or widowed). Over half had been to college, yet 70 percent reported that they were nonworking housewives. Ninety-eight percent of the women claimed to be church members, with two-thirds identifying themselves as being affiliated with Protestant fundamentalist religious groups. Finally, the investigators found that the women interviewed had histories of political activism; the ERA was not the only issue to lure these women to action.[89]

A study in Boston, Massachusetts, in 1976, revealed similar attributes among those "anti" groups opposed to the ERA. In the Boston study, it was found that 92.3 percent of the anti-ERA leaders were married at the time of the survey, in comparison to 47.1 percent of proponents. One hundred percent of the anti-ERA leaders claimed religion to be "very important" in their lives; however, unlike the Texas women, the Boston leaders were predominantly Catholic. The Boston investigators found also that a significant number of the anti-ERA leaders held prominent positions within groups that were concerned with children, including Scouts, the YMCA, school committees, and church auxiliaries.[90] Thus, these women were having an influence upon the younger baby boomers and the generation that followed.

Overall, the women opposing the Equal Rights Amendment during the 1970s had very much in common with the women involved in right-wing campaigns of the 1950s and 1960s. Indeed, a large number of anti-ERA activists had participated in other rightist campaigns. Such organizations as Pro America, Minute Women, DAR, and Patriotic Letter Writers were among women's groups that carried on their rightist activities to include protests against the ERA. At least some of those women opposing the amendment believed that it was another example of government *forcing* equality onto Americans.[91] In the past, it was government mandated fluoridation, school desegregation, busing, and polio vaccination that drew right-wing women to take action. Now, they came to fight what they believed was forced adherence to new gender roles.

Despite recent agreements between the United States and the Soviet Union, such as the 1968 Treaty on Non-Proliferation of Nuclear Weapons and the establishment of commercial air service between the United States and USSR, 88 percent of the 154 women surveyed during their anti-ERA lobbying efforts in Austin, Texas, in 1976, considered American communists either a "great danger" or a "very great danger." Ninety-one percent agreed with the statement "the federal government is taking away our basic freedoms." Eighty-six percent agreed that morality in America was "pretty bad and getting worse."[92] With other anti-ERA activists, such as Dorothy Frooks, expressing similar opinions about domestic communism and other issues, the survey shows that rightist women's views had changed very little over twenty-five years.

In August 1976, the Republican Party came close to leaving the amendment off its platform for the first time since 1940. At the GOP's National Convention in Kansas City, Missouri, proponents and opponents waged a battle of words. Signaling that much of the conflict was between generations, fifty-two-year-old Phyllis Schlafly led the opposition, while twenty-nine-year-old baby boomer Betsy Griffith represented the feminist cause. The conspicuously pregnant Griffith pointed to her pregnancy as proof that she was not a "man hater," a charge that the right often leveled at those in favor of the ERA. Griffith professed that she was a Republican before she was a feminist and had joined the Young Republicans during her junior year at Wellesley College. In 1976, she was an officer of the National Women's Political Caucus and a member of the Republican Women's Task Force, which was affiliated with the former group. When the platform committee's fifty-one to forty-seven decision to include the ERA on the party platform prevailed, Griffith claimed victory.[93]

As years passed and the deadline for ratification by the states approached,[94] women's issues continued to receive the government's and the public's attention. Recognizing the United Nations International Women's Year, Congress sponsored the IWY National Women's Conference held in Houston, Texas, in November 1977. It was the first meeting of its kind since the 1848 Seneca Falls, New York, Women's Rights Convention. Between 15,000 and 20,000 women, of whom approximately 2,000 were official delegates from all fifty states and six United States territories, assembled at Houston's Albert Thomas Convention Center.[95] A reporter described the delegates as "a kaleidoscope of American womanhood," noting that while almost two-thirds were white, 17 percent were black, 8 percent were Hispanic, 3 percent were Asian-American, and another 3 percent were American Indian. They were of varied backgrounds—including doctors, lawyers, welfare mothers, farmers, nuns, secretaries, and factory workers. Ages of delegates ranged from sixteen to eighty, and styles of dress ranged from T-shirts and blue jeans to designer dresses. Although most supported the ERA, approximately 20 percent described themselves as "pro-family" and argued against the amendment and other progressive resolutions. Even while the crusade for the ERA was by then meeting strong opposition, delegates passed a twenty-five point National Plan of Action, intending to better the lives of all Americans. Their resolutions included such issues as the ERA, health care, and women's access to credit. Despite opposition from "pro-family" delegates and some ERA supporters who were uneasy over the issues of abortion and homosexuality, the two resolutions deemed the most sensitive—supporting reproductive freedom and gay and lesbian rights—passed with overwhelming support.[96]

A month after the IWY National Women's Conference, Dorothy Frooks complained that some members of a group with which she was active, Women World War Veterans, Inc., were given tickets to the event, but not voting rights.[97] Despite Frooks's colleagues' lack of recognition at the conference, the anti-ERA right was fighting back in a big way. Indeed, they were doing so just across town from the conference. Lottie Beth Hobbs of Fort Worth, Texas, cofounder of Women Who Want to be Women, had developed the idea for a Pro-Family Rally to counter the IWY National Women's Conference. Hobbs and Schlafly cooperated as leaders of anti-ERA forces, with Hobbs reaching out to the Christian fundamentalist women that Roman Catholic Schlafly had a more difficult time attracting. Schlafly and STOP ERA agreed to sponsor the counterrally.[98]

Of the more than 15,000 women attending the Pro-Family Rally at Houston's Astro Arena, most were white, well-dressed, and middle-aged. This homogeneous group was in sharp contrast to the "kaleidoscope" of participants at the National Women's Conference, for minority groups had more to lose than most white, middle-class women if they remained unequal in status to men. Many participants at the rally were affiliated with fundamentalist Christian churches. As was the case at many rightist gatherings, it included spiritual and patriotic music, prayers, and a large display of flags. In addition to Schlafly's STOP ERA and Eagle Forum, representatives came from the Conservative Caucus, March for Life, the National Council of Catholic Women, the Mormon Church, the National Right to Life Movement, the Daughters of the American Revolution, and the John Birch Society.[99] Rally organizers launched an advertising campaign in Houston newspapers, which included at least one advertisement that made clear its position on homosexual rights. It showed a little girl clutching a bouquet of flowers and asking, "Mommy, when I grow up, can I be a lesbian?"[100]

Their emphasis on homosexuality was an important tool in rightist women's fight against ratification of the ERA. It was particularly effective when they used it in combination with their stress on "pro-family" values. In his study of gay rights debates in Florida during the 1970s, Gillian Frank found similarities between right-wing arguments against both busing for purposes of integration and gay rights. He points out that the idea of sexual danger underwrote activism on both issues. Miscegenation was the fear voiced in response to integration, while gay adoption and alleged gay recruitment of children were fears voiced in antigay campaigns.[101] The right's message was clear: If Americans wished to save their families from the dangers of moral decay and destruction, the Equal Rights Amendment had to die.

For Schlafly the events in Houston marked a turning point. In addition to doing its own propagandizing, the anti-ERA gathering received considerable media coverage and the conference served as an organizing tool to draw in more supporters. Schlafly and others on the right found the lesbian issue to be an especially useful recruitment tool, as was the debate over abortion.[102] The right continued to emphasize the two topics throughout the ERA battle and beyond.

Several months after the gatherings in Houston, Schlafly continued to criticize the IWF Conference. During a speech before 700 participants at a Southern Baptist family life seminar in Orlando, Florida, she focused her wrath upon four of the delegates' resolutions—support for the ERA, day-care centers, what she described as "lesbian rights," and "government funding for abortions." At least one woman at the seminar challenged her to discuss the other twenty-one resolutions, which Schlafly refused to do. James M. Wall, an observer at the meeting, noted that Schlafly was unable to win over her audience of Southern Baptists, many of whom were young mothers. He predicted that despite Schlafly's STOP ERA movement's appearance of being on the verge of successfully preventing the amendment's ratification, the pro-ERA movement had served its purpose for many women. Wall believed that many of the women who "quietly fought for its passage have gained a sense of who they are." Such young women would not allow their roles to be narrowly defined as "baby-raisers" and helpers to male breadwinners, as Schlafly wanted women to do. These women believed they should not be limited to stereotypical sex roles, but that they had "the right to serve society as interest, talent and opportunity dictate[d]—and it certainly include[d] marriage, motherhood, the task of raising children and the creation of mutuality within a family structure."[103]

Wall's predictions were sound. Although the ERA failed, women have indeed made progress since the late 1960s, when the latest large-scale movement for women's rights began. Title IX of the Education Amendments of 1972, which President Richard Nixon signed into law, was of great importance to women. The law, which prohibits sex discrimination in any education program or activity within an institution receiving any type of federal financial assistance, led to a tremendous increase in women entering law and medical schools and nontraditional fields of study and employment. The Pregnancy Discrimination Act of 1978, which prohibited employers from firing, refusing to hire, and otherwise discriminating against women because of pregnancy or related circumstances, was another success for women's rights activists.

Women have accomplished much since the 1970s but, as baby boomer and Congresswoman Carolyn B. Maloney writes, there are many more obstacles that need to be overcome before they can claim equality. For example, in the year 2000, women managers made only 79.7 cents to a man's dollar, a proportion that was actually 0.7 percent less than what they made in 1983.[104] Maloney and other feminists maintain that the lack of an Equal Rights, or Women's Equality Amendment, to the Constitution is responsible for many of the obstacles that continue to hold women back from achieving their full potential.[105]

Conclusion

The battle over the Equal Rights Amendment was a culmination of conflicts over the direction that change should take in American culture and society. Although men entered the conflict on both sides, it was largely seen as a struggle of women against women as women led the fight on both sides of the issue. Because the majority of the anti-ERA women were middle-aged or older, while the majority of the pro-ERA women were young adults (particularly among those who were the most radical), it was, in general, also a conflict between generations. For many, it was a battle of professional and single women versus homemakers. But overall it was a fight to gain control over the amount and the direction of change. For instance, conservative Americans, including some of the baby boom generation, saw the ERA as going too far.

Although the baby boomers were the largest generation in American history, in the 1970s they were just beginning to have an impact upon the country's politics. Boomers born in the late 1950s and early 1960s were not yet eligible to vote, and few of those who were voting had made their way into positions of political power. Thus, despite their high rate of support for the Equal Rights Amendment, the older generation was still in control. Yet had the younger feminists conducted their campaigns somewhat differently, they might have experienced greater success and have won the approval of the final three states that were needed to ratify the amendment.

One baby boomer regretfully recalls that she and other radical feminists deserved a great amount of the blame for the ERA's defeat. Many feminists, she remembers, were becoming too arrogant; they acted as though they believed they were better than men. As a result, men felt threatened.[106] If such was the case, that did not bode well for the women's movement, for it was males who had the power in state legislatures and in Congress. Some of the female radicals went so far as to say that marriage and families needed to be abolished as institutions, and others expressed disdain, and even hatred, for men. Meanwhile, the younger feminists, whether it was true or not, were often perceived as being associated with the loosening of American morals and with earlier movements, such as those promoting black civil rights, student free speech, or peace in Vietnam.

Conservative opponents considered the ERA campaign as the latest example of growing threats from the left, and pointed these women out as representative of the movement and of what the future might hold should the amendment be passed. One Illinois legislator who voted against the ERA was undoubtedly thinking of the "bra burners," who had extensive media coverage, when he repeatedly referred to amendment proponents as "braless, brainless broads." ERA supporters in Illinois were roused to write defensive letters to their state representatives as proof that they were intelligent women who represented a "wide majority of the people."[107]

Continuing their rhetoric of the 1950s and 1960s, the anti-ERA rightists frequently referred to both American tradition and God. For them, the ERA, as well as such personal matters as abortion and homosexual marriage, challenged the Divine fundamentals of human identity—both male and female. Once again, many of these rightists saw a conspiracy—one that involved government and youth whom, they believed, had fallen to communistic ideas. Of course, not all ERA opponents were right-wing. Many were homemakers who feared the loss of security should the amendment be ratified. While they absorbed rightist propaganda that instilled doubt about the future under the ERA, they did not adhere to the entire right-wing agenda.

The use of emotionally laden slogans to defeat the ERA was similar to tactics that earlier rightist women employed to support such causes as antifluoridation. Such tactics identified their specific cause with the larger and deeply rooted emotions that at heart guide so many human actions. Using the term "pro-family" was an especially effective tactic. Although not widely used during the 1950s and 1960s, it was an expression that could also describe rightist women's campaigns of that era, for those women also emphasized their concerns about the raising of future generations of Americans. For rightist women, the term "pro-family" was one that encompassed numerous issues. The American family had been undergoing considerable change since the end of World War II. As historian Marisa Chappell points out, by the early 1980s the "traditional" family of male breadwinner, female homemaker, and dependent children had practically disappeared, with only 13 percent of American families conforming to that model.[108] For the right then, the threat of disintegration of the traditional family was dire. The debate over the ERA revealed that it was no longer only the working mother who posed the threat to the family's moral structure but also single mothers, gays, lesbians, and women's easier access to abortion.

By the 1980s, "pro-family" was associated with the New Right, providing a link between the ideologies of the Old Right and the New. Yet, while the term applies to the campaigns of both generations of rightists, the issues are not always the same. The moral issues of abortion and homosexuality are topics that the New Right emphasized much more than did the Old. This is because homosexuality and abortion, always present in American society, were now emerging out of the silences. The earlier rightists did at times raise the issue of homosexuality, but usually in discussions of communist-backed conspiracies to undermine American morality. During the ERA fight, there was still talk of communists manipulating youth to destroy American values; however, by the end of the 1970s, large moves by government toward mitigating the Cold War were making progress and, overall, the New Right was much less concerned with communist conspiracy.

Many of those studying the successes of the New Right in the latter decades of the twentieth century have concluded that the politics of the family, sexuality, and reproduction were important to the right-wing ascent during the latter half of the 1970s. In 1981, political scientist Rosalind Pollack Petchesky argued that the New Right's focus on reproductive and sexual issues gave it both ideological legitimacy and organizational coherence, and historian Catherine E. Rymph points out that conservative women's campaigns, addressing the ERA and other social issues, not only enhanced women's power in political parties but also enabled the women to become critical parts of a growing New Right coalition.[109]

ERA opponents Phyllis Schlafly and Dorothy Frooks are but two examples of the older generation of rightist women whose social activism carried them from the Old Right to the New. Both challenged the New Deal ideology of big government, were ardent anticommunists, and believed in conspiracy theories.[110] Both joined patriotic groups that sought to defend America, Schlafly in the DAR and Frooks in veterans' organizations. Both women defended the traditional family, yet were modern women who took advantage of twentieth-century women's opportunities to expand their roles into the public sphere. Thus, they were accepting of some change, but only such changes that benefitted them and women like them.

In her study of the women's rights movement, political scientist Christina Wolbrecht surmises that when the meaning and definition of an issue changes, equilibrium disruption results. When such disruption occurs, perceptions of an issue are likely to change, with the result being loss of electoral support. Although Wolbrecht places the beginning of the "equilibrium disruption" at about 1970, when women's rights issues were receiving widespread news coverage, the issue became considerably more disrupted beginning in 1973, following *Roe v. Wade*.[111] By the mid-1970s, with the introduction of a variety of new issues that became linked to the

Equal Rights Amendment, including gay and lesbian rights in addition to abortion, the resulting chaos opened the door for rightists to enhance their base of support.

Yet while rightists gained new supporters, women as a whole won greater opportunities. Prior to the ERA campaign, a few women reached high office, including state governorships and seats in Congress, but those numbers increased significantly once the movement was under way. From 1920, when American women won the vote, until 1968, only three women had held state governorships. Between 1975—when the Equal Rights Amendment push was at its height—and 2014, nearly three dozen women served as governors of their states. No woman ever served on the United States Supreme Court until 1981, when President Reagan appointed Justice Sandra Day O'Connor. Although the United States has yet to elect a woman president, Senator Hillary Rodham Clinton came very close to winning the Democratic Presidential Primary in 2008. Progress has been slower than most feminists wanted, but increasing numbers of women are making their way into executive offices and into powerful positions in government. Most of the baby boomers interviewed here voiced support for the Equal Rights Amendment, but they were almost unanimous in their belief that there was little chance of its revival in the foreseeable future. Most agreed that the majority of young women today are either apathetic about equal rights, believe that women have already achieved that goal, or both.[112] A boomer, who was a Florida state representative in the early 2000s, when Jeb Bush (also a boomer) was governor, remembers broaching the idea of introducing equal rights legislation. She recalls that he told her to forget it. The ERA, he said, was passé. It had "gone the way of bell bottoms."[113]

Historian Elinor Burkett found similar results during the late 1990s when she interviewed numerous right-wing women, both baby boomers and the Generation Xers who followed. Burkett learned that whether or not these women admitted it, the feminist movement of the 1960s and 1970s gave young women opportunities to make many choices in their lives, choices they could not have made in earlier decades. She noted, too, that while almost all women enjoy the fruits of feminism, few even think about where their opportunities came from.[114]

While it was under way, the push for the Equal Rights Amendment gave women, both on the left and the right, experience in the world of politics.

This was true for baby boomers in particular, since they were the most active in the pro-ERA campaign. They learned how to organize like-minded women for rallies, marches, and conferences and how to prepare proposals and resolutions. Even those who did not hold positions of leadership experienced the camaraderie of working alongside other women to achieve their goals. On the other side of the issue, the antifeminists politicized a different group of women. Some were baby boomers, but their mothers also discovered their political voices and left their homes to join the anti-ERA crusade. While the ERA controversy erupted into verbal battles of women against women, it served to remind their fellow Americans that women were capable of leading political fights; for it was the first time since women achieved suffrage in 1920 that the nation saw women at the forefront of a long-lasting, major campaign. Although legislators voting on the amendment were mostly male, and both men and women voted on state ERA referenda, the women's campaigns played important roles in swaying the votes in one direction or another. Despite the amendment's eventual defeat, women of 1980 found considerably more doors open for them than were available in the early 1960s. Thus, those women who had fought for greater opportunities for their sex deserved to emerge from the battle feeling a great degree of satisfaction.

CONCLUSION

With World War II over, and the country growing both economically and in population as returned veterans and others produced the largest generation of youth in American history, public attention turned to trying to decide what kind of America people wanted to live in. Whatever their politics, American adults sought to regain what they had lost during the Depression and the war and to adjust to postwar realities. Americans' social, political, and religious traditions faced challenges that included the worldwide spread of communism, the expanding black civil rights movement, and rapid advances in science, technology, and medicine. This, combined with concerns about the futures of their rapidly growing families, led increasing numbers of people to speak out and act from the grassroots. As the young baby boom generation grew toward maturity, it began to play an increasingly important role in American politics, society, and culture. Although boomers differed from one another in many ways, such factors as the new ease of moving around the country, the rapid development of mass media, the development of a youth culture, and their close contact with each other in colleges or in the military (as it grew once more to fight new wars) helped many of them to develop a sense of their potential power.

The right itself was undergoing change during the postwar years. Unlike the right-wing women of the Depression and World War II eras who often exposed their extreme anti-Semitic—and in some instances pro-fascist—attitudes, the women studied here mostly avoided blatant attacks on Jews. On that and other issues, most did not display the fiery rhetoric and militancy that had set many of the earlier generation of right-wing activists on the fringe. However, as historian Lisa McGirr has shown, before they could become a vital force in American politics and society, they would need to shed their overwhelming preoccupation with communism.[1] Yet it was not only their extreme fear of communism that put the far right on the fringe but also their notion of a general conspiracy.

For most of the rightist women examined here, communism was a sign of what was to come if their warnings were not heeded. They saw communists as being the farthest down the path toward disaster, for they were collectivist, totalitarian, antireligious, and most adept at manipulating other individuals and groups. Many of these rightist women considered the government's social programs, dating from the Roosevelt administration's New Deal, as part of the nation's decay. Particularly from the 1950s onward, the women believed the Supreme Court was involved, too, finding evidence in *Brown v. Board of Education of Topeka* and other court decisions. They also distrusted those who were introducing new chemicals and health programs that scientists alleged would improve Americans' physical and mental health. While they usually focused their anger upon the left, government, scientists, and the intellectual elite, there were several occasions when some of these women also took capitalists to task. On the issue of fluoridation, for instance, some charged that the sugar industry was hoping to profit as a result of parents not having to worry about sugar decaying their children's teeth if the chemical was added to the nation's public water systems. Overall, right-wing women saw themselves as fighting major battles for just causes, and most believed that if they intended to win, they needed to join forces with like-minded citizens. As time passed, they became increasingly active and visible in their campaigns and played a larger role in influencing society and politics.

These women created new organizations that addressed their concerns and also joined older ones, such as Pro America and the Daughters of the American Revolution. Their organizations were valuable. They made friends there and often built networks across the country. The mass media had an especially important effect on right-wing women in helping them to form their worldview. Earlier many had remained on the sidelines in regard to political and social matters. Especially via electronic media, right-wing leaders had the ability to spread their messages to women living in all regions of the country. Such opportunities were particularly apparent during the anti-ERA campaign, when the media was attracted to the clash between feminist and traditionalist women. The expanding media allowed rightist women to both build an image of reality that accorded with their beliefs and to draw to their causes women from the grassroots who discovered they shared common concerns with the right over the direction the country was moving. At the same time, the media was reporting on such events as race riots, student protests, hippies using drugs, and bra-burnings that challenged the basic beliefs of millions of Americans, especially those who held conservative ideals. For rightist women, such reports emphasized the need to take counteractions.

As their numbers and self-confidence grew, rightist women showed greater independence from men and male-led organizations. With some exceptions, including the DAR and Phyllis Schlafly's Eagle Forum (the latter of which welcomes both women and men), most of the organizations discussed here no longer exist. Those with narrow agendas, such as anti-fluoridation groups, were usually the first to dissolve once their goals were accomplished or were deemed lost forever. But new groups developed as new issues arose. In 1920, when women were granted suffrage, many Americans predicted that gender-related issues would lead women to vote as a block. That did not occur. However, gender did play a role in women's political activism, both for those on the left (NOW, for example) and on the right. Forming autonomous women's groups was an effective way for American women of the twentieth century to achieve political influence. In the twenty-first century, realizing that there remain differences in the ways that men and women see the world—and that women are yet to be equally represented within the halls of government—rightist women continue to found new gender-specific organizations. Smart Girl Politics and a second organization, Conservative Women, established in 2008 and 2012 respectively, both founded with the purpose of encouraging activism among conservative women, are among the more recent groups.[2]

Many rightist women of the postwar era were active in several right-wing organizations simultaneously. A woman might be in one group that was overwhelmingly comprised of women, while also in another that was predominantly male. Lucille Cardin Crain is an example of one who involved herself in numerous rightist organizations. Although her primary emphasis during the 1950s and 1960s was on education, she campaigned on behalf of many rightist causes. Another example is Jane Crosby of Pasadena, who, in 1961, founded the South Pasadena chapter of the male-dominated John Birch Society, while maintaining active roles in the Network of Patriotic Letter Writers, an organization in which women outnumbered men by a ratio of about two to one.[3]

The attitudes of those women who were most vehement in their anticommunism campaigns support the findings in a 1963 report on Americans' thoughts on communist conspiracies. Surveys of women aged twenty-one and over, from all regions, educational backgrounds, small towns and large, found that, overall, women were less interested than men in the matter of domestic communism. However, once an individual or group was identified as socialist, communist, or atheist, women tended to be less tolerant than men. They considered people with such ideologies to be disloyal to the United States.[4] Crain, Phoebe Courtney, Ida Darden, and many others examined here showed no mercy to those who did not share their definitions of patriotism.

Anticommunism, which had been a major theme for rightists of the 1930s and 1940s, became an even more important issue during the postwar era, attracting much larger sections of the American population. Combined with knowledge of communist involvement in labor strikes and racial issues in the 1930s and the tremendous spread of communism worldwide during the latter half of the 1940s and the 1950s, the right was able to identify their nemesis. Yet, for rightists in particular, blame for what they saw as undesirable changes coming to the United States could not be laid solely upon communists. Communists could not do it alone. Many of the new programs and ideas coming into American society were arriving as the result of scientific advancements and decisions in government. Still, communists could not be left out of the equation because there was also evidence that communists and sympathizers were in, or had recently held, government positions.

Rightists, especially those on the far right, began promoting the idea of a wide conspiracy. Senator Joseph McCarthy's allegations regarding communists in government added to such perceptions. The idea of "conspiracy" was an advantage for the right. The term provided a simple explanation for all the forces that the right, including hundreds of organizations of right-wing women, were struggling against. This "conspiracy" represented the opposite to what right-wing women stood for: the family as the primary structure of society throughout the ages, as opposed to the disintegration of the family; the authority of the individual to make his or her own moral and practical decisions versus collectivism; and God as the source of political order, ensuring stability and upholding morality versus absence of God and the fall of the moral order. The most rigid of the women studied here saw all of these factors as closely linked to one another and believed that they were all part of a common conspiracy. Others, however, only accepted parts of it.

Whether or not they accepted this claim of "conspiracy," right-wing women were not going to allow such forces to take over without a fight. However, some, even among the women themselves, did not believe they were fully capable of taking on such actions. In 1960, Ida Darden, herself a leader of the right, reflected upon the contributions of "patriotic" American women and their organizations. She contended that although these women were doing "excellent work in alerting the American people" about the expansion of communism into American institutions, women had not been able to break into "rough-and-tumble, down-to-earth, practical politics." She declared that despite their activism women had achieved very little, particularly in light of their "loud and strident boasts before they got the ballot about how they were going to 'clean up politics' when once granted the right of franchise." As Darden put it, "In party decisions and policy-making they are just the bubbles on the champagne and the foam on the beer." In other words, they were full of air, with little substance. Women, she wrote, were too inclined to be followers and to avoid taking stands on controversial issues. It was only when women were willing to take a stand and "hold out for principles and policies" that they will have "reached the kind of political maturity which will justify the passage of the nineteenth amendment."[5]

Darden and other such women may have had cause to be disillusioned with the progress of right-wing women's activism in the 1960s as their campaigns against such government mandated reforms as the integration of public schools and the banning of prayer in schools failed. Having been an antisuffragist during the early years of the twentieth century, Darden may have felt triumphant that her earlier assessment that women were incapable of intelligently casting a ballot was proving to be justified.[6] She was, however, overlooking rightist women's many accomplishments during the 1950s. The women had successes in their attempts to influence school districts in their selection of textbooks and in removing some progressive educators from their jobs. They scored some important victories in preventing fluoridation programs in cities nationwide. While their greatest victory—preventing the ratification of the Equal Rights Amendment—was yet to come, the women deserved more credit than Darden was willing to give.

In California in the 1960s, some conservative Republican women's groups were connecting themselves to the future of the conservative movement when they sponsored tributes to Ronald Reagan. The Sierra Madre Republican Women's Club in East Pasadena held a special program in June 1965, which included a luncheon for the actor/politician.[7] Reagan, who had charged Republican women to work hard at the grassroots level in anticipation of the 1964 election, and who had admonished them to unify when he saw them dividing into factions during the California Federation of Republican Women Convention in 1967, realized that women were an important force in politics.[8] He did, however, warn them to not be militant in their conservatism, but to "convert" Democrats instead of just seeking to beat them at the polls.[9] It seems he was laying out his plan to create a following among Democrats, a plan that would be successful, eventually propelling him to the forefront of the Republican Party and to a two-term presidency.

This idea of reaching out to others who shared similar concerns played an important part in the broadening of the right-wing movement, taking it from the smallness and narrowness of the 1930s and 1940s to its growth during the 1950s and 1960s and to its much greater expansion during the 1970s and 1980s. Rightist women experienced their greatest successes at drawing others into their crusades when they tapped into issues and concerns of other women.

Their extreme fear of communism links the generations of right-wing women, from the activists such as Elizabeth Dilling and Lyrl Clark Van Hyning of the New Deal/World War II era to Crain, Darden, Phoebe Courtney, and the many other individuals and rightist organizations of the 1950s and 1960s. This same theme carried onward into the 1970s when Phyllis Schlafly, a strong anticommunist, led the anti-ERA campaign. A common link for most of these women was their support for Senator Joseph McCarthy's fight against communism.[10]

Other issues, too, descended from one generation of rightists to the next. Textbook censorship did not begin with the *Educational Reviewer* in 1949, and there is little sign that the issue will ever die. Later arrivals to the textbook censorship crusade, including rightist Texans Mel and Norma Gabler who established Educational Research Analysts in 1961, helped carry the movement into the twenty-first century, where it continues.[11] While anticommunism became a lesser issue in battles over textbooks after the 1970s, new issues emerged. In more recent decades, diverse groups of New Rightists, particularly those among the Christian right, have kept close watch on textbooks for examples of "secular humanism" or of acceptance of homosexual relationships. The right-wing women's organization, Concerned Women for America (CWA), is one such group.[12] Founded in January 1979 by Christian activist Beverly LaHaye, currently under the leadership of Penny Young Nance, the CWA continues to include education among its core issues. The CWA also sponsors Young Women for America, which is designed to train the next generation to promote Christian fundamentalist values in schools and society.[13]

As Janice M. Irvine notes in her study of the battles over sex education in the United States, sex education was another bridge issue between the Old and the New Right.[14] It is an issue that has not been resolved. Despite periodic attempts, mostly from the right, to focus on sexual abstinence, there is still no consensus as to what students should be taught in school. At the same time, studies of sexuality among teenagers present mixed conclusions as to whether their sex education courses really have much of an impact upon young people's sexual behavior.[15] The New Right, however, does at times score some successes, such as preventing representatives from Planned Parenthood Federation of America from visiting local schools.

The focus on the family is an important issue connecting the Old Right with the New. Phyllis Schlafly, who played a large part in establishing the "pro-family" theme as an important element of the New Right's agenda, had strong ties with the Old Right.[16] The rise of the Tea Party movement of the twenty-first century, with its quick turn to the right, reveals that issues that were important to right-wing women of the Cold War era remain so today. Antistatism also has carried forth from the Old Right to the New. Too much government interference—especially in health care ("Obamacare") and gun control—are major arguments of Tea Partiers. Also familiar is their stress on the words of God and the founding fathers.

Rightist women of today, including Jenny Beth Martin, cofounder of the Tea Party Patriots, are proving themselves to be very influential leaders of political movements. Tea Party women such as Congresswoman Michele Bachmann and former Alaska governor Sarah Palin set their sights on even higher office. Whereas most right-wing women's activities of the earlier decades were usually lucky to receive notice in the inner pages of newspapers, what right-wing women do and say today is frequently in the national news, giving them greater influence than their predecessors. Through the growth of media, especially cable television, rightist women are able to reach significantly larger audiences than rightist women of the past. Rabble-rousing Ann Coulter, whose vituperative language denouncing liberals might once have placed her at the margins of the right, has gained much of her following as a result of her appearances on conservative talk shows.

The disintegration of the Soviet Union and its satellites deprived the right of what had been a major factor upon which it based its conspiracy theories. But, this does not mean that conspiracy theories disappeared. For example, Beverly LaHaye is among the New Christian rightists who charge that secular humanists are conspiring to take over the world.[17] As time passes, new faces emerge, but the old ways of looking at issues often remain. Nevertheless, the Old Right was at the margins of American society while the right of today is much larger. It phrases issues in broader terms, such as "big government," "pro-family" or "family values" that appeal to a wider audience. The technology of today, including the Internet, has impacted the New Right as it has all groups, enabling them to communicate instantly and interact with the world at large. But, because of its size, the New Right is also much more amorphous and includes much broader aspects of American life and culture. The struggle over how this culture should evolve continues to this day. But, to those on the right, the basic "threat" is still there: widespread secularism, moral decay, and rapid government growth, which they consider to be interfering with their version of how society should be structured.

Most of the grassroots organizations in which women were the leaders and comprised the majority of the membership were centered on social and cultural issues. These were also issues regarding which women had more influence than their male counterparts. The strength of their emphasis on family and morality continues to set rightist women apart from most right-wing men.[18] Most right-wing women did not express comprehensive ideologies in the manner of such rightist intellectuals as

Russell Kirk, Friedrich Hayek, or Ayn Rand. Much of the motivation for grassroots action came from how specific issues affected individuals or their families. When a matter bothered them, rightist women would look for others who shared their concerns. Often the issue would grow into something larger, as in the case of fluoridation. From worries about the chemical's effects upon their children's teeth, the matter might broaden to include anger against the scientists who developed the water fluoridation program, local government for administering it, and the federal government for allowing government interference.

For others, the matter of patriotism—or the question: What would our forefathers do?—was an important theme. Religion, too, held significant importance for many. Followers of Lucille Cardin Crain viewed her as an intellectual and relied upon her pronouncements on a variety of issues because of her writings, lectures, and associations with educators. For the baby boom generation also it was frequently not ideology, but specific circumstances, that determined how they chose their issues. For example, viewing her mother's difficulties finding well-paying employment, or discovering she held an identical job to that of a man yet received considerably lower pay, led many a female baby boomer to value legislation that supported equal opportunities for women. Seeing friends going to Vietnam and returning with major wounds, or not returning at all, led both male and female boomers to join protests against the war. These decisions were more personal than ideological, although they often had ideological implications.

During the first three decades following World War II, right-wing women struggled with many important issues. They sometimes expressed the unease felt by large numbers of Americans. Fears about consequences connected with fluoridation, the elimination of school prayer, and the introduction of forced school busing are but some examples. Nevertheless, the far right's extreme reactions to government-supported changes and their highly charged rhetoric when denouncing their opponents led some critics to give them such labels as "lunatic fringe." Rightist women, especially those on the far right, differed from moderates in that they often viewed matters in black and white, and were unwilling to compromise or to listen to both sides of arguments. They failed to see the contradictions between their convictions and reality. Rightist women stressed American principles of freedom and liberty, yet many could not understand why

African Americans fought for civil rights. Nor were many of these women willing to admit that such government- and science-backed health programs as fluoridation and polio vaccinations could have positive effects. Women on the right were frustrated that more groups and individuals did not agree with them. Nevertheless, their movement did expand as they found issues that more moderates agreed with and rightist women were able to connect with them via the media.

Many Americans today express concerns over the rapid and often secret extension of government surveillance; the growing extent of mass murders in schools, places of employment, and shopping malls; the threat of long-term worldwide terrorism; and a host of other issues. The right as a whole puts forth specific explanations as to the causes of the problems and proffers decisive pathways to action in dealing with these issues. Rightist women, especially, are motivated by anxieties about the future of their families and their desires to extend the roles of women within American political culture. Often attempts to solve problems in one area creates new problems. As Americans have to face increasingly complex issues, some new and some longstanding, the right, with its strong accent on tradition and individual rights, has a particularly challenging task.

APPENDIX

Right-Wing Women and Organizations That Address Multiple Issues and Appear in More Than One Chapter of This Book

Individuals

ANN ACKLEY, COLORADO
Interests: education, fluoridation, vaccination. Coeditor, with husband, Russell, of Christian fundamentalist newsletter *Portions in Due Season*

FRANCES BARTLETT, CALIFORNIA
Interests: education—textbooks, sex education, mental health testing. Editor of *FACTS in Education*; a founder and member of School Development Council

TAYLOR CALDWELL (BORN IN ENGLAND), NEW YORK AND CONNECTICUT
Interests: education, Young Americans for Freedom. Popular novelist who warned of conspiracies in her books; member of Minute Women of the U.S.A.

PHOEBE COURTNEY, COLORADO AND LOUISIANA
Interests: integration, busing, fluoridation, polio vaccination, sex education, school prayer. Coeditor, with husband, Kent, of *Free Men Speak* (later *Independent American*). She later became sole editor of the publication. Wrote series of pamphlets, *Tax Fax*, and authored *Sex Education Racket* (1969)

LUCILLE CARDIN CRAIN, NEW YORK

Interests: education, patriotism, voting age, fluoridation, Vietnam War. Editor of the *Educational Reviewer* (1949–1954); coauthor of *Packaged Thinking for Women* (1948). Wrote numerous articles, appeared on radio, and gave lectures before rightist groups
Member of Minute Women of the U.S.A., New York Citizens Committee Opposing Fluoridation, Mothers Crusade for Victory over Communism, and New York City Branch of Victory in Vietnam Committee

IDA DARDEN, TEXAS

Interests: mental health, integration, patriotism. Published the *Southern Conservative*

EDITH KERMIT ROOSEVELT

Interests: student rebellion, patriotism

MARTHA ROUNTREE, WASHINGTON, D.C.

Interests: busing, morality, school prayer, Equal Rights Amendment. Television personality. Established Leadership Foundation to mobilize conservative women to action

PHYLLIS SCHLAFLY, ILLINOIS

Interests: Vietnam War, Equal Rights Amendment, abortion. Authored books in support of conservative causes. Founded such organizations as Eagle Forum, STOP ERA, and American Women Are Richly Endowed (AWARE)

JOYCE ZUCK, CALIFORNIA

Interests: student rebellion, patriotism. Led East Pasadena-Sierra Madre Women's Club

Organizations

DAUGHTERS OF THE AMERICAN REVOLUTION (DAR), FOUNDED 1890

Interests: education, fluoridation, integration, school prayer, sex education, Vietnam War, Equal Rights Amendment

EAST PASADENA-SIERRA MADRE REPUBLICAN WOMEN'S CLUBS,
CALIFORNIA

Interests: patriotism, student rebellion

MINUTE WOMEN OF THE U.S.A., FOUNDED IN 1949

Interests: education, fluoridation, patriotism, mental health programs, polio vaccine, sex education, Equal Rights Amendment

NATIONAL ASSOCIATION OF PRO-AMERICA (SEE PRO-AMERICA)

NETWORK OF PATRIOTIC LETTER WRITERS, FOUNDED IN
CALIFORNIA

Interests: school prayer, patriotism, sex education, Vietnam War, Equal Rights Amendment

PRO-AMERICA

Founded in Seattle in 1932 as an anti–New Deal organization
Interests: education, integration, school prayer, patriotism, Equal Rights Amendment

WOMAN'S RIGHT TO KNOW, INC., LAKELAND, FLORIDA

Interests: education, integration, patriotism. Published the *Spirit*, later known as *American Spirit*

NOTES

Abbreviations

BHS	Bay Haven School
ED	Education
HU	Human Rights
LBJ Library	Lyndon B. Johnson Presidential Library, Austin, Texas
LCC	Lucille Cardin Crain Collection
MMC	Margaret Meier Collection of Extreme Right Ephemeral Material
NA II	National Archives II, College Park, Maryland
NA SE	National Archives Southeast Region, Morrow, Georgia
NAC	Norman Allderdice Collection
NPP	Nixon Presidential Papers
NYPL	New York Public Library Manuscripts Division
NYT	*New York Times*
OHS	Oregon Historical Society Library, Portland, Oregon
PCP	Phoebe Courtney Papers
PR	Public Relations
RM	Religious Matters
RRC	Radical Right Collection
RWC	Right Wing Collection
SMOF	Staff Member and Office Files
SU	Stanford University
UI	University of Iowa
UO	University of Oregon
WE	Welfare
WHCF	White House Central Files

Introduction

1. Taylor Caldwell, *The Devil's Advocate*, 9–22.

2. Caldwell, *Devil's Advocate*, 31.

3. See June Melby Benowitz, *Days of Discontent: American Women and Right-Wing Politics, 1933–1945*.

4. For census information regarding baby boomers, see http://www.census.gov/population/socdemo/age/.

5. Kim E. Nielsen, "Doing the 'Right' Right," 169.

6. Benowitz, *Days of Discontent*.

7. Jerome L. Himmelstein, *To the Right: The Transformation of American Conservatism*, 13–14. Rebecca Klatch, studying right-wing women of the 1980s, found two distinct ideologies among women of the New Right: what she describes as "laissez-faire conservative" and "social conservative." She writes that the former group views the world "through the lens of liberty, particularly the economic liberty of the free market, and political liberty based on the minimal state." The social conservatives see America as a morally decaying country, and moral problems outweigh all other issues. They hope to restore America to health by renewing religious faith, morality, and decency, and returning the country to the America envisioned by the Founding Fathers. See Klatch, "The Two Worlds of Women of the New Right," 529–32. The anticommunism strand was no longer apparent.

8. George H. Nash, *The Conservative Intellectual Movement in America Since 1945*, 52–60, 109.

9. Some recent studies that address the right wing and the issue of communism include: Sara Diamond, *Roads to Dominion: Right-Wing Movements and Political Power in the United States*; Mary C. Brennan, *Wives, Mothers, and the Red Menace: Conservative Women and the Crusade against Communism*; Himmelstein, *To the Right*; Nancy MacLean, *Freedom Is Not Enough: The Opening of the American Workplace*; Stuart J. Foster, *Red Alert! Educators Confront the Red Scare in American Public Schools*; Lisa McGirr, *Suburban Warriors: The Origins of the New American Right*; William J. Billingsley, *Communists on Campus: Race, Politics, and the Public University in Sixties North Carolina*; and Clyde Wilcox, *God's Warriors: The Christian Right in Twentieth Century America*.

10. Donald T. Critchlow, *Phyllis Schlafly and Grassroots Conservatism: A Woman's Crusade*, 8.

11. "Extremist," list compiled by the Extremist Committee, ca. March 1966, Box 9, file 45, BHS, Sarasota County History Center, Sarasota, Florida.

12. Catherine E. Rymph, *Republican Women: Feminism and Conservatism from Suffrage through the Rise of the New Right*, 213; Jean Hardisty, *Mobilizing Resentment: Conservative Resurgence from the John Birch Society to the Promise Keepers*, 38–39.

13. Randall Balmer, *The Making of Evangelicalism: From Revivalism to Politics and Beyond*, 59–65.

14. See, for example, McGirr, *Suburban Warriors*; MacLean, *Freedom Is Not Enough*; and Critchlow, *Phyllis Schlafly and Grassroots Conservatism*; David Farber and Jeff Roche, eds., *The Conservative Sixties*; Mary C. Brennan, *Turning Right in the Sixties: The Conservative Capture of the GOP*; Donald G. Mathews and Jane Sherron DeHart, *Sex, Gender, and the Politics of ERA: A State and the Nation;* Catherine E. Rymph, *Republican Women*; Jonathan M. Schoenwald, *A Time for Choosing: The Rise of Modern American Conservatism*; Kirsten Marie Delegard, *Battling Miss Bolsheviki: The Origins of Female Conservatism in the United States*; Kim Phillips-Fein, *Invisible Hands: The Making of the Conservative Movement from the New Deal to Reagan*.

15. David Bennett's *The Party of Fear* gives an excellent overview of right-wing campaigns and movements from the middle of the nineteenth century to the 1980s. As with Brennan's informative book *Wives, Mothers, and the Red Menace*, which examines women leaving their homes to fight communism, most other studies of the right in the twentieth century have focused on right-wing activities as they pertained to specific issues, regions of the country, or individuals.

16. Elizabeth Dilling Papers, Newsletters 1946 to 1965, Christian Liberty Church and School, Arlington, Illinois, especially newsletters June-July and August-September, 1964.

17. Grace Wick Papers, letters to and from Marilyn Allen, Box 1, file 1, OHS, Portland, Oregon.

18. For example, on their newsletter the Minute Women of the U.S.A., Inc., included the prayer, "If we are to be the instrument of thy will, O Lord, please help us." Newsletter, January 1958, Reel 76, M19, RWC, UI.

19. Paul A. Carter, in *Another Part of the Fifties*, 85–90, explores the 1950s male's perception of the role of the "dream wife" and reveals that young women perhaps did not always share the male point of view. Most of the women studied here wanted more out of life than what was available within their homes.

20. See for example, Kathleen McCourt, *Working-Class Women and Grass-Roots Politics*; Rymph, *Republican Women*.

21. McCourt, *Working-Class Women and Grass-Roots Politics*, 38.

22. Sara Evans, *Personal Politics: The Roots of Women's Liberation in the Civil Rights Movement and the New Left*, 168–69. Rymph found that a similar situation existed within the national Republican Party. Women staffed local headquarters, did much of the fund-raising, helped voters on election day, and organized speaking events, all of which were considered women's work. Rymph, *Republican Women*, 135–37.

23. Lucille Cardin Crain and Anne Burrows Hamilton, *Packaged Thinking for Women*, 1948.

24. Newsletter, Minute Women of the U.S.A., Inc., June, 1957, Reel 76, M19, and newsletter, Pasadena Anti-Communist League, March and April 1956, "The Octopus Seduces America's Womanhood," Reel 92, P4, RWC, UI.

25. Elizabeth Churchill Brown, "The Secret of Political Success: How to Convert the Unconverted," *Human Rights*, August 25, 1958, 3.

26. This is a conservative estimate based upon the documents found in my research.

27. Editorial, "The DAR Supplies Leadership," *The American Mercury*, August 1958, in Box 33, RRC, Hoover Institution.

28. Don E. Carleton, *Red Scare!: Right-Wing Hysteria, Fifties Fanaticism, and Their Legacy in Texas*, 113–16.

29. League of Women Voters, accessed August 9, 2014, http://www.lwv.org/.

30. Carleton, *Red Scare!*, 132.

31. Critchlow, *Phyllis Schlafly and Grassroots Conservatism*, 221.

32. For more on Dilling see Benowitz, *Days of Discontent*, 22–53, and Glen

Jeansonne, *Women of the Far Right: The Mothers' Movement and World War II*; Elizabeth Dilling, Bulletin, September 1952, Box 35, file "Patriotic Research Bureau," NAC, Hoover Institution.

33. Carleton, *Red Scare!*, 118–19.

34. Mrs. James W. Perry, chairman, and Mrs. Charles N. Allen, secretary, Charleston Chapter Minute Women, to Dorothy Frankston, June 30, 1966, and Frances Bartlett to Crain, September 22, 1966, Box 17, file 2, LCC, Special Collections, UO.

Chapter 1. Shaping American Education

Epigraph source: Crain, copy of speech before Rotary Club, Freeport, New York, January 25, 1951, Box 67, file 9, LCC, UO.

1. Both titles are from *McCall's*. Arthur D. Morse's article, "Who's Trying to Ruin Our Schools?" appeared in the September 1951 issue. John Bainbridge's series on public education appeared in *McCall's* under titles "Save Our Schools" (September 1952), and "Danger's Ahead in the Public Schools" (October 1952). At least three dozen other titles appeared in less widely circulated publications, including M. M. Morrison's "The Enemy at Work," *Virginia Journal of Education* (September 1950); Carey McWilliams's "The Enemy in Pasadena," *Christian Century* (January 3, 1951); and Ernest O. Melby's booklet *American Education Under Fire*, Freedom Pamphlet Series (New York: Anti-Defamation League of B'nai B'rith, 1951).

2. Morse, "Who's Trying to Ruin Our Schools?"; Arnold Forster and Benjamin R. Epstein, *Danger on the Right*.

3. Paul S. Boyer, "Boston Book Censorship in the Twenties," 3–24; Joseph Schafer, "Popular Censorship of History Texts," 450–61.

4. Eric F. Goldman, *The Crucial Decade—And After, 1945–1960*, 28.

5. This is not to say that these women were not anti-Semitic to one degree or another. For example, Lucille Cardin Crain, whose story will be covered in the following pages, collected anti-Semitic material but, it seems, deliberately avoided comments regarding Jews in her correspondence and publications. See LCC, UO. And, as Philip Wylie remarked when discussing American anti-Semitism in 1955, "Communism is widely regarded as 'Jew dominated.'" See *Generation of Vipers*, 147.

6. Foster, *Red Alert!*, 8.

7. "Report on the Conspiracy," *Time Archive 1923 to the Present* August 3, 1953, http://www.time.com/time/archive. This was taken from the report by the Senate subcommittee, investigating subversives in U.S. education. David Caute, in *The Great Fear: The Anti-Communist Purge Under Truman and Eisenhower*, 432, notes that in 1941 there were approximately 35,000 public school teachers in New York City. While ex-Communist Bella Dodd, who was a leader of the Teacher's Union in the early 1940s, claimed that 1,000 of the 4,000 union members belonged to the Communist Party, Caute believes 500 to be a more plausible estimate.

8. For more on right-wing women of the FDR era, see Benowitz, *Days of Discontent*.

9. As Nancy MacLean discusses in *Freedom Is Not Enough*, 35, white conservatives were stressing such traditions as small government and economic liberty, all contrary to the political and economic systems that had emerged from the New Deal and World War II. Carter, in *Another Part of the Fifties*, 28–30, notes how conservative Republicans were not happy with President Eisenhower due to his maintenance of his predecessors' programs, and in some cases proposing to enlarge them, e.g., Social Security.

10. Speech, Crain to Rotary Club, Freeport, New York, January 25, 1951, Box 67, file 9, LCC, UO.

11. Crain, "Iron Curtain Over the Schools," an address before Michigan Women's National Security Council, Detroit, February 13, 1953, Box 17, John T. Flynn Papers, UO.

12. The term "progressive education" was often used during the middle part of the twentieth century, harking back to the Progressive Era when John Dewey introduced changes in the approach to education. The term took on a derogatory meaning when the right voiced opposition to various changes that had occurred in education during the intervening years. While their protests became heated and widespread during the post–World War II Red Scare, many dated the problem back to the late 1910s or early 1920s. See Crain documents, Boxes 23–68, LCC, UO.

13. Susan F. Semel and Alan R. Sadovnik, eds., *"Schools of Tomorrow," Schools of Today: What Happened to Progressive Education*, 5–7; James B. MacDonald, introduction to James R. Squire, ed., *A New Look at Progressive Education*, 2. Bode found flaws in progressive education, but wrote that it had "a unique opportunity of serving as a clearinghouse for the meaning of democracy and thus making a significant contribution toward bringing to fruition the great hope and promise of our American civilization." Boyd H. Bode, *Progressive Education at the Crossroads*, 61.

14. Diane Ravitch, *The Troubled Crusade: American Education, 1945–1980*, 43.

15. Michelle M. Nickerson, *Mothers of Conservatism: Women and the Postwar Right*; Nickerson, "Moral Mothers and Goldwater Girls," 51–61; McGirr, *Suburban Warriors*; Critchlow, *Phyllis Schlafly and Grassroots Conservatism*.

16. Crain, address before the Study Group on Communism, Women's National Republican Club, New York City, December 1, 1953, Box 67, file 12, LCC, UO.

17. See also Ravitch, *The Troubled Crusade*, 43–45.

18. See especially Melby, *American Education Under Fire*, 26–36.

19. Morse, "Who's Trying to Ruin Our Schools?" *McCall's*, September 1951. Pasadena is near Orange County, which was known as a center of conservatism during the 1950s and 1960s. Kurt Schuparra, *Triumph of the Right: The Rise of the California Conservative Movement, 1945–1966*, xiv; McGirr, *Suburban Warriors*; Neal R. Peirce, *The Pacific States of America: People, Politics, and Power in the Five Pacific Basin States*, 37.

20. See especially letters of September 7, 1948, and September 13, 1948—Buckley to Crain and Crain to Buckley, respectively. It was George Montgomery who had introduced Crain to Buckley, and he would serve for a time on the board of

the Educational Reviewer. Montgomery dedicated *The Return of Adam Smith* "To those parents who have watched in bewilderment as their children emerge from American schools and colleges mouthing strange and alien philosophies. . . . And to those of America's youth who have as yet escaped complete enthrallment of the propaganda that is daily leveled at them from lecture hall and library." Box 26, file 15, LCC, UO.

21. Crain to Buckley, July 31, 1948, and exchange of letters between Buckley and Crain during January 1950. In letter of January 4, 1950, Crain writes Buckley, "Scoop flash, bulletin—a personal check for $500 from Mr. Lammot DuPont." Box 26, file 21, LCC, UO.

22. Box 26, files 14–25. Patricia worked as a secretary and in other capacities for the Educational Reviewer for about a year. See also Box 27 for correspondence with and regarding William F. Buckley Jr., and Box 72, file 3 for advertisement. LCC, UO.

23. For more on Crain's World War II-era activities, see Benowitz, *Days of Discontent*, 125–26, 146–47.

24. Illness prevented Crain's coauthor, attorney Anne Burrows Hamilton, from doing much promotional work for the booklet. In the early months of their collaboration on the Reviewer, William F. Buckley Sr., expressed interest in her work on "Communistic Infiltration in Women's Organizations." See Box 26, file 14, especially Buckley to Crain, March 16, 1948, LCC, UO. Crain and Hamilton, *Packaged Thinking for Women*, 23.

25. The right-wing Friends of the Public Schools used *Packaged Thinking* as the base of their editorial, "Who Is Doing Your Thinking for You: or Who Controls Your Thoughts," in their August 1949 *Bulletin*. See Reel 18, B11, RWC, UI.

26. In a letter to Lee H. Bristol, dated September 21, 1951, Crain wrote, "The truth is that I have no association whatever with either [of the two groups with which the article's author linked her] . . . except to receive their materials as they do mine. I do not mean to imply, however, that I decry with the author of the article the activities of these organizations." Box 26, file 4, LCC, UO.

27. "Pleadings," Box 62, file 11, LCC, UO.

28. Crain placed much of the blame for the Educational Reviewer's financial woes on board member George Montgomery, who she claimed initiated the lawsuit against *McCall's* without first consulting her. She also believed that Montgomery was conspiring to have her removed from the Reviewer, and succeeded in having him censured at a board meeting during the summer of 1954. The failure of the Educational Reviewer, coupled with Crain's arguments with Montgomery, led to an uncomfortable relationship with William F. Buckley when he continued to voice support for Montgomery. June 24, 1954, Crain to Buckley; and June 30, 1954, Buckley to Crain, Box 27, file 4, LCC, UO.

29. Phillips-Fein, *Invisible Hands*, 10–21; LCC, UO, Box 26, file 21, January 4, 1950, Crain to William Buckley; Box 29, files 2 and 3; and Crain to Lee H. Bristol, Bristol-Myers Company, September 21, 1951, Box 26, file 4, LCC, UO.

30. Edna Brinkman to Crain, May 1, 1954, Box 6, file 21, LCC, UO.

31. Crain to Scanlon, May 8, 1961, Box 27, file 13, LCC, UO.

32. "A Philosofer's Stone for Textbooks," *Chicago Daily Tribune*, January 18, 1950, 20.

33. "Advice on Text Books," *Chicago Sunday Tribune*, January 29, 1950, 16.

34. Deposition, ca. 1951. She taught elementary school in rural Minnesota towns of Fisher and Dorothy, until she developed tuberculosis in the early 1920s, Box 62, file 3, LCC, UO.

35. See, for example, newsletter from Pro America, Inc., East Orange, New Jersey, announcing a luncheon on January 22, 1953, at which Crain was scheduled to be featured speaker, Box 51, file 5; June 28, 1953, newsletter from Pro America, Illinois Chapter saying that highlight of year's activities was talk by Crain on May 5, 1953, entitled "Let's Keep America in the Schoolroom." Also, "Stress Needed on 'Right' Editor Tells Minute Women," *Charlotte Gazette*, October 6, 1953, Box 64, file 4, LCC, UO.

36. U.S. Congress, 82nd Congress, Second Session, "The UNESCO Threat to Our Schools," Remarks of Hon. Paul W. Shafer of Michigan, Wednesday, July 2, 1952.

37. See correspondence with Flynn, Box 34, file 22, LCC, UO.

38. Correspondence between Palmer and Crain. Quoted from letter of May 18, 1951, Palmer to Crain, Box 51, file 15, LCC, UO.

39. Crain to Cassel Publishers Service, November 19, 1952, Box 17, file 17, LCC, UO.

40. MacBride to Crain, December 3, 1952, Box 17, file 17, LCC, UO.

41. T. J. Ross to Crain, June 20, 1950, Box 29, file 2, LCC, UO.

42. Boxes 23–61, LCC, UO.

43. Behrhorst to Crain, 14 November 1950, Box 25, file 7, LCC, UO.

44. For example, see memo to John Flynn, September 1, 1950, Box 34, file 21; J. B. Withee to Crain, Box 24, file 6; "Investigation of Subversive Text-Books," Mrs. E. L. Harwell (copy of state report given at State Conference at Waco, Texas, March 1952), Box 30, file 10, LCC, UO.

45. Foster, *Red Alert!*, 98–99.

46. Crain to Buckley, December 16, 1949, Box 26, file 20, LCC, UO.

47. Crain to Flynn, September 15, 1951, Box 34, file 21, LCC, UO.

48. Ravitch, *The Troubled Crusade*, 85–89.

49. Crain to Buckley, July 20, 1950, Box 26, file 22, LCC, UO.

50. *Educational Reviewer*, vol. 1, no. 4, April 15, 1950, 1, Box 61, file 6, LCC, UO.

51. MacBride would also lead a student libertarian group at Harvard, become a state representative in Vermont, and play an important role in the Libertarian Party during the 1970s, including running for the presidency as a Libertarian Party candidate in 1976. See Brian Doherty, *Radicals for Capitalism: A Freewheeling History of the Modern American Libertarian Movement*, 131 and 397. Clark Woodroe was another student. Woodroe to Crain, November 27, 1954, Box 7, file 13, LCC, UO.

52. Box 24, files 16–21, LCC, UO. For more on the Pasadena affair, see David Hurlburd, *This Happened in Pasadena*. Bartlett was a fan of the *Educational Reviewer*,

and when she learned it was ceasing publication, she expressed regrets to its editor, saying "Au revoir—a big job well done." In "Sad Facts," *FACTS in Education*, November-December 1953, Reel 46, RWC, UI.

53. Carleton, *Red Scare!*, 114.

54. Mary Lamar Knight, who preceded Bartlett as editor of *FACTS*, had been a foreign correspondent for the United Press. In January 1953, she went on an extended speaking tour, culminating in a role as a chief speaker at the Women's Patriotic Societies meeting in Washington, D.C., where she spoke on "Progressive Education and UNESCO." It appears that Bartlett took over the reins of editing and publishing the newsletter from Knight sometime in 1953. "Facts Editor on Lecture Tour," *FACTS in Education*, January 1953 and "Five Years and Now," *FACTS*, April-May 1955 and August-September 1955, Reel, 46, RWC, UI.

55. "Five Years and Now," *FACTS in Education*, April-May 1955, and August-September 1955, Reel 46, RWC, UI.

56. Newsletter, January 1953, 3, Reel 76, M19, RWC, UI; Carleton, *Red Scare!*, 111–12.

57. Newsletter, January 1953, 3, Reel 76, M19, RWC, UI.

58. John R. Crippen, "And Now 'McCallism,'" Reel 76, M19, RWC, UI.

59. For more on the Minute Women's influence in Texas, and especially in Houston, see Carleton, *Red Scare!*, and the Houston *Post*, October 11–28, 1953.

60. Carleton, *Red Scare!*, 128; Houston *Post*, October 11–28, 1953.

61. Helen Holt, regent, Sara De Soto Chapter, Daughters of the American Revolution, in essay, "What the Daughters Do," writes that the Daughters operate schools for poor children, spending millions of dollars. They also offer scholarships. They stress in their schools the teaching of American history, familiarity with the Constitution, and other historic documents, and instill a "reverence for the American flag." From unidentified newspaper, October 12, 1958, in file "Associations: DAR, Sarasota," Sarasota History Center. Kim E. Nielsen, *Un-American Womanhood: Antiradicalism, Antifeminism, and the First Red Scare*, 57.

62. Nielsen, *Un-American Womanhood*, 34.

63. Benowitz, *Days of Discontent*, 28.

64. Richard M. Ketchum, *The Borrowed Years: America on the Way to War*, 114.

65. Osie Smith Coolbaugh, "Our Most Powerful Weapon of Defense," *Daughters of the American Revolution Magazine*, July 1953, Box 32, RRC, Hoover Institution.

66. Francs B. Lucas, "A New Social Order Being Taught—'Progressive Education,'" September 1953, Box 41, RRC, Hoover Institution.

67. Editorial, "The DAR Supplies Leadership," *American Mercury*, August 1958, in Box 33, RRC, Hoover Institution. The article stated further that such organizations as the League of Women Voters, the PTA, the National Federation of Business and Professional Women, the American Association of University Women, and the YWCA "are only too frequently counted in the ranks of the political left, on vital issues."

68. For example, correspondence from the DAR came from such states as Vir-

ginia, Minnesota, Ohio, Kansas, Indiana, Idaho, Louisiana, Kentucky, and Texas. Box 30, files 9–11, LCC, UO.

69. Friends of the Public Schools Bulletin, "The Daughters of the American Revolution Explain Their Stand on Federal Aid to Education," March 1951, RWC, UI.

70. Daughters of the American Colonies, minutes, January 11, 1952. However, the Oregon Chapter of the Colonial Dames of America made efforts in the 1960s to develop in schoolchildren "attitudes of *patriotism* as opposed to *nationalism*" (Colonial Dames' emphasis). "A History of the Colonial Dames as Resident in the State of Oregon 1923–1967," 23. Box 3, "Daughters of the American Colonies" and "Colonial Dames of America," Associations, Institutions Collection, OHS.

71. Carleton, *Red Scare!*, 125.

72. Pamphlet, "Pro America: National Organization of Republican Women, Inc.," 1936, Grace Wick Papers, OHS; Benowitz, *Days of Discontent*, 16.

73. Hurlburd, *This Happened in Pasadena*, 57–58, and 60.

74. *The Pasadena Story* (Washington, D.C.: National Commission for the Defense of Democracy through Education of the National Educational Association of the United States, 1951) 14, 21.

75. Bonny to Crain, June 10, 1949, Box 25, file 21, LCC, UO.

76. Alexander to Crain, July 1953, Box 24, file 9, LCC, UO.

77. Dorothy Frank, "I Was Called a Subversive," *Collier's*, March 28, 1953, 68–73.

78. Ibid.

79. Justus D. Doenecke, "Irene Corbally Kuhn," in *Women in World History*, ed. Anne Commire.

80. Irene Corbally Kuhn, "Your Child Is Their Target," *American Legion Magazine*, June 1952, in Box 64, file 4, LCC, UO.

81. Ibid.

82. Jonathan Zimmerman, *Whose America?: Culture Wars in the Public Schools*, 95–96.

83. Carleton, *Red Scare!*, 114, 125.

84. Myrtle G. Hance, "A Report on Our San Antonio Public Libraries Communist Front Authors and Their Books Therein," n.d., ca. 1952. Box 37, files 19-20, LCC, UO.

85. J. C. Phillips, "Patriot Crusades to Label All Communist Books," *Free Men Speak*, March 21, 1955, Box 1, PCP, UO.

86. Caldwell to Mr. Roche, October 16, 1957, Federal Bureau of Investigation, the Vault, "Taylor Caldwell," accessed January 25, 2014, http://vault.fbi.gov/Taylor%20 Caldwell.

87. Caldwell to Flynn, May 2, 1953, Box 17, file C, John T. Flynn papers, UO.

88. Ibid.

89. Newsletter, Minute Women of the U.S.A., Inc., December 1952, Reel 76, M19, RWC, UI.

90. Caldwell, *Devil's Advocate*, 30.

91. Ibid., 35.

92. Ibid., 47.

93. For example, see "Report on the Conspiracy," *Time Archive 1923 to the Present*, August 3, 1953. Also, "Communist Teachers," *Tampa Tribune*, September 19, 1952.

94. Bella Dodd, *School of Darkness*, 151.

95. Box 30, files 22 and 23, LCC, UO.

96. Anne Atkins to Senator Lyndon Johnson, October 1, 1953, U. S. Senate, General Files, Box 491, LBJ Library.

97. Dodd, *School of Darkness*, 248–49.

98. Mary L. Allen, *Education or Indoctrination?* More information regarding Allen and other right-wing women playing active roles in the Pasadena affair can be found in chapter 3 of Nickerson's *Mothers of Conservatism*.

99. Rosalie Gordon, *What's Happened to Our Schools?*, 4–5, 20–22.

100. Dorothy Thompson, "Report on the American Communist," *Ladies Home Journal*, January 1953.

101. Dorothy Thompson, "Do Our Schools Need an SOS?," *Ladies Home Journal*, February 1953, 14.

102. Ibid., 86.

103. Dorothy Thompson, "Do American Educators Know What They Are Up To?," *Ladies Home Journal*, January 1958.

104. Lillian Bellison, "State Women Split on School Survey," *NYT*, November 14, 1951, 19.

105. "Scarsdale Women Criticize Program," *NYT*, November 8, 1951, 32.

106. "Scarsdale Reports No Reds in Schools," *NYT*, April 24, 1953, 25.

107. Zimmerman, *Whose America?*, 103–4.

108. David M. Oshinsky, *A Conspiracy So Immense: The World of Joe McCarthy*, 464.

109. "Textbook Study, 1958–1959," National Defense Committee, National Society, Daughters of the American Revolution, in Box 46, RRC, Hoover Institution.

110. Marian M. Strack, "How Government Agencies Changed Our History Textbooks," reprinted from *DAR Magazine*, December 1960, in Box 30, file 11, MMC, SU, Department of Special Collections.

111. Harry Schwartz, "Peril to Doing Sums Seen in 'New Math,'" *NYT*, December 31, 1964; Open letter from Dorothy, newsletter, Minute Women of the U.S.A., Inc., January 1967, 2.

112. Open letter from Dorothy, newsletter, Minute Women of the U.S.A., Inc., January 1967, 2.

113. Dick Turpin, "Vote on Social Studies Textbooks Faces Delay," *Los Angeles Times*, January 9, 1962; "New Texts Protested by Parents," *Los Angeles Times*, January 5, 1962. Both articles in Box 30, file 10, MMC, SU.

114. "School Bill On Communism Passes Senate," *Jackson County Floridian*, May 3, 1961; "Anti-Red Course Called Dangerous," *Miami Daily News*, June 4, 1964.

115. Eckard V. Toy Jr., "The Right Side of the 1960s: The Origins of the John

Birch Society in the Pacific Northwest," 260–83; Barbara S. Stone, "The John Birch Society: A Profile," 184–97.

116. Daniel R. Campbell, "Right-Wing Extremists and the Sarasota Schools, 1960–1966," 17.

117. Ibid., 18.

118. Ibid., 20.

119. Newspaper clipping, "SHS Graduate Comments," letter to the editor *Sarasota Herald-Tribune* from Julia Kiger, September 16, 1964, Box 7, file 36, BHS, Sarasota County History Center.

120. "Sees Schools Infiltrated," letter to the editor from Margaret G. Crosby, *Sarasota Herald-Tribune* September 25, 1964, Box 7, file 36, BHS, Sarasota County History Center.

121. Letter to the editor from Mrs. James Takores, *Sarasota Herald-Tribune*, October 11, 1964, Box 7, file 36, BHS, Sarasota County History Center

122. Mrs. J. P. [Elizabeth] McCall to Mrs. Sam Spencer, March 13, 1966, Box 7, file 34, BHS, Sarasota County History Center.

123. E-mails, Elizabeth McCall to author, September 19, 2006, and September 20, 2006; Jennelle Moorhead to Mrs. J. P. McCall, October 20, 1965, Box 7, file 34, BHS, Sarasota County History Center.

124. Harold Rummell, "PTA Shies from Right-Wing Ties," *Evening Independent*, June 15, 1964, *American Spirit*, Reel 8, A49, RWC, UI.

125. "P.T.A.," *Spirit*, July-August 1964, Reel 8, A49, RWC, UI.

126. Dick Turpin, "PTA Shaken by Losses," *Atlanta Journal*, April 24, 1966, in Box 8, file 40, BHS, Sarasota County History Center.

127. Marjorie Niles Kime, "The Little Red Hens," in Box 49, RRC, Hoover Institution.

128. U.S. Senate, Cong. Rec., 89th Congress, First Session, September 14, 1965, vol. 111, no. 169, "PTA Under Attack," includes transcript of article printed in *Look*, September 7, 1965, "The Plot to Take Over the PTA," in Box 8, file 40, BHS, Sarasota County History Center.

129. Untitled John Birch Society publication, ca. November 1960, "Politics and Miscellaneous, Radical Groups #1," Box 17, file 10, OHS.

130. John Birch Society, "Responsible Leadership through the John Birch Society," n.d., ca. April 1965, in Box 14, file 16, MMC, SU.

131. Schoenwald, *A Time for Choosing*, 82.

132. Nickerson, *Mothers of Conservatism*, 141.

133. Betsy to Crain, May 5, 1963, Box 15, file 4, LCC, UO.

134. Joseph N. Bell, with Mrs. Alice Hollenbeck, "I Fought Against Hatred among My Neighbors," reprint of article from *Good Housekeeping*, [no month given] 1965, in Box 41, NAC, Hoover Institution.

135. Stephanie Coontz illustrates the change in marital status among young American women after World War II, noting that in 1940, 24 percent of women

aged eighteen to twenty-four were married; however, by 1950, more than 60 percent of women in that age group were married. See Coontz, *A Strange Stirring: The Feminine Mystique and American Women at the Dawn of the 1960s*, 51.

136. A broad look at women's anticommunist activism during the 1950s can be found in Brennan, *Wives, Mothers, and the Red Menace*.

137. Zimmerman, *Whose America?*, 81–106.

138. David Caute estimates that at least 600 teachers and professors lost their jobs as a result of political purges in American colleges and schools during those years. See Caute, *The Great Fear*, 406. Julia L. Mickenberg, *Learning from the Left: Children's Literature, the Cold War, and Radical Politics in the United States*, 134.

139. Mickenberg, *Learning from the Left*, 135.

140. However, political propaganda could have an opposite effect. Baby boomer Tim Novak recalled that a high school teacher's lesson regarding communism was so obviously anticommunist propaganda that he lost all respect for that teacher. Personal interview with author August 6, 2009.

141. Rebecca E. Klatch, *A Generation Divided: The New Left, the New Right, and the 1960s*, 65.

142. Ibid., 66–67, 69.

143. Attachment to personal e-mail from Jane Roberts, August 17, 2008.

144. Discussion with participants Jane, Kerry, Deborah, and others at National Association of Social Workers educational workshop, Sarasota, Florida, September 1, 2009.

145. Boxes 11–23 and 69, LCC, UO. In focusing on textbooks, right-wing women may have been too narrow in their search for communist influences. Julia L. Mickenberg provides abundant evidence in *Learning from the Left* that leftists played an important role in the children's book field during the middle of the twentieth century. Mickenberg found that children's series books such as *Penny Parker, Hardy Boys*, and *Nancy Drew* attracted less scrutiny by those searching out communist influences. Thus leftists wrote a sizable number of the series books.

146. Evidence of Crain's work with and influence upon others is scattered throughout the Lucille Cardin Crain Collection. For some examples of her correspondence with right-wing English professor E. Merrill Root, see Box 52, file 22 and Box 80, files 4 and 5; and see Box 69, file 7, for more on her work with Professor Russell Kirk, LCC, UO.

Chapter 2. Public Health

Epigraph source: Beverly Chase Perroni to Lucille Cardin Crain, n.d., ca. November 1956, Box 10, file 11, LCC, UO.

1. Committee for the Study of the Future of Public Health, Division of Health Care Services, Institute of Medicine, the Future of Public Health (Washington, D.C.: National Academies Press, 1988), 62–67, e-book http://www.nap.edu/openbook.php?record_id=1091&page=56.

2. "Beware of Fluoridation," newsletter, New Mexico Women Speak!, February 1956, Reel 86, N39, RWC, UI.

3. For more on the history of the beginnings of fluoridation in the United States see Kai Hunstadbraten, "Fluoride in Caries Prophylaxis at the Turn of the Century," *Bulletin of the History of Dentistry* 30, no. 2 (October 1982): 117–20; Brian Martin, *Scientific Knowledge in Controversy: The Social Dynamics of the Fluoridation Debate*, 1–5.

4. Martin, *Scientific Knowledge in Controversy*, 4.

5. "Treated Waters Held Dental Aid," *NYT*, January 17, 1951.

6. Warren Weaver Jr., "Fluoridation Plan Held 'Liquidation,'" *NYT*, March 5, 1953. Brian Martin, in *Scientific Knowledge in Controversy*, 121, notes that while fertilizer companies did profit from sales of fluoride wastes these profits were a small portion of their overall profits.

7. Quoted in Weaver, "Fluoridation Plan."

8. Weaver, "Fluoridation Plan."

9. "Fluoridated Water," *NYT*, May 3, 1953. The cities were San Diego, California; Baltimore, Maryland; Northampton, Massachusetts; Chehalis, Washington; and Fargo, North Dakota.

10. Letter to the editor *NYT*, from Charlotte A. Koch, October 19, 1954.

11. Letter to the editor, *NYT*, from Eva L. Collins, February 25, 1957.

12. "Opposes Fluoridation Plan," *NYT*, March 6, 1955.

13. Letter to the editor, *NYT*, from Emily Mehr, April 20, 1955.

14. Murray Illson, "Fluoride's Value in Water Argued," *NYT*, April 11, 1955.

15. Illson, "Fluoride's Value in Water Argued"; "Pattern—Fluoridation," newsletter, New Mexico Women Speak!, February 1956, Reel 86, N39, RWC, UI.

16. Emily Mehr, "Report on Fluoridation from New York City," newsletter, Minute Women of the U.S.A., Inc., January 1958, Reel 76, M19, RWC, UI. Mehr at this time was president of the Greater New York Committee Opposed to Fluoridation, Inc.

17. "Women's Club Federation Fights Fluoridation of the Water Supply," *NYT*, May 7, 1955.

18. Quoted in "Fluoridation Opposed," *NYT*, January 21, 1956.

19. Delegard, *Battling Miss Bolsheviki*, 58.

20. "Hearing Divided on Fluoridation," *NYT*, March 1, 1956.

21. Thomas F. A. Plaut, "Analysis of Voting Behavior on a Fluoridation Referendum," 213–22.

22. Ibid.

23. "Cincinnati Rejects Fluoridation," *NYT*, November 4, 1953.

24. Letters, Massachusetts Women's Political Club, ca. 1954–1957, Reel 77, M26, RWC, UI.

25. Russell and Ann Ackley, eds., *Portions in Due Season*, July 1956, Reel 96, P28, RWC, UI. While *Portions*, published in Denver, Colorado, was mainly a religious

tract, most issues contained one or more short articles regarding political and social topics.

26. Clarence Dean, "Hundreds Crowd All-Day Hearing on Fluoridation," *NYT*, March 7, 1957.

27. Herb Bailey, "Found—a new curb on tooth decay!" *Better Homes and Gardens* (September 1953).

28. Letters to the editor, *NYT*, from Theresa Murphy, Leda Sanford, Ernestine Jaediker, and Shirley J. Anderson, March 17, 1957.

29. Donald R. McNeil, "Fluoridation, Pro and Con," *NYT*, March 3, 1957.

30. Donald R. McNeil, *The Fight for Fluoridation*, 123–24.

31. Open letter to Americans from Leona Scannell, n.d., ca. spring 1952, Reel 13, A100, RWC, UI.

32. Mrs. Herman J. Kuppers, "The Fluoridation Lie," *Right*, June 1957, Reel 103, R25, RWC, UI.

33. McNeil, "Fluoridation, Pro and Con," *NYT*, and *Fight for Fluoridation*, 166. For more on the National Blue Star Mothers during their earlier campaigns, see Benowitz, *Days of Discontent* and Jeansonne, *Women of the Far Right*.

34. "The Magic of Fluorine: The New Way to Reduce Tooth Decay," *Parents Magazine*, May 1952, 145. A recent calculation of the annual cost of fluoridating water systems places the annual cost in a range from 95 cents to ten dollars per person, depending upon the size of the community. See Jane E. Brody, "Dental Exam Went Well? Thank Fluoride," *NYT*, January 24, 2012.

35. Letter to the editor from Edna Muchnic, *NYT*, September 23, 1959.

36. McNeil, *Fight for Fluoridation*, 164.

37. Flyer, "Does New York Want Poison (Sodium Fluoride) in its Drinking Water?," n.d., Box 77, file 13, LCC, UO.

38. "D.A.R. Congress Adjourns After Accolade to New Officers," *NYT*, April 19, 1958.

39. Newsletter, Pasadena Anti-Communist League, July 1958, Reel 92, P4, RWC, UI.

40. Gerald Walker, "Fluoride or No: An Emotional Debate," *NYT*, May 25, 1958.

41. Ibid.

42. Ibid.

43. Martin, *Scientific Knowledge in Controversy*, 7. Most scientists disputed Waldbott's conclusions, arguing that he failed to test his patients under blind conditions. Martin writes that "*some* of his patients were tested in blind conditions" (Martin's emphasis).

44. Walker, "Fluoride or No," *NYT*, May 25, 1958.

45. Pamphlet, Salem Pure Water Committee, "Why Fluoridation?," 1953, Politics Collection, MSS 1513, OHS.

46. Walker, "Fluoride or No," *NYT*, May 25, 1958.

47. Ibid.

48. Plaut, "Analysis of Voting Behavior," 216.

49. "Mt. Kisco Drops Plan to Fluoridate Water," *NYT*, December 2, 1958.

50. Open letter from Dorothy Frankston, national chairman, newsletter, Minute Women of the U.S.A., Inc., January 1958, Reel 76, M19, RWC, UI.

51. List, "The following communities have had artificial fluoridation and have stopped it," n.d., Box 77, file 13, LCC, UO.

52. The discussion of the Mausners's findings is found in Gerald Walker, "Fluoride or No," *NYT*, May 25, 1958.

53. Plaut, "Analysis of Voting Behavior," 220.

54. Short summaries of data in unpublished manuscripts by Arnold L. Green and Jean L. Briggs, and George F. Taylor, Michael S. Munro, and H. B. Fuqua can be found in Plaut, "Analysis of Voting Behavior," 214–22.

55. Herbert S. Parmet, *Jack: The Struggles of John F. Kennedy*, 209–17.

56. Plaut, "Analysis of Voting Behavior," 214–22.

57. Gretchen Ann Reilly, "'Not a So-Called Democracy': Anti-Fluoridationists and the Fight over Drinking Water"; Robert L. Crain, Elihu Katz, and Donald B. Rosenthal, *The Politics of Community Conflict*.

58. James Q. Wilson in preface to Crain, Katz, and Rosenthal, *The Politics of Community Conflict*.

59. Crain, Katz, and Rosenthal, *The Politics of Community Conflict*, xi, 36–40, 148.

60. "43 Million in U.S. Drink Fluorides," NYT, September 15, 1959.

61. "Fluoridation Is Here to Stay," *Journal of the American Dental Association* (November 1962): 578–80.

62. Letter to the editor from Emily Mehr, *NYT*, July 7, 1961.

63. Hazel Kramer to President Johnson, May 25, 1965, HE 8–4, WHCF, Box 25, LBJ Library.

64. Ibid.

65. Fannie B. McCoy to the president, October 21, 1968, and Mary DeRemer to the president, February 7, 1968, Box 26, HE 8–4, WHCF, LBJ Library.

66. Deborah Atkinson, telephone conversation with author, October 12, 2007.

67. Fluoridation was first introduced as a resolution in New York City in August 1954. "Fluoridation Loses in 8 Towns, Wins in 2," *NYT*, November 5, 1954, and Peter Khiss, "Fluoridation Foes Press Fight Against City Plan," *NYT*, November 28, 1965.

68. Juan M. Vasques, "Pros and Cons Are Heard on Statewide Fluoridation," *NYT*, September 21, 1972.

69. Walter H. Waggoner, "Foes of State Fluoridation Dominate Hearing on Plan," *NYT*, March 1, 1974.

70. Ibid.

71. Centers for Disease Control, "Achievements in Public Health, 1900–1999: Fluoridation of Drinking Water to Prevent Dental Caries," *MMWR Weekly*, October 22, 1999, 933–40; Jane E. Brody, "Dental Exam Went Well? Thank Fluoride," *NYT*, January 24, 2012; "Fluoridation Status of Largest 50 U.S. Cities," M. W. Easley, National Center for Fluoridation Policy and Research, revised April 4, 2001, accessed online; National Institute of Dental Research, "The Story of Fluoridation,"

accessed July 21, 2007, http://www.nidcr.nih.gov/oralhealth/Topics/Fluoride/The StoryofFluoridation.htm. Among the opponents is Christopher Bryson, who in *The Fluoride Deception*, argues that the safety of fluoride was firmly accepted without having been thoroughly studied. He argues that the government and the scientific community have been covering up studies that suggest fluoridation is harmful. "After 60 Years of Success, Water Fluoridation Still Lacking in Many Communities," *Medical News Today*, July 19, 2005, accessed July 31, 2007, http://www.medical newstoday.com/releases/27595.php; Centers for Disease Control, "Achievements in Public Health, 1900–1999: Fluoridation of Drinking Water to Prevent Dental Caries," *MMWR Weekly*, October 22, 1999, 933–40.

72. Ida Darden, "If You're a Good Conservative American Patriot—Let's Face It—You're Nuts," *Southern Conservative*, April 1957, Reel 114, S18 RWC, UI.

73. For example, in 1955, the institutionalization of mentally disturbed patients in New York State peaked at 93,600. By 1984, that state's inpatient population was down to 32,000. "Overview of Mental Health in New York and the Nation," New York State Archives, accessed April 4, 2011, http://www.archives.nysed.gov/com mon/archives/files/res_topics_health_mh_hist.pdf.

74. Roger Boyvey, "Mental Health and the Ultra-Concerned," *Social Service Review* 38, no. 3 (September 1964): 282.

75. U.S. Government, U.S. Senate, 84th Congress, Second Session, "Hearings before the Subcommittee on Territories and Insular Affairs of the Committee on Interior and Insular Affairs," H.R. 6376, "An Act to Provide for the Hospitalization and Care of the Mentally Ill of Alaska, and for other Purposes (With Proposed Substitute)," S. 2518, A Bill to Provide for the Hospitalization and Care of the Mentally Ill of Alaska, and for Other Purposes; S. 2973, "A Bill to Provide for the Hospitalization and Care of the Mentally Ill of Alaska, and for Other Purposes (and Also the Provisions of S. 1027 and S. 1028)," February 20, 21, and March 5, 1956, U.S. Government Printing Office, 1956, Box 45, RRC, Hoover Institution. Francis Carroll, "Senators Study Alaska Project for U.S. Siberia," *Tablet*, March 3, 1956, in Box 9, file 13, LCC, UO. The article includes notes in the margins written by Florence Walker, who pointed out that there were twenty-two "patriotic" groups associated with the Women's Patriotic Conference on National Defense.

76. Florence Walker to Crain, March 7, 1956, Box 9, file 13, LCC, UO.

77. Donna R. Kemp, *Mental Health in America: A Reference Handbook*, 131; Gerald N. Grob, *From Asylum to Community: Mental Health Policy in Modern America*, 53–54.

78. 84th Congress, 2d Sess., 1956, H.R. 6376, Senate Report 2053.

79. W. Henry MacFarland, "A Report to the American People on the Alaska Mental Health Act," newsletter, American Flag Committee, March 1956, Box 45, RRC, Hoover Institution. None of the many files examined in this study give any indication of the right's objections to the idea of Alaskans having their own mental institution. Although MacFarland, a male, was editor and executive chairman of the American Flag Committee, women held prominent positions in that group. The

only others listed as officers were four women, who led the chapters in New Jersey, California, Maryland, and Illinois.

80. Texas Women for Constitutional Government, "H.R. 6376—Alaska Mental Health Bill," Box 82, file 11, LCC, UO.

81. 84th Congress, 2d Sess., 1956. H.R. 6376, Senate Report 2053.

82. Michelle M. Nickerson, "The Lunatic Fringe Strikes Back: Conservative Opposition to the Alaska Mental Health Bill of 1956," 126.

83. American Public Relations Forum, Inc., "New Alaska Area Exploration Likely," Bulletin no. 53, May 1956, Box 82, file 8, LCC, UO.

84. M. Klein, "Mental Health Laws Bring Problems," *Albuquerque Tribune*, November 1964.

85. Newsletter, Pasadena Anti-Communist League, April 1956, Reel 92, P4, RWC, UI. The USSR did have mental health institutions and programs. One way of dealing with political deviants there was to incarcerate them in mental institutions.

86. Grob, *From Asylum to Community*, 280; E. Fuller Torrey, *Nowhere to Go: The Tragic Odyssey of the Homeless Mentally Ill*, 88–89.

87. Elizabeth Chesnut Barnes hints at anti-Semitism in "Are You Mental?" Reprinted from *DAR Magazine* (May and October 1960), Box 81, file 8, LCC, UO; Torrey, *Nowhere to Go*, 89. Torrey did not give the date of the series; Donald Robinson, "Conspiracy USA," *Look*, January 26, 1965, 31; Roger Boyvey, "Mental Health and the Ultra-Concerned," 288.

88. Texas Women for Constitutional Government, "H.R. 6376—Alaska Mental Health Bill," Box 82, file 11, LCC, UO.

89. Ibid.

90. Ibid.

91. Letter to the editor, from Gladice G. Woolf, "Mental Health Bill for Alaska Called Vicious," and a reprint of a report by columnist Drew Pearson, "Alaskan Measure Nets Barrage," both in the *Post-Standard*, Syracuse, New York, March 25, 1956, 6. For more on Mrs. Burkeland's influence, see Roger Boyvey, "Mental Health and the Ultra-Concerned," 282–83.

92. Newsletter, Minute Women of the U.S.A., February 1956, Reel 76, M19, RWC, UI.

93. "Pattern of Mental Health," New Mexico Women Speak! February 1956, Reel 86, N39, RWC, UI. In *The Paranoid Style in American Politics*, Hofstadter gives T. W. Adorno and his associates credit for the term "pseudo-conservative."

94. Hofstadter, *The Paranoid Style in American Politics*, 45.

95. Leo R. O'Brien to Crain, April 25, 1956, Box 9, file 18, LCC, UO.

96. After the mid-1950s the number of inpatients sharply declined, to approximately 130,000 in 1980. Torrey, *Nowhere to Go*, 1–3; Kemp, *Mental Health in America*, 133.

97. Coontz, *A Strange Stirring*, 73; Carol A. B. Warren, *Madwives: Schizophrenic Women in the 1950s*.

98. Warren, *Madwives*, 129; Torrey, *Nowhere to Go*, 1–3.

99. California State Bulletin of Minute Women of the U.S.A., Inc., Box 82, file 11, LCC, UO.

100. Michel Foucault, *History of Madness*.

101. T. W. Adorno, et al. *The Authoritarian Personality*, 765; Leo Lowenthal and Norbert Guterman, *Prophets of Deceit: A Study of the Techniques of the American Agitator*, 63–64.

102. Ibid.

103. "Mental Health," *New Mexico Women Speak!*, December 1955, Reel 86, N39, RWC, UI.

104. "Children Seized to Silence Anti-Communists," *New Mexico Women Speak!*, June 1956, Reel 86, N39, RWC, UI.

105. Letter, Beverly Chase Perroni to Crain, n.d., ca. November 1956, Box 10, file 11, LCC, UO.

106. Schreiber quoted in "Mental Health: It's [sic] Political Implications," newsletter, Minute Women of the U.S.A., Inc. The article also referred to work done by Dr. Nathan Ackerman and Marie Jahoda, purportedly for the American Jewish Committee. No date was given. Reel 76, M19, RWC, UI.

107. Roger Boyvey, "Mental Health and the Ultra-Concerned," 288; Alfred Auerback, "The Anti-Mental Health Movement," *American Journal of Psychiatry* 120 (August 1963): 107.

108. Texas Women, "Who Is Mentally Ill?" n.d., ca. March 1956, Box 82, file 11, LCC, UO.

109. Elizabeth Chesnut Barnes, "Are You Mental?" Reprinted from *D.A.R. Magazine*, May and October 1960, Box 81, file 8, LCC, UO.

110. "Alaska Measure Nets Letter Barrage," reprint of some comments of Drew Pearson, *Syracuse Post-Standard*, New York, March 25, 1956, 6.

111. Copy of speech by Anne Smart to Marin County, California, Real Estate Board, July 1958. Reproduced by the National Americanism Committee of the Catholic War Veterans, August 1958, Box 81, file 8, LCC, UO.

112. Judd Marmor, *Psychiatry in Transition*, 356.

113. Auerback, "The Anti-Mental Health Movement," 108–9.

114. Donald Robinson, "Conspiracy USA: The Far Right's Fight Against Mental Health," *Look*, January 26, 1965, 30; Auerback, "The Anti-Mental Health Movement," 105–12.

115. "Brief Summary of Mental Health Movement in the United States," California State Bulletin of Minute Women of the U.S.A., Inc., n.d., Box 81, file 11, LCC, UO.

116. "Mental Health," *New Mexico Women Speak!* (December 1955), Reel 86, N39, RWC, UI.

117. Ibid.

118. California State Bulletin of Minute Women of the U.S.A., Inc., Box 81, file 11, LCC, UO.

119. Warren, *Madwives*, 112–24.

120. Ida Darden, "If You're a Good Conservative American Patriot—Let's Face It—You're Nuts," *Southern Conservative*, April 1957, Reel 114, S18, RWC, UI.

121. Ibid.

122. Bulletin, Mrs. Fred A. Weser, State Mental Health Chairman, West Virginia Federation of Women's Clubs, n.d., ca. June-July 1956, Box 10, file 4, LCC, UO. The seven-point program included: encouraging the establishment of Mental Health Chapters and working with them; promoting state legislation or regulations that would require periodic health and psychiatric examinations of teachers; developing summer workshops for clergy, teachers, or for everyone in the community; raising "funds for scholarships and fellowships for research and training in mental health field"; knowing "the needs and support[ing] state legislation for personnel, state hospitals, local clinics, etc.; educating and preparing the community to accept patients who are released from mental hospitals"; and "promoting one's own mental health."

123. Frances Bartlett, "Post Mortem," *FACTS in Education*, June-July, 1955.

124. Jean Ward, "Mental Health Plan Scored," reprint from *Los Angeles Examiner*, March 27, 1958, Box 45, RRC, Hoover Institution.

125. L. A. Alesen, *Mental Robots*, 11.

126. Helen Hayne, "Mental Health: People a Science?," *Educational Signpost* (August-September 1959), "Caxton Printers," Box 10, NAC, Hoover Institution.

127. Jo Hindman, "The Fight for Your Child's Mind," *American Mercury* (November 1957): 7.

128. Barnes, "Are You Mental?" Reprint from *D.A.R. Magazine*, May and October, 1960, Box 81, file 8, LCC, UO; Jo Hindman, "The Fight for Your Child's Mind," *American Mercury*, November 1957, 7–12.

129. "Psychological Testing Grows," *NYT*, December 11, 1960; "Foreseeing Baby's Future," *NYT*, December 13, 1959; Fred M. Hechinger, "New Test Debate: Amateur Psychology Is Criticized in Group Analysis of Pupils," *NYT*, September 30, 1962.

130. Copy of Speech by Anne Smart to Marin County, California, Real Estate Board, July 1958, reproduced by the National Americanism Committee of the Catholic War Veterans, August 1958, Box 81, file 8, LCC, UO; newsletter, Minute Women of the U.S.A., June 1956, Reel 76, M19, RWC, UI.

131. Frances Bartlett, "The Power of Suggestion by Remote Control. Part II—Personality Tests," *FACTS in Education*, November-December 1961, Box 47, RRC, Hoover Institution.

132. Ibid.

133. Kenneth D. Hopkins, *Educational and Psychological Measurement and Evaluation*, 418–19; Robert Gerdy, "The A.B.C. of the I.Q." *NYT*, September 6, 1953.

134. Fred M. Hechinger, "New Test Debate: Amateur Psychology is Criticized in Group Analysis of Pupils," *NYT*, September 30, 1962.

135. See, for example, Harrison G. Gough, "A New Dimension of Status, II," 534–37; Hopkins, *Educational and Psychological Measurement and Evaluation*, 418–19.

136. Kevin R. Murphy and Charles O. Davidshofer, *Psychological Testing: Principles and Applications*, 6th ed., 60, 496–97.

137. Dorothy Barclay, "Have Parents a Right to Know?" *NYT*, February 12, 1961.

138. Nickerson, "The Lunatic Fringe Strikes Back" 129–30.

139. Lisa Appignanesi, *Mad, Bad, and Sad*, 349–51; Raymond M. Weinstein, "Goffman's Asylums and the Social Situation of Mental Patients," 267–74.

140. Jacob Heller, *The Vaccine Narrative*, 16–20.

141. James Colgrove, *State of Immunity: The Politics of Vaccination in Twentieth-Century America*, 46–47; Michael Willrich, *Pox: An American History*, 264–65.

142. Quoted in Colgrove, *State of Immunity*, 52–61.

143. Colgrove, *State of Immunity*, 57; Robert D. Johnston, *The Radical Middle Class: Populist Democracy and the Question of Capitalism in Progressive Era Portland, Oregon*, 192–213.

144. David Oshinsky, *Polio: An American Story*, 16.

145. Aaron E. Klein, *Trial by Fury: The Polio Vaccine Controversy*, 4–7; Oshinsky, *Polio*, 22.

146. Klein, *Trial by Fury*, 10; Oshinsky, *Polio*, 22.

147. Klein, *Trial by Fury*, 20–21 and 42–63.

148. Oshinsky, *Polio*, 118–21.

149. Howard A. Rusk, "Gamma Globulin Gives Hope that Polio Can Be Checked," *NYT*, August 25, 1952; Arthur Allen, *Vaccine: The Controversial Story of Medicine's Greatest Lifesaver*, 168, 177.

150. Klein, *Trial by Fury*, 42–63, 71; Jane S. Smith, *Patenting the Sun: Polio and the Salk Vaccine*, 107–27; Howard A. Rusk, "Gamma Globulin Gives Hope that Polio Can Be Checked," *NYT*, October 25, 1952.

151. Klein, *Trial by Fury*, 80–84; Jane Smith, *Patenting the Sun*, 177; "May Help Combat Polio," *Wall Street Journal*, March 28, 1953.

152. Arthur Allen, *Vaccine*, 161; Kurt Link, *The Vaccine Controversy: The History, Use, and Safety of Vaccinations*, 31–32; Klein, *Trial by Fury*, 103–19.

153. Ibid., 119.

154. Oshinsky, *Polio*, 231.

155. "Two Regions Balk at Polio Program," *NYT*, May 12, 1955; "Polio Shot Brings a $500,000 Claim," *NYT*, February 7, 1956.

156. "Polio Spreads in Chicago," *NYT*, July 18, 1956.

157. "Is It Salk?" in *Portions in Due Season*, August 1957, Reel 96, P28, RWC, UI.

158. Klein, *Trial by Fury*, 7–9; Jane Smith, *Patenting the Sun*, 35.

159. "Salk Vaccine Against Polio," *New Mexico Women Speak!* January 1956, Reel 86, N39, RWC, UI.

160. Jeffrey Kluger, *Splendid Solution: Jonas Salk and the Conquest of Polio*, 209–10.

161. Newsletter, Minute Women of the U.S.A., February 1960, Reel 76, M19, RWC, UI. See also letter to the editor from T. G. Flanagan, *NYT*, May 9, 1959.

162. Quoted in "Pattern No. 3 'A Step Toward Socialized Medicine,'" *New Mexico Women Speak!* February 1956, Reel 86, N39, RWC, UI.

163. Ibid.

164. Ralph E. Ellsworth and Sarah M. Harris, "The American Right Wing," 13. The article was distributed by Gold Star Sons and Daughters of the American Revolution, originally appearing in *Free Men Speak*, February 15, 1955.

165. Morris Kominsky, *The Hoaxers, Plain Liars, Fancy Liars, and Damned Liars*, 129–30.

166. "Paralytic Polio Up, House Group Hears," *NYT*, October 13, 1953; Foster Hailey, "Doctor Criticizes Polio Vaccine Use," *NYT*, March 12, 1954; Klein, *Trial by Fury*, 123, 138.

167. Klein, *Trial by Fury*, 146; "4 Polio Cases Push Total in Iowa to 87," *NYT*, July 13, 1959; "Polio Death Here the First of 1959," *NYT*, July 18, 1959; "Texas Sets a Drive to Fight Polio Rise," *NYT*, July 19, 1962.

168. Klein, *Trial by Fury*, 146–47; "Big Test in Mexico for Polio Vaccine," *NYT* (May 12, 1960); "Health Service Approves Output of Sabin's Oral Polio Vaccine; Lederle's Is Rejected," *Wall Street Journal*, August 25, 1960. Kominsky, in *The Hoaxers, Plain Liars, Fancy Liars, and Damned Liars*, notes that Sabin, like Salk, was Jewish. Those charging a Jewish-Communist conspiracy might have found it difficult to explain why Sabin gave the purportedly "poisonous" oral vaccine to millions of Soviet children.

169. Arthur Allen, *Vaccine*, 209.

170. Oshinsky, *Polio*, 268; Link, *The Vaccine Controversy*, 94.

171. Debbie Bookchin and Jim Schumacher, *The Virus and the Vaccine: The True Story of a Cancer-Causing Monkey Virus, Contaminated Polio Vaccine, and the Millions of Americans Exposed*; Arthur Allen, *Vaccine*, 211–13.

172. Keerti V. Shah, "Simian Virus 40 and Human Disease," 2061–64. Immunization Safety Review Committee, Kathleen Stratton, et al., eds., *Immunization Safety Review: SV40 Contamination of Polio Vaccine and Cancer*.

173. Virginia R. Wilson, ed., *Count Down*, August 1970, Reel 35, C59, RWC, UI.

174. Warren, *Madwives*, 41.

175. Klein, *Trial by Fury*, 131–33.

176. Idaho Department of Environmental Quality, "How Did We Get Here? History of Waste Disposal at the SDA 1950-Present," accessed September 29, 2008. http://www.deq.state.id.us/inl_oversight/waste/history.cfm.

Chapter 3. Right-Wing Women and Desegregation of the Public Schools

Epigraph source: Mrs. J. M. Burke Sr., to Senator Lyndon Johnson, December 7, 1958, Box 652, Civil Rights, LBJ Library.

1. H. Warren Button and Eugene F. Provenzo Jr., *History of Education and Culture in America*, 55–62; Kathryn Kish Sklar, "The Schooling of Girls and Changing Community Values in Massachusetts Towns, 1750–1820," 511–42.

2. Button and Provenzo, *History of Education and Culture in America,* 141–48; Thomas J. Sugrue, *Sweet Land of Liberty: The Forgotten Struggle for Civil Rights in the North,* 449–55.

3. Joseph Crespino, *In Search of Another Country: Mississippi and the Conservative Counterrevolution,* especially pp. 4, 12, 51. Crespino notes how rightist leaders' appeals to concerns of white Mississippians contributed to the tremendous expansion of conservatism in America by the time of the presidency of Ronald Reagan.

4. Nancy MacLean, "Neo-Confederacy Versus the New Deal: The Regional Utopia of the Modern American Right," in *The Myth of Southern Exceptionalism,* ed. Matthew D. Lassiter and Joseph Crespino, 313.

5. Christine Benagh, "The American Dream: A Southern Nightmare?" 379.

6. Lillian Smith, *Killers of the Dream,* 27–28, 83, 85.

7. Elizabeth Gillespie McRae, "White Womanhood, White Supremacy, and the Rise of Massive Resistance," in *Massive Resistance: Southern Opposition to the Second Reconstruction,* ed. Clive Webb, 181–201.

8. Lillian Smith, *Killers of the Dream,* particularly see pp. 26–27.

9. Interview with Deborah Atkinson, July 25, 2009.

10. Harvey Klehr and John Earl Haynes, *The American Communist Movement: Storming Heaven Itself,* 75, 88.

11. James A. Miller, Susan D. Pennybacker, and Eve Rosenhaft, "Mother Ada Wright and the International Campaign to Free the Scottsboro Boys, 1931–1934," 387–430.

12. Historian Thomas J. Sugrue notes that black poet Langston Hughes was sympathetic to the Communist Party for a short while during the 1930s and that both W.E.B. DuBois and Paul Robeson were committed to the party throughout most of their lives. Sugrue, *Sweet Land of Liberty,* 23. However, John Egerton writes that both Robeson and DuBois were more committed to liberty and equality than to the Communist Party. See *Speak Now Against the Day: The Generation Before the Civil Rights Movement in the South,* 529. Robert Gid Powers, in *Not Without Honor: The History of American Anticommunism,* 187, notes that at the end of World War II, the American Communist Party had a total of approximately 73,000 members, of which 10 percent were black.

13. Powers, *Not Without Honor,* 58–59; Benowitz, *Days of Discontent,* 30, 125; Crespino, *In Search of Another Country,* 50–51.

14. Allen's politics were more radical that those of the Minute Women, whom Allen criticized as not being true Patriots since they had "crucified" another woman for distributing some of Allen's literature. See Marilyn L. Allen, *I Love America* Series No. 5, April 23, 1951, Reel 13, RWC, UI.

15. Marilyn L. Allen, "The Supreme Court Decision, Outlawing Segregation in Our Schools," *I Love America* Series No. 17, June 1954, Reel 13, RWC, UI.

16. Ibid.

17. Grace Wick Papers, Box 1, File 1, OHS; Ralph Lord Roy, *Apostles of Discord,* 107–10.

18. David Burner, *Making Peace with the Sixties*, 16. "Eleanor Joins Communist Plot to Integrate South," *White Sentinel*, June 1958; "History," Highlander Research and Education Center website, accessed June 28, 2008, http://highlandercenter. org/about-us/history/.

19. Memorandum, DAR, August 1958, Box 75, file 5, LCC, UO.

20. "Maddox Cites 'Red Threat,'" *Sarasota Herald Tribune*, October 13, 1969.

21. Phoebe and her husband Kent Courtney copublished both the *Independent American* and *Tax Fax*. The Courtneys divorced, and Phoebe moved to Littleton, Colorado, taking the *Independent American* and *Tax Fax* with her. Kent Courtney was active in right-wing circles, including chairing the John Birch Society's New Orleans chapter during the late 1950s. Together, they headed the New Orleans-based Conservative Society of America (CSA). See PCP, UO.

22. "Communist Agitation and Racial Turmoil," *Tax Fax* No. 46, 1963, in RRC, Box 38, Hoover Institution. See also, "Integrate or Else . . . ! *Tax Fax* No. 80, 1967, Box 1, PCP, UO.

23. Susan L. M. Huck, "Insurrection: Is America Sleeping Through Civil War?" June 1968, Box 33, RRC, Hoover Institution.

24. Memo, Mrs. Robert V. H. Duncan to the National Board of Management, NSDAR, August 1963; Marie Smith, untitled article, *Washington Post*, July 11, 1963; Frances Lide, "DAR Head Writes Kennedy," *Evening Star*, July 11, 1963. All Box 32, RCC, Hoover Institution.

25. Marie Smith, untitled article, *Washington Post*, July 11, 1963, Box 32, RRC, Hoover Institution.

26. Mrs. P. D. Williams to senators, December 9, 1953, Box 652, Senate Subject Files, Civil Rights, LBJ Library.

27. Mrs. Albert Davis to Senator Lyndon Johnson, Box 590, Senate Subject Files, LBJ Library.

28. Ella Ellisar, et al., to Senator Lyndon Johnson, July 15, 1954, Box 528, U.S. Senate General Files, LBJ Library.

29. Mrs. L. H. Chaney to Senator Lyndon Johnson, October 22, 1958, Box 590, Senate Subject Files, LBJ Library, and Maude Willis to President Johnson, August 30, 1964, WHCF, PR 3, Box 14, LBJ Library, are other examples.

30. Jane Dailey, "The Theology of Massive Resistance: Sex, Segregation, and the Sacred after *Brown*," 151–80.

31. Mrs. L. H. Chaney to Senator Lyndon Johnson, October 22, 1958, Box 590, Senate Subject Files, LBJ Library.

32. In letters to Lyndon Johnson, it was usually women who referred to integration as being in violation of God's plan for the universe. See Senate Subject Files, Civil Rights, and WHCF, Religious Matters (RM) files, LBJ Library. Jane Dailey found that similar letters to Virginia governor Thomas B. Stanley were mostly from women. Dailey, "The Theology of Massive Resistance," 162.

33. Mrs. J. M. Burke Sr., to Senator Lyndon Johnson, December 7, 1958, Box 652, Senate Subject Files, Civil Rights, LBJ Library.

34. Katie Lou Brown, "Which Eye Has the Mote?" n.d., ca. 1960, RWC, UI, Reel 19, B32.

35. Ibid.

36. For example, Alice Elizabeth Treleaven to President Johnson, July 15, 1964, Box 30, WHCF, PL, LBJ Library; Helen Thornton to the president, December 1, 1965, Box 3, WHCF, RM, LBJ Library.

37. Margaret Black to the president, June 18, 1966, Box 2, WHCF, RM, LBJ Library.

38. Mrs. J. M. Burke Sr., to Senator Lyndon Johnson, December 7, 1958, Senate Subject Files, Box 652, Civil Rights, LBJ Library.

39. "More Than 88 Billion Dollars Are Required to Educate Texas Negroes," *Southern Conservative*, June 1958.

40. Oral history interview of Frances Pauley by Cliff Kuhn, May 3, 1988, pp. 57–58, Folder 6, Box 7, Georgia Government Documentation Project, Series B, Special Collections and Archives, Georgia State University Library, Atlanta.

41. Letter to the editor, from "Mrs. E.C.," "Hypocrisy Exposed," *White Sentinel*, June 1958, Box 20, RRC, Hoover Institution.

42. "Little Rock School Board Asks Court to Suspend Integration Order," *Southern Conservative*, March 1958; "Teachers in Integrated Detroit Schools Are Pleading for Protection," *Southern Conservative*, April 1958. "Communist Party and Supreme Court Are in Line on Integration," and "Integrationists Achieve Part of Their Objective in Little Rock," *Southern Conservative*, March 1959.

43. "New Orleans Mothers Given the Works by Irate Woman Writer," *Southern Conservative*, January 1961.

44. Claude Sitton, "2 White Schools in New Orleans Are Integrated," *NYT*, November 15, 1960; Claude Sitton, "Tension Rises Over New Orleans School Integration," *NYT*, November 16, 1960; Morton Inger, "New Orleans: The Failure of an Elite," in *The Politics of School Desegregation*, ed. Robert L. Crain, 263, 283–84.

45. John Steinbeck, *Travels with Charley in Search of America*, 195.

46. "New Orleans Mothers Given the Works by Irate Woman Writer," *Southern Conservative*, January 1961.

47. "New Orleans Schools Are Integrated under Police State Proceedings," *Southern Conservative*, October 1961.

48. William Henry Kellar, *Make Haste Slowly: Moderates, Conservatives, and School Desegregation in Houston*, 107.

49. "Mrs. White Charges Board's 'Impression' is 'Anti-American,'" *Houston Chronicle*, December 10, 1963, 1.

50. "Mrs. White Charges Board's 'Impression' is 'Anti-American,'" and "Mrs. White Explains Attitude," *Houston Chronicle*, December 10, 1963, 1.

51. Kellar, *Make Haste Slowly*, 109. On p. 114, Kellar writes that many years later, White recalled that Cullen did not speak to her once during the entire two terms that the two women served together on the school board.

52. Kellar, *Make Haste Slowly*. See in particular pp. 93–139.

53. Mrs. W. B. Zedler to President Johnson, December 12, 1963, Box 53, WHCF, HU, LBJ Library.

54. Kellar, *Make Haste Slowly*, 107–14.

55. U.S. Department of Health, Education and Welfare, "Enrollment of Negro Pupils in Southern and Border States," December 7, 1966, Box 53, WHCF, HU, LBJ Library.

56. W. G. Mazill to Mr. Christian, September 18, 1967, Box 53, WHCF, HU, LBJ Library.

57. Zimmerman, *Whose America?*, 106–19.

58. Sugrue, *Sweet Land of Liberty*, 192–99.

59. Allen, *Education or Indoctrination?*, 57–58.

60. Julie Salley Gray, "'To Fight the Good Fight': The Battle Over Control of the Pasadena City Schools, 1969–1979," 1–2.

61. Benjamin Fine, "Pupils Declared Integration Key," *NYT*, February 24, 1956.

62. Cabell Philips, "Integration: Battle of Hoxie, Arkansas," *NYT*, September 25, 1955.

63. Letter to the editor from Carol Isermann, "Morality by Law," *NYT*, June 5, 1955.

64. "Students Differ on Segregation," *NYT*, May 12, 1955.

65. Rebecca J. Linn to President Johnson, October 19, 1965, Box 70, WHCF, HU, LBJ Library.

66. Billingsley, *Communists on Campus*, 42–44.

67. "Two Letters—Two Views—Negro Maturity, White Immaturity," *Spirit*, July-August 1964, 12–13.

68. Ibid., 13.

69. Ibid., 12.

70. Ibid., 13.

71. Personal interview with Barbara Needleman, March 1, 2006.

72. Personal interview with Larry Kelleher, August 4, 2009; personal interview with Tim Novak, August 6, 2009; personal interview with Leigh Ann Novak, August 6, 2009.

73. Frank Denton, "One Family's Story of School Integration," *Anniston Star*, Alabama, Box 1, Emergency School Assistance Program files, Record Group 12, National Archives, Southeast Region, Morrow, Georgia.

74. Ibid.

75. Personal e-mail from Claire Cole Curcio, August 5, 2008.

76. Joseph Crespino, "Civil Rights and the Religious Right," 90–105.

77. Lyn Tornabene, "Murder in Alabama: American Wives Think Viola Liuzzo Should Have Stayed Home," *Ladies Home Journal*, July 1965, 42–44.

78. Ibid.

79. Grif Stockley, "Daisy Lee Gatson Bates." Sugrue, *Sweet Land of Liberty*, 452. See also, Jeanne Theoharis, "'I'd Rather Go to School in the South': How Boston's School Desegregation Complicates the Civil Rights Paradigm," 126–41.

80. *White Sentinel*, June 1958, Box 20, RRC, Hoover Institution.

81. McRae, "White Womanhood, White Supremacy, and the Rise of Massive Resistance," 191.

82. Kathleen M. Blee, *Women of the Klan: Racism and Gender in the 1920s.*

83. David Frum, *How We Got Here: The 1970s*, 251–52.

84. U.S. Commission on Civil Rights, *Southern School Desegregation, 1966–1967*, Washington, D.C., U.S.G.P.O., 107–10, in William Anton Vrame, "A History of School Desegregation in Chicago Since 1954" (PhD diss., University of Wisconsin, 1970), 5.

85. "Education Czar Harold Howe 'Buses' His Son," *Independent American*, November-December 1966, reprinted from *Chattanooga News-Free Press*, PCP, UO.

86. "Keep Up Anti-Busing Fight," *Independent American*, September-October 1972, reprinted from *Chattanooga News-Free Press*, PCP, UO.

87. Kevin P. Phillips, "How to Stop Forced Busing," *Independent American*, September-October 1977, PCP, UO.

88. Personal interview with Stanley Harris, Sarasota, Florida, September 2007.

89. Personal interview with Rhonda Moraca, June 29, 2009. On the other side of the country, Shawn Spangle Looney, who attended public schools in Portland, Oregon, remembers the tensions at her high school in 1970. As racial tensions rose at school, a black friend no longer responded when Looney spoke to her. On one day in particular, racial tensions were at a height. Talk spread around the school that a riot was about to take place, and students, black and white, gathered outside of the school. Suddenly, almost out of nowhere, Portland Police appeared in riot gear, marching in formation. It struck the students as such a strange and comic scene that all the students began to laugh, and the crowd dispersed. The situation at the high school was never so tense again. Personal interview with Shawn Spangle Looney, August 31, 2009.

90. See, for example, Box 11, WHCF, HU 2-1, NPP, NA II.

91. Mrs. Robert Mason to President Nixon, July 2, 1969, Box 11, WHCF, HU 2-1, NPP, NA II.

92. Paper, Mothers Support Neighborhood Schools, "A Critical Review of the Report by the U.S. Commission on Civil Rights Entitled 'Racial Isolation in the Public Schools,'" Reel 78, M67, RWC, UI.

93. Newsletter, Parents of New York United (October 1971), Box 88, files 1 and 4, LCC, UO.

94. Mrs. Thomas DeGeorge to President Johnson, n.d., ca. June 1964 (based on reply from Lee C. White, Associate Special Counsel to the president, July 2, 1964), Box 54, WHCF, HU, LBJ Library.

95. For example, one baby boomer recalls her mother's desire to move the family to the outskirts of Buffalo, New York, to avoid race riots in the city. Her mother was not a racist. Indeed, she had hosted blacks in her home. Her concern was for her daughter's safety. Personal interview with Donna Paganello, July 10, 2009.

96. Kathleen Blee, "Mothers in Race-Hate Movements," 250.

97. Ibid., 251.

98. Letter, Lillabel H. West to Hon. Sidney O. Smith Jr., March 7, 1973, Box 55A, Record Group 21, District Courts of United States, NA SE. At about the same time, the Executive Board of the Morningside Elementary School Parent-Teacher Association filed suit in U.S. District Court for the Northern District of Georgia, objecting to a Compromise Desegregation Plan that they claimed would cause turmoil at their school. See *Vivian Calhoun, et al. v. Ed S. Cook, et al.*, filed March 16, 1973, Box 55A, Record Group 21, NA SE.

99. Helen P. Taylor to Lonnie King, February 6, 1973, Box 55A, Record Group 21, District Courts of United States, NA SE.

100. Helen P. Taylor to Lonnie King, February 6, 1973, Box 55A, Record Group 21, District Courts of United States, NA SE.

101. Letter, Mr. and Mrs. James H. Taylor, March 25, 1973, Record Group 21, Box 55A, District Courts of United States, NA SE.

102. Untitled newspaper article, *Austin American Statesman*, December 26 [year missing], in Farenthold (Frances Tarlton) Papers, Center for American History, University of Texas at Austin (UT).

103. "Busing Foe Fades from Limelight," *NYT*, May 21, 1973; McCabe quoted in untitled newspaper article, *Austin American Statesman*, December 26 [year missing], in Farenthold (Frances Tarlton Papers, Center for American History, UT.

104. McCabe quoted in untitled newspaper article, *Austin American Statesman*, December 26 [year missing], in Farenthold (Frances Tartlon) Papers, Center for American History, UT.

105. "Busing," in *Powerline* newsletter, 1, no. 1, December 1971, Anne Armstrong, file "Rountree," Box 48, WHCF, SMOF, NPP, NA II.

106. Maurice Isserman and Michael Kazin, *America Divided: The Civil War of the 1960s*, 218; John Kifner, "A Tense, Troubled City," *NYT*, October 11, 1974.

107. Theoharis, "'I'd Rather Go to School in the South,'" 140–41.

108. Ronald P. Formisano takes a broad look at the antibusing campaign in *Boston Against Busing: Race, Class, and Ethnicity in the 1960s and 1970s*, and Julia Wrigley explores the prominent roles of women in that crusade in "From Housewives to Activists: Women and the Division of Political Labor in the Boston Antibusing Movement," 251–88. Jean Theoharis gives evidence that the middle-class women have been overlooked in many accounts of the antibusing campaign in Boston. See, "'I'd Rather Go to School in the South,'" 126–37.

109. Formisano, *Boston Against Busing*, particularly p. 105.

110. Julia Wrigley, "From Housewives to Activists," 263.

111. John Kifner, "A Tense, Troubled City," *NYT*, October 11, 1974.

112. Wrigley, "From Housewives to Activists," 268–69.

113. Ibid., 264–68.

114. Margaret (Mrs. John S.) Langford to Judge Sidney O. Smith, January 29, 1973, Box 55A, Record Group 21, District Courts of United States, NA SE.

115. "Section IV—Project Narrative," n.d., ca. 1972, Box 1, Record Group 12, Emergency School Assistance Program, Alabama, NA SE. This report was from Anniston City, Alabama, school district. Other districts had similar projects.

116. Thomas A. Johnson, "Black Delegates Seek More Contacts," *NYT*, May 19, 1972; "National Black Political Convention Collection, 1972–1973," Indiana Historical Society, http://www.indianahistory.org.

117. Ronald P. Formisano, *Boston Against Busing*, 146–50; Wrigley, "From Housewives to Activists," 283–84.

118. League of Women Voters, "LWVUS Opposes Anti-Busing Legislation," news release, February 22, 1972, in BX 173, League of Women Voters, Box 18, file "Education-Busing," UO.

119. Ibid.

120. Harvard Graduate School of Education, "Busing in Boston: Looking Back at the History and Legacy," *HGSE News*, September 1, 2000, http://www.gse.harvard.edu/news/features/busing09012000_page6.html; "The Legacy of School Busing: Decades after '*Brown*,' Desegregation Efforts Yield Mixed Results," NPR, http://www.npr.org/templates/story/story.php?storyId=1853532.

121. Egerton, *Speak Now Against the Day*, 10.

122. Nancy MacLean, "Neo-Confederacy versus the New Deal: The Regional Utopia of the Modern American Right," 308–29.

123. MacLean, *Freedom Is Not Enough*, 232–33.

Chapter 4. Sex, God, and the American Flag: Tradition and Change in Moral Values

Epigraph source: Holly Holmes, "The ABC's of America," reprint of talk given on radio show *Life Lines*, May 1, 1961, in newsletter from Temple City Letter Shop (California), ed. Mae K. Hughes. In Box 19, file 3, MMC, SU.

1. Loretta Killian to President Nixon, n.d., ca. 1969, Box 48, WHCF, WE 9, Box 48, NPP, NA II.

2. Linda Kerber coined the term in her book *Women of the Republic: Intellect and Ideology in Revolutionary America*.

3. David J. Pivar, *Purity Crusade: Sexual Morality and Social Control, 1868–1900*, 41–42.

4. Peggy Pascoe, *Relations of Rescue: The Search for Female Moral Authority in the American West, 1874–1939*, 4–5; Nancy F. Cott, *The Bonds of Womanhood: "Woman's Sphere" in New England, 1780–1835*, 6–8; Pivar, *Purity Crusade*, 26; Benowitz, *Encyclopedia of American Women and Religion*, 380.

5. D'Ann Campbell, *Women at War with America: Private Lives in a Patriotic Era*, 216.

6. Benowitz, *Days of Discontent*, 133–34; Blanche Winters, American Woman's Party, pamphlet, "Men . . . Let us call to your attention . . . These Facts," n.d., ca. 1952, Reel 13, RWC, UI.

7. Isserman and Kazin, *America Divided*, 202.

8. Not all adults were pessimistic about the future of the younger generation. Some were like Mrs. Alden Carlson of Worcester, Massachusetts, who wrote President Johnson to express her agreement with the president that "the youth of this country have improved . . . in the past generation." Box 22, WHCF, "Welfare," LBJ Library.

9. Jeffrey P. Moran, "'Modernism Gone Mad': Sex Education Comes to Chicago, 1913," 481–82, 502.

10. Johannah Cornblatt, in "The Sin of Yielding to Impure Desire," *Newsweek*, October 27, 2009, estimates that somewhere between 20 to 40 percent of schools had programs in social hygiene and sexuality.

11. Susan K. Freeman, *Sex Goes to School: Girls and Sex Education Before the 1960s*, 3.

12. Howard Whitman, "Youth and 'The Natural Urge,'" *Better Homes and Gardens*, July 1957, 43, 102, 112–14, 120.

13. Bryan Strong, "Ideas of the Early Sex Education Movement in America, 1890–1920," 129–61; Janice M. Irvine, *Talk About Sex: The Battles Over Sex Education in the United States*.

14. Frances Bartlett, "'Modern' Morality: Is it Moral?" *FACTS in Education*, May-June, 1963, Box 47, RRC, Hoover Institution.

15. Frances Bartlett, "A Moral Crisis: The Disarming of Youth," *FACTS in Education*, July-August 1963, Box 24, file 5, MMC, SU.

16. Ibid.

17. Report, Textbook Study Committee, Alabama Society, Daughters of the American Revolution, April 2, 1964, Circuit Riders, Inc., Collection 167, Box 4, UO.

18. Janice M. Irvine, in her comprehensive book, *Talk About Sex*, includes considerable information regarding SIECUS and about the leaders of that organization. Jeffrey P. Moran, *Teaching Sex: The Shaping of Adolescence in the 20th Century*, 162–63.

19. Gloria Lentz, *Raping Our Children: The Sex Education Scandal*, 19.

20. Irvine, *Talk About Sex*, 23.

21. Established in 1950, the National Council of Churches was an integration of Protestant interdenominational agencies. At the outset, the twenty-five Protestant and four Eastern Orthodox denominations entering the organization claimed a total of approximately thirty million church members, mainly of the long established "mainstream" churches. See Carter, *Another Part of the Fifties*.

22. Letter to the editor from Arlene Steinmeyer, "Anaheim Woman Tells Deep Concern," *Anaheim Bulletin*, November 1, 1968.

23. John Steinbacher, "Parent Reads Textbooks, Causes Gasps and Giggles at Sex Education Hearing," *Anaheim Bulletin*, November 15, 1968, 1.

24. Ibid.

25. Letter to editor from Florence M. Vollman, "Shocked at Sex Classes," *Anaheim Bulletin*, November 1, 1968.

26. Copy of broadcast of reply to an editorial, KCBS News Radio 74, Spokesman: Mrs. Margaret Scott, September 21, 1968, Box 4, Collection 167, Circuit Riders, Inc., UO.

27. Lloyd Shearer, "Classroom Sex" in "Intelligence Report," *Parade*, November 2, 1969, 26.

28. George C. Wallace, "Pornographic Sex Education Sure Way to Destroy Morals of Youth," *George C. Wallace Newsletter*, n.d., reprinted in *Independent American*, June-July-August 1969, in Box 28, file 7, MMC, SU.

29. Phoebe Courtney, *The Sex Education Racket*, 1–5.

30. Viola R. Hanson, "Sexploitation," reprint of letter to the editor of *Daily Breeze*, n.d., ca. 1960s, reproduced by the Network of Patriotic Letter Writers, Box 34, file "Network of Patriotic Letter Writers," NAC, Hoover Institution.

31. Ibid.

32. Larry Schulz, "Sex Education Is Raging Battle," *Arcadia News-Post*, November 18, 1969, in Box 20, file 14, MMC, SU. In 1969, the JBS reported that nationwide it had 2,000 of these committees, aimed at protecting Americans' morality. MOTOREDE believed that communists and SIECUS were conspiring to destroy the moral character of the upcoming generation. The leadership of MOTOREDE was mostly male, although women were among its members.

33. Lloyd Shearer, "Classroom Sex" in "Intelligence Report," *Parade*, November 2, 1969, 26.

34. Lentz, *Raping Our Children*, 48.

35. Marilyn A. Angle, Jean E. Sumrall, and Nell J. Seagraves, "Supplementary Evaluation of Curriculum Guides on Family Life and Sex Education and an Overview of the Guides," March 6, 1969, Minute Women, Reel 76, RWC, UI.

36. Minute Women, newsletter, January-February 1969, Reel 76, M19, RWC, UI.

37. Neil Ulman, "The Facts of Life," *Wall Street Journal*, September 19, 1967; "'Sensitivity' Course Stirs Parental Anger," *Los Angeles Times*, January 24, 1969; in newsletter, Minute Women, January-February 1969, Reel 76, M19, RWC, UI.

38. Petition, filed June 5, 1969, from Anna Dow and fourteen additional women, Box 5, WHCF, ED, NPP, NA II.

39. Ibid.

40. Letter/petition, Alice P. Lewis, et al., to President Nixon, September 23, 1969, Box 5, WHCF, ED, NPP, NA II.

41. Ibid.

42. Gwen Mote to President Johnson, ca. November 1965, Box 9, WHCF, "Education," LBJ Library.

43. Ibid.

44. Lloyd Shearer, "Classroom Sex" in "Intelligence Report," *Parade*, November 2, 1969, 26.

45. Janice M. Irvine, "Doing It with Words: Discourse and the Sex Education Culture Wars," 59, 63; personal interview with Peggy Melby, April 4, 2009.

46. Philip Wylie, *Sons and Daughters of Mom*, 81.

47. Walter Trohan, "Skinny Dippin' with President is the Latest D.C. Status Symbol," news clipping from unidentified newspaper, n.d., ca. January, 1964, Box 11, WHCF PR 3, LBJ Library.

48. Stephanie Wnek to President Johnson, January 24, 1964 and W. D. Cavanaugh and Jean Cavanaugh to the president, January 24, 1964. Similar letters came from Alta London, January 27, 1964, and Mrs. Estelle Marie Deres, January 30, 1964, all Box 11, WHCF, PR 3, LBJ Library.

49. Mary Southward to the president, May 12, 1966, Box 14, WHCF, PR 3, LBJ Library.

50. Mrs. Johnnie Ramsey to President Nixon, March 25, 1969, Box 48, WHCF, WE 9, NPP, NA II.

51. Personal interview with Rhonda Moraca, June 29, 2009. She adhered to her parents' expectations in her early adulthood, but later did go to college.

52. For an example of how the issue has changed, see Rob Stein, "Teen-sex Study Focuses on TV," *Washington Post*, reprinted in *Sarasota Herald-Tribune*, November 3, 2008.

53. Bruce J. Dierenfield, *The Battle Over School Prayer: How* Engel v. Vitale *Changed America*, 18–19.

54. Elaine Tyler May, *Homeward Bound: American Families in the Cold War Era*, 25.

55. Benowitz, *Encyclopedia of American Women and Religion*, particularly 310–11 and 338–39; Susan Hill Lindley, *"You Have Stepped Out of Your Place": A History of Women and Religion in America*.

56. For instance, in 1986 fundamentalist Christian parents sought rulings in two separate cases in federal District Courts in Alabama and Tennessee that would remove from public schools reading materials "that are colored by anti-Christian themes." Concerned Women for America was reportedly financing the Tennessee plaintiffs. See Dudley Clendinen, "Conservative Christians Again Take Issue of Religion in Schools to Courts," *NYT*, February 28, 1986.

57. DAR, "Religion and the New Social Order," Box 10, file 7, LCC, UO.

58. Vivian Utterson Sullivan, California Chapter, Pro America, "School Affairs Report," May 13, 1959, RRC, Hoover Institution.

59. Ibid.

60. The first case was *Engel v. Vitale*, in which the Supreme Court ruled against the recitation of an official prayer in the New York state public schools. The second ruling combined two cases, *School District of Abington Township Pennsylvania v. Schempp* and *Murray v. Curlett*. Marianne M. Meier examines these cases and other controversies on the question of religion in school, in *Understanding the School Prayer Issue and the Related Character Education and Charter School Movements*, particularly 18–77. Also see Bruce J. Dierenfield, *The Battle Over School Prayer*.

61. Dierenfield, *The Battle Over School Prayer*, 163, 170; Eugene F. Provenzo Jr., *Religious Fundamentalism and American Education: The Battle for the Public Schools*, 77.

62. Dierenfield, *The Battle Over School Prayer*, 170 and 175.

63. C. P. Trussell, "Sheen Criticizes Court Prayer Ban," *NYT*, May 1, 1964; "The School Prayer Issue," *NYT*, May 10, 1964; Zimmerman, *Whose America?*, 164.

64. Letter to the editor, "How Readers View Religion in Schools," from Bette Pforr, *Wall Street Journal*, May 19, 1964, 18. In *Battle Over School Prayer*, Dierenfield notes that at the time of the second Supreme Court case, thirty-nine states either required or permitted Bible reading in public school classrooms.

65. For example, Helen Thornton, a mother of four, wrote President Johnson on December 1, 1965, "if one woman who believed in nothing can do this much damage to a country and get away with it, I can do something to counteract it, because I believe in God and my country." Box 3, WHCF, RM, LBJ Library.

66. Untitled document, Network of Patriotic Letter Writers, Box 34, file "The Network of Patriotic Letter Writers," NAC, Hoover Institution.

67. For example, Virginia Ingalls, a Catholic woman, raises a number of questions surrounding the issue of religious freedom and the Supreme Court decision in a letter to President Johnson, January 2, 1964, Box 152, WHCF, Legislation, LBJ Library.

68. Phoebe Courtney, "Let Our Children Pray! How to Reverse the Supreme Court's Atheistic Decision Which Bans Prayer in Schools," *Tax Fax* No. 48, Independent American, 1963, in Box 1, PCP, UO.

69. Untitled document, Network of Patriotic Letter Writers, Box 34, file "The Network of Patriotic Letter Writers," NAC, Hoover Institution.

70. "Resolutions: Seventy-First Continental Congress National Society Daughters of the American Revolution," April 16–20, 1962, Box 32, RRC, Hoover Institution.

71. Letter to the editor, "Denial of Our Heritage," from Veronica S. Cassidy, *NYT*, June 29, 1962, 26.

72. Marguerite Geis to President Johnson, February 11, 1966, Box 3, WHCF, RM, LBJ Library.

73. Mabel Hanlen to the president, April 21, 1966, Box 24, WHCF, "Welfare," LBJ Library.

74. Untitled document, Network of Patriotic Letter Writers, Box 34, file "The Network of Patriotic Letter Writers," NAC, Hoover Institution.

75. Mrs. Henry W. Rowell to President Johnson, October 4, 1967, Box 2, WHCF, RM, and Helen Thornton to President Johnson, December 1, 1965, Box 3, WHCF, RM, LBJ Library. See also, editorial, "The War Against Religion," *Wall Street Journal*, May 6, 1964, 12; Ann Lockhart to the editor in "How Readers View Religion in Schools," *Wall Street Journal*, May 19, 1964, 18.

76. Flyer, "Evelyn Wyatt, Director of the world wide ministry of WINGS OF HEALING, Invites You to the American Heritage Rally," in Box 36, file 6, MMC, SU.

77. "Miss Pickford Tells of Voter Prayer Rally," *Los Angeles Times*, October 17, 1964, in Box 25, file 6, MMC, SU.

78. Zimmerman, *Whose America?*, 174.

79. Bernice Batterton, "Voluntary Prayers Endorsed," *Evening Carrier*, Prescott,

Arizona, April 18, 1966; We, The People! "Public Affairs Opinion Poll," Box 44, NAC, Hoover Institution.

80. Bernice Batterton, "Voluntary Prayers Endorsed," *Prescott (Az.) Evening Carrier*, April 18, 1966, We, The People! "Public Affairs Opinion Poll," and open letter, "We Must Poll Millions," from Harry T. Everingham on flyer in Box 44, NAC, Hoover Institution.

81. Open Letter, Dear Friend, We, The People! May 2, 1966, Box 44, NAC, Hoover Institution.

82. Dierenfield, *Battle Over School Prayer*, 138, 145, 153–55.

83. Thomas G. Rees, "Ohio Woman Is Staging Prayer Fight," *Uniontown (Pa.) Morning Herald—Evening Standard*, August 19, 1971; "Prayer Ban Foes Applaud Mother," *NYT*, September 26, 1971.

84. Rees, "Ohio Woman Is Staging Prayer Fight," *Uniontown Morning Herald—Evening Standard*, August 19, 1971, 12; Marjorie Hunter, "School Prayer Vote Is Forced in House," *Special to the NYT*, September 22, 1971; "Prayer Ban Foes Applaud Mother," *NYT*, September 26, 1971.

85. Florence Matthews and thirty-three additional women to President Johnson, October 20, 1967, Box 11, WHCF, PR 3, LBJ Library.

86. Marian E. Murphey Cansler to the president, January 20, 1966, and Mrs. James Dobson to the president, n.d., ca. January 1966, Box 3, WHCF, RM, LBJ Library; Carter, *Another Part of the Fifties*, 127; Himmelstein, *To the Right*, 113–14; Wilcox, *God's Warriors*, 70; Justus D. Doenecke, "McIntire, Carl Curtis."

87. Marian E. Murphey Cansler to President Johnson, January 20, 1966; Mrs. James Dobson to the president, n.d., ca. January 1966; Ruth Briggs to the president, February 23, 1966, Box 3, WHCF, RM, LBJ Library.

88. Letter, to Douglas Cater Jr., White House, November 15, 1965, Box 9, WHCF, "Education," LBJ Library.

89. Telegram to the president from Miss Tevis Graham, July 27, 1966, Box 2, WHCF, RM, LBJ Library.

90. Margaret Blake to President Johnson, June 18, 1966, Box 2, WHCF, RM, LBJ Library.

91. Marjorie Maloy to the president, July 13, 1966, Box 2, WHCF, RM, LBJ Library.

92. For example, see Mary E. Tyler to the president, February 2, 1964, Box 2, WHCF, RM, LBJ Library; and Yvonne Weiberg of Portola Valley, California, to the president, May 31, 1965; and Anne Culbertson, of Cleveland, Ohio, to the president, May 31, 1965, both Box 3, WHCF, RM, LBJ Library.

93. While men and women often worked together, historian Jonathan Zimmerman found that "aggrieved mothers" were frequently the instigators of letter-writing campaigns to return prayer to the schools. This study supports his findings. Zimmerman, *Whose America?*, 174.

94. Jacqueline Mutone to the president, October 5, 1967, Box 72, WHCF, HU, LBJ Library.

95. Jeannie Norris to the president, April 13, 1967, Box 72, WHCF, HU, LBJ Library.

96. Ida Darden, "Compassion Tempers Our Judgment of Brain-Washed College Students," *Southern Conservative*, November-December 1955, Reel 114, S18, RWC, UI.

97. For more on the founding of the YAF see John A. Andrew III, *The Other Side of the Sixties: Young Americans for Freedom and the Rise of Conservative Politics*, 5, 11, 31, 53–74 and Klatch, *A Generation Divided*, 1, 18–19, 20–21, 23. Among the former YAF members whom she interviewed, Klatch found that nearly one-quarter joined the organization during high school (89). Brennan, *Turning Right in the Sixties*, 65.

98. James H. Hijiya, "The Conservative 1960s," 208.

99. Douglas Caddy to Crain, August 16, 1960, Box 13, file 8, LCC, UO.

100. One-page document, "National Advisory Board, Young Americans for Freedom (Still in Formation)," ca. late 1960, Box 13, file 15, LCC, UO. For more on Taylor, Dodd, and Kuhn see chapter 1.

101. John A. Andrew III, *The Other Side of the Sixties*, 82.

102. Klatch, *A Generation Divided*, 59.

103. "The Red Diaper Babies Grow Up," *New Guard*, September 1965, MMC, SU. About one-third of the SDS activists whom Rebecca Klatch interviewed were "red diaper babies," although by the time their children were growing up, many of the parents were no longer sympathetic to communism. See Klatch, *A Generation Divided*, 43.

104. Everette Dennis, "'Go to Oak St. and turn right' for latest conservative books," *Oregon Daily Emerald*, November 8, 1961, in BX 173, League of Women Voters, Box 10, file "Anti-League," OHS.

105. Flyer distributed by Patriot Bookshop, Box 24, file 7, MMC, SU; "GOP Unit to Discuss Red Theory," *Los Angeles Times*, Box 28, file 1, MMC, SU.

106. See MMC, SU. See also McGirr, *Suburban Warriors*; Isserman and Kazin, *America Divided*, 212; and Schuparra, *Triumph of the Right*; Nickerson, *Mothers of Conservatism*.

107. McGirr, *Suburban Warriors*, especially pp. 8–9.

108. James Gregory, *American Exodus: The Dust Bowl Migration and Okie Culture in California*; Darren Dochuk, *From Bible Belt to Sunbelt: Plain-Folk Religion, Grassroots Politics, and the Rise of Evangelical Conservatism*.

109. McGirr, *Suburban Warriors*, especially pp. 8–9.

110. See MMC, SU. Also, the Pasadena's Sierra Madre community was one that Julie Salley Gray designated "solidly conservative to extremely conservative" in "'To Fight the Good Fight,'" 2.

111. "Republican Club Topic Hear 'Crime' Speaker," *Arcadia Tribune*, February 2, 1967, in Box 28, file 6, MMC, SU. Browning was also reported to have served on the antisubversive committee of the American Legion and on the Board of Trustees of the Covina Unified School District.

112. "Dr. William Fort to Speak Before Republican Club," *Arcadia Tribune*, June 11, 1964, in Box 28, file 7, MMC, SU. More on Walter Knott can be found in the MMC, particularly in Box 28.

113. Bulletin, Arcadia Republican Women's Club, Federated, June 1964, and Bulletin, Arcadia Republican Women's Club, October 1964, in Box 28, file 1, MMC, SU.

114. Ruth Billheimer, "Climate of Patriotism Needed, Says Defector," unidentified newspaper, Pasadena, September 22, 1965, in Box 12, file 14, MMC, SU.

115. Sarah Watson Emery, "Recruiting for the 'New Community' America's Trojan Horse," *American Spirit*, January 1965, 16.

116. Ibid., 17–18.

117. Ibid., 18.

118. Statement, Joyce Zuck, n.d., ca. late 1964–early 1965, in Box 28, file 5, MMC, SU.

119. Bulletin, East Pasadena-Sierra Madre Republican Women's Club, March 1965, in Box 28, file 5, MMC, SU.

120. Brennan, *Turning Right in the Sixties*, 113.

121. "Bits and Pieces," *American Spirit*, February-March 1965, Reel 8, A49, RWC, UI. In an interview for a documentary of his life, Pete Seeger recalled it was around 1949 that he had "drifted out of the Communist Party." Nevertheless, he continued to espouse left-wing ideals, which led to his being hounded by the FBI throughout the 1950s and blacklisted from commercial television until 1967. PBS, *American Masters*, "Pete Seeger: The Power of Song" (Live Nation Worldwide, Inc., 2007).

122. "Bits and Pieces," *American Spirit*, February-March 1965, Reel 8, A49, RWC, UI.

123. Isserman and Kazin in *America Divided*, 163.

124. Glenn C. Altschuler, *All Shook Up: How Rock 'n' Roll Changed America*, 6.

125. "Folk Songs Push Communist Line," Box 34, file "The Network of Patriotic Letter Writers," NAC, Hoover Institution.

126. "Folk Songs Push Communist Line," Box 34, file "The Network of Patriotic Letter Writers," NAC, Hoover Institution.

127. This letter was described and quoted in "Republican Women Seek Speakers' Policy Review," *Arcadia News Post*, July 18, 1967, in Box 28, file 6, MMC, SU.

128. "Pro-America Club to Have Police Talk, 'Hippie' Film," *San Marino News*, October 5, 1967, Box 25, file 7, MMC, SU.

129. Mary Erb to Crain, September 11, 1968, Box 20, file 11, LCC, UO.

130. Helen M. Peters, "A Red Front: Young Americans for Freedom," Reel 114, S14, RWC, UI.

131. John A. Andrew III, *The Other Side of the Sixties*, 61–62, 88; Diamond, *Roads to Dominion*, 124; Sandra Scanlon, *The Pro-War Movement*, 260; Klatch, *A Generation Divided*, 81.

132. Nash, *Conservative Intellectual Movement Since 1945*, 235–86, 531.

133. Crain to Lukens, August 26, 1968, Box 20, file 10, LCC, UO; Harry Gilroy, "U.S. and Belgium Sign Amity Pact," *NYT*, February 22, 1961; "Unity of the Atlan-

tic," *NYT*, June 13, 1961; "Rockefeller Asks a Union of Nations," *NYT*, November 21, 1964, 16.

134. Lukens served in Congress from 1966 to 1990. John A. Boehner defeated him in the Ohio Republican primary, but Lukens resigned from Congress in October 1990 following a House Ethics Committee vote to investigate charges that he had propositioned a young House of Representatives elevator operator. Douglas Martin, "Donald Lukens, Scandal-Tainted Lawmaker, Dies at 79," *NYT*, May 25, 2010.

135. Mrs. George W. Hewlett, corresponding secretary, Long Island Federation of Women's Clubs, Inc., to President Johnson, May 29, 1968, with memorandum attachment, Box 73, WHCF, HU, LBJ Library.

136. Homer Joseph Dodge, "Let's Not Have Infant Suffrage," *USA*, Reel 136, U2, RWC, UI.

137. Crain to the Honorable J. Mercorella, July 1, 1966, Box 17, file 3, LCC, UO.

138. Richard L. Madden, "Voting at 18 Asked as Constitution Convention Begins Recess," *NYT*, April 18, 1967; "Rockefeller Proposes Cutting the Voting Age to 18," *NYT*, December 14, 1969; letter, Julia B. Steiner to Andrew R. Tyler, July 5, 1968, Box 20, file 7, LCC, UO.

139. Mervin D. Field, "18–20 Year Olds Consider Themselves Liberal and Identify Themselves with Democratic party in Larger Proportions than Present Voting Population," Field Research Corporation, November 27, 1970, Robert H. Finch, Box 43, NPP, NA II.

140. Carl Leubsdorf, "Mrs. Armstrong Opposes GOP Change to Woo Young Voters," *Corpus Christi Caller*, April 21, 1971, in Farenthold (Frances Tarlton) Papers, Box 3 G91, Center for American History.

141. Telegram to president from ? (illegible), August 6, 1967, Box 24, WHCF, "Welfare," LBJ Library.

142. Joyce McLewin to president, n.d., ca. June 1968, Box 2, WHCF, RM, LBJ Library.

143. Debra Clement to president, July 26, 1968, Box 24, WHCF, "Welfare," LBJ Library. Another girl, June Frederick of Ames, Iowa, wrote Johnson about the changes in her attitude regarding world problems that her membership in the MRA had brought her. Frederick to president, July 10, 1964, Box 3, WHCF, "Welfare," LBJ Library.

144. Debra Clement to president, July 26, 1968, Box 24, WHCF, "Welfare," LBJ Library; Up With People, "History of Up With People," accessed August 23, 2008, http://www.upwithpeople.org/about/history.htm; Boxes 17–19, LCC, UO.

145. Up With People, "History of Up With People," http://www.upwithpeople.org/about/history.htm.

146. Andrew Preston, "Evangelical Internationalism: A Conservative Worldview for the Age of Globalization," in Laura Jane Gifford and Daniel K. Williams, *The Right Side of the Sixties: Reexamining Conservatism's Decade of Transformation*, 235.

147. Lee Storey, director. *Smile 'Til It Hurts: The Up With People Story*, Documen-

tary, 2012; Jason Zasky, "Smile 'Til It Hurts: A Behind the Music-like look at the perpetually perky, ideologically-motivated singing phenomenon Up With People," *Failure Magazine*, 2014, accessed April 6, 2014, http://failuremag.com/index.php/site/print/smile_til_it_hurts/.

148. Pamela Jones to President Johnson, June 17, 1968, Box 24, WHCF, "Welfare," LBJ Library.

149. Susan Ward to the president, August 16, 1967, Box 72, WHCF, HU, LBJ Library.

150. Letter to the president from "A Teenager from Sherwood Junior High School," no name given, February 12, 1968, Box 72, WHCF, HU, LBJ Library.

151. "Stars Join Teens in Decency Rally," *Atlanta Journal*, March 24, 1969.

152. "Stars Join Teens in Decency Rally," *Atlanta Journal*, March 24, 1969; Michael Lienesch, *Redeeming America: Piety and Politics in the New Christian Right*, 21. In 1976, in the Miami, Florida, region, Bryant led the religious crusade that used a referendum to repeal the Dade County commissioners' vote in favor of granting homosexuals equality in housing, employment, and public accommodation, and inspired a similar campaign in California. See Hardisty, *Mobilizing Resentment*, 100; and Gillian Frank, "'The Civil Rights of Parents': Race and Conservative Politics in Anita Bryant's Campaign Against Gay Rights in 1970s Florida," 126–60.

153. Bruce J. Schulman, *The Seventies: The Great Shift in American Culture, Society, and Politics*, 16.

154. See Lienesch, *Redeeming America*, 11.

155. Walter H. Capps, *The New Religious Right: Piety, Patriotism and Politics*, 7–8. For more discussion of major themes of the New Religious Right, see Capps pp. 186–89.

156. Unidentified writer of "The Hippies," reprinted in flyer of Network of Patriotic Letter Writers, Reel 89, N93, RWC, UI.

Chapter 5. The Vietnam War and Student Rebellion

Epigraph source: Alice Widener, "SOS for Our Viet Nam Wounded," reprint from *Human Events*, March 19, 1966.

1. Crain to David (last name not given), August 4, 1965, Box 16, file 3, LCC, UO.

2. David W. Levy, *The Debate Over Vietnam*, 44–45, 125; George C. Herring, *America's Longest War: The United States and Vietnam, 1950–1975*, 20–145.

3. Crain to David (last name not given), August 4, 1965, Box 16, file 3, LCC, UO.

4. Press release, Mothers' Crusade for Victory over Communism, March 6, 1966, file 2; Flyer, Mothers' Crusade for Victory over Communism, ca. March-April 1967, file 3; newsletter, Mothers' Crusade for Victory over Communism, June 1967, files 3 and 7. All Box 84, LCC, UO.

5. List of officers, Victory in Vietnam Committee, New York City, ca. 1969, Box 84, LCC, UO.

6. Ada B. Gourdin to President Johnson, January 4, 1966, Box 3, WHCF, RM, LBJ Library.

7. Edwin A. Walker, "To Mothers: Why Viet Nam?" *American Mercury,* September 1965, Box 32, RRC, Hoover Institution.

8. Levy, *The Debate Over Vietnam,* 46–59.

9. Press Release, Mrs. Jess Conant, Mothers' Crusade for Victory over Communism, March 6, 1966, in Box 20, file 13, MMC, SU.

10. Bea Zeegler to Mrs. Kirkpatrick, chairperson of Mothers of Servicemen, October 30, 1966; flyer and brochure, Mothers' Crusade for Victory over Communism, "Why Should We Help Communists to Kill Our Sons?" September 1966, both in Box 20, file 13, MMC, SU.

11. Phyllis Schlafly, *A Choice Not an Echo,* 84.

12. Ethel Johnson to Crain, July 31, 1966, Box 17, file 5, LCC, UO.

13. Ibid.

14. Transcripts, August 21, 1966, and September 25, 1966, Crain, speaking with Charles Videla on radio station WLGN, Sag Harbor, New York, Box 84, file 8, LCC, UO.

15. Ethel Johnson to Crain, July 31, 1966, Box 17, file 5, LCC, UO.

16. Bea Zeegler, chairperson of Mothers of Servicemen, to Mrs. Kirkpatrick, October 30, 1966; flyer and brochure, Mothers' Crusade for Victory over Communism, "Why Should We Help Communists to Kill Our Sons?" September 1966, both in Box 20, file 13, MMC, SU.

17. "An Open Letter to Our U.S. Senators and Representatives," Mothers' Crusade for Victory over Communism, n.d., ca. January 1967, Reel 78, M66, RWC, UI.

18. Telegram, Peggy Ferebee, Mrs. W. McLail, and Lois Whitten to the president, Box 70, WHCF, HU, LBJ Library. "White House Pickets Urge End to Communist Trade," *Washington Post,* May 5, 1967.

19. "Mothers Crusade," *Arcadia News-Post,* April 14, 1967, Box 20, file 13, MMC, SU.

20. "Mothers Crusade," *Arcadia News-Post,* April 14, 1967, Box 20, file 13, MMC, SU; Mothers' Crusade for Victory over Communism, "Rules of Conduct to Be Observed by Rally Participants," Box 84, file 2, LCC, UO; Ethel Johnson to Crain, July 31, 1966, Box 17, file 5, LCC, UO.

21. Ethel Johnson to Crain, July 31, 1966, Box 17, file 5, LCC, UO.

22. "White House Pickets Urge End to Communist Trade," *Washington Post,* May 5, 1967; "Women Hold Washington Talks Today," unidentified newspaper article, May 5, 1967, Box 84, file 7, LCC, UO.

23. Benowitz, *Days of Discontent,* 126–27, 146.

24. "White House Pickets Urge End to Communist Trade," *Washington Post,* May 5, 1967; "Women Hold Washington Talks Today," unidentified newspaper article, May 5, 1967, Box 84, file 7, LCC, UO.

25. No title, *Houston Tribune,* May 18, 1967, 6.

26. Statement of Mrs. C. B. Johnson, Box 84, file 7, LCC, UO.

27. Ethel Johnson to Crain, July 31, 1966, Box 17, file 5, LCC, UO.

28. Mothers' Crusade for Victory over Communism, "Aims and Purposes of Mothers' Crusade," Box 84, file 3, LCC, UO.

29. Mothers of Servicemen, "Surrender—Never! (Negotiations=Surrender) A Military Victory Is Our Only Hope for Peace in Asia," broadside (South Pasadena: Mothers of Servicemen, ca. 1969–1972), MMC, SU.

30. Flyer, Mothers of Servicemen, "This Nation under God," n.d., ca. 1967, MMC, SU.

31. Sandra Scanlon, The Pro-War Movement, 56.

32. Flyer, Mothers of Servicemen, "This Nation under God," n.d., ca. 1967, MMC, SU.

33. "Resolutions Adopted by 76th Continental Congress, National Society of the Daughters of the American Revolution, April 14–21, 1967, p. 3, Reel 89, N85, RWC, UI.

34. Sam Pope Brewer, "Thant Urges U.S. Declare a Halt in Vietnam War," NYT, April 2, 1967.

35. Mrs. Dennis Lorance to President Johnson, January 3, 1966, Box 3, WHCF, RM, LBJ Library.

36. Among the others were Ruth Briggs, February 23, 1966, and Ada B. Gourdin, January 4, 1966, Box 3, WHCF, RM, LBJ Library.

37. Andrew Preston, "Evangelical Internationalism," in The Right Side of the Sixties, ed. Gifford and Williams, 227.

38. A 1967 Lou Harris Poll revealed that for a while, at least, television coverage likely had the opposite effect, as 64 percent of Americans surveyed stated that they believed that television coverage made them more supportive of the war. See Levy, The Debate Over Vietnam, 54.

39. Schulman, The Seventies, 9.

40. In 1970 there were reports of some American Legion posts distributing the flyers, as well as the John Birch Society. See Linda Greenhouse, "Flyer about Peace Symbol Disturbs Many," NYT, August 3, 1970. "Their Peace Symbol—The Broken Cross,'" reprint of article in Free Enterprise, July 1968, Network of Patriotic Letter Writers, Reel 89, N93, RWC, UI.

41. Linda Greenhouse, "Flyer about Peace Symbol Disturbs Many," NYT, August 3, 1970.

42. Mauralee Z. Clark to the president, March 8, 1968, Box 72, WHCF, HU, LBJ Library, is one example. Frances K. Whitcraft to Mr. [Jay] Wilkinson, February 26, 1969, Box 47, WHCF, WE 9, NPP, NA II, offers a rightist perspective with her charges that the troublemakers were lower class socialists and parasites, living off of taxpayers' money.

43. Clyde Brown and Gayle K. Pluta Brown, "Moo U and the Cambodian Invasion: Nonviolent Anti-Vietnam War Protest at Iowa State University," 119.

44. Herring, America's Longest War, 234–37; Mark Hamilton Lytle, America's Uncivil Wars: The Sixties Era from Elvis to the Fall of Richard Nixon, 252–53; Vivian Ballentine, et al., to President Nixon, May 20, 1970, Box 29, WHCF, HU 3-1, NPP, NA II.

45. Herring, *America's Longest War*, 246–47.

46. Memo from Eleanor W. Spicer to members of the National Board of Management, Anne Armstrong, Box 59, WHCF, SMOF, NPP, NA II; letter from Louise Brown to president, May 11, 1972, Anne Armstrong, Box 61, WHCF, SMOF, NPP, NA II.

47. Herring, *America's Longest War*, 273. Brennan, in *Turning Right in the Sixties*, p. 136, notes that while mainstream conservatives like William F. Buckley Jr. accepted the peace, the John Birch Society took the position that Nixon had sold out to radical forces in both the United States and North Vietnam.

48. "Campus Protests a Ban on Politics," *NYT*, November 1, 1964, 28; Wallace Turner, "796 Students Arrested as Police Break Up Sit-In at University of California," *NYT*, December 4, 1964.

49. Lytle, *America's Uncivil Wars*, 168–73. Some books that examine the protests in detail are Gerard J. DeGroot, ed., *Student Protest: The Sixties and After*; Marc Jason Gilbert, ed., *The Vietnam War on Campus: Other Voices, More Distant Drums*; and Tom Wells, *The War Within: America's Battle over Vietnam*.

50. Bulletin, East Pasadena-Sierra Madre Republican Women's Club, Federated (March 1965), Box 28, file 5, MMC, SU.

51. "The Kerr Resignation," *NYT*, March 11, 1965; "Sale of Magazine Halted on Campus at Berkeley," *NYT*, March 20, 1965; Wallace Turner, "Students Protest Berkeley Ouster," *NYT*, April 23, 1965.

52. Jennifer Burns, *Goddess of the Market: Ayn Rand and the American Right*, 196–204.

53. Ayn Rand, "Check Your Premises: The Cashing-in: 'The Student Rebellion,'" *Objectivist Newsletter*, September 1965, Box 25, file 12, MMC, SU.

54. Ibid.

55. Stephen Hess, *America's Political Dynasties*, 206, 256.

56. Edith Kermit Roosevelt, "A New Profession for Youth: Insurrection," *Independent American*, September-October 1965, 1.

57. John Andrew, "Pro-War and Anti-Draft: Young Americans for Freedom and the War in Vietnam," 1–11.

58. "Nixon Supporters Planning War Rallies," *NYT*, November 9, 1969.

59. Roosevelt, "A New Profession for Youth," *Independent American*, September-October 1965, 1.

60. Ibid.

61. Ibid.

62. Lytle, *America's Uncivil Wars*, 199.

63. Neil Sheehan, "A Student Group Concedes It Took Funds from CIA," *NYT*, February 14, 1967; John Herbers, "President Bars Agency Influence over Education," *NYT*, February 16, 1967; Steven V. Roberts, "C.I.A. Is Criticized by Conservatives," *NYT*, February 23, 1967; Ben A. Franklin, "Students Assail C.I.A. 'Whitewash,'" *NYT*, February 25, 1967; "N.S.A. is Opposed," *NYT*, February 22, 1969.

64. Lytle, *America's Uncivil Wars*, 241.

65. Tom Wells, *The War Within*, 312.

66. Kenneth J. Heineman, "American Schism: Catholic Activists, Intellectuals, and Students Confront the Vietnam War," 103.

67. This is based upon my examination of Boxes 29–37, White House Central Files, Human Rights, NPP, NA II.

68. Mrs. William Coldsnow to the President Nixon, with fourteen additional signatures (mostly women). Box 37, WHCF, HU 3-1, NPP, NA II.

69. Muriel Roberts to the president, May 9, 1970, Box 29, WHCF, HU 3-1, Box 29, NPP, NA II.

70. Muriel Roberts to William Hitch, Nathan Pusey, Fred Harrington, William Friday, Alexander Heard, Edward Levi, Malcolm Moos, and W. Allen Wallis, May 8, 1970, Box 29, WHCF, HU 3-1, Box 29, NPP, NA II.

71. Angela Re, Carol Stephenson, and four others to President Nixon, May 8, 1970, Box 28, WHCF, HU 3-1, NPP, NA II.

72. Mrs. William T. Wilkerson to the president, May 16, 1970, Box 29, WHCF, HU 3-1, NPP, NA II.

73. Lunette Haselwood, et al., to the president, November 11, 1969, Box 22, WHCF, HU 2-5. For another example, see Muriel Carroll, et al., to President Nixon, July 6, 1970, WHCF, HU 3-1, NPP, NA II.

74. For example, see Peggy Young, et al., to the president, February 1, 1969, Box 47, WHCF, WE 9, NPP, NA II.

75. Linda Pennington, secretary Student Council to the president, May 25, 1970, with attachments, Bob-Ray Sanders, "Teens Ask Action on Violent Protest, *Fort Worth Star-Telegram*, May 22, 1970, and "Resolution: Campus Disorder," May 12, 1970, Box 29, WHCF, HU 3-1, NPP, NA II.

76. Art Linkletter, "The Drug Society," n.d., ca. 1969, distributed by National Teen Age Republicans, Box 20, "Drug Abuse—Education," NAC, Hoover Institution; Robert Semple Jr., "Linkletter Talks to Nixon on Drugs," *NYT*, October 24, 1969.

77. "Facts on Marijuana," copied from *Powerline*, Leadership Foundation, Inc., n.d., ca. 1971, in Anne Armstrong, Box 48, file "Martha Rountree," WHCF, SMOF, NPP, NA II.

78. Fact Sheet, "President Leads Fight Against Drug Abuse," n.d., ca. 1972, Anne Armstrong, Box 42, Barbara Franklin Reference File—Drugs, WHCF, SMOF, NPP, NA II.

79. Some of that spiritualism led many baby boomers to the discovery of evangelical Christianity, writes Paul Boyer in "The Evangelical Resurgence in 1970s American Protestantism," 41.

80. Personal interview with Janice Daigle, April 20, 2009; William C. Robbins, "Vortex I," *The Oregon Encyclopedia*, accessed October 11, 2009, http://www.oregonencyclopedia.org/entry/view/vortex_i/.

81. Peg Zwecker to President Nixon, January 9, 1969, and Joan Levine to the president, May 27, 1970. Both in Box 47, WHCF, WE 9, NPP, NA II.

82. Louis Harris and Associates, Inc., "A Survey of the Attitudes of College Students," June 1970, Box 43, Robert H. Finch, NPP, NA II.

83. John D. Rockefeller 3rd Task Force on Youth, "A Study of Youth and the Establishment," December 1970, Box 43, Robert H. Finch, NPP, NA II.

84. John D. Rockefeller 3rd Task Force on Youth, "A Study of Youth and the Establishment," December 1970, Box 43, Robert H. Finch, NPP, NA II.

85. George Gallup, "Students Reject Radical Politics," *Washington Post*, February 17, 1971, in Box 43, Robert H. Finch, NPP, NA II.

86. Louis Harris and Associates, Inc., "A Survey of the Attitudes of College Students," June 1970, in Box 43, Robert H. Finch, NPP, NA II.

87. Memo James Tanck to Constance Stuart, March 16, 1970, Box 6, Susan A. Porter, WHCF, SMOF, NPP, NA II.

88. Memo Coral Schmid to Constance Stuart, May 6, 1970, Box 6, Susan A. Porter, WHCF, SMOF, NPP, NA II.

89. Jean Strauss to President Nixon, May 19, 1969; Gayle Goolsby to president, July 9, 1969; and Andrea White to president, March 18, 1969, Box 48, WHCF, WE 9. See also boxes 47–51, NPP, NA II.

90. Ann Blackman, "Back on the Ranch in '72," *Washington Post*, October 24, 1971, E25.

91. Personal interview with Donna Clarke, September 27, 2009.

92. J. Justin Gustainis, *American Rhetoric and the Vietnam War*, 9–14.

93. Philip Wylie, *Sons and Daughters of Mom*, 41–55, 115.

94. A boomer, who was living with her politically conservative parents in North Carolina during the war, recalls watching Buddhist monks burning themselves to protest the war. "Watching that, I began to think about my own ethics," she said, and began to support the peace movement. Personal interview with Deborah Atkinson, July 25, 2009.

95. Personal interview with Shawn Spangle Looney, August 31, 2009.

Chapter 6. "Women's Liberation" and the Equal Rights Amendment

Epigraph source: Cathy Pitts, "ERA: After the Defeat," letter to the editor, *NYT*, November 12, 1975, 42.

1. *S.J. Res. 21* and H.J. Res. 75, 68th Cong., 1st sess.

2. Martha Sonntag Bradley, *Pedestals and Podiums: Utah Women, Religious Authority, and Equal Rights*, 37–38; Jane J. Mansbridge, *Why We Lost the ERA*, 9.

3. Mansbridge, *Why We Lost the ERA*, 9.

4. Ibid., 10.

5. "Mrs. Ford to Continue Equal Rights Lobbying," *NYT*, February 15, 1975; "Mrs. Ford Terms Right Plan Vital," *NYT*, October 25, 1975.

6. Ruth Murray Brown, *For a "Christian America": A History of the Religious Right*; Carol Mueller and Thomas Dimieri, "The Structure of Belief Systems Among Contending ERA Activists," *Social Forces* 6, no. 4 (March 1982), 657–76; Mathews and DeHart, *Sex, Gender, and the Politics of ERA*; Bradley, *Pedestals and Podiums*.

7. Letter, Anna O. Nisbet to Members, newsletter, New York State Minute Women, Inc., July 1954, Reel 89, N95, RWC, UI.

8. Elizabeth Singer More, "'The Necessary Factfinding Has Only Just Begun': Women, Social Science, and the Reinvention of the Working Mother in the 1950s," 974–1005.

9. Kathleen M. Blee, *Women of the Klan*, especially pp. 33–46.

10. Benowitz, *Days of Discontent*, 137–53; Jeansonne, *Women of the Far Right*.

11. Benowitz, *Days of Discontent*, 133–34.

12. Blanche Winters, American Woman's Party, pamphlet, "Men . . . Let us call to your attention . . . These Facts, "n.d., ca. 1952, Reel 13, RWC, UI.

13. Ibid.

14. Ibid.

15. Christina Wolbrecht, *The Politics of Women's Rights: Parties, Positions, and Change*, 11.

16. "Human Rights: Status of Women," newsletter, Minute Women of the U.S.A., March 1962, Reel 76, M19, RWC, UI.

17. Paul Boyer, et al., *The Enduring Vision: A History of the American People*, 1019.

18. For a full account of how at least one group of feminists viewed the situation of women during the 1960s, see the paper of Heather Booth, Evie Goldfield, Sue Munaker, "Towards a Radical Movement," Box 3, Circuit Riders, Inc., Coll. 167, UO.

19. Bureau of the Census, *Consumer Income*, P-60, No. 66 (December 23, 1969), cited in *Twentieth-Century America: Recent Interpretations*, ed. Barton J. Bernstein and Allen J. Matusow, 556.

20. For a detailed account of the New Left and the beginnings of the women's rights movement see Evans, *Personal Politics*. Another good source on the women's movement is Rymph, *Republican Women*. See also, Marlene Dixon, "Why Women's Liberation," 557–60. An example of their using the word "radical" to describe themselves is the New York Radical Women who protested at the Miss America pageant in 1968. See Mark Hamilton Lytle, *America's Uncivil Wars*, 274.

21. Klatch, *A Generation Divided*, 166–77.

22. Ibid., 163.

23. Alison Lefkovitz, "The Problem of Marriage in the Era of Women's Liberation," (PhD diss., University of Chicago, 2010), 41.

24. Booth, Goldfield, and Munaker, paper, "Towards a Radical Movement," Box 3, Circuit Riders, Coll. 167, UO; Rymph, *Republican Women*, 188; Schulman, *The Seventies*, 164–65.

25. Quoted in Pat Brazeel, "Women Need to Clean House Politically, Female Leader Says," *Birmingham, Alabama Post-Herald*, ca. November 9, 1971, in Anne Armstrong, file "Rountree," WHCF, SMOF, NPP, NA II.

26. Statistics from Schulman, *The Seventies*, 166–67.

27. For more on this event, and its impact, see Schulman, *The Seventies*, 159–60.

28. Marilyn Mercer, "ERA: What Would it Really Mean?" *McCall's*, July 1976,

107; Lisa Levenstein, "'Don't Agonize, Organize!': The Displaced Homemakers Campaign and the Contested Goals of Postwar Feminism," 1114–38.

29. Carol Mueller and Thomas Dimieri, "The Structure of Belief Systems among Contending ERA Activists," 657–76.

30. Elinor Langor, in "Why Big Business Is Trying to Defeat the ERA," *Ms.*, May 1976, 64–66, 100–108, writes that big business was aligned with anti-ERA forces. They worried that the ERA would result in employers being told who they should hire and fire, be forced to pay men and women equal wages, and forecasted huge financial losses should it be ratified. Ruth Murray Brown, in *For a "Christian America,"* 35–50, writes that the JBS published an anti-ERA article as early as 1972, and a number of both its male and female members were active participants in the movement against the amendment.

31. Virginia Sapiro's "News from the Front: Intersex and Intergenerational Conflict over the Status of Women," 260–77, studies generational perceptions of one another. She examines how the generations, beginning with those who reached age twenty-one prior to 1920 through those reaching twenty-one between 1967 and 1976 perceived their own stands on equal rights for women, in comparison with how they perceive other generations' positions on the issue.

32. Critchlow, *Phyllis Schlafly and Grassroots Conservatism* 4, 217; Phyllis Schlafly, "What's Wrong with 'Equal Rights' for Women?" *Phyllis Schlafly Report*, February 1972, 1; Marjorie J. Spruill, "Gender and America's Right Turn," 78.

33. Phyllis Schlafly, "ERA's Assist to Abortion," flyer, n.d., ca. December 1974, Reel 153, W54, RWC, UI.

34. Stephanie Gilmore, *Groundswell: Grassroots Feminist Activism in Postwar America*, 31–32, 105.

35. Letter to President Nixon from Bonnie Pilkington, et al., April 25, 1970, Box 32, WHCF, WE 3, NPP, NA II. Many of the letters came from baby boomers enrolled in Catholic schools in many regions of the country. One girl wrote that the first week of October 1972 was "Respect Life Week" at her school. During that week, teacher Sister Mary Ann Stoltz and her eighth-grade students from Thorp Catholic School, Thorp, Wisconsin, signed a letter to President Nixon protesting abortion (Karen Benzschwel, et al., October 4, 1972); some appealed directly to the president to take action, pointing out that they were too young to vote. Letters from Gail Younie, October 6, 1972, and Lynne Ann Greenop, October 19, 1972. All letters in Box 33, WHCF, WE, 3, NPP, NA II.

36. Meryle Secrest, "The Radicalizing of a Catholic Girl," *Washington Post*, August 20, 1972, in Anne Armstrong, Box 46, WHCF, SMOF, NPP, NA II.

37. Ibid.

38. Eugene L. Meyer, "Rally Hits Abortion, 'Mercy Killing,'" *Washington Post*, September 4, 1972, in Anne Armstrong, Box 46, WHCF, SMOF, NPP, NA II.

39. Ibid.

40. George Gallup, "Abortion Seen Up to Woman, Doctor," *Washington Post*, August 26, 1972, in Anne Armstrong, WHCF, SMOF, NPP, NA II.

41. Interview with Elizabeth Larkin, June 4, 2009; David W. Brady and Kent L. Tedin, "Ladies in Pink: Religion and Political Ideology in the Anti-ERA Movement," 564–75; Critchlow, *Phyllis Schlafly and Grassroots Conservatism*, 219.

42. Open letter from JoAnn (Mrs. Norbert) Budde, Housewives for ERA, April 23, 1973, Box 67, folder 4, Georgia Lloyd Papers, NYPL, Manuscripts Division.

43. Levenstein, "'Don't Agonize, Organize!'" 114–38.

44. Klatch, *A Generation Divided*, 266.

45. "Mrs. Ford to Continue Equal Rights Lobbying," *NYT*, February 15, 1975.

46. Olga Coren, "Surface comparisons," letter to the editor, *NYT*, May 9, 1976. Another middle-aged woman protesting the same article was Phyllis Pollard in "Overprotected?" letter to the editor, *NYT*, May 9, 1976.

47. Annette Stern, "Honest concerns," letter to the editor, *NYT*, May 9, 1976.

48. Annette Stern, "Sneak Attack on the Family," *Newsday*, October 27, 1975, 41.

49. Ibid.

50. Levenstein, "'Don't Agonize, Organize!'" 114–38.

51. Gilmore, *Groundswell*, 55.

52. Janet K. Boles, *The Politics of the Equal Rights Amendment: Conflict and the Decision Process*, 67–69; Gilmore, *Groundswell*; Bradley, *Pedestals and Podiums*, 116–17.

53. Elinor Langor, "Why Big Business Is Trying to Defeat the ERA," *Ms.*, May 1976, 66; Ricki Fulman, "ERA Stock Drops as Wall St. Rally Challenges Amendment," *New York Daily News*, October 10, 1974, in Box 2, folder 9, Dorothy Frooks papers, NYPL.

54. Phyllis Schlafly, "What's Wrong with 'Equal Rights' for Women?" *The Phyllis Schlafly Report*, February 1972, 1.

55. Patricia S. Caplan, "Pop and apple pie?" letter to the editor, *NYT*, May 9, 1976.

56. Letter to the editor from Lila Anastas, "Onward!," *NYT*, May 9, 1976.

57. Ruth Bader Ginsburg, "ERA: A Vote 'For' and a Vote 'Against,'" letters to the editor, *NYT*, October 28, 1975.

58. Annette Stern, "ERA 'Pandora's Box,'" letter to the editor, *NYT*, October 21, 1975.

59. Jane Dedman, "The Conspiracy to Kill the ERA," *Playgirl*, July 1976, 34–35, 42, 52, 71–73, 86, 108.

60. See, for example, "The Battlefields of Home," reprint from *Mindszenty Report*, January 1975, the Network of Patriotic Letter Writers, Reel 89, N93, and Virginia L. Wilson, ed., "Equal Rights Amendment," in *Count Down: Faith, Facts and Freedom*, February 1973, Reel 35, C59, RWC, UI; "Mrs. Ford Scored on Equality Plan," *NYT*, February 1, 1975.

61. Letter, Frooks to Hon. John S. Thorpe Jr., February 10, 1975, Box 2, folder 8, and flyers in Box 2, Dorothy Frooks papers, NYPL.

62. Annette Stern, president of Operation Wake Up, mentions a number of these issues in "Sneak Attack on the Family," *Newsday*, October 27, 1975, 41; "Unsocial Security," *NYT*, July 24, 1974, 40; "Hand-to-Hand Combat Over Equal Rights," *NYT*, March 4, 1977. The latter article reports on the U.S. Supreme Court voiding

the requirement that widowers had to prove they were dependent upon their deceased wives to receive Social Security benefits based upon their spouse's earnings. There was no such requirement for widows.

63. Personal interview with Peggy Melby, July 14, 2009.

64. Lefkovitz, "The Problem of Marriage in the Era of Women's Liberation," 272.

65. Letter to Dorothy Frooks from Mary Margaret Hober, n.d., ca. 1976, Dorothy Frooks papers, NYPL.

66. Ricki Fulman, "ERA Stock Drops as Wall St. Rally Challenges Amendment," *New York Daily News*, October 10, 1974, clipping, Box 2, folder 9, Dorothy Frooks papers, NYPL.

67. Jane Dedman, "The Conspiracy to Kill the ERA," *Playgirl*, July 1976, 42. Mathews and DeHart, in *Sex, Gender, and the Politics of the ERA*, 54–90, relate that pro-ERA women in North Carolina did not realize how difficult a task it would be to see the ERA become law.

68. Historian Donald T. Critchlow gives an in-depth look at Schlafly and her activism in *Phyllis Schlafly and Grassroots Conservatism*. For more on Edmonson see Jane Dedman, "The Conspiracy to Kill the ERA," *Playgirl*, July 1976, 35, 42.

69. Ruth Murray Brown, *For a "Christian America,"* 31–32, 36–37.

70. Robin Morris, "Kathryn Dunaway's ERA Battle and the Roots of Georgia's Republican Revolution," in *Entering the Fray: Gender, Politics, and Culture in the New South*, ed. Jonathan Daniel Wells and Sheila R. Phipps, 164–65.

71. Morris, "Kathryn Dunaway's ERA Battle and the Roots of Georgia's Republican Revolution," 167; Mueller and Dimieri, "The Structure of Belief Systems among Contending ERA Activists," 657–76; Mathews and DeHart, *Sex, Gender, and the Politics of the ERA*, 59–60.

72. Boles, *The Politics of the Equal Rights Amendment*, 78–79.

73. Mansbridge, *Why We Lost the ERA*, 174.

74. Ruth Murray Brown looks closely at how religion played a large role in bringing fundamentalist Christians into the anti-ERA campaign in *For a "Christian America."* Mathews and DeHart address the issue in *Sex, Gender, and the Politics of ERA*. See also contemporary investigations, Brady and Tedin, "Ladies in Pink," 564–75, and Mueller and Dimieri, "The Structure of Belief Systems among Contending ERA Activists," 657–76.

75. Bradley, *Pedestals and Podiums*, 26, 65.

76. Deborah Turk, national president, Women's Branch, Union of Orthodox Jewish Congregations of America, letter to the editor, December 23, 1978, "ERA: The Doubts and the Fears," *NYT*, January 1, 1979. Rabbi Sol Roth, First Vice President Rabbinical Council of America, raised the issue of female draftees sharing barracks and fighting alongside males in a letter to the editor, December 5, 1978, "ERA: A Religious Community's Dilemma," *NYT*, December 12, 1978.

77. Eleanor R. Schwartz, executive director, National Federation of Temple Sisterhoods, letter to the editor, December 12, 1978, "ERA and Religion: 'We Have No Dilemmas,'" *NYT*, December 20, 1978.

78. Critchlow, *Phyllis Schlafly and Grassroots Conservativism*, 218–19.

79. Dedman, "The Conspiracy to Kill the ERA," *Playgirl*, July 1976, 34, 43, 52.

80. Marisa Chappell, *The War on Welfare: Family, Poverty, and Politics in Modern America*, 161.

81. Rymph's *Republican Women*, provides an in-depth look at the history of women of the Republican Party and their positions on the roles of women in society and politics. According to conservative writer Lee Edwards, political analyst Kevin Phillips was the first, in 1975, to use the term "New Right" when discussing "social conservatives." Lee Edwards, *The Conservative Revolution: The Movement That Remade America*, 184.

82. Joseph Modzelewski, "Ex-Suffragette Votes No," *New York Daily News*, August 27, 1970, 3; "Dorothy Frooks . . . Lawyer, Judge, Crusader, Publisher . . . speaks her mind like Hepburn," *Empire State Legionnaire*, January 1980, 12; flyer, "Dorothy Frooks—America's Modern Portia," n.d., Box 3, folder 22, NYPL.

83. Dorothy Frooks, *Lady Lawyer*, 180.

84. "Dorothy Frooks . . . Lawyer, Judge, Crusader, Publisher . . . speaks her mind like Hepburn," *Empire State Legionnaire*, January 1980, 12, Dorothy Frooks papers, NYPL.

85. Modzelewski, "Ex-Suffragette Votes No," *New York Daily News*, August 27, 1970, 3.

86. Letter, Dorothy Frooks to editor, *NYT*, August 27, 1975, letter to John D. Rockefeller III, May 12, 1977, and letter to Hon. John S. Thorpe Jr., February 10, 1975, Box 2, folder 8, Dorothy Frooks papers, NYPL.

87. Statement of Dorothy Frooks at City Hall, Women World War Veterans, Inc., December 14, 1977, Box 2, folder 5, Dorothy Frooks papers, NYPL.

88. Brady and Tedin, "Ladies in Pink," 570.

89. Ibid., 572–73.

90. Mueller and Dimieri, "The Structure of Belief Systems among Contending ERA Activists," 657–76.

91. Mathews and DeHart, *Sex, Gender, and the Politics of ERA*, 173.

92. Brady and Tedin, "Ladies in Pink," 569. For more on changes in American-Soviet relations, see Schulman, *The Seventies*, 6.

93. "ERA Action Stuns Betty Ford," *NYT*, August 12, 1976; Joseph Lelyveld, "Normally Proper G.O.P. Women Come Out Fighting Over E.R.A.," *NYT*, August 17, 1976. The feminist victory did not last, however, as Rymph discusses in *Republican Women*, 212–38.

94. Initially, the deadline was March 1979, but Congress later extended it until 1982.

95. Debbie Mauldin Cottrell, "National Women's Conference, 1977," *The Handbook of Texas Online*, https://tshaonline.org/handbook/online/articles/pwngq.

96. Judy Klemesrud, "At Houston Meeting, 'A Kaleidoscope of American Womanhood,'" *NYT*, November 19, 1977. The resolutions, in their entirety, are found

in Caroline Bird and the Members and Staff of the National Commission on the Observance of International Women's Year, *What Women Want* from the official report to the President, the Congress and the People of the United States (New York: Simon and Schuster, 1977); Wolbrecht, *The Politics of Women's Rights*, 43.

97. Statement of Dorothy Frooks at City Hall, Women World War Veterans, Inc., December 14, 1977, Box 2, folder 5, Dorothy Frooks papers, NYPL.

98. Brown, *For a "Christian America,"* 36, 51, 66.

99. Judy Klemesrud, "Equal Rights Plan and Abortion Are Opposed by 15,000 at Rally," *NYT*, November 20, 1977; Critchlow, *Phyllis Schlafly and Grassroots Conservatism*, 246–47; Schulman, *The Seventies*, 186–87. Kim E. Nielsen, *Un-American Womanhood*, 57. While the rightward-leaning DAR was usually associated with the anti-ERA movement, not all of the organization's members shared the majority view. One baby boomer recalls that both she and her mother, a DAR member (who "always voted Republican"), favored the ERA. Personal interview with Elizabeth Larkin, June 4, 2009.

100. Judy Klemesrud, "Houston Hosts, if Not Toasts, Feminists," *NYT*, November 18, 1977.

101. Frank, "'The Civil Rights of Parents,'" 126–60.

102. Critchlow, *Phyllis Schlafly and Grassroots Conservatism*, 248.

103. James M. Wall, "The Gospel According to Schlafly," *Christian Century* (April 11, 1978): 395–96.

104. Carolyn B. Maloney, *Rumors of Our Progress have been Greatly Exaggerated: Why Women's Lives Aren't Getting Any Easier and How We can Make Real Progress for Ourselves and Our Daughters*, 2.

105. Maloney, *Rumors of Our Progress Have Been Greatly Exaggerated*, 75–80. Political scientist Jane J. Mansbridge did not believe the passage of the ERA would have immediately brought about major changes in relations between men and women, as the general public did not want change in gender roles. However, she did see the ERA's defeat as a setback for equality. Mansbridge, *Why We Lost the ERA*.

106. Personal interview with Andrea Weissleder, July 11, 2009.

107. Schulman, *The Seventies*, 165; Wolbrecht, *The Politics of Women's Rights*, 159; Flyer, "ERA," n.d. ca. June 1972, Box 67, folder 5, Georgia Lloyd Papers, NYPL; interviews with baby boomers, particularly Janice Daigle, John Howard, Lynne Koons, Tim Novak, Leigh Ann Novak, Elizabeth Larkin, and Stephen Graves.

108. Chappell, *War on Welfare*, 157.

109. Rosalind Pollack Petchesky, "Antiabortion, Antifeminism, and the Rise of the New Right," 206–46. Others addressing the abortion issue as an important reason for the failure of the ERA include Mansbridge, *Why We Lost the ERA*; Wolbrecht, *The Politics of Women's Rights*, 158. Sara Diamond, in *Roads to Dominion*, 168, notes how the fight against the ERA was a "boon to the budding coalition between the New Right and the Christian Right." Rymph, *Republican Women*, 1.

110. Critchlow, *Phyllis Schlafly and Grassroots Conservatism*, 39.

111. Wolbrecht, *The Politics of Women's Rights*, 120.

112. Personal interviews with baby boomers listed in bibliography, and particularly Larry Kelleher, Janice Daigle, Lynne Koons, Donna Clarke, Donna Paganello, Rhonda Moraca, and John Howard.

113. Personal interview with Donna Clarke, September 27, 2009.

114. Elinor Burkett, *The Right Women: A Journey through the Heart of Conservative America.*

Conclusion

1. McGirr, *Suburban Warriors*, 4, 272.

2. Alicia M. Cohn, "Conservative Spotlight: Smart Girl Politics," *Human Events* .com, 65, no. 35, October 12, 2009, http://www.humanevents.com/article.php?print =yes&id=33950; "About Us," Conservative Women website accessed September 19, 2014, http://www.conservative-women.com/.

3. Untitled article, *Los Angeles Times*, March 12, 1961, in Box 14, file 12, MMC, SU; Nickerson, *Mothers of Conservatism*, 51, 142.

4. Samuel A. Stouffer, *Communism, Conformity, and Civil Liberties: A Cross-Section of the Nation Speaks Its Mind*, 132–33. Brennan, in *Wives, Mothers, and the Red Menace*, shows what a motivating force the fight against domestic communism could be for some homemakers.

5. "Women May Be the Last Great Hope of Saving the American Republic," *Southern Conservative*, June 1960.

6. Elna C. Green, in "From Antisuffragism to Anti-Communism: The Conservative Career of Ida M. Darden," 87–316, discusses Darden's antisuffragism in detail.

7. Bulletin, East Pasadena-Sierra Madre Republican Women's Club, Federated, June 1965; Mrs. Joyce Zuck, president. In Box 28, file 5, MMC, SU.

8. "Ronald Reagan Spurs GOP Women Campaign, *Los Angeles Times*, October 22, 1963, in Box 28, file 7, MMC, SU.

9. Ibid.

10. For example, Van Hyning praised the senator's fight against communism in a 1952 issue of *Women's Voice*, and Portland, Oregon, right-wing activist Grace Wick rallied to McCarthy's side when criticism against him intensified. Benowitz, *Days of Discontent*. Fred and Phyllis Schlafly continued to admire McCarthy after his censure in the U.S. Senate in 1954. Critchlow, *Phyllis Schlafly and Grassroots Conservatism*, 64.

11. In 1992 the state of Texas fined publishers of U.S. history textbooks a million dollars as a result of the Gablers finding hundreds of errors in ten books, including a passage mistakenly reporting that President Truman dropped an atomic bomb to end the Korean War. These were books the state had approved. Joe Holley, "Norma Gabler: Conservative Texan Influenced Textbooks Nationwide," *Washington Post* (August 2, 2007), B07, http://www.washingtonpost.com/wp-dyn/content/article /2007/08/01/AR2007080102421_pf.html. In 2010 the Texas Board of Education

voted 10–5 to purchase textbooks that presented conservative views on history and economics. James C. McKinley Jr., "Texas Board OKs Shift on Curriculum," *Sarasota Herald-Tribune*, March 13, 2010, 4, from *NYT*.

12. Fundamentalist Christian Tim LaHaye, husband of Beverly LaHaye, the founder of Concerned for America, defines secular humanism as man's attempt to solve his problems independently of God. The result, Tim LaHaye believes, is an amoral democratic society. See Provenzo Jr., *Religious Fundamentalism and American Education*, xii.

13. CWA information packet (1997); "Biblical Support for CWA Core Issues," Concerned Women for America website, accessed May 16, 2011, and September 19, 2014, http://www.cwfa.org/coreissues.asp (page no longer available).

14. Irvine, *Talk About Sex*, 9.

15. Moran, *Teaching Sex*, 225, argues that the courses did little to decrease the teenage birth rate, while Zimmerman, *Whose America?*, 202, writes that the birth rate for teenage women was nearly halved from 1960 to 1975.

16. Critchlow, *Phyllis Schlafly and Grassroots Conservatism*.

17. Tim LaHaye also promotes this theory, as does female writer Pat Brooks. For more on this subject, see Lienesch, *Redeeming America*, 160–65, and Stephen Bates, *Battleground: One Mother's Crusade, the Religious Right, and the Struggle for Control of Our Classrooms*.

18. A large percentage of conservative women were attracted to Senator Rick Santorum's campaign for president of the United States in 2012. Sixty percent of the visitors to Santorum's website were women. They identified moral issues and his support for "family values" as the most important reasons for their support. Susan Saulny, "On the Right, Santorum Has Women's Vote," *NYT*, March 23, 2012, http://www.nytimes.com/2012/03/24/us/politics/rick-santorum-attracts-votes-of-conservative-women.html?pagewanted=all.

BIBLIOGRAPHY

Primary Sources

MANUSCRIPTS, ARCHIVAL COLLECTIONS, BOOKS, JOURNALS, AND WEBSITES

"After 60 Years of Success, Water Fluoridation Still Lacking in Many Communities." *Medical News Today*, July 19, 2005, http://www.medicalnewstoday.com/releases/27595.php.

Alesen, L. A. *Mental Robots*. Caldwell, Idaho: Caxton Printers, 1957.

Allderdice, Norman Collection. Hoover Institution on War, Revolution, and Peace. Stanford University, Palo Alto, California.

Allen, Mary L. *Education or Indoctrination?* Caldwell, Idaho: Caxton Printers, 1955.

Auerback, Alfred. "The Anti-Mental Health Movement." *American Journal of Psychiatry* 120 (August 1963): 105–12.

Bainbridge, John. "Danger's Ahead in the Public Schools." *McCall's*, October 1952.

———. "Save Our Schools." *McCall's*, September 1952.

Benagh, Christine. "The American Dream: A Southern Nightmare?" *Modern Age* (Fall 1958): 377–82.

Bird, Caroline, and Members and Staff of the National Commission on the Observance of International Women's Year. *What Women Want*. New York: Simon and Schuster, 1977.

Bloomberg, Wilfred, and Myron John Rockmore. "Interstate Compact on Mental Health." *American Journal of Psychiatry* 124 (October 1967): 520–26.

Boyvey, Roger. "Mental Health and the Ultra-Concerned." *Social Service Review* 38, no. 3 (September 1964): 281–93.

Brown, Elizabeth Churchill. "The Secret of Political Success: How to Convert the Unconverted." *Human Rights* (August 25, 1958).

Budnick, Nick. "Fluoride Foes Get Validation. *Portland Tribune*, March 24, 2006, http://www.portlandtribune.com/news/story.php?story_id=34527.

Caldwell, Gladys, and Philip E. Zafagna. *Fluoridation and Truth Decay*. Reseda, California: Top-Ecol Press, 1974.

Caldwell, Taylor. *The Devil's Advocate*. New York: Crown Publishers, 1952.

Campbell, Carol Ann. "State Hears Pros and Cons of Fluoridation Plan." *Star-Ledger*, June 7, 2005, http://fluoridealert.org/news/2286.html.

Cohn, Alicia M. "Conservative Spotlight: Smart Girl Politics." *Human Events.com* 65, no. 35, October 12, 2009, http://www.humanevents.com/article.php?print =yes&id=33950.

Colburn, Don. "Oregon Fluoridation Bill Sidetracked." *Oregonian*, May 16, 2007, http://www.oregonlive.com/news/oregonian/index.ssf?base/news/11798222 53940.xml&coll=7.

Concerned Women for America website. Accessed online May 16, 2011, and September 19, 2014. http://www.cfa.org/coreissues.asp.

Conservative Women. "About Us." Accessed online September 19, 2014. http:// www.conservative-women.com/.

Courtney, Phoebe. *The Sex Education Racket*. New Orleans: Free Men Speak, Inc., 1969.

Crain, Lucille Cardin, Papers. University of Oregon, Special Collections Library, Eugene.

Crain, Lucille Cardin, and Anne Burrows Hamilton. *Packaged Thinking for Women*. New York: National Industrial Conference Board, 1948.

"The DAR Supplies Leadership." *American Mercury*, August 1958.

Dilling, Elizabeth, Papers. Library of the Christian Liberty Church and School, Arlington Heights, Illinois.

Dodd, Bella. *School of Darkness*. New York: Kennedy and Sons, 1954.

Easley, M. W. "Fluoridation Status of Largest 50 U.S. Cities." National Center for Fluoridation Policy and Research. Revised April 4, 2001. http://www.waterfluoridationcenter.org.

Education in Florida Collection. P. K. Yonge Library of Florida History. University of Florida, Gainesville.

Ellsworth, Ralph E., and Sarah M. Harris. "The American Right Wing." *Occasional Papers* 59 (November 1960). University of Illinois Library School.

Farenthold, Frances Tarlton, Papers. Center for American History. University of Texas at Austin.

"Fluoridation Is Here to Stay." *Journal of the American Dental Association* 69, no. 5 (November 1962): 578–80.

Flynn, John T. *The Roosevelt Myth*. New York: Devin-Adair Company, 1948.

Frank, Dorothy. "I Was Called a Subversive." *Collier's*, March 28, 1953, 68–73.

Frooks, Dorothy. *Lady Lawyer*. New York: Robert Speller and Sons, Publishers, Inc., 1975.

Frooks, Dorothy, Papers. Manuscripts Division. New York Public Library.

Georgia Government Documentation Project, Series B. Special Collections and Archives. Georgia State University Library, Atlanta.

Gordon, Rosalie. *Nine Men Against America*. New York: Devin-Adair, 1958.

———. *What's Happened to Our Schools?* New Rochelle, New York: America's Future, Inc., 1956.

Gough, Harrison G. "A New Dimension of Status II." *American Sociological Review* (October 1948): 534–37.

Highlander Research and Education Center website. Accessed online September 8, 2012. www.highlandercenter.org/a-history.asp.

Hindman, Jo. "The Fight for Your Child's Mind." *American Mercury* (November 1957): 7.

"History of Up With People." Up With People, Inc. Accessed online June 1, 2012. http://www.upwithpeople.org/about/history.htm.

Holley, Joe. "Norma Gabler: Conservative Texan Influenced Textbooks." *Washington Post*. http://www.washingtonpost.com/wp-dyn/content/article/2007/08/01/AR2007080102421_pf.html.

"How Did We Get Here?: History of Waste Disposal at the SDA 1950 to Present." Idaho Department of Environmental Quality. Accessed online July 21, 2012. http://www.deq.state.id.us/inl_oversight/waste/history.cfm.

Hurlburd, David. *This Happened in Pasadena.* New York: MacMillan Company, 1951.

Immunization Safety Review Committee, and Kathleen Stratton, et al., eds. *Immunization Safety Review: SV40 Contamination of Polio Vaccine and Cancer.* National Academies Press, 2003.

Johnson, Lyndon Baines, Presidential Library, Austin, Texas. Presidential Papers, White House Central Files. U.S. Senate, General Files.

Klein, M. "Mental Health Laws Bring Problems." *Albuquerque Tribune*, November 1964, A-4.

Lentz, Gloria. *Raping Our Children: The Sex Education Scandal.* New York: Arlington House, 1972.

Manion, Clarence E., Collection. Chicago Historical Society.

McNeil, Donald R. *The Fight for Fluoridation.* New York: Oxford University Press, 1957.

McWilliams, Carey. "The Enemy in Pasadena." *Christian Century*, January 3, 1951.

Meier, Margaret, Collection of Extreme Right Ephemeral Material, 1930–1980. Stanford University Libraries Department of Special Collections, Palo Alto, California.

Melby, Ernest O. *American Education Under Fire.* New York: Anti-Defamation League of B'nai B'rith, 1951.

Montgomery, George. *The Return of Adam Smith.* Caldwell, Idaho: Caxton Printers, 1949.

Morrison, M. M. "The Enemy at Work." *Virginia Journal of Education* (September 1950).

Morse, Arthur D. "Who's Trying to Ruin Our Schools?" *McCall's*, September 1951.

National Archives, Southeast Region. Morrow, Georgia. Collections cited: District Courts of United States; Emergency School Assistance Program Files, Record Group 12.

National Association for the Advancement of Colored People (NAACP) Collection (microfilm). Manuscript Division. Library of Congress.

Nixon, Richard M. Presidential Papers. National Archives II. College Park, Maryland.

Oregon Historical Society Library, Portland, Oregon. Collections cited: Colonial Dames Papers; Daughters of the American Colonies Papers; Politics and Miscellaneous Collection; Radical Groups Collection; Grace Wick Papers.

"Overview of Mental Health in New York and the Nation." New York State Archives. Accessed April 4, 2011. http://www.archives.nysed.gov/common/archives/files/res_topics_health_mh_hist.pdf.

The Pasadena Story. Washington, D.C.: National Commission for the Defense of Democracy through Education of the National Educational Association of the United States, 1951.

Plaut, Thomas F. A. "Analysis of Voting Behavior on a Fluoridation Referendum." *Public Opinion Quarterly* 23, no. 2 (Summer 1959): 213–22.

Radical Right Collection. Hoover Institution on War, Revolution, and Peace. Stanford University, Palo Alto, California.

Right-Wing Collection of the University of Iowa Libraries, 1918–1977 (Microfilm Corporation of America, 1977). Collections cited: *American Spirit*; American Woman's Party; Katie Lou Brown; Gladys Caldwell; *Countdown*; *FACTS in Education*; *I Love America*; Massachusetts Women's Political Club; Minute Women of the U.S.A., Inc.; Mothers Support Neighborhood Schools; National Society of the Daughters of the American Revolution; Network of Patriotic Letter Writers; New Mexico Women Speak!; Pasadena Anti-Communist League; *Portions in Due Season*; *Right*; *Southern Conservative*; *USA: An American Magazine of Fact and Opinion.*

Robinson, Donald. "Conspiracy USA: The Far Right's Fight Against Mental Health." *Look*, January 26, 1965, 31.

Roosevelt, Edith Kermit. "A New Profession for Youth: Insurrection." *Independent American*, September-October, 1965, 1.

Sarasota County History Center, Sarasota, Florida. Collections cited: Bay Haven School Papers; Daughters of the American Revolution Papers.

Schlafly, Phyllis. *A Choice Not an Echo.* Alton, Illinois: Pere Marquette Press, 1964.

———. *The Power of the Positive Woman.* New Rochelle, New York: Arlington House, 1977.

———. "What's Wrong with 'Equal Rights' for Women?" *Phyllis Schlafly Report* (February 1972).

Shah, Keerti V. "Simian Virus 40 and Human Disease." *Journal of Infectious Diseases* 190, no. 12: 2061–2064. Accessed online July 9, 2015. http://jid.oxfordjournals.org/content/190/12/2061.

Tucker, Cornelia Dabney Papers. South Caroliniana Library. University of South Carolina, Columbia.

U.S. Congress. House. "The UNESCO Threat to Our Schools." 82nd Congress, 2nd Session, July 1952.

University of Oregon Libraries, Eugene. Collections cited: Circuit Riders, Inc.; Phoebe Courtney; John T. Flynn; League of Women Voters.

Wall, James M. "The Gospel According to Schlafly." *Christian Century*, April 11, 1978, 395–96.

Widener, Alice, "SOS for Our Viet Nam Wounded." *Human Events*, March 19, 1966.

Personal Interviews

*These individuals did not want their surnames listed.

Atkinson, Deborah, October 12, 2007, August 16, 2008, and July 25, 2009

Clarke, Donna, September 27, 2009

Curcio, Claire Cole, August 6, 2008

Daigle, Janice, April 20, 2009

Deborah, September 1, 2009*

Fowler, Linda (Christa), September 4, 2009

Graves, Stephen, June 4, 2009

Harris, Stanley, September 2007

Howard, John, July 3, 2009

Irene, May 2, 2009*

Kelleher, Larry, August 4, 2009

Kerry, September 1, 2009*

Koons, Lynne, September 27, 2009

LaMontagne, Wanda, July 25, 2009

Larkin, Elizabeth, June 4, 2009

Looney, Shawn Spangle, August 31, 2009

McCall, Elizabeth. September 19, 2006

Melby, Peggy, July 4, 2009

Moraca, Rhonda, June 29, 2009

Needleman, Barbara. March 1, 2006

Novak, Leigh Ann, August 6, 2009

Novak, Tim, August 6, 2009

Paganello, Donna, July 10, 2009

Roberts, Jane, August 17, 2008, September 1, 2009

Snider, JoAnne, July 20, 2008

Valentine, Martha, October 21, 2008

Weissleder, Andrea, July 11, 2009

Secondary Sources

Adorno, T. W., Else Frenkel-Brunswik, Daniel J. Levinson, and R. Nevitt Sanford. *The Authoritarian Personality*. New York: Harper and Brothers, 1950.

Allen, Arthur. *Vaccine: The Controversial Story of Medicine's Greatest Lifesaver*. New York: W. W. Norton and Company, 2007.

Altschuler, Glenn C. *All Shook Up: How Rock 'n' Roll Changed America*. New York: Oxford University Press, 2003.

Andrew, John. "Pro-War and Anti-Draft: Young Americans for Freedom and the War in Vietnam." In *The Vietnam War On Campus: Other Voices, More Distant Drums*, edited by Marc Jason Gilbert, 1–19. Westport, Connecticut: Praeger Publishers, 2001.

Andrew, John A., III. *The Other Side of the Sixties: Young Americans for Freedom and the Rise of Conservative Politics*. New Brunswick, New Jersey: Rutgers University Press, 1997.

Appignanesi, Lisa. *Mad, Bad, and Sad: Women and the Mind Doctors*. New York: W. W. Norton and Company, 2008.

Balmer, Randall. *The Making of Evangelicalism: From Revivalism to Politics and Beyond*. Waco, Texas: Baylor University Press, 2010.

Bates, Stephen. *Battleground: One Mother's Crusade, the Religious Right, and the Struggle for Control of Our Classrooms*. New York: Poseidon Press, 1993.

Bell, Donald, ed. *The Radical Right*. Garden City, New York: Anchor Books, 1963.

Bennett, David. *The Party of Fear*. Chapel Hill: University of North Carolina Press, 1988.

Benowitz, June Melby. *Days of Discontent: American Women and Right-Wing Politics, 1933–1945*. DeKalb: Northern Illinois University Press, 2002.

———. *Encyclopedia of American Women and Religion*. Santa Barbara, California: ABC-CLIO, 1998.

———. "Reading, Writing, and Radicalism: Right-Wing Women and Education in the Post-War Years." *History of Education Quarterly* 49, no. 1 (February 2009): 89–111.

Bernstein, Barton J., and Allen J. Matusow, eds. *Twentieth-Century America: Recent Interpretations*. New York: Harcourt Brace Jovanovich, Inc., 1972.

Billingsley, William J. *Communists on Campus: Race, Politics, and the Public University in Sixties North Carolina*. Athens: University of Georgia Press, 1999.

Blee, Kathleen. "Mothers in Race-Hate Movements." In *The Politics of Motherhood: Activist Voices from Left to Right*, edited by Alexis Jetter, Annelise Orleck, and Diana Taylor, 247–56. Hanover, New Hampshire: University Press of New England, 1977.

———. *Women of the Klan: Racism and Gender in the 1920s*. Berkeley: University of California Press, 1991.

Bode, Boyd H. *Progressive Education at the Crossroads*. New York: Arno Press and New York Times, 1971.

Boles, Janet K. *The Politics of the Equal Rights Amendment: Conflict and the Decision Process*. New York: Longman, 1979.

Bookchin, Debbie, and Jim Schumacher. *The Virus and the Vaccine: The True Story of a Cancer-Causing Monkey Virus, Contaminated Polio Vaccine, and the Millions of Americans Exposed*. New York: St. Martin's Press, 2004.

Boyer, Paul. "Boston Book Censorship in the Twenties." *American Quarterly* (Spring 1963): 3–24.

——. "The Evangelical Resurgence in 1970s American Protestantism." In *Rightward Bound: Making American Conservative in the 1970s*, edited by Bruce J. Schulman and Julian E. Zelizer, 29–51. Cambridge, Massachusetts: Harvard University Press, 2008.

Boyer, Paul, Clifford Clark, Joseph F. Kett, Neal Salisbury, and Harvard Sitkoff. *The Enduring Vision: A History of the American People.* Lexington, Massachusetts: D. C. Heath and Company, 1993.

Bradley, Martha Sonntag. *Pedestals and Podiums: Utah Women, Religious Authority, and Equal Rights.* Salt Lake City, Utah: Signature Books, 2005.

Brady, David W., and Kent L. Tedin. "Ladies in Pink: Religion and Political Ideology in the Anti-ERA Movement." *Social Science Quarterly* 56, no. 4 (March 1976): 564–75.

Brennan, Mary C. *Turning Right in the Sixties: The Conservative Capture of the GOP.* Chapel Hill: University of North Carolina Press, 1995.

——. *Wives, Mothers, and the Red Menace: Conservative Women and the Crusade against Communism.* Boulder: University Press of Colorado, 2008.

Bridges, Linda, and John R Coyne Jr. *Strictly Right: William F. Buckley, Jr. and the American Conservative Movement.* Hoboken, New Jersey: John Wiley and Sons, Inc., 2007.

Brokaw, Tom. *Boom!: Voices of the Sixties.* New York: Random House, 2007.

Brown, Clyde, and Gayle K. Pluta Brown. "Moo U and the Cambodian Invasion: Nonviolent Anti-Vietnam War Protest at Iowa State University." In *The Vietnam War on Campus: Other Voices, More Distant Drums*, edited by Marc Jason Gilbert, 119–41. Westport, Connecticut: Praeger Publishers, 2001.

Brown, Ruth Murray. *For a "Christian America": A History of the Religious Right.* Amherst, New York: Prometheus Books, 2002.

Bryson, Christopher. *The Fluoride Deception.* New York: Steven Stories Press, 2004.

Burkett, Elinor. *The Right Women: A Journey through the Heart of Conservative America.* New York: Touchtone, 1998.

Burner, David. *Making Peace with the Sixties.* Princeton, New Jersey: Princeton University Press, 1996.

Burns, Jennifer. *Goddess of the Market: Ayn Rand and the American Right.* New York: Oxford University Press, 2009.

Button, H. Warren, and Eugene F. Provenzo Jr. *History of Education and Culture in America.* Englewood Cliffs, New Jersey: Prentice-Hall, Inc., 1983.

Campbell, Daniel R. "Right-Wing Extremists and the Sarasota Schools, 1960–1966." *Tampa Bay History* 6 (Spring/Summer 1984): 16–26.

Campbell, D'Ann. *Women at War with America: Private Lives in a Patriotic Era.* Cambridge, Massachusetts: Harvard University Press, 1984.

Capps, Walter H. *The New Religious Right: Piety, Patriotism, and Politics.* Columbia: University of South Carolina Press, 1990.

Carleton, Don E. *Red Scare!: Right-Wing Hysteria, Fifties Fanaticism, and Their Legacy in Texas.* Austin: Texas Monthly Press, 1985.

Carter, Paul A. *Another Part of the Fifties*. New York: Columbia University Press, 1983.

Caute, David. *The Great Fear: The Anti-Communist Purge Under Truman and Eisenhower*. New York: Simon and Schuster, 1978.

Chafe, William H. *Paradox of Change: American Women in the Twentieth Century*. New York: Oxford University Press, 1991.

Chafetz, Janet Saltzman, and Anthony Gary Dworkin. *Female Revolt: Women's Movements in World and Historical Perspective*. Totowa, New Jersey: Rowman and Allanheld, 1986.

Chappell, Marisa. *The War on Welfare: Family, Poverty, and Politics in Modern America*. Philadelphia: University of Pennsylvania, 2010.

Colgrove, James. *State of Immunity: The Politics of Vaccination in Twentieth-Century America*. Berkeley: University of California Press, 2006.

Committee for the Study of the Future of Public Health, Division of Health Care Services, Institute of Medicine. *The Future of Public Health*. Washington, D.C.: National Academy Press, 1988.

Coontz, Stephanie. *A Strange Stirring: The* Feminine Mystique *and American Women at the Dawn of the 1960s*. New York: Basic Books, 2011.

Cott, Nancy F. *The Bonds of Womanhood: "Woman's Sphere" in New England, 1780–1835*. New Haven, Connecticut: Yale University Press, 1977.

Cottrell, Debbie Mauldin. "National Women's Conference 1977." *The Handbook of Texas Online*. Texas State Historical Association, 1999.

Crain, Robert L. *The Politics of School Desegregation*. Chicago: Aldine Publishing Co., 1968.

Crain, Robert L., Elihu Katz, and Donald B. Rosenthal. *The Politics of Community Conflict: The Fluoridation Decision*. Indianapolis and New York: Bobbs-Merrill Co., Inc., 1969.

Crespino, Joseph. "Civil Rights and the Religious Right." In *Rightward Bound: Making America Conservative in the 1970s*, edited by Bruce J. Schulman and Julian E. Zelizer, 90–105. Cambridge, Massachusetts: Harvard University Press, 2008.

———. *In Search of Another Country: Mississippi and the Conservative Counterrevolution*. Princeton, New Jersey: Princeton University Press, 2007.

Critchlow, Donald T. *The Conservative Ascendancy: How the GOP Right Made Political History*. Cambridge: Harvard University Press, 2007.

———. *Phyllis Schlafly and Grassroots Conservatism: A Woman's Crusade*. Princeton, New Jersey: Princeton University Press, 2005.

Critchlow, Donald T., and Nancy MacLean. *Debating the American Conservative Movement, 1945 to the Present*. Lanham, Maryland: Rowman and Littlefield Publishers, Inc., 2009.

Dailey, Jane. "The Theology of Massive Resistance: Sex, Segregation, and the Sacred after *Brown*." In *Massive Resistance: Southern Opposition to the Second Reconstruction*, edited by Clive Webb, 151–80. New York: Oxford University Press, 2005.

DeGroot, Gerard J., ed. *Student Protest: The Sixties and After*. London: Longman, 1998.

Delegard, Kirsten Marie. *Battling Miss Bolsheviki: The Origins of Female Conservatism in the United States*. Philadelphia: University of Pennsylvania Press, 2012.

Detwiler, Fritz. *Standing on the Premises of God: The Christian Right's Fight to Redefine America's Public Schools*. New York: New York University Press, 1999.

Diamond, Sara. *Roads to Dominion: Right-Wing Movements and Political Power in the United States*. New York: Guilford Press, 1995.

Dierenfield, Bruce J. *The Battle Over School Prayer: How Engel v. Vitale Changed America*. Lawrence: University Press of Kansas, 2007.

Dixon, Marlene. "Why Women's Liberation." In *Twentieth-Century America: Recent Interpretations*, edited by Barton J. Bernstein and Allen J. Matusow, 555–70. New York: Harcourt Brace Jovanovich, Inc., 1972.

Dochuk, Darren. *From Bible Belt to Sunbelt: Plain-Folk Religion, Grassroots Politics, and the Rise of Evangelical Conservatism*. New York: W. W. Norton and Company, 2011.

Doenecke, Justus D. "Irene Corbally Kuhn." In *Women in World History*, edited by Anne Commire. Waterford, Connecticut: Yorkin Publications, 2000.

———. "McIntire, Carl Curtis." In *The Scribner Encyclopedia of American Lives*, vol. 6, edited by Kenneth T. Jackson, et al., 2003.

Doherty, Brian. *Radicals for Capitalism: A Freewheeling History of the Modern American Libertarian Movement*. New York: Public Affairs, 2007.

Edwards, Lee. *The Conservative Revolution: The Movement That Remade America*. New York: Free Press, 1999.

Egerton, John. *Speak Now Against the Day: The Generation Before the Civil Rights Movement in the South*. New York: Alfred A. Knopf, 1994.

Evans, Sara. *Personal Politics: The Roots of Women's Liberation in the Civil Rights Movement and the New Left*. New York: Vintage Books, 1979.

Farber, David, and Jeff Roche, eds. *The Conservative Sixties*. New York: Peter Lang, 2003.

Formisano, Ronald P. *Boston Against Busing: Race, Class, and Ethnicity in the 1960s and 1970s*. Chapel Hill: University of North Carolina Press, 1991.

Forster, Arnold, and Benjamin R. Epstein. *Danger on the Right*. New York: Random House, 1964.

Foster, Stuart J. *Red Alert!: Educators Confront the Red Scare in American Public Schools*. New York: Peter Lang Publishing, Inc., 2000.

Foucault, Michael. *History of Madness*. Edited by Jean Khalfa. Translated by Jonathan Murphy and Jean Khalfa. First published in French in 1961. London: Routledge, 2006.

Frank, Gillian. "'The Civil Rights of Parents': Race and Conservative Politics in Anita Bryant's Campaign Against Gay Rights in 1970s Florida." *Journal of the History of Sexuality* 22, no. 1 (January 2013): 126–60.

Freeman, Susan K. *Sex Goes to School: Girls and Sex Education Before the 1960s*. Urbana: University of Illinois Press, 2008.

Frum, David. *How We Got Here: The 1970s*. New York: Basic Books, 2000.

George, John, and Laird Wilcox. *American Extremists: Militias, Supremacists, Klansmen, Communists, and Others*. Amherst, New York: Prometheus, 1996.

———. *Nazis, Communists, Klansmen, and Others on the Fringe: Political Extremism in America*. Buffalo: Prometheus, 1992.

Gifford, Laura Jane, and Daniel K. Williams, eds. *The Right Side of the Sixties: Reexamining Conservatism's Decade of Transformation*. New York: Palgrave Macmillan, 2014.

Gilbert, James. *A Cycle of Outrage: America's Reaction to the Juvenile Delinquent in the 1950s*. New York: Oxford University Press, 1986.

Gilbert, Marc Jason, ed. *The Vietnam War on Campus: Other Voices, More Distant Drums*. Westport, Connecticut: Praeger, 2001.

Gilmore, Stephanie. *Groundswell: Grassroots Feminist Activism in Postwar America*. New York: Routledge, 2013.

Glen, John M. "Highlander Folk School." In *The Tennessee Encyclopedia of History and Culture*. Knoxville: University of Tennessee Press, 1998.

Glenn, Brian J., and Steven M. Teles. *Conservatism and American Political Development*. New York: Oxford University Press, 2009.

Goldman, Eric F. *The Crucial Decade—And After, 1945–1960*. New York: Vintage Books, 1962.

Gray, Julie Salley. "'To Fight the Good Fight': The Battle over Control of the Pasadena City Schools, 1969–1979." *Essays in History* 37 (1995). http://etext.virginia.edu/journals/EH/EH37/Gray.html.

Green, Elna C. "From Antisuffragism to Anti-Communism: The Conservative Career of Ida M. Darden." *Journal of Southern History* 65, no. 2 (May 1999): 287–316.

Gregory, James. *American Exodus: The Dust Bowl Migration and Okie Culture in California*. New York: Oxford University Press, 1991.

Grob, Gerald N. *From Asylum to Community: Mental Health Policy in Modern America*. Princeton, New Jersey: Princeton University Press, 1991.

Gustainis, J. Justin. *American Rhetoric and the Vietnam War*. Westport, Connecticut: Praeger, 1993.

Hardisty, Jean. *Mobilizing Resentment: Conservative Resurgence from the John Birch Society to the Promise Keepers*. Boston: Beacon Press, 1999.

Hartmann, Susan M. *From Margin to Mainstream: American Women and Politics since 1960*. Philadelphia, Pennsylvania: Temple University Press, 1989.

Heale, M. J. *American Anticommunism: Combating the Enemy Within, 1830–1970*. Baltimore, Maryland: Johns Hopkins University Press, 1990.

Heineman, Kenneth J. "American Schism: Catholic Activists, Intellectuals, and Students Confront the Vietnam War." In *The Vietnam War on Campus: Other Voices, More Distant Drums*, edited by Marc Jason Gilbert, 89–118. Westport, Connecticut: Praeger Publishers, 2001.

Heller, Jacob. *The Vaccine Narrative*. Nashville, Tennessee: Vanderbilt University Press, 2008.

Herring, George C. *America's Longest War: The United States and Vietnam, 1950–1975*. New York: Alfred A. Knopf, 1986.

Hess, Stephen. *America's Political Dynasties*. Garden City, New York: Doubleday, 1966.

Hijya, James H. "The Conservative 1960s." *Journal of American Studies* 37, no. 2 (August 2003): 201–27

Himmelstein, Jerome L. *To the Right: The Transformation of American Conservatism*. Berkeley: University of California Press, 1990.

Hofstadter, Richard. *The Paranoid Style in American Politics*. Chicago: University Press of Chicago, 1952.

Hopkins, Kenneth D. *Educational and Psychological Measurement and Evaluation*, 8th ed. Boston: Allyn and Bacon, 1998.

Inger, Morton. "New Orleans: The Failure of an Elite." In *The Politics of School Desegregation*, edited by Robert L. Crain, 250–308. Chicago: Aldine Publishing Co., 1968.

Irvine, Janice M. "Doing It with Words: Discourse and the Sex Education Culture Wars." *Critical Inquiry* 27, no. 1 (Autumn 2000): 58–76.

———. *Talk About Sex: The Battles Over Sex Education in the United States*. Berkeley: University of California Press, 2002.

Isserman, Maurice, and Michael Kazin. *America Divided: The Civil War of the 1960s*. New York: Oxford University Press, 2000.

Jackson, Kenneth, ed. *The Scribner Encyclopedia of American Lives*, vol. 6. New York: Charles Scribner's Sons, 2004.

Jeansonne, Glen. *Women of the Far Right: The Mothers' Movement and World War II*. Chicago, Illinois: University of Chicago Press, 1996.

Jetter, Alexis, Annelise Orleck, and Diana Taylor, eds. *The Politics of Motherhood: Activist Voices from Left to Right*. Hanover, New Hampshire: University Press of New England, 1997.

Johnston, Robert D., ed. *The Politics of Healing: Histories of Alternative Medicine in Twentieth-Century North America*. New York and London: Routledge, 2004.

———. *The Radical Middle Class: Populist Democracy and the Question of Capitalism in Progressive Era Portland, Oregon*. Princeton, New Jersey: Princeton University Press, 2003.

Kellar, William Henry. *Make Haste Slowly: Moderates, Conservatives, and School Desegregation in Houston*. College Station: Texas A & M University Press, 1999.

Kemp, Donna R. *Mental Health in America: A Reference Handbook*. Santa Barbara, California: ABC-CLIO, 2007.

Kerber, Linda. *Women of the Republic: Intellect and Ideology in Revolutionary America*. Chapel Hill: University of North Carolina Press, 1980.

Ketchum, Richard M. *The Borrowed Years: America on the Way to War*. New York: Random House, 1989.

Klatch, Rebecca E. *A Generation Divided: The New Left, the New Right, and the 1960s.* Berkeley: University of California Press, 1999.

———. "The Two Worlds of Women of the New Right." In *Women, Politics, and Change*, edited by Louise A. Tilley and Patricia Gurin, 529–52. New York: Russell Sage Foundation, 1990.

———. *Women of the New Right.* Philadelphia, Pennsylvania: Temple University Press, 1987.

Klehr, Harvey, and John Earl Haynes. *The American Communist Movement: Storming Heaven Itself.* New York: Twayne Publishers, 1992.

Klein, Aaron E. *Trial by Fury: The Polio Vaccine Controversy.* New York: Charles Scribner's Sons, 1972.

Kluger, Jeffrey. *Splendid Solution: Jonas Salk and the Conquest of Polio.* New York: G. P. Putnam's Sons, 2004.

Kominsky, Morris. *The Hoaxers, Plain Liars, Fancy Liars, and Damned Liars.* Boston: Branden Press, 1970.

Lassiter, Matthew D. *The Silent Majority: Suburban Politics in the Sunbelt South.* Princeton, Jersey: Princeton University Press, 2006.

Lassiter, Matthew D., and Joseph Crespino, eds. *The Myth of Southern Exceptionalism.* New York: Oxford University Press, 2010.

Lefkovitz, Alison. "The Problem of Marriage in the Era of Women's Liberation." PhD diss., University of Chicago, 2010.

Lehman, Elyse Branch, and Carol J. Erdwins. "The Social and Emotional Adjustment of Young Intellectually Gifted Children." In *Social/Emotional Issues, Underachievement and Counseling of Gifted Students*, edited by Sidney Moon, 1–8. Thousand Oaks, Calif.: Corwin Press and National Association for Gifted Children, 2004.

Levenstein, Lisa. "'Don't Agonize, Organize!': The Displaced Homemakers Campaign and the Contested Goals of Postwar Feminism." *Journal of American History* 100, no. 4 (March 2014): 114–38.

Levine, Murray. *The History and Politics of Mental Health.* New York: Oxford University Press, 1981.

Levy, David W. *The Debate Over Vietnam.* Baltimore, Maryland: Johns Hopkins University Press, 1991.

Lienesch, Michael. *Redeeming America: Piety and Politics in the New Christian Right.* Cambridge, Massachusetts: DaCapo Press, 2002.

Lindley, Susan Hill. *"You Have Stepped Out of Your Place": A History of Women and Religion in America.* Louisville, Kentucky: Westminster John Knox Press, 1996.

Link, Kurt. *The Vaccine Controversy: The History, Use, and Safety of Vaccinations.* Westport, Connecticut, and London: Praeger, 2005.

Lowenthal, Leo, and Norbert Guterman. *Prophets of Deceit: A Study of the Techniques of the American Agitator.* New York: Harper and Brothers, 1949. 2nd edition, Palo Alto, California: Pacific Books, 1970.

Lowndes, Joseph E. *From the New Deal to the New Right: Race and the Southern Origins of Modern Conservatism.* New Haven: Yale University Press, 2008.

Lyons, Paul. *American Conservatism: Thinking It, Teaching It*. Nashville, Tennessee: Vanderbilt University Press, 2009.

Lytle, Mark Hamilton. *America's Uncivil Wars: The Sixties Era from Elvis to the Fall of Richard Nixon*. New York: Oxford University Press, 2006.

MacDonald, James B. Introduction to *A New Look at Progressive Education*, edited by James R. Squire, 1–13. Washington, D.C.: Association for Supervision and Curriculum Development, 1972.

MacLean, Nancy. *Freedom Is Not Enough: The Opening of the American Workplace*. Cambridge, Massachusetts: Harvard University Press, 2006.

———. "Neo-Confederacy Versus the New Deal: The Regional Utopia of the Modern American Right." In *The Myth of Southern Exceptionalism*, edited by Matthew D. Lassiter and Joseph Crespino, 308–29. New York: Oxford University Press, 2010.

Maloney, Carolyn B. *Rumors of Our Progress Have Been Greatly Exaggerated: Why Women's Lives Aren't Getting Any Easier and How We Can Make Real Progress for Ourselves and Our Daughters*. New York: Modern Times, 2008.

Mansbridge, Jane M. *Why We Lost the ERA*. Chicago: University of Chicago Press, 1986.

Marmor, Judd. *Psychiatry in Transition*. New York: Brunner/Mazel Publishers, 1974.

Martin, Brian. *Scientific Knowledge in Controversy: The Social Dynamics of the Fluoridation Debate*. Albany: State University of New York Press, 1991.

Mathews, Donald G., and Jane Sherron DeHart. *Sex, Gender, and the Politics of ERA: A State and the Nation*. New York: Oxford University Press, 1990.

May, Elaine Tyler. *Homeward Bound: American Families in the Cold War Era*. New York: Basic Books, 1988.

McCourt, Kathleen. *Working-Class Women and Grass-Roots Politics*. Bloomington: Indiana University Press, 1977.

McGirr, Lisa. "Piety and Property: Conservatism and Right-Wing Movements in the Twentieth Century." In *Perspectives on Modern America: Making Sense of the Twentieth Century*, edited by Harvard Sitkoff, 33–54. New York: Oxford University Press, 2001.

———. *Suburban Warriors: The Origins of the New American Right*. Princeton, New Jersey: Princeton University Press, 2001.

McRae, Elizabeth Gillespie. "White Womanhood, White Supremacy, and the Rise of Massive Resistance." In *Massive Resistance: Southern Opposition to the Second Reconstruction*, edited by Clive Webb, 181–202. New York: Oxford University Press, 2005.

Meier, Marianne M. *Understanding the School Prayer Issue and the Related Character Education and Charter School Movements*. Pittsburgh, Pennsylvania: Dorrance Publishing Company, Inc., 2002.

Mickenberg, Julia L. *Learning from the Left: Children's Literature, the Cold War, and Radical Politics in the United States*. New York: Oxford University Press, 2006.

Miller, James A., Susan D. Pennybacker, and Eve Rosenhaft. "Mother Ada Wright and the International Campaign to Free the Scottsboro Boys, 1931–1934." *American Historical Review* 106, no. 2 (April 2001): 387–430.

Moon, Sidney, ed. *Social/Emotional Issues, Underachievement and Counseling of Gifted Students.* Corwin Press and National Association for Gifted Children, Thousand Oaks, California, 2004.

Moran, Jeffrey P. "'Modernism Gone Mad': Sex Education Comes to Chicago, 1913." *Journal of American History* 83, no. 2 (September 1996): 418–513.

——. *Teaching Sex: The Shaping of Adolescence in the 20th Century.* Cambridge: Harvard University Press, 2000.

More, Elizabeth Singer. "'The Necessary Factfinding Has Only Just Begun': Women, Social Science, and the Reinvention of the Working Mother in the 1950s." *Women's Studies: An Interdisciplinary Journal* 40, no. 8 (2011): 974–1005.

Morris, Robin. "Kathryn Dunaway's ERA Battle and the Roots of Georgia's Republican Revolution." In *Entering the Fray: Gender, Politics, and Culture in the New South*, edited by Jonathan Daniel Wells and Sheila R. Phipps, 161–83. Columbia, Missouri: University of Missouri Press, 2009.

Moser, John E. *Right Turn: John T. Flynn and the Transformation of American Liberalism.* New York: New York University Press, 2005.

Mueller, Carol, and Thomas Dimieri. "The Structure of Belief Systems among Contending ERA Activists." *Social Forces* 6, no. 4 (March 1982): 657–76.

Murphy, Kevin R., and Charles O. Davidshofer. *Psychological Testing: Principles and Applications*, 6th ed. Upper Saddle River, New Jersey: Pearson Prentice Hall, 2005.

Nash, George H. *The Conservative Intellectual Movement in America since 1945.* Wilmington, Delaware: ISI Books, 2008.

Nickerson, Michelle M. "The Lunatic Fringe Strikes Back: Conservative Opposition to the Alaska Mental Health Bill of 1956." In *The Politics of Healing: Histories of Alternative Medicine in Twentieth-Century North America*, edited by Robert D. Johnston, 117–30. New York: Routledge, 2004.

——. "Moral Mothers and Goldwater Girls." In *The Conservative Sixties*, edited by David Farber and Jeff Roche, 51–61. New York: Peter Lang, 2003.

——. *Mothers of Conservatism: Women and the Postwar Right.* Princeton, New Jersey: Princeton University Press, 2012.

——. "The Lunatic Fringe Strikes Back: Conservative Opposition to the Alaska Mental Health Bill of 1956." In *The Politics of Healing: Histories of Alternative Medicine in Twentieth-Century North America*, edited by Robert D. Johnston, 117–30. New York: Routledge, 2004.

Nielsen, Kim E. "Doing the 'Right' Right." *Journal of Women's History* 16, no. 3 (2004): 168–72.

——. *Un-American Womanhood: Antiradicalism, Antifeminism, and the First Red Scare.* Columbus: Ohio State University Press, 2001.

Oshinsky, David M. *A Conspiracy So Immense: The World of Joe McCarthy.* New York: Free Press, 1983.

———. *Polio: An American Story*. New York: Oxford University Press, 2005.

"Overview of Mental Health in New York and the Nation." New York State Archives. Accessed online July 7, 2011. http://www.archives.nysed.gov/a/research/res_topics_health_mh_timeline.

Parmet, Herbert S. *Jack: The Struggles of John F. Kennedy*. New York: Dial Press, 1980.

Pascoe, Peggy. *Relations of Rescue: The Search for Female Moral Authority in the American West, 1874–1939*. New York: Oxford University Press, 1990.

Peirce, Neal R. *The Pacific States of America: People, Politics, and Power in the Five Pacific Basin States*. New York: W. W. Norton and Company, Inc., 1972.

Petchesky, Rosalind Pollack. "Antiabortion, Antifeminism, and the Rise of the New Right." *Feminist Studies* 7, no. 2 (Summer 1981): 206–46.

Phillips-Fein, Kim. *Invisible Hands: The Making of the Conservative Movement from the New Deal to Reagan*. New York: W. W. Norton and Company, Inc., 2009.

Pivar, David J. *Purity Crusade: Sexual Morality and Social Control, 1868–1900*. Westport, Connecticut: Greenwood Press, 1973.

Powers, Richard Gid. *Not Without Honor: The History of American Anticommunism*. New York: Free Press, 1995.

Provenzo, Eugene F., Jr. *Religious Fundamentalism and American Education: The Battle for the Public Schools*. Albany: State University of New York Press, 1990.

Radl, Shirley Rogers. *The Invisible Woman: Target of the Religious New Right*. New York: Dell Publishing Co., Inc., 1983.

Ravitch, Diane. *The Troubled Crusade: American Education, 1945–1980*. New York: Basic Books, 1983.

Reilly, Gretchen Ann. "'Not a So-Called Democracy': Anti-Fluoridation and the Fight over Drinking Water." In *The Politics of Healing: Histories of Alternative Medicine in Twentieth-Century North America*, edited by Robert D. Johnston, 131–50.

Robbins, William C. "Vortex I." In *The Oregon Encyclopedia*. Accessed online October 11, 2011. http://www.oregoneyeyclopedia.org/entry/view/vortex_i/.

Roy, Ralph Lord. *Apostles of Discord*. Boston: 1953.

Rymph, Catherine E. *Republican Women: Feminism and Conservatism from Suffrage through the Rise of the New Right*. Chapel Hill: University of North Carolina Press, 2006.

Sapiro, Virginia. "News from the Front: Intersex and Intergenerational Conflict Over the Status of Women." *Western Political Science Quarterly* 33, no. 2 (June 1980): 260–77.

Scanlon, Sandra. *The Pro-War Movement: Domestic Support for the Vietnam War and the Making of Modern Conservatism*. Amherst and Boston: University of Massachusetts Press, 2013.

Schafer, Joseph. "Popular Censorship of History Texts." *Wisconsin Magazine of History* 6, no. 4 (June 1923): 450–61. Wisconsin Historical Society, http://www.jstor.org/stable/4630458.

Schoenwald, Jonathan M. *A Time for Choosing: The Rise of Modern American Conservatism*. New York: Oxford University Press, 2001.

Schreiber, Ronnee. *Righting Feminism: Conservative Women and American Politics*. New York: Oxford University Press, 2008.

Schulman, Bruce J. *The Seventies: The Great Shift in American Culture, Society, and Politics*. Cambridge: DaCapo Press, 2001.

Schulman, Bruce J., and Julian E. Zelizer, eds. *Rightward Bound: Making America Conservative in the 1970s*. Cambridge, Massachusetts: Harvard University Press, 2008.

Schuparra, Kurt. *Triumph of the Right: The Rise of the California Conservative Movement, 1945–1966*. Armonk, New York: M. E. Sharpe, 1998.

Semel, Susan F., and Alan R. Sadovnik, eds. *"Schools of Tomorrow," Schools of Today: What Happened to Progressive Education*. New York: Peter Lang Publishing, Inc., 2006.

Sklar, Kathryn Kish. "The Schooling of Girls and Changing Community Values in Massachusetts Towns, 1750–1820." *History of Education Quarterly* 33, no. 4 (Winter 1993): 511–42.

Smith, Jane S. *Patenting the Sun: Polio and the Salk Vaccine*. New York: William Morrow and Company, Inc., 1990.

Smith, Lillian. *Killers of the Dream*. 1949. Reprint, New York: W. W. Norton Company, 1994.

Spruill, Marjorie. "Gender and America's Right Turn." In *Rightward Bound: Making America Conservative in the 1970s*, edited by Bruce J. Schulman and Julian E. Zelizer, 71–89. Cambridge, Massachusetts: Harvard University Press, 2008.

Squire, James R., ed., *A New Look at Progressive Education*. Washington, D.C.: Association for Supervision and Curriculum Development, 1972.

Steinbeck, John. *Travels with Charley in Search of America*. New York: Penguin Books, 1997.

Stockley, Grif. "Daisy Lee Gatson Bates." In *The Encyclopedia of Arkansas History and Culture* (2012), http://www.encyclopediaofarkansas.net/encyclopedia/entry-detail.aspx?entryID=591.

Stone, Barbara S. "The John Birch Society: A Profile." *Journal of Politics* 36, no. 1 (February 1974): 184–97.

"The Story of Fluoridation." National Institute of Dental Research, July 31, 2007. http://www.nidcr.nih.gov/oralhealth/topics/fluroide/thestoryoffluoridation.htm.

Stouffer, Samuel A. *Communist, Conformity, and Civil Liberties: A Cross-Section of the Nation Speaks Its Mind*. Gloucester, Massachusetts: Peter Smith, 1963.

Strong, Bryan. "Ideas of the Early Sex Education Movement in America, 1890–1920." *History of Education Quarterly* 12, no. 2 (Summer 1972): 129–61.

Sugrue, Thomas J. *Sweet Land of Liberty: The Forgotten Struggle for Civil Rights in the North*. New York: Random House, 2008.

Swerdlow, Amy. *Women Strike for Peace: Traditional Motherhood and Radical Politics in the 1960s*. Chicago: University of Chicago Press, 1993.

Theoharis, Jeanne. "'I'd Rather Go to School in the South': How Boston's School Desegregation Complicates the Civil Rights Paradigm." In *Freedom North: Black Freedom Struggles Outside the South, 1940–1980*, edited by Jeanne Theoharis and Komozi Woodard, 126–41. New York: Palgrave Macmillan, 2003.

Tilley, Louise A., and Patricia Gurin, eds. *Women, Politics, and Change*. New York: Russell Sage Foundation, 1990.

Torrey, E. Fuller. *Nowhere to Go: The Tragic Odyssey of the Homeless Mentally Ill*. New York: Harper and Row Publishers, 1998.

Toy, Eckard V., Jr. "The Right Side of the 1960s: The Origins of the John Birch Society in the Pacific Northwest." *Oregon Historical Quarterly* 105, no. 2 (Summer 2004): 260–83.

Vrame, William Anton. "A History of School Desegregation in Chicago Since 1954." PhD diss. University of Wisconsin, 1970.

Warren, Carol A. B. *Madwives: Schizophrenic Women in the 1950s*. New Brunswick, New Jersey: Rutgers University Press, 1987.

Webb, Clive, ed. *Massive Resistance: Southern Opposition to the Second Reconstruction*. New York: Oxford University Press, 2005.

Weinstein, Raymond M. "Goffman's Asylums and the Social Situation of Mental Patients." *Orthomolecular Psychiatry* 11, no. 4 (1982): 267–74.

Wells, Jonathan Daniel, and Sheila Phipps, eds. *Entering the Fray: Gender, Politics, and Culture in the New South*. Columbia: University of Missouri Press, 2010.

Wells, Tom. *The War Within: America's Battle over Vietnam*. Berkeley: University of California Press, 1994.

Whitfield, Stephen J. *The Culture of the Cold War*. Baltimore, Maryland: Johns Hopkins University Press, 1991.

Wilcox, Clyde. *God's Warriors: The Christian Right in Twentieth Century America*. Baltimore, Maryland: Johns Hopkins University Press, 1992.

Willrich, Michael. *Pox: An American History*. New York: Penguin Press, 2011.

Wolbrecht, Christina. *The Politics of Women's Rights: Parties, Positions, and Change*. Princeton, New Jersey: Princeton University Press, 2000.

Woods, Jeff. *Black Struggle Red Scare: Segregation and Anti-Communism in the South, 1948–1968*. Baton Rouge: Louisiana State University Press, 2004.

Wrigley, Julia. "From Housewives to Activists." In *No Middle Ground*, edited by Kathleen M. Blee, 251–88. New York: New York University Press, 1998.

Wylie, Philip. *Generation of Vipers*. New York: Rinehart and Company, Inc., 1955.

———. *Sons and Daughters of Mom*. Garden City, New York: Doubleday and Company, Inc., 1971.

Zimmerman, Jonathan. *Whose America?: Culture Wars in the Public Schools*. Cambridge, Massachusetts: Harvard University Press, 2002.

INDEX

Abortion: anti-ERA women and, 236, 245, 247; baby boomers and, 245–47, 326n35; conflict over, 245–46; *Roe v. Wade* ruling on, 236, 243, 245

Ackley, Ann and Russell, 71, 105, 106, 279

Activism: civil rights movement, 126, 130, 135, 136–37; teachers, books and baby boomer, 60–61. *See also* Antiwar activism; Campaigns; Education activism; Rightist activism; Women's rights activism

Adorno, Theodor W., 91

African Americans. *See* Blacks

Alaska Mental Health Bill: anti-Semitism and, 88; debate over, 85; mental health conspiracy theories about, 87–89, 93; overview, 85–86; rightists and, 86–87, 94, 101, 298n79; rightist women and, 63, 85, 89, 93, 94; rightist women's organizations and, 86–89, 93, 94

Alesen, Lewis A., 97–98

Alexander, Kathryn G., 42

Allen, Marilyn R., 120, 123, 304n14

Allen, Mary Louise, 48

American Council on Education, student survey, 225–26

American Flag Committee, 86, 298n79

Americanism, 53, 73, 93, 178, 179, 181. *See also* Patriotism; Traditionalism

American Legion, 43, 44, 224, 316n111, 321n40

American Legion Magazine, 43, 44

Americans: concerns about public health programs, 64; current problems and, 278; during postwar years, 2, 269; rightist women's education activism impact on, 62; rightist women's public health campaigns and, 64; student rebellion and, 199, 219–21, 226; Vietnam War and, 199, 200–202, 210, 212, 213, 215, 229, 321n38

American Spirit, 134, 183, 184–85

American Woman's Party, 238

American Women Are Richly Endowed (AWARE), 249

Antibusing: far right and, 144, 145, 148; moderates and, 143–44, 147–49; overview, 148; physical safety and, 143, 149, 308n95; racists and, 139, 140, 143, 144, 145, 149; rightists and, 115–16, 138–42, 148–49; rightist women and, 139–41, 148–49; women and, 143, 145–47, 309n98, 309n108

Antibusing activism: protests, *141*, 141–42, *142*, 144–47, 157; rightist organizations and, 142, 145; rightist women's organizations and, 141, 148; violence in, 146

Antibusing campaigns: Boston, 145–47, 309n108; boycotts in, 144; men in, 146; racism of, 142; rightist women and, 144–45, 147; women and, 145–47, 309n108

Anticommunism: of anti-ERA women, 260; baby boomers and, 294n140; of mainstream, 51, 52; mainstream women's education activism and, 50; militant, 7; of mothers, 201, 203–10; of patriotic organizations, 201, 203–13, 321n40;

SDS. *See* Students for a Democratic Society

Seeger, Pete, 185, 317n121

Segregated schools: northern, 115; southern, 114–15. *See also* School desegregation

Segregation, 114. *See also* Anti-integration

Segregationists, 115; busing and, 139; civil rights movement and, 138; desegregation and, 117; rightists and, 116–17, 120, 138, 304n3; rightist women and, 116, 119, 121–22. *See also* Anti-integrationists; Southern segregationists

Sex, and school desegregation, 124, 125, 126, 127

Sex discrimination, 240, 241; ERA and, 250; Pregnancy Discrimination Act of 1978 and, 263; Title IX of Education Amendments of 1972 and, 263; Title VII of Civil Rights Act of 1964 and, 235–36, 239

Sex education: mainstream and, 162; mothers and, 165–66; overview, 156–68, 196, 275, 311n10, 332n15; parents and, 159–61, 164–65; progressives and, 156–57, 159; religion and, 159; rightist morality and, 159, 165, 167; rightist women's morality and, 154, 156–58, 160–66; rightist women's organizations and, 158, 162–63; youth morality and, 156–67

Sex Information and Education Council of the United States (SIECUS), 158–59, 161, 163, 165, 167, 312n32

Sexism, 240–41

Sharon Conference, 179, 180

SIECUS. *See* Sex Information and Education Council of the United States

Sixties: rightist women and, 184; women's equal rights during and beyond, 240–63; youth and, 232

Smart, Anne, 99

Smith, Chester A., 66

Smith, Lillian, 118, 119

Social conservatives, 284n7, 329n81. *See also* New Right

Social Frontier, 34

Socialism: polio vaccine and, 107; rightist women's education activism against, 45, 48. *See also* Communism

Social traditionalism, 7

Southern Conservative, 18, 38, 96, 126, 179

Southerners: attitudes regarding blacks, 119; baby boomer, 132; civil rights movement and, 117, 119; culture of white, 116–18, 149; segregated schools of, 114–15

Southern segregationists: school desegregation and, 115–20, 123–24, 134–35. *See also* Anti-integrationists

Southern segregationist white women: racism of, 123, 127–29, 131; rightist women and, 116–18, 122–24; school desegregation and, 122–29, 131

Soviet Union, 108–9, 276, 303n168. *See also* Communism; Russia

Spirit, 56, 132–34

Statism, 2

Steiner, Julia B., 190–91

Stern, Annette, 248, 251, 253

Stevenson, Suzanne Silvercruys, 18–19, 37

STOP ERA campaigns, 244–45, 247, 248, 256, 262

Strack, Marian M., 51–52

Student demonstrations: antiwar, 213, 216, 220–22; free speech, 216, 218, 221; rightist women and, 184, 215. *See also* Student protests

Student organizations: leftist, 60, 180, 218, 240–41, 316n103; rightists and, 218, 219–20

Student protesters: Portland State University, 224, 224, 225. *See also* Antiwar demonstrators

Student protests, 216, 220, 224. *See also* Student demonstrations

Student rebellion: Americans and, 199, 219–21, 226; communism and, 191, 197–98; cultural change indicated by, 226; free speech and, 216–18, 221; Johnson and, 195, 220; leftists and, 218; media and, 217, 219, 222; Nixon and, 220–22; overview, 215–28, 230–32; rightist organizations and, 216; rightist women and, 13, 191, 199, 216–19, 221–22, 226, 228, 230, 321n42; Vietnam War and, 198, 213, 215–16, 218, 220–21, 226; women and, 213, 221–22, 231; young rightists and, 222. *See also* Youth rebellion

JUNE MELBY BENOWITZ is associate professor of history at the University of South Florida Sarasota-Manatee. She is the author of *Encyclopedia of American Women and Religion* and *Days of Discontent: American Women and Right-Wing Politics, 1933–1945*.